COHESION AND DISSENSION
IN EASTERN EUROPE

Foreign Policy Issues
A Foreign Policy Research Institute Series

Series Editor
NILS H. WESSELL

Managing Editor
CHARLES B. PURRENHAGE

COHESION AND DISSENSION IN EASTERN EUROPE

Six Crises

---

by
Jeffrey Simon

PRAEGER

PRAEGER SPECIAL STUDIES • PRAEGER SCIENTIFIC

Library of Congress Cataloging in Publication Data

Simon, Jeffrey.
  Cohesion and dissension in Eastern Europe.

  (Foreign policy issues)
  Includes index.
  1. Europe, Eastern—Politics and government.
2. World politics—1965–1975. 3. World politics—
1975–1985. I. Title. II. Series.
DJK50.S57 1983   947′.0009′046   83-4157
ISBN 0-03-063751-1

Series text design by Gordon Powell.
Text set in Goudy Oldstyle.

Published in 1983 by Praeger Publishers
CBS Educational and Professional Publishing
a Division of CBS Inc.
521 Fifth Avenue, New York, NY 10175 USA

© 1983 by Praeger Publishers

456789 052 98765432

Printed in the United States of America
on acid-free paper

To my parents

Foreword

This volume is another in the Foreign Policy Research Institute's book series, *Foreign Policy Issues*. Established in cooperation with Praeger Publishers, the series will include both collectively and individually authored works on contemporary international affairs. The series will provide a publications outlet for work by the staff of the Foreign Policy Research Institute and by other authors in the academic and policy communities.

In this volume Jeffrey Simon argues that Western interest in Eastern Europe in recent years has focused on growing domestic instability, largely as a result of the virtual revolt of the Polish working class (and, in fact, the entire population) against a Marxist regime perceived as the agent of a foreign power. To invert Lenin, martial law may be seen as the highest stage of socialism.

But the deepening socio-economic and political crisis besetting most of Eastern Europe should not distract us from another significant trend of the past two decades: the increasing East European deviation from Soviet foreign policies. As Jeffrey Simon points out in this study, several non-Soviet Warsaw Pact states, despite Soviet trumpeting of the Pact's purported "fraternal unity," have separated themselves from Moscow's foreign policy initiatives on various occasions. The unwillingness of the Soviet Union to acknowledge the political unreliability of several of its allies has not kept Romania, Yugoslavia, Poland, and Hungary from pursuing foreign policies that are sometimes at variance with the Kremlin's preferences.

In the decade between 1967 and 1977, Simon argues, at least four factors combined to further this process of differentiation: détente, the invasion of Czechoslovakia, the Sino-Soviet rift, and Arab-Israeli conflict. The author concludes not only that these political differences widened over the decade but also that U.S. foreign policy contributed to the process. By heightening the differentiation in our policies toward individual East European countries, based on their willingness to resist Soviet pressures, the United States in the future may materially complicate the Soviet Union's diplomatic and military problems in its own asserted sphere of influence.

Charles B. Purrenhage and Elizabeth D. Dunlap ably supervised production of the volume, accepted for publication at a time when Alan Ned Sabrosky shared the role of Series Editor.

Nils H. Wessell
Series Editor
Foreign Policy Issues
A Foreign Policy Research Institute Series

Preface

This book traces the development of differences in the foreign policy outlook of the countries of Eastern Europe by examining their increasing dissension and deviation from critical Soviet policies toward NATO, the People's Republic of China (PRC), the Middle East, and regional security. Based on comparative analysis of East European media commentary, government statements and actions, and public diplomatic activities of party and government leaders, I measure the degree of each state's adherence to Soviet policy during six international events that challenged Soviet and East European unity over a ten-year period: the Middle East war of June 1967; the invasion of Czechoslovakia in August 1968; the Ussuri incident of March 1969; Nixon's visit to Peking in March 1972; the October 1973 Middle East war; and Sadat's visit to Jerusalem in November 1977.

Each of the case studies represents a problem that demanded the attention of the Soviet leadership. Each involved a Soviet response coupled with varying degrees of intensified diplomatic interaction with East European allies, client state(s), other socialist states, and the United States. Finally, each involved a different perception of threat for the Soviet leadership, affecting both its public political response and the degree of its military commitment. The responses of the East European states differed from those of the USSR and each other, and may well cause Soviet leaders to question the political reliability of some of their allies.

January 1983
Washington, D.C.

Acknowledgments

The work leading to this study was supported in large part by a Project Air Force study effort of the Rand Corporation, which assisted the Net Assessment Task Force, Directorate of Concepts, Assistant Chief of Staff/Intelligence, Headquarters, U.S. Air Force. I am indebted to Major General Jasper A. Welch, Jr. for invaluable comments on an earlier draft of the manuscript, and to Colonel Alton L. Elliott, Lt. Colonel Richard D. Walsh (Ret.), and Major Thomas Cason for their enthusiasm and encouragement during the course of this project.

I must acknowledge the contributions of Milton Weiner, Edmund Dews, A. Ross Johnson, Charles Gati, Nils H. Wessell, Alan Ned Sabrosky, Charles B. Purrenhage, and others for their incisive comments and reviews of portions of the manuscript. For her assistance in editing of the manuscript, I am greatly indebted to Erma Packman, who has taught me the value of succinct expression, and to Rosalie Fonoroff, whose professional and efficient typing made this volume possible. I am also indebted to Jacky L. Simon for her suggestions and patience. It goes without saying that responsibility for all errors and oversights remain mine alone.

Contents

Glossary

Agerpres	Romanian Press Agency
ADN	East German News Agency
BTA	Bulgarian Telegraph Agency
CC	central committee
CCP	Chinese Communist Party
Ceteka	Czechoslovak News Agency
CMEA	Council of Mutual Economic Assistance
CPCS	Communist Party of Czechoslovakia
CPSU	Communist Party of the Soviet Union
CTK	Czechoslovak News Agency
CSSR	Czechoslovak Socialist Republic
DR	Daily Report
EE	Eastern Europe
FBIS	Foreign Broadcast Information Service
FRG	Federal Republic of Germany
GDR	German Democratic Republic
GMT	Greenwich Mean Time
Hsinhua	New China News Agency
HSWP	Hungarian Socialist Workers' Party
JPRS	Joint Publications Research Service
KGB	Committee of State Security
KYODO	Japan Press Agency
LCY	League of Communists of Yugoslavia
ME-A	Middle East and Africa
MENA	Middle East News Agency
MTI	Hungarian Press Agency
NCNA	New China News Agency
NSWP	Non-Soviet Warsaw Pact (members, forces, etc.)
OPEC	Organization of Petroleum Exporting Countries
PAP	Polish Press Agency
PCC	Political Consultative Committee (of the Warsaw Pact)
PLO	Palestine Liberation Organization
PRC	People's Republic of China
PUWP	Polish United Workers' Party
RCP	Romanian Communist Party
RFE	Radio Free Europe
SED	Socialist Unity Party

SU	Soviet Union
Tanjug	Telegraph Agency of Yugoslavia
TASS	Telegraph Agency of the Soviet Union
UAR	United Arab Republic

COHESION AND DISSENSION
IN EASTERN EUROPE

1

Introduction

This book traces the development of differences in the foreign policy outlook of the countries of Eastern Europe by examining their increasing dissension and deviation from critical Soviet policies toward NATO, the People's Republic of China (PRC), the Middle East, and regional security, as reflected in the East European press from 1967 to 1977. Significant extra- and intraregional influences beyond the USSR's control nurtured these foreign policy differences. Events since 1977 suggest that they will worsen before they show any sign of improvement.

Extraregional influences have appeared in the form of:

1) U.S. (and European NATO) détente, which has brought varying degrees of economic, social, and political influence to Eastern Europe.
2) Open challenges to the Soviet concept of proletarian internationalism from the PRC's two-superpower thesis and Yugoslavia's policy of nonalignment, which found a receptive ear in Romania, Poland, and Hungary.
3) Third-area (particularly Middle East) politics.

These extraregional factors contributed to Soviet bloc tension in November–December 1978 when, at a Moscow session of the Warsaw Pact Political Consultative Committee (PCC), the Soviet Union pressured its allies to increase defense expenditures to match NATO's 3 percent increase; to condemn the Camp David Middle East Accords of September 1978; and to condemn the PRC, with whom the Soviets had exchanged hostilities along the Ussuri River in May 1978 and with whom the United States was about to establish full diplomatic relations. Significant dissension among the non–Soviet Warsaw Pact

(NSWP) countries, influenced in part by these extraregional factors, resulted from the Soviet demands and contributed to extreme tension in Soviet–Eastern European relations.[1]

Intraregional pressures, which have also become more pronounced in Eastern Europe over the past 15 years, have appeared in the form of:

1) Economic problems exacerbated by higher costs for increasingly scarce energy resources.
2) Social and political tensions, resulting in part from wider contact with the outside (particularly Western) world.
3) Local conditions and national aspirations increasingly in collision with Soviet organizational norms (for example, Poland's private agricultural sector, Hungary's New Economic Mechanism, Romania's New Mechanism, and Yugoslavia's self-management system).

These intraregional pressures were much in evidence between July 1980 and December 1981, when the Polish Solidarity movement was building momentum. Although economics were also the catalyst for the social and political movements in 1970 and 1976, Solidarity exhibited a Western leaning and a degree of social mobilization much greater than anything that Poland had experienced during the 1970s. On the other hand, the mechanism for reestablishing social control—martial law—suggests greater subtlety and sophistication in the resolution of an intraregional crisis.

The Warsaw Pact, which came into existence on 14 May, 1955,[2] primarily as a Soviet response to the inclusion of the Federal Republic of Germany (FRG) in NATO, serves as a major organ for maintaining Soviet influence in Eastern Europe.[3] According to General Sergey Shtemenko, Warsaw Pact Chief of Staff from 1968 to 1976, the pact is "the *chief* center for the coordination of the fraternal countries' foreign policy activity" (emphasis added).[4] Control (as well as military) functions are performed by the 30 Soviet divisions (Groups of Soviet Forces) in Eastern Europe, of which 19 (nine tank) are stationed in East Germany, two (tank) in Poland, four (two tank) in Hungary, and five (two tank) in Czechoslovakia.[5] Particularly since the 1968 invasion of Czechoslovakia, Warsaw Pact institutions have undergone significant structural and functional differentiation to more effectively resolve intraregional problems.[6]

The Soviets never refer publicly to their allies' political unreliability, nor do they publicly differentiate among their allies. Rather, they extol the "fraternal unity," "proletarian internationalism," and "monolithic cohesion" of the Warsaw Pact. During internal crises, however, they rely on the following mechanisms to rally the support of their more reliable allies and to criticize, control, and/or punish the less reliable ones:

1) Bilateral and multilateral meetings with NSWP leaders (ad hoc or extraordinary—in contrast to normal periodic—meetings).

2) Domestic media discussions ("theoretical" discussion or criticism of a surrogate obviously meant to refer specifically to the actions of the offending ally) or native language broadcasts (over the heads of the ally's dissident leaders) to a foreign populace.
3) Military exercises (often joint) to pressure a recalcitrant ally.
4) Warsaw Pact invasion and occupation or the establishment of martial law to restore "order."

Some variation or combination of these control mechanisms was used in each of the six crises between 1967 and 1977 outlined below and examined in the following chapters.

SIX SOVIET CRISES

The existence of differences between East European and Soviet behavior in a given crisis and the extent of NSWP deviation from Soviet positions should provide some indication of the political reliability of the NSWP member states as allies. To this end, this book analyzes the behavior of NSWP leaders during six significant international events occurring between 1967 and 1977, each of which was a crisis for the USSR in terms of the similarities and differences between the positions of the NSWP and Soviet leaders. Significant deviations by NSWP leaders from Soviet positions and from behavior expected of them by the Soviets may well raise Soviet doubts as to the political reliability of the NSWP states in future crises.

I do not discuss *how* decisions in the six events were formulated, nor do I document the directives that were issued and the resulting NSWP responses in each crisis.[7] Rather, I describe the results of a comparative investigation of the *general* behavior of these states as expressed in the media, government decrees and actions, and the public diplomatic activities of party and government leaders. The six international events serving as case studies are summarized below.

The Middle East War, 1967

Following the outbreak of the Middle East War, on 5 June 1967, the USSR called an emergency meeting of the Warsaw Pact in Moscow, severed diplomatic relations with Israel, and began a massive military assistance program to Egypt, Syria, and Iraq. The Soviets threatened to do everything necessary to help the Arabs "rebuff the aggressor" but, significantly, also made the first use of the hot line, ostensibly to assure the United States that they contemplated no direct Soviet military intervention. Several instances of different perceptions of the situation on the parts of NSWP and Soviet leaders contributed to the modification of NSWP policies and to the development of tensions within the pact between the Soviets and their allies and among the NSWP members.

The Invasion of Czechoslovakia, 1968

Events in Prague that demanded the Soviet leadership's attention differed fundamentally from the situation in the Middle East. The Soviet leadership perceived the post-January developments in Czechoslovakia as a challenge to all its vital interests in Eastern Europe: The USSR's efforts to preserve the integrity of the Warsaw Pact and the Northern Tier security system in Europe were jeopardized, and international communist legitimacy was challenged by the reformists' attempts to destroy the monopoly of the Czechoslovak Communist Party.

Soviet propaganda justified the invasion of Czechoslovakia by arguing that the Western imperialist powers were attempting to wrest Czechoslovakia from the socialist camp; however, some significant differences in nuance appeared in the NSWP media. Whatever the Soviet leaders' real motives and perceptions, their response to the Prague uprising—a military commitment in the form of a Warsaw Pact invasion and the continued presence of five Soviet divisions on Czechoslovak soil—was severe. Resultant tensions within the pact soon became obvious: Albania, an inactive member of the pact, formally withdrew, and Romania, which did not participate in the invasion of Czechoslovakia, reactivated the Patriotic Guards.

The Ussuri Incident, 1969

To the Soviet media, China represented twin threats: ideological and military. First, China was challenging the Soviet model of socialism and competing for influence within the socialist community. In the Soviet view, China was pursuing a policy of anti-Sovietism and was attempting to undermine socialist unity by splitting the communist states. Second, Soviet leaders were beginning to perceive China as a potential military problem.

The Ussuri conflict, involving the outbreak of fighting between Soviet and Chinese troops on Damanskiy Island in the Ussuri River, which separates China and the USSR, in March 1969 created a crisis for the Soviet leadership that led to rapid and impressive military buildup in the area. Although numerous incidents had been reported along the Sino–Soviet border since 1967, the Soviets apparently had not viewed these as a source of serious military concern until the Ussuri incident. Up to then, only 15 divisions were stationed along the long frontier east of Lake Baykal, ten at full strength and the other five in the second category of readiness as of September 1968. Within three years, the Soviets were deploying approximately 45 divisions in the region, with about half in the first and second categories of readiness. Furthermore, they were alleged to have sounded out the United States in August 1969 and July 1970[8] about the possibility of establishing an alliance against other nuclear powers (read China) planning provocative actions or attacks.

The immediate Soviet reaction to the Ussuri clash was unprecedented in Soviet diplomatic practice. Their ambassadors called on NATO leaders to express their concern about the incident and the danger posed by the Chinese. Second, they attempted to get symbolic political commitment to their anti-Chinese stance from their Warsaw Pact allies at a meeting of the PCC on 17 March 1969 in Budapest. Although this effort failed, the reactions of the media and some NSWP leaders indicated that the issue had generated tremendous tension within the pact.

Nixon's Visit to China, 1972

President Nixon's visit to China in February 1972 jarred both the United States and the USSR. In light of how seriously the Soviets took the Chinese threat (evidenced by the Soviet troop increase along the eastern frontier), they must have seen the Sino–American rapprochement as perhaps a greater danger—or even the specter of a two-front war.

Soviet attempts to gain support for their position at the Crimea meetings of the Warsaw Pact in July 1971 created strains among the members that were still evident during Nixon's visit. Even though the rapprochement did not result in the feared Sino–American collusion, it created a situation of uncertainty for the Soviets and was clearly against their national interest. Both the potential for Sino–American rapprochement and the resulting Soviet uncertainty were clearly in the national interest of some NSWP members.

The Middle East War, 1973

The Soviets had advance warning that Egypt and Syria planned to attack Israel in October 1973, and they apparently engaged in some fairly extensive political and military arrangements with pact members that enabled them to resupply the Arabs during the war. The Soviets not only airlifted and shipped extensive military resources but also threatened to introduce Soviet military force into the region, an act that would have placed them on a collision course with the United States.

Significant differences among Warsaw Pact members were evident before, during, and immediately after the war. Soviet awareness of the different NSWP orientations and sensitivity to their inherent dangers were apparent in their careful prewar preparations as well as in their media and diplomatic actions during the war.

Sadat's Visit to Israel, 1977

Like Nixon's 1972 visit to China, Sadat's to Jerusalem in November 1977 was an event of great international significance that challenged old assumptions and suggested new potentialities. The USSR had special interests in both.

Despite the extensive military assets committed to the Middle East since 1967, the Soviets had experienced some significant political setbacks. While Kissinger's step-by-step diplomacy was effectively eliminating the Soviets from the process of seeking a regional political settlement, Sadat unilaterally abrogated the Soviet–Egyptian treaty of friendship and cooperation in April 1976, and Soviet–Syrian relations deteriorated over the issue of Assad's intervention in Lebanon.

When President Carter, in a change of U.S. policy, called for a Geneva conference to settle Middle Eastern problems under joint USA–USSR sponsorship, the Soviets were quite receptive. The resulting 1 October, 1977 joint communiqué provided the Soviets with an opportunity to recoup lost political influence and prestige. Sadat's visit to Jerusalem not only undermined these Soviet gains but also strained Soviet relations with the United States and the Warsaw Pact countries. Differing degrees of commitment to the Arab cause generally and the Geneva conference specifically contributed to further tensions within the pact.

WHY STUDY CRISIS?

The fundamental difference between everyday international political situations and the six international events represented in the case studies is that the latter could not be ignored—each *demanded* the attention of the Soviet leadership. At the minimum, each event involved a Soviet response coupled with varying degrees of intensified diplomatic interaction with Warsaw Pact allies, with client state(s) involved in the specific situation, and/or with the United States.

In everyday situations, political leaders are more or less free to decide which issue to focus on and which to put off for the future. At such times, they may have correspondingly little concern as to their allies' behavior. Soviet leaders did not have this freedom in dealing with the events covered in the case studies. Each situation demanded their attention, and each required them to make policy decisions and—in varying degrees—to obtain the support of their allies. Under these circumstances, the behavioral deviance of an ally is likely to weigh heavily on Soviet perceptions of that ally's political reliability. Thus, in recognizing the differences in the degree of Soviet concern from one situation to another, we assume a fundamental difference between everyday behavior and that in response to the six international events.[9]

The unique attributes of the case studies should be noted. First, each involved a different perception of threat for the Soviet leaders, and each affected not only their public political response but also the degree of their military commitment (contributing military assistance, threatening to employ force, actually doing so) and the pressure for support they would exert on their allies. Although it is clear that the Czechoslovak liberalization that ultimately resulted in the Soviet-led Warsaw Pact invasion involved a higher level of threat perception than either the 1972 Nixon visit to China or the 1977 Sadat visit to Jerusalem, the last two cases nevertheless generated significant tension within the pact. It is probable that the Soviets mobilized military force along the Romanian frontier because they perceived Romanian support for the PRC in July 1971 and for Egypt in 1976.

The fact that the Soviets threatened to introduce military force in the Middle East in 1973 but not in 1967 does not necessarily reflect qualitative differences in the degree to which they felt threatened. Perhaps they did not threaten in 1967 because they lacked the military capability to make such a threat credible; correspondingly, their greater political restraint in 1973 may have been influenced by their enhanced military capability. The degree of threat perceived undoubtedly affected the Soviet leaders' responses, just as it undoubtedly contributed to their demands on their Warsaw Pact allies and, correspondingly, on the Warsaw Pact responses.

Two other interrelated factors linked to threat perception—time and surprise—probably also affected Soviet behavior during these six events. The greater the perception of threat, the more likely it is that time becomes a critical factor in the particular decison-making situation.[10] Time may have played a significant role in the Soviet decision to invade Czechoslovakia.

Coupled with time and similarly related to threat perception is the question of the surprise engendered by a particular international event. For example, the 1967 Middle East war, the 1969 Ussuri conflict, and the 1977 Sadat visit to Jerusalem appear to have surprised the Soviet leaders. In contrast, Nixon's visit to China caused no surprise; it had been announced seven months earlier. (However, Soviet surprise at the announcement in July 1971 that the visit would take place may have contributed somewhat to their military response.) The Soviets also knew in advance of the impending hostilities in the Middle East in 1973.

Even in those events for which the Soviets had foreknowledge, there are apt to be elements of time-stress and surprise. For instance, they may have been surprised by the degree of tension generated within the Warsaw Pact by the invasion of Czechoslovakia; they may also have been surprised by Nixon's decision to go on military alert during the October war or by Carter's sudden shift from supporting a jointly sponsored Geneva settlement to supporting Sadat's initiative for a "separate peace." Qualitative judgments about the degree of perceived threat and the effects of time-stress and surprise are impossible. One can only speculate based on Soviet responses, which have ranged from emergency consultations with top-level NSWP party and government officials to the threatened or actual use of military assistance or force.

Thus, while each of the six cases studied contains unique attributes—based on varying threat perceptions, time, and surprise—they are similar in that they are all outside the considerations of everyday politics. Each tested the Warsaw Pact, engendered a broad range of NSWP behavior, and probably influenced Soviet leaders' perceptions of NSWP political reliability. To this one must add a final factor related to threat perception, time, and surprise, namely, the factor of Soviet leadership stability during this entire period. The top political leaders,

Leonid Brezhnev and Aleksey Kosygin, as well as Mikhail Suslov and Andrey Gromyko, were present during all of the crises, and Nikolai Podgorny and Andrey Grechko during most. In other words, what lessons were learned during these crises were not lost through leadership attrition.[11]

DATA LIMITATIONS

It should be noted that there are limits to the use of media responses as a source of evidence. First, there is some question as to what in the communist media (whether Soviet, Chinese, or NSWP) is instrumental (propaganda) as against what is "real" (reflecting perceptions and belief). Although media content cannot necessarily be equated with leadership attitudes or beliefs, it is generally accepted that communist public communications do afford a useful basis for political analyses: that open commentary contains meaningful clues or political "grain," which, supplemented by other information, can provide reliable evidence.[12]

Second, differences between Soviet and NSWP media may not necessarily represent measurements of disunity or political unreliability. There may be situations where the Soviets expect conformity; in fact, they may write specific articles for the non-Soviet media. On the other hand, there are situations where the Soviets may evidence no particular concern about the editorial comments of NSWP media. There are also situations where the Soviets may, for diplomatic and political purposes, refrain from making explicit and specific charges through their own media and at the same time actively encourage NSWP media to do so for them. Thus, what may appear to be an indication of deviation may, in reality, be a sign of conformity.

Because of this situation, a comparison of NSWP media with Soviet media as representing a measurement of NSWP conformity with Soviet behavior must be highly qualified. Media analyses should be examined in the context of such forms of objective behavior as (1) the long-term national policies and goals of specific NSWP members that are likely to affect, to varying degrees, their threat perception and (2) the immediate governmental decrees and actions, diplomatic activities, and statements of party and government officials. A comparison of the two factors—NSWP long-range policies and threat perceptions coupled with immediate behavior—will better enable us to differentiate between a significant media nuance representing potential deviation from Soviet behavior and an apparent nuance that may not necessarily constitute a deviation.

SOME METHODOLOGICAL NOTES

It is imperative to note that reliability is a function not only of measurements of objective behavior but also of subjective factors. Our knowledge of NSWP behavior is limited; the Soviet leadership presumably has a more intimate knowledge of specific personalities, national proclivities, and special bonds than we. At the very least, their evidential sources are likely to differ from ours.

This creates further potential methodological problems: First, the tactical information that I have incorporated into this strategic calculation of political reliability may not necessarily be included in the Soviet leaders' calculations if they are using different information. Thus, if we perceive a NSWP member as adhering quite closely to Soviet behavior during crisis, the Soviets may perceive a different "reality."[13]

Second, if Soviet leaders have different strategic assumptions from those held in the West, even sharing the same tactical information, they could arrive at different conclusions. Historical examples abound of leaders having factored out or ignored tactical information that pointed in directions different from their expectations. This apparently was the case for U.S. leaders in the attack on Pearl Harbor and the 1973 Middle East war.[14] In other words, because political leaders sometimes expect or want different things to happen, they do not perceive the signals that lead toward conclusions that are either unbelievable or undesirable. This is as true of the Soviet Union as it is of the United States.

Third, even if U.S. and Soviet evidential sources of behavior and strategic assumptions were similar, it is possible that the Soviet leaders (as has occurred with their U.S. counterparts) could misperceive the behavior of other states[15] or simply make mistakes.[16]

A fourth factor that should be taken into account is the relationship between predictability or unpredictability and reliability or unreliability in the eyes of the Soviet leadership. From an American perspective, Romania (and perhaps Hungary) may be considered unreliable because its behavior has consistently differed from the USSR's during crisis. But from the Soviet perspective, Romania's behavior has been consistent and is therefore predictable.[17] If consistency, not conformity, is the premier psychopolitical need of the Soviet leadership (and we have no way of determining this), it may be able to cope with Romania's predictable unreliability.

On the other hand, although Poland and Czechoslovakia may have behaved in conformity with the USSR more often than Romania did, each has evidenced inconsistency in its support of the USSR during crisis. Poland's and Czechoslovakia's inconsistency may have a more negative effect than Romania's consistency on the Soviet leaders' perceptions of their reliability. Thus, from the Soviet perspective, because Poland and Czechoslovakia have been less predictable, they may be considered less reliable than Romania (or Hungary).

This book makes no attempt to deal definitively with these subjective problems, which are perceptual and psychological and relate to Soviet leaders about whom we have very little information. However, it is essential to keep in mind that subjective factors, which are unobservable and unmeasurable, are as likely to affect Soviet leaders' perceptions of NSWP reliability as are measurements of objective behavior. In addition, when these subjective factors operate on NSWP leaders and citizens, they are, in many instances, favorable forces for the West.

Each of the six international situations examined in this study has tested the Warsaw Pact, has resulted in a broad range of behavior, and has probably influenced Soviet perceptions of the reliability of its allies. I have argued here, in recognition of the limits of the methodology, first, that measurements of objective behavior—particularly an analysis of media in isolation from other observations—must be treated with care; second, that Soviet leaders' perceptions are likely to be based on evidential sources, strategic assumptions, misperceptions, and psychology, all of which are unobserved, unknown, and perhaps unknowable to Western analysts; and third, that these perceptions are likely to affect Soviet assessments of the reliability of their allies.

NOTES

1. For a more complete account of these events see Jeffrey Simon, *Warsaw Pact Reliability*, System Planning Corporation, SPC 620 (September 1980), pp. 61–70. System Planning Corporation, a "think tank" located in Arlington, Va., produces technical reports on national security policy for various U.S. government agencies.

2. The original signatories of the treaty were Albania, Bulgaria, Czechoslovakia, the German Democratic Republic (GDR), Hungary, Poland, Romania, and the USSR. For a general overview see Robin Allison Remington, *The Warsaw Pact: Case Studies in Communist Conflict* (Cambridge: MIT Press, 1971); Raymond Garthoff, *Soviet Military Policy: A Historical Analysis* (New York: Praeger, 1966); and John Erickson, *Soviet Military Power* (London: Royal United Services Institute, 1971).

3. The Soviets also utilize other institutions to maintain influence and control over the region, including party-to-party contacts, KGB links with Eastern European security services, and the Council of Mutual Economic Assistance (CMEA) for coordinating economic policy.

4. General S. Shtemenko, "Indestructible Combat Alliance," *Izvestiya* (May 14, 1971), p. 2; in *Foreign Broadcast Information Service (FBIS), Daily Report (DR), Soviet Union (SU)* (May 18, 1971), p. E11. Items from foreign-language sources are translated by FBIS, a component of the U.S. Department of Commerce. Daily Reports are on file for public reference at the Library of Congress and at many specialized and university libraries throughout the United States.

5. International Institute for Strategic Studies, *The Military Balance 1980–1981* (London: International Institute for Strategic Studies, 1981), p. 10.

6. For an evaluation of the 1969 and 1976 institutional reforms, see Malcolm Mackintosh, "The Evolution of the Warsaw Pact," *Adelphi Papers*, No. 58 (London: International Institute for Strategic Studies, June 1969); Malcolm Mackintosh, "The Warsaw Pact Today," *Survival*, 16 (May–June 1974): 122–26; Lawrence T. Caldwell, "The Warsaw Pact Directions of Change," *Problems of Communism*, 24 (September–October 1975); John Erickson, *Soviet–Warsaw Pact Force Levels* (Washington, D.C.: United States Strategic Institute, 1976); and Simon, *Warsaw Pact Reliability*.

7. Such data are, of course, unavailable. Nevertheless, one can speculate on specifics, much as the Kremlinologist does when discussing motive–belief patterns of top political leaders.

8. Henry Kissinger, *White House Years* (Boston: Little, Brown, 1979), p. 183; John Newhouse, *Cold Dawn: The Story of SALT* (New York: Holt, Rinehart and Winston, 1973), pp. 188–89.

9. At the same time, Soviet leaders' perceptions of reliability are probably heavily colored by the actions of Warsaw Pact states in all situations in which support is demanded. Hence, our six case studies remain only one indicator among many.

10. The phenomenon of time-stress and its effect on crisis decision-making has been outlined in Robert Kennedy, *Thirteen Days: A Memoir of the Cuban Missile Crisis* (New York: W. W. Norton, 1969), pp. 89–106.

11. During the same period, the United States had four presidents, secretaries of state, and national security council advisers, and seven defense secretaries.

12. Propaganda analysis techniques were developed during World War II with respect to Nazi Germany. See Alexander George, *Propaganda Analysis: A Study of Inferences Made from Nazi Propaganda in World War II* (Evanston, Ill.: Row, Peterson, 1959). These methods have been further refined in the communist-country context to allow the observer to extrapolate from the propaganda context of the media to concerns of the respective political leadership. See particularly Donald S. Zagoria, "A Note on Methodology," *The Sino–Soviet Conflict, 1956–1961* (Princeton: Princeton University Press, 1962), pp. 24–35; and Thomas M. Gottlieb, "A Postscript on Methodology," *Chinese Foreign Policy Factionalism and the Origins of the Strategic Triangle*, The Rand Corporation, R-1902-NA (November 1977), pp. 135–45. The Rand Corporation, a "think tank" located in Santa Monica, Calif., produces technical reports on national security policy. These are available to the public at the Library of Congress and at many university libraries.

13. This is similar to the parable of three men in a hole. Although all three men share the same physical condition (being in the hole), if one entered voluntarily, the other slipped in accidentally, and the third was forced in against his will, each probably would not perceive his condition to be the same. More important, if we, the analysts, were to come on the scene only in time to witness the third man being forced into the hole (the other two already being there), we might come to the wrong conclusion regarding the condition of all three men.

14. Roberta Wohlstetter, *Pearl Harbor: Warning and Decision* (Stanford: Stanford University Press, 1962), p. 397; and Abraham Ben-Zvi, "Hindsight and Foresight: A Conceptual Framework in the Analysis of Surprise Attack," *World Politics*, 28 (April 1976): 394.

15. A provocative study on the United States concludes that, although American decision-makers are often influenced by beliefs about what history teaches or portends in framing foreign policy, they ordinarily use history badly: "When resorting to an analogy, they tend to seize upon the first that comes to mind. They do not search more widely. Nor do they pause to analyze the case, test its fitness, or even ask in what ways it might be misleading. Seeing a trend running toward the present, they tend to assume that it will continue into the future, not stopping to consider what produced it or why a linear projection might prove to be mistaken." Ernest R. May, *"Lessons" of the Past: The Use and Misuse of History in American Foreign Policy* (New York: Oxford University Press, 1975), p. xi.

16. A recent study of U.S. intelligence failures concludes that "the most crucial mistakes have seldom been made by collectors of raw information, occasionally by professionals who produce finished analysis, but most often by the decision-makers. . . ." Richard K. Betts, "Analysis, War and Decision: Why Intelligence Failures Are Inevitable," *World Politics*, 31 (October 1978): 61. See also Irving L. Janis, *Victims of Groupthink* (Boston: Houghton Mifflin, 1972).

17. I do not mean to suggest that specific actions can be predicted in human affairs. By *predictable*, I mean that the general behavior accords with expectations.

2

The Middle East War, June 1967

WARSAW PACT TENSIONS

Prior to Nikita Khrushchev's removal from power in October 1964, the Soviets had been experiencing major problems with fellow communist states. First, the Sino–Soviet rift, publicly aired for the first time at the Twenty-second Congress of the Communist Party of the Soviet Union (CPSU) in October 1961, continued unabated. Second, Romania, a member of the Warsaw Pact, announced its intention of developing an independent policy in an April 1964 declaration of the Central Committee (CC) of the Romanian Communist Party (RCP) that stressed the Romanian right to national independence.[1] Third, Khrushchev's inclinations toward détente with the FRG met with strong opposition within the pact from Walter Ulbricht, first secretary of the Socialist Unity Party of Germany (SED), and Wladyslaw Gomulka, first secretary of the Polish United Workers' Party (PUWP).

Immediately after Khrushchev's ouster, the new Soviet leadership shifted to a harder line on relations with West Germany. This was evident at the meeting of the Warsaw Pact PCC in January 1965, which issued a harsh condemnation of West Germany. Romania, on the other hand, continued to approach the FRG, despite a change in RCP leadership in March of that year, when Nicolae Ceausescu succeeded Gheorghiu-Dej on the latter's death. The USSR, in response, attempted in late 1965 to increase its control over its allies by enhancing military integration and foreign policy coordination within the Warsaw Pact.[2] That the Soviets failed in this objective became clear in July 1966 when the Warsaw Pact PCC issued its Bucharest declaration.

Romania's establishment of diplomatic relations with the FRG on 31 January 1967 created a new crisis within the pact.[3] Ulbricht vehemently opposed the Romanian move because the FRG did not recognize de jure the German Democratic Republic (GDR); Gomulka, because the FRG refused officially to accept Poland's Oder–Neisse boundary. The Soviet leadership backed Ulbricht and Gomulka to thwart similar diplomatic activities by other Warsaw Pact countries and called European socialist leaders together at Karlovy Vary in April. Romania (and Yugoslavia) boycotted the conference.

Although the boycott created great tension within the pact, the Romanians remained undeterred. On 7 May, Ceausescu took the occasion of the forty-sixth anniversary of the founding of the RCP to reiterate (in the unusual form of a signed article in *Scinteia*) his determination to pursue an independent line, stressing the importance of bilateral relations to the RCP. In this context, he noted specifically that since the beginning of 1966 the RCP had held bilateral meetings with all 13 ruling communist parties, including Albania, China, and Yugoslavia, 20 nonruling communist parties, eight socialist parties, and social organizations from three countries.[4]

Getting to the heart of the matter, Ceausescu justified the RCP's failure to participate at Karlovy Vary:

Each communist party has the legitimate right to participate in an international meeting if it considers it necessary and useful, just as it has the legitimate right not to participate. Internationalist solidarity is not a conference. . . . The representatives of communist parties who uphold that nonparticipation in a conference must not affect, in any way whatsoever, the comradely relations between parties . . . are perfectly correct.[5]

According to Ceausescu, the unity of the communist movement could be achieved only if the movement (and, implicitly, its leadership) recognized the right of each individual party to act independently. To justify this new unity, Ceausescu quoted Friedrich Engels on historical relationships among communists, further arguing that this lesson should have been learned from the failure of the Comintern in 1943.

Of particular significance was Ceausescu's implicit charge that the CPSU had attempted to subvert his leadership of the RCP:

An attempt by a party to establish relations with members or groups within another party outside the organized framework means an encroachment upon the principle of proletarian internationalism, an action splitting the unity of that party. Any support given by a party, regardless of the reasons submitted, to members or groups within another party signifies interference in its internal affairs, disregard of the norms which must govern the relations between communist parties, leading to weakening the unity of the party, and entailing serious consequences to the class struggle it is waging and—in the socialist countries—to the work of building socialism. Under such circumstances, each party is fully entitled to take every measure it considers necessary to insure its political and organizational unity and to implement its political line.[6]

Thus, without naming the USSR or the CPSU, Ceausescu made clear his view of the limits to Soviet authority, not only in the communist movement, but also inside Romania, where he considered the authority of the RCP to be sovereign.

The Middle East war began on 5 June 1967, with tensions continuing to be felt within the communist movement, Romania still pursuing greater independence, disagreement over the rapprochement with West Germany unabated, and the breach with the People's Republic of China unresolved.

This chapter will examine the responses of the Warsaw Pact states to the Middle East war. By comparing the behavioral and rhetorical responses of the individual member nations in relationship to each other and to the USSR during June 1967, the chapter will attempt to assess how these responses may have further strained the pact, as well as how they may have affected Soviet perceptions of each state's political reliability.

AN UNWELCOME SURPRISE

The war enabled the USSR to establish its presence in the Middle East. Nevertheless, it probably came as an unwelcome surprise to the Soviet leadership. Although the Soviets had been supplying arms to and politically supporting the Arabs, when the fighting began Brezhnev hastened to contact President Johnson—making the first use of the hot line—to assure the United States that the USSR contemplated no military intervention.[7] This Soviet initiative suggested that the avoidance of confrontation was a primary concern. Despite this caution, Moscow actively sought to rally international political support for the Arab cause, to unite the Warsaw Pact on a common line toward the Arab states and Israel, and to drive a wedge into NATO.

Before the war began, the Soviets' publicly stated view of the positions of the United States and Great Britain was that these two countries, to carry out their colonialist program, actually did not want to end the Middle East crisis. The United States was generally portrayed as wanting:

1) To maintain colonial power over the region to obtain oil.
2) To control the eastern Mediterranean to protect the southern flank of NATO.
3) To exploit the situation in the Middle East to draw attention away from its problems in Vietnam and thus distract its NATO and domestic critics.[8]

The Soviets particularly highlighted the differences between the interests of the United States and those of its NATO allies in an attempt to undermine the relationship and sow discord within the alliance.[9]

The initial Soviet response to the war was to side with the Arabs and to accuse the Israelis of aggression. Moscow Domestic Service interrupted a broadcast to announce that "Israel had attacked the UAR [United Arab Republic] . . . [and that] Egyptian Armed Forces are resisting the enemy."[10] A few hours later, the Telegraph Agency of the Soviet Union (TASS) quoted the following statement of the UAR foreign ministry: "The Israeli conspiracy has been unmasked. . . . It is obvious that Israel is pursuing two goals: (1) to violate shipping in the Suez Canal; and (2) to provoke a third state to support Israel's aggression."[11]

On 5 June, the USSR condemned the aggression and demanded that the Israelis withdraw:

> The Soviet Government demands that the aggression on the part of Israel be stopped immediately and that the troops be withdrawn behind the armistice lines. Only compliance with the justified demands mentioned in this statement can restore the disturbed peace.[12]

The Soviet press further accused the Israelis of imperialist expansion, [13] made possible by aid from the United States, Britain, and West Germany.[14]

The Soviets supported the UN resolution of 6 June, which urged all governments in the Middle East, as a first step, to take all measures toward an immediate cease-fire and cessation of all military actions. In their media coverage of the UN action, the Soviets criticized the United States, arguing that the Americans were employing a delaying tactic to allow the Israelis to penetrate deeply into the Sinai Peninsula.[15]

Threatening on 7 June to break relations with Israel, the Soviet government said:

> If the Israeli Government now does not immediately fulfill the common demand of states for an immediate ending of fire, which is expressed in the Security Council's resolution, the Soviet Union will revise its attitude with respect to Israel and adopt a decision concerning the further maintenance of diplomatic relations with Israel, which by its actions is opposing itself to all peace-loving states. It goes without saying that the Soviet Government will consider and implement other necessary measures stemming from Israel's aggressive policy.[16]

The next Soviet action, and the major focus of this case study, involved the attempt to coordinate the policies of the Warsaw Pact members. The USSR held an emergency meeting in Moscow on 9 June 1967, attended by all members of the pact,[17] as well as by Yugoslavia, which was not a member. But the delegates were apparently unable to achieve a consensus. The official statement, issued by the participants—all of which were listed, with the notable omission of Romania[18]—warned:

> The participants in the meeting find it necessary to draw appropriate conclusions from the fact that Israel did not comply with the decision of the Security Council and did not stop military actions against Arab states.

The *states participating in this meeting* demand that Israel immediately stop military actions against the neighboring Arab countries and withdraw all its troops from their territories behind the truce line.

If the Government of Israel does not stop the aggression and withdraw its troops behind the truce line, *the socialist states which signed this statement* will do everything necessary to help the peoples of Arab countries to administer a resolute rebuff to the aggressor, to protect their lawful rights, and to extinguish the hotbed of war in the Middle East and restore peace in that area [emphasis added].[19]

The distinction made in the official text between "the states participating in this meeting" and "the socialist states which signed this statement" implied that Ceausescu and Ion Maurer, the Romanian leaders who attended, had supported the demand that Israel stop fighting and withdraw but had refused to sign the statement committing Romania to "help the peoples of Arab countries to administer a resolute rebuff to the aggressor."

The Soviet broadcasts covering the Moscow meeting reflected none of the dissension. One such broadcast to the Arab world, after listing the participants and again omitting Romania, declared: "The Moscow statement is an historical international document. . . . The participants . . . *unanimously* agreed . . . that the Israeli aggression came as a result of a conspiracy by certain imperialist circles, headed by the United States, against the Arab states" (emphasis added).[20]

On 10 June, the Soviet government carried out its earlier threat and broke diplomatic relations with Israel:

The Soviet Government states that in view of the continued Israeli aggression against Arab states and the gross violation of the Security Council decisions by it, the Soviet Government has taken a decision on the severance of the Soviet Union's diplomatic relations with Israel.[21]

It was noteworthy that there were no qualifications in the announcement of the break. The Soviets did not stipulate that if the Israelis stopped fighting and withdrew to the truce line they would then reestablish relations.

If, for the moment, the Soviets were reluctant to make a public issue over Romania's behavior in Moscow, they did not hesitate to attack the "leftist revisionist" People's Republic of China. They portrayed the Israeli action not as a Middle Eastern phenomenon, but as an imperialist aggression linked to the Vietnam war.[22] Once this linkage had been established, the Soviet media drew attention to the fact that the U.S. and Chinese ambassadors to Poland had been meeting in Warsaw since August 1954, and claimed that outbursts of Chinese "anti-Sovietism"[23] had followed such meetings, indicating that a "secret agreement existed between Peking and Washington."[24] The Soviets condemned the PRC for its policies in the Middle East and Vietnam,[25] its "collusion" with the United States,[26] and its "splitting" of the communist movement.[27] With increasing frequency, the Soviet media stressed the need for maintaining communist unity, reiterating that such unity was the aim of the April 1967 Karlovy Vary conference.[28]

Although communist unity and the importance of the statement signed by the Moscow meeting participants became a predominant theme of the Soviet press and radio, the media did not say outright that Romania had not signed the statement; they simply omitted to list Romania among the signers.[29] Soviet broadcasts to Romania condemned China for "splitting" communist unity. For example, one broadcast highlighted USA–PRC collusion; another stressed the importance of unity.[30] A week later, Soviet broadcasts to Romania reiterated these charges against China.[31] Particularly noteworthy here is the implicit criticism of Romanian policy, for, during this period, Romania had also been pursuing a policy of increased trade with the West as well as with China, while cutting its trade with the CMEA (Council of Mutual Economic Assistance) countries.[32] The warning, if not explicit, was nevertheless clear—those who undermine the unity of the communist camp face ostracism.

In summary, the Soviets responded to the Middle East war by:

- Charging that Israel was the aggressor, aided primarily by American and British "imperialists" and secondarily by West German "revanchists."
- Demanding that Israel cease fighting and withdraw to the prewar truce lines.
- Severing without qualification diplomatic relations with Israel on 10 June, immediately following the meeting of socialist leaders in Moscow.
- Refraining from criticizing Warsaw Pact member Romania while explicitly attacking the People's Republic of China for what the Soviets evidently considered to be Romania's sins.

By examining the responses of the other members, we may get a better picture of what tensions were generated within the Warsaw Pact during this period.

BULGARIAN ORTHODOXY

The Bulgarian response to the June 1967 war in the Middle East was almost a carbon copy of the Soviet response. Todor Zhivkov, first secretary of the Bulgarian Communist Party, on the eve of an official visit to Belgrade, told three Yugoslav journalists: "As for events in the Near East, our sympathies are on the side of the Arab people."[33] The joint communiqué issued by Josip Broz Tito and Zhivkov on 6 June at the end of the two-day visit also echoed the Soviet line on the Middle East.[34]

Bulgaria issued another official declaration on 6 June containing the same two demands on Israel that the Soviets had made the day before.[35] The Bulgarian media also ascribed the same motives to Israel, the United States, and Britain that the Soviets had.[36] The Bulgarian delegates to the 9 June meeting in Moscow apparently supported the Soviets on all points. On 10 June, Radio Sofia broadcast the text of the Moscow statement of 9 June and later that day, following the USSR's lead, broke diplomatic relations with Israel (and, like the USSR, said nothing about resuming them).[37]

The Bulgarians also held an orthodox view of communist unity during the crisis. *Rabotnichesko Delo* condemned the PRC for its slander against the USSR,[38] and relations between Bulgaria and China appeared to deteriorate. Radio Free Europe reported that, according to Reuters and Hsinhua dispatches of 10 June from Peking, China had charged the Bulgarians with undermining the Sino–Bulgarian agreement on student exchange by expelling three Chinese students.[39] On 11 and 12 June, anti-Bulgarian demonstrations were held in Peking;[40] the next day, Ivan Popov, a deputy minister of foreign affairs, summoned the Chinese chargé d'affaires to protest the Peking government's "anti-Bulgarian campaign."[41]

While condemning the Chinese quite explicitly, the Bulgarians remained silent on the Romanians' actions at the Moscow conference and, during the next two weeks, frequently upheld the Soviet position. They followed the Soviet formula for maintaining communist unity. For example, in reference to the 9 June Moscow statement, Politburo member Pencho Kubadinski noted that "the resolute voice of the seven socialist countries resounded in Moscow during the most critical times for the Arab countries."[42] It is significant that Kubadinski referred to the seven signers of the statement and not to the eight participants in the meeting, Romania being the eighth. Kubadinski also stressed the importance of the Karlovy Vary conference in strengthening communist unity, without mentioning Romania's absence. Zhivkov, in a speech to the UN General Assembly on 20 June 1967, also spoke only of the signers of the Moscow statement: "The socialist states which have signed this declaration will do everything possible to help the peoples of the Arab countries give resolute resistance to the aggression."[43]

It seems reasonable to assume, then, that the USSR, seconded by Bulgaria, had consciously decided to pursue a policy of:

- Stressing the success of the Karlovy Vary and Moscow conferences in achieving communist unity.
- Ignoring the failure of one of their number, Romania, to attend the former conference and to sign the solidarity statement of the latter.
- Concentrating all criticism and condemnations for "splitting" the communist movement on the People's Republic of China.

PRAGUE SPEAKS

Czechoslovakia consistently sided with the Arab countries in its prewar statements. On 25 May, the Czechoslovak foreign ministry accused Israel of having created the Middle East tension in complicity with "imperialist circles directly connected with oil monopolies."[44] President Antonin Novotny, who was also the first secretary of the Communist Party of Czechoslovakia (CPCS), in an address at a Czechoslovak–Soviet friendship rally at Devin on 4 June blamed "reactionary forces [who], with the help of extremist circles of Israel, are endeavoring to bring to a halt the independent and progressive development of the Arab states and to suppress the national liberation movement in this area."[45]

The Czechoslovaks responded immediately and extensively to the outbreak of the war. Taking a stand similar to that of the Soviets and Bulgarians, they branded Israel the aggressor and implicated the United States, Great Britain, and West Germany as the accessories.[46]

Novotny told the Fifth Congress of the Czechoslovak Youth Federation, which opened in Prague on 5 June: "According to the latest news, an armed attack by Israel against the UAR has already broken out. . . . We must condemn these Israeli provocations which threaten peace throughout the world."[47] The Youth Federation passed a resolution expressing solidarity with the Arab countries.[48] The next day the foreign ministry made the same demands as those found in the 5 June Moscow declaration: "In the interests of the reestablishment of peace it is necessary for Israel to cease immediately its aggression against the Arab states and to withdraw its troops behind the armistice line."[49] On 8 June, following the lead of the 7 June Soviet threat to sever relations if Israel did not withdraw, the foreign ministry issued a similiar ultimatum.[50] The Czechoslovaks also signed the 9 June Moscow statement. And, like the Soviets, they announced an unqualified break in relations with Israel.[51]

The Czechoslovaks, like the Soviets, blamed the Chinese (but not the Romanians) for creating tension within the communist camp and undermining communist unity. The press explicitly charged the Chinese not only with criticizing Soviet policy on the Middle East but also with acting in collusion with the United States.[52]

The media reiterated the importance of the Karlovy Vary and Moscow conferences. Writing in *Rude Pravo*, Otto Klicka, a deputy foreign minister, noted that the Karlovy Vary conference had "made a correct estimate of the trends and processes which are shaping Europe's new face."[53] In references to the Moscow conference, the reports on both Novotny's return to Prague[54] and his speech at Lidice on 11 June ignored the issue of Romania's behavior. Novotny said with regard to the Moscow conference:

> The socialist countries are unanimous in the opinion that if Israel does not stop its military actions and withdraw its troops from the territory of the Arab countries to behind the armistice line they will draw the necessary conclusions from this and undertake everything to make Israel feel the solidarity of the people of the socialist countries with the Arab people [emphasis added].[55]

Nor was Romania excluded from among the socialist countries in an article in *Prace* a week later: "Since their Moscow meeting and their joint statement, the

Soviet Union and all the socialist countries, with the exception of China and Albania, have firmly held the initiative in the . . . Middle East."[56]

ULBRICHT SNARLS AT WEST GERMANY

East Germany, in an awkward position during this period because of its political isolation, shared full diplomatic relations only with other communist states (except for Albania, which had recalled its ambassador in December 1961).[57] This isolation resulted, in part, from the West German Hallstein doctrine of 1955, which stipulated that the FRG would sever relations with any state that recognized the German Democratic Republic (GDR). As a result, the East Germans perceived the FRG as their primary enemy and the USSR as their major supporter. The establishment of diplomatic relations between Romania and the FRG in January had distressed Ulbricht, and one may assume that the German leader had done his best at Karlovy Vary to keep the other Warsaw Pact members from recognizing the Federal Republic. The situation was causing considerable tension within the pact at the time the Middle East war broke out.

The GDR, like the USSR and its orthodox allies, supported the Arab position.[58] But the East German media tended to pay less attention to the Middle East and more to the FRG than did the other Warsaw Pact media. Even before the Arab–Israeli fighting began, the East German radio and press highlighted West German links with Israel, citing rumors to the effect that the FRG had been sending arms, aid, and "volunteers" to Israel.[59]

With the commencement of hostilities, the East Germans stood solidly behind the Arabs, whom they portrayed as the victims of Israeli aggression. Premier Willi Stoph, speaking in Dresden on 5 June, said:

> Full of indignation we received the news a few hours ago that Israel has started large-scale action by land and air against the Arab peoples. . . . In view of this aggression, we express our entire support for the assaulted Arab peoples . . . [and] condemn this new imperialist plot in the Middle East.[60]

The East Germans followed the Soviet line in interpreting the motives of the United States, Britain, and West Germany in the Middle East and in accusing the West Germans of pursuing a policy of revenge.[61] The most authoritative interpretation came from Ulbricht. In three major addresses in two weeks, he essentially reiterated the Soviet position, emphasizing the themes of U.S. oil and strategic needs and West German militarism and revanche.[62]

But as before the war, the East German media's emphasis, because of GDR political sensitivities, differed on one fundamental issue from that of the other socialist media. Specifically, the Soviets, after declaring Israel the aggressor, claimed that Israel was being aided primarily by the United States and Great

Britain and secondarily by the FRG. The East Germans, however, portrayed the Americans and West Germans primarily and the British secondarily as Israel's main supporters.[63] The GDR media continued to hint at a conspiracy between the FRG and Israel that included West Germany's foreknowledge of the Israeli "aggression," as evidenced by Bonn's having sent volunteers, mercenaries, and weapons to Israel before the Israelis attacked.[64]

The East German media adopted the Soviet statement of 5 June condemning the Israeli aggression and demanding that the Israeli forces withdraw. The next day, ADN Domestic Service repeated the Soviet demands,[65] as did a Council of Ministers declaration on 7 June: "The GDR Government . . . emphatically demands the immediate cessation of the aggressive actions of Israel and the withdrawal of the Israeli forces to the positions occupied prior to the aggression."[66] On 9 June, the GDR delegation signed the Moscow conference statement. The question of severing diplomatic relations with Israel did not arise, as the two states had never recognized each other. Kosygin's demands and threats against Israel at the UN General Assembly on 19 June were repeated the next day in the same forum by Stoph[67] and by Ulbricht on 22 June in Potsdam.[68]

Criticism of the Chinese for undermining socialist unity began on 1 June when the GDR foreign ministry sent a strong note to the PRC chargé d'affaires in the GDR protesting alleged violations of the diplomatic immunity of East German diplomats in Peking.[69] After the Moscow conference, the polemic against China, which centered on the Chinese attacks on Soviet policy, also betrayed the GDR's distrust of the FRG by linking Bonn with Peking:

> When Israel attacked its Arab neighbors on the morning of 5 June, it was not surprising that Bonn applauded this war. . . . What is less understandable is that Bonn is able to enjoy the fellowship of a companion hardly dreamed of, that of the present Peking leaders around Mao Tse-tung.
>
> The more vigorously the Soviet Union and the other socialist and anti-imperialist states in the Security Council, and by other means at their command, insisted on calling a halt to Israel's aggression, the more strident became Peking's anti-Soviet propaganda. . . . Peking is thus playing directly into the hands of Washington and Bonn with their imperialist aims.[70]

One area of fundamental difference with the USSR, and one that may well have contributed to increased tension within the pact, involved Romania's dissidence. The East Germans, unlike the USSR and other orthodox states, explicitly criticized Romania for its position during the crisis.[71] Immediately after the Moscow conference, *Neues Deutschland* published an article, "Economic Agreement between Israel and Romania," which quoted directly from the official West German Foreign Trade Information Office journal, *Nachrichten fuer den Aussenhandel*. The article revealed that on 14 April 1967 Israel and Romania had signed a treaty on the expansion of mutual trade and on the intensification of economic, technical and scientific cooperation. . . . Romania thus becomes the only socialist state with which Israel has concluded an agreement on economic and technological cooperation.[72]

The point of the article was obvious: Romania was in "collusion" with a country that the other Warsaw Pact members had branded an imperialist aggressor.

East Germany remained suspicious of Romania's loyalty. Toward the end of the year, General Heinz Kessler, a deputy minister of national defense, in an article on the Israeli aggression and the Soviet peace policy, omitted Ceausescu from his list of pact leaders on whose support East Germany could count if attacked.

It would be a dangerous mistake to think that this foreign policy and military policy of the CPSU constitutes weakness. The CC of the CPSU repeatedly warned the imperialist circles: do not try to test the strength and resistance and solidarity of the Socialist defense coalition! The statements by Comrades Brezhnev, Gomulka, Novotny, Kadar, and Zhivkov as to the readiness of their peoples and armies to defend the borders of East Germany as if they were their own—those statements are quite unmistakable.[73]

Thus, although East Germany did adhere to Soviet positions during this crisis, its behavior may have begun to be a source of concern for the Soviets. The GDR's hatred for the FRG, its desire for diplomatic recognition, and its antipathy toward Romania were creating problems within the pact. Soviet leaders may have begun to perceive East Germany as yet another threat to socialist unity.

POLAND'S UNPREDICTABLE POPULACE

Poland announced its pro-Arab Middle East position before the 1967 war began. Replying to a 27 May message from President Gamal Nasser explaining the UAR's stand in the Arab–Israeli conflict, Edward Ochab, president of the Polish State Council,

expressed the full support of the Polish Government for the UAR struggle against imperialism and neocolonialism and stated that Poland sees the main source of the present conflict in the growing pressure of the imperialist powers, which regard the progressive transformations taking place in the UAR and other Arab countries as a threat to their own interests.[74]

Trybuna Ludu, the Polish party organ, echoed Ochab's reassurances several days later.[75]

But while Polish officialdom clearly stood behind the Arabs as tension rose in the Middle East, some elements of Polish society appeared to question the

Soviet (and Polish) policy in that part of the world. Bernard Margueritte, a French journalist writing from Warsaw, quoted "an outstanding Polish journalist" as saying:

> It is clear that in this new crisis one has to see a new diversionary operation engineered, not by the United States, as the press in our country is bound to say, but by the Soviet Union. The Russians cannot answer the American escalation in Vietnam. Therefore they wanted to warn Washington that they can answer to the new escalation in Vietnam by opening a second front in a region where the possibilities of Soviet intervention are much greater.[76]

With the outbreak of war, the Polish media condemned Israel as the aggressor,[77] and on 6 June, the Polish government made the same demands of Israel that the USSR had made a day earlier: "The Polish nation and government express their deepest indignation over Israel's aggression, condemn the perpetrators, and demand the immediate cessation of the aggression and the withdrawal of Israeli forces to previous positions."[78] Still following the Soviet line, the Poles held the United States and Britain (and later, the FRG) responsible for supporting Israeli aggression.[79]

Popular sentiment, however, diverged significantly from the official position. *Le Monde*'s Warsaw correspondent reported:

> There is no doubt that almost the whole population is on the side of Israel. . . .
> Evidence has been provided by countless messages of sympathy and solidarity, which the [Israeli] embassy in Warsaw received from the very beginning of the crisis by telephone, through telegrams and letters.[80]

No official public notice was taken of pro-Israel public opinion. Gomulka and Premier Jozef Cyrankiewicz went to Moscow for the 9 June emergency meeting and on behalf of Poland signed the official statement condemning Israel. The full text of the statement, including the list of signatories, was broadcast to the Polish people the following day.[81] An editorial in *Trybuna Ludu* on 11 June repeated the paragraph of the Moscow statement threatening that unless Israel stopped fighting and withdrew the signers would do everything necessary to "help the Arab states to give a decisive rebuff to the aggressor."[82]

Warsaw continued to follow Moscow's lead in attributing imperialist motives to the U.S. desire to maintain colonial domination in the region,[83] protect its oil sources, control the Mediterranean, and draw the attention of its NATO allies away from Vietnam,[84] and in implicating the United States, Britain, and the FRG[85] in the Israeli aggression. The Poles, however, introduced an original theme. After noting the Israeli–French–British military attack on the UAR in October 1956, they specifically dissociated France from the activities of the Israelis in the 1967 war.[86] Thus, the traditional Polish–French relationship was not compromised.

Polish divergence from the Soviet line began to show after the Moscow meeting in the timing and conditions of severing relations with Israel. While the USSR, Bulgaria, and Czechoslovakia broke without qualification on 10 June, the Poles waited two days, until 12 June, to act. Moreover, the break was qualified. The official announcement read:

> The Government of the Polish People's Republic has decided to break diplomatic relations with Israel, and states that it will be ready to establish them when Israel withdraws from the territories of Arab states it has seized by force and ceases the policy of aggression toward these states.[87]

Press commentaries over succeeding days repeatedly emphasized to the public not the break itself but the conditions for reestablishing diplomatic relations between the two countries.[88]

This moderation of the official Polish position probably represented a concession to public opinion by the Polish leadership. Popular feeling was described at this time as "running strongly in favor of Israel."[89] The officially encouraged demonstrations held in the USSR and the more orthodox states to protest the Israeli aggression did not occur in Poland. Although Radio Warsaw reported that "rallies and meetings were held today in various parts of Poland to protest Israeli aggression in the Middle East,"[90] it gave only one example.

The top leadership apparently held a number of policy briefings for party and government officials.[91] On 10 June, Adam Rapacki, the Polish foreign minister, briefed a joint meeting of the Sejm Assembly of Seniors and the Sejm foreign relations committee. Konstanty Lubienski, a ZNAK (liberal Catholic coalition) deputy, expressed disapproval of the government's support of the 6 June Moscow statement and the government's failure to reaffirm "Israel's right to existence."[92] The Polish media, without noting the disagreement, said: "After discussion and additional explanations by . . . Rapacki, the assembly . . . adopted a resolution which expressed full support for the stand of the Polish government."[93]

That public opinion favoring Israel had affected Polish official policy was indicated by Gomulka himself. Addressing the Sixth Trade Union Congress in Warsaw on 19 June, the party leader said: "Poland, together with other socialist states, always stood behind and continues to adhere to the position of the existence of the Israeli state. But we condemn most emphatically the aggressive anti-Arab policy of the Israeli government."[94] The following excerpt from Gomulka's speech reveals the extent to which the party and government leaders had been forced to accede to Jewish and pro-Israeli demands, as well as the moral pressure they used to curb these dissident demands:

> We made no difficulties for Polish citizens of Jewish nationality in moving to Israel if they desired it. We hold the position that every Polish citizen should have one country only—People's Poland. . . .

Every citizen of our country enjoys equal rights, and every citizen has identical citizen's duties toward People's Poland. But we cannot remain indifferent toward people who, in the face of a threat to world peace—that is, also to the security of Poland and the peaceful work of our nation—come out in favor of the aggressor, for the wreckers of peace, and for imperialism. Let those who feel that these words are addressed to them, irrespective of their nationality, draw from them proper conclusions.[95]

Clearly Gomulka was caught between Soviet pressure for Warsaw Pact unity and Polish public pressure for greater national self-expression.

Polish policy followed the Soviet course with regard to the problem of Romanian dissidence (that is, ignored it), but differed on the PRC, which the Polish press never explicitly condemned. While the Soviet media were charging the Chinese with pursuing "irresponsible" policies on the Middle East and Vietnam, the Poles remained notably silent.[96] Polish reluctance to engage China may have been due in part to the fact that the Sino–American talks were being held in Warsaw[97] and in part to the fact that the Poles and Chinese were negotiating a trade agreement.[98]

Thus, although the Poles took a "softer" line on China than the Soviets did, under the circumstances the latter may not have seen this difference as cause for alarm. But when the Soviets viewed this behavior in conjunction with the unpredictability of Polish popular support of official policy and the modifications that public opinion could force in official policy, they may well have questioned Poland's reliability as an ally.

HUNGARY SUPPORTS
ROMANIAN DISSIDENCE

Hungary followed the Soviet line in siding with the Arab countries in the Middle East crisis of 1967, accusing Israel of aggression, and implicating the United States and Britain as the imperialist powers backing Israel.[99] The Hungarian media ascribed to the "imperialists" much the same motives for intervention in the Middle East that the Soviet and other orthodox media did, namely, oil and strategic interests.[100] On 6 June, the Hungarian government issued a statement containing the Soviet 5 June demand that the Israelis cease fighting and withdraw.[101]

The Hungarian delegation to the 9 June emergency meeting in Moscow signed the official statement condemning Israel. The following day all the Budapest dailies published the statement of the Moscow meeting, including the names of the signatories, on page one. Lengthy editorials in these dailies on 11 June highlighted the significance of the 9 June statement.[102] Zoltan Komocsin, party secretary and politburo member, reaffirmed Hungary's support of the official position in a radio interview on 14 June:

[The] leaders of seven European countries, including those of our party and government, ... by their signature ... reaffirmed their view that aggression had taken place and that Israel was the aggressor; that they condemn the aggression and with it the imperialist powers, the United States and Britain, its backers.[103]

Hungary may have been somewhat less inclined than some of its socialist neighbors to associate the West Germans with American and British imperialism in the Middle East. The Hungarians were evidently only a step or two behind the Romanians in readiness to take up formal ties with the FRG.[104] Although they fell into line at Karlovy Vary, they continued to show signs of independence in other ways. Nevertheless, Premier Jeno Fock, speaking on 23 June to the UN General Assembly, like other communist leaders in that same forum referred specifically to "the revanchist ... more and more overtly, fascist-inclined military circles" of the FRG.[105] The Hungarians apparently did not, however, specifically associate the FRG with the U.S. and British imperialist intervention in the Middle East.

Hungary, unlike the USSR, Bulgaria, and Czechoslovakia, which severed relations with Israel resolutely and unequivocally on 10 June (the day after the Moscow meeting), made the break awkwardly and with qualifications. Ambassador Istvan Beck, a department head in the Hungarian foreign ministry, called in the Israeli chargé d'affaires on 10 June. According to MTI Domestic Service:

On behalf of the Hungarian government Beck told him that unless the Israeli government complies without delay with the UN Security Council appeal for a cease-fire, the government of the Hungarian People's Republic will take the necessary steps as regards relations between the two countries.[106]

Beck called in the Israeli chargé again on 12 June, telling him that:

In view of the fact that this warning failed to yield the expected result, the government of the Hungarian People's Republic has decided to break off diplomatic relations with the state of Israel. ... Should the state of Israel ... continue its aggression or fail to withdraw its forces to positions occupied before the start of military operations, then the government of the Hungarian People's Republic will carry into effect further steps as well. ... Should the Israeli government draw the necessary conclusions from the Hungarian note, and act accordingly, the Hungarian government sees no obstacle in the way of restoring normal interstate relations.[107]

Indications of internal opposition to official policy regarding Israel appeared in Hungary as they had in Poland.[108] Gyula Kallai, a member of the Hungarian Socialist Worker's Party (HSWP) politburo and speaker of the National Assembly, in an address to party leaders in Szombathely on 15 June, implied the existence of such opposition:

The cease-fire and the declarations of the socialist countries, our party and government declaration included, generally speaking, have met with our people's approval and appreciation. At the same time the remnants of internal reaction once again began to stir. Discredited elements, of whose political countenance anti-Semitism forms an inseparable part, in the days of armed aggression hoped for the victory of the aggressive leading circles in Israel simply because they acted in alliance with American imperialism and against the progressive forces of the world. However, when the peace-loving forces halted the aggressor they once again resorted to anti-Semitic incitement within. These elements must be firmly called to order. On the other hand there are some people, who because of relatives, cannot understand our firm and unequivocal stand against the Israeli aggressor.[109]

The Hungarians reacted initially to the issue of communist unity by supporting the Romanian position and ignoring the Chinese. (The Soviets had ignored the Romanian dissidence and criticized the PRC for "splintering" the movement.) Ceausescu and Maurer had led a delegation on an official visit to Budapest on 24–26 May 1967. While the communiqué issued after the talks indicated some policy differences between the two states, it also suggested some critical areas of consensus. The omission of any reference to the question of diplomatic relations with West Germany—in the aftermath of Karlovy Vary—was noteworthy. More important, Hungary supported Romania's right to act independently of the other communist countries, specifically, the right not to attend conferences.

The Romanian Communist Party did not attend the Karlovy Vary conference of European communist parties. It is, therefore, a great surprise that a Romanian party delegation has visited Hungary immediately after the conference. Janos Kadar's speech in Karlovy Vary said quite plainly that Hungary and the Hungarian party are of the opinion that the communists of the socialist countries are cooperating in the most essential international problems of Europe and the world, whether they attended the conference or not. The Hungarian and Romanian party delegations exchanged their views in Budapest, in the spirit of this statement.[110]

Even after the emergency meeting in Moscow on 9 June, when the Romanian leaders refused to sign the statement in which the socialist states pledged to "help the peoples of the Arab countries to administer a resolute rebuff to the aggressor," Hungary appeared to support the Romanian position. The Budapest newspapers carried a summary of Romania's version of the statement on the Middle East of 10 June, albeit without comment.[111]

On 18 June, in what appears to have been a reversal of policy, Deputy Premier Antal Apro, speaking in Oroshaza, stressed again the importance of communist unity in the wake of the Middle East crisis and specifically warned that a "neutral standpoint" would favor Israeli aggression.[112] That he meant Romania's neutral standpoint was obvious.

Also noteworthy for its deviation from the usual pattern was the low visibility maintained by party leader Janos Kadar during this period. While Zhivkov, Ulbricht, Novotny, and Gomulka spoke publicly and frequently on the issues involved, Kadar seemed to prefer to remain silent and out of public sight.

To conclude, Hungary differed from the USSR and the more orthodox countries in its responses to this crisis, playing down the FRG's role in the Middle East, ignoring the divisive activities of the PRC, hesitating to break with Israel, and overtly supporting, then criticizing the Romanian stand.

CEAUSESCU REFUSES
TO CRITICIZE ISRAEL

Outlining Romania's foreign policy position in a major speech to the Romanian armed forces in Bucharest on 31 May 1967,[113] Ceausescu carefully balanced Romania's adherence to the traditional goals of the socialist states with the demand for full equality and sovereignty.[114] His stand on the Middle East crisis differed basically from that of the USSR and orthodox socialist states; whereas the Soviets were as highly critical of the Israelis as they were supportive of the Arabs, Ceausescu, continuing to weigh his words, offered highly qualified support of the Arabs, but no criticism of the Israelis:

> In our opinion a war or an armed conflict between the Arab states and Israel would not serve the one or the other, but only reactionary circles and international imperialism. This is why our people express their hope that all will be done to avoid an armed conflict, that divergencies will be solved by way of understanding between the sides, and that rational and fair agreements will be reached that will take into account the legitimate rights of the interested peoples.[115]

The Romanians had seen fit, meanwhile, to expand their trade with Israel.[116]

The official Romanian reaction to the outbreak of hostilities between Israel and the UAR clearly deviated from Moscow's 5 June response. Instead of branding Israel the aggressor and demanding its immediate withdrawal, the Romanian first deputy foreign minister on 5 June called in first the UAR ambassador, then the Israeli minister, and handed them similar notes, appealing to each side "to stop hostilities immediately." The notes said also that Romania "would welcome with particular satisfaction the solving by means of negotiations of divergences, the reaching of fair and rational agreements which would take into account the legitimate rights of the interested peoples."[117]

The Romanian media supported the party and government position. Israel was not portrayed as the aggressor, nor were there long commentaries analyzing the "imperialist" motives of the United States, Britain, and the FRG. In fact, the

United States was described as playing a positive role. On 9 June, Radio Bucharest announced that the UN Security Council had met in an extraordinary session the evening before, at the request of both the United States and the USSR, to examine the situation in the Middle East. According to Bucharest Domestic Service:

> The U.S. representative submitted a draft resolution asking Israel and the Arab countries to cease fire and start negotiations for the withdrawal and disengagement of military forces, for renunciation of the use of force and the establishment of a durable peace in the Middle East.[118]

Avoiding the critical polemic style of the Soviets and reporting factually on the Middle East, the Romanian media were the first in any Warsaw Pact country to reveal the Arab military setbacks.[119] Bucharest Domestic Service reported the 9 June UAR communiqué on the cessation of military operations, but unlike the USSR and other pact states, Romania did not at that time demand the withdrawal of Israeli forces. Nor did the media criticize the 6 June UN cease-fire resolution, either for vagueness or for its failure to demand the withdrawal of Israeli forces.[120]

The Romanians attended the 9 June Moscow emergency meeting on the Middle East but were the only ones who refused to sign the statement issued by the participants. After Ceausescu's return to Bucharest, the Romanian party and government put out a separate statement on the Middle East situation.

The Romanian statement of 10 June diverged from the Moscow document in that it did not call Israel the aggressor and, although it demanded that Israel stop fighting and withdraw, it did not threaten "to do everything necessary" to help the Arabs rebuff Israel. In their statement, the Romanian party and government called

> for the immediate and definitive cessation of all military action in the Near East, for the adoption of measures which would insure that such actions would not be resumed, and for the withdrawal of the Israeli forces from the occupied territories as well as that of all forces to the limits of the borders existing before the outbreak of the conflict. For the liquidation of the consequences of the military operations and the solution of the problems in dispute in this part of the world, it is necessary for the respective parties to sit down at the negotiating table with a view to finding solutions corresponding to the interests of the respective peoples and insuring and consolidating peace.[121]

Romania's actions at the Moscow meeting obviously further aggravated tensions with its allies. The USSR and other members of the Warsaw Pact (except for the GDR and Hungary) chose to ignore—at least publicly—the Romanian dissidence. Romania's position apparently also created some strain in its relationship with Yugoslavia. A 12 June broadcast announced that it had been "jointly agreed"[122] to postpone a scheduled visit between Ceausescu and Tito.

But on 16 June it was reported that Foreign Minister Corneliu Manescu had gone to Yugoslavia, presumably to iron out differences.[123] Tito's telegram to Ceausescu on the occasion of his birthday on 19 June seemed to indicate that the differences had been smoothed over.[124]

Although the Romanians were able to patch up their relations with the Yugoslavs, this was not the case with their deep and long-standing differences with the Soviets. As noted above, Romania had announced its intention of developing an independent policy in April 1964. More recently, it had created considerable tension within the Warsaw Pact by establishing diplomatic relations with the FRG on 31 January 1967 and, three months later, by refusing to attend the conference of socialist leaders at Karlovy Vary. Ceausescu had made clear his view of Romania's right to act independently within its own borders, within the Warsaw Pact, and within the communist movement. Romania's statements on 5 and 10 June with reference to the Middle East hostilities again demonstrated independence of Moscow.[125]

Ignoring the displeasure of their allies, the Romanians pursued their independent policy toward the Middle East and finally went so far as to try to use their good offices to bring about negotiations between the warring parties, arguing that it was only those involved who could solve the problem.[126] Foreign Minister Manescu called in both the Israeli minister and the UAR ambassador again on 13 June to explain the Romanian government's position.[127] Significantly, the Romanians neither severed nor threatened to sever diplomatic relations with Israel, which remain intact to this day.

In light of Romania's show of independence, the activities of its top leaders— RCP chief Ceausescu and Premier Maurer—following the 9 June Moscow meeting take on added significance. Ceausescu made so many speeches between 15 and 17 June in the Brasov region[128] that his movements took on the aspect of an election campaign. This, coupled with his 7 May charges that the Soviets were trying to undermine his authority over the RCP, makes it appear that Ceausescu was building a public constituency, both to resist pressures to undermine him and to support Romanian policy in the Middle East.

On 17 June, Ceausescu gave his final speech—the tenth in three days—to the Brasov party organization. Reiterating Romania's position on the Middle East and then turning to the matter of Romania's place in the Warsaw Pact, Ceausescu repeated what he had said to the armed forces on 31 May:

> We declare ourselves, as you know, for the abolishment of the aggressive NATO pact and at the same time of the Warsaw Pact within the framework of implementing security in Europe. Of course, as long as the Warsaw Pact exists, Romania, as a member of this pact, is developing and will continue to develop cooperation and joint combat training of our armies, proceeding certainly from the principles which govern the relations between socialist countries . . .

But he added a new and important condition:

And from the fact that each country and each army must be well organized, powerful from all points of view, and possess its own command, able to answer any call.[129]

In specifying the need for a national command of the armed forces, Ceausescu took his demand for national sovereignty and equality within the Warsaw Pact and the communist movement one step further.[130]

Evidence of Soviet pressure on the Romanian leadership appeared in two actions that it took. First, on 21 June it postponed until 24 July the seventh session of the State Council of Romania, which had been scheduled to begin on 28 June.[131] Second, a plenary meeting of the CC RCP on 26–27 June "established measures for steadily perfecting the activity of the Ministry of Internal Affairs and improving its organizational structure."[132] In light of Ceausescu's 7 May accusations that the CPSU had tried to subvert his leadership of the RCP, the decision to strengthen the ministry charged with internal security took on particular significance.

Premier Maurer, in the United States to represent Romania at the UN General Assembly emergency session on the Middle East, engaged in some extraordinary diplomacy in New York and Washington. Interacting with Western leaders (including the President of the United States) independently of the Soviets and his Warsaw Pact counterparts, he became deeply involved in seeking a compromise solution to the Middle East crisis. On 19 June, after Soviet Premier Aleksey Kosygin addressed the General Assembly,[133] Maurer discussed with Abdul Rahman Pazhwak, the General Assembly chairman, "problems connected with the present extraordinary session."[134] The following day, Maurer met with U.S. Secretary of State Dean Rusk,[135] then with the Danish Prime Minister and Foreign Minister Jens Otto Krag, who had also met with Dean Rusk. Observers speculated on the possibility that Krag and Maurer were trying to work out a compromise aimed at persuading the Arabs and Israelis to agree on certain concessions.[136]

Maurer's peacemaking activities in New York continued. On 21 June, he gave a luncheon honoring Krag,[137] then met with Italian, American, and French delegates to discuss "problems of international affairs."[138] The next day, he hosted a luncheon for delegates from the socialist and Arab states.[139]

On 23 June, Maurer delivered a major address to the UN General Assembly in which he deviated from the stand of the other communist countries by calling for negotiations and agreements for a lasting Middle East settlement:[140]

The Romanian Government, expressing its confidence in the capacity of the peoples to solve problems, no matter how complicated, and to imprint a rational course of events, has pronounced and pronounces itself for an approach which, taking into account the fundamental interests of all the states in that region, should lead to a viable settlement by peaceful means.[141]

Refraining from naming an aggressor, and recognizing that all involved had legitimate interests, Maurer demanded first, a cease-fire and withdrawal to prewar truce lines as necessary conditions for achieving peace; second, the elimination of foreign interference in the affairs of the countries in that region; and third, "the observance of the fundamental interests of each state in the Near East region, based upon its independent and sovereign existence."[142]

Finally, Maurer got to the essence of Romanian policy: the encouragement of direct negotiations between participants.

> We consider that no effort from the outside can replace a genuine settlement, by the countries of a region, of their common problems, the only lasting solutions being those which emanate from the thorough acquaintance and long experience of the sides concerned. In the case in which the circumstances hinder the direct contact between these sides, the international community has the duty of creating a climate favoring the realization of this dialog in the future.[143]

Maurer saw Israeli Foreign Minister Abba Eban on 24 June; that evening Rusk gave a dinner party in his honor at which "there was a broad exchange of opinions regarding the current state of Romanian–United States relations and regarding problems on the agenda of the current UN session and other international problems."[144]

President Johnson and Kosygin ended their Glassboro, New Jersey, meeting on 25 June. The next day, Maurer flew to Washington and became the first communist head of government to be received by Johnson in the White House.[145] At a press conference following the meeting, Maurer said that the talks had been useful and frank[146] and that a number of problems had been discussed, including U.S.–Romanian relations, the Middle East, and other world issues. He said also that an expansion of U.S.–Romanian trade was likely, adding that he had "no reason not be be content with the way in which the President looks upon the development of the relationships between the U.S. and Romania."[147]

Maurer's Western diplomacy continued. Flying from Washington, via New York, to Paris for a visit that was officially described as "private," he was received by President de Gaulle on 28 June.[148] The talk with de Gaulle took on added significance, coming as it did immediately after Maurer's meeting with Johnson and in the wake of rumors that Maurer was going to visit Chou En-lai in Peking.[149] Maurer returned to Bucharest on 29 June. The London *Times* of 3 July reported that he had left for Peking, and on 4 July, Reuters quoted a Romanian spokesperson at the UN as saying that Maurer had arrived in Peking. Up to this time there had been no official confirmation in either Bucharest or Peking.[150]

Maurer's Peking visit made him the only communist leader to have had contacts with both the Arabs and Israelis and the Americans, Soviets, and Chinese. These contacts gave Maurer a unique negotiating position regarding not only the Middle East but also Vietnam.[151]

Romania, unlike the other Warsaw Pact states, was enjoying increased cultural and economic exchanges with the PRC.[152] Moreover, although Peking criticized the Soviet Middle East policies and the Johnson–Kosygin Glassboro meeting, it remained silent about the Romanian Middle East stand, which was surely less orthodox from the Chinese perspective.[153]

That Romania's actions during this period had a further deleterious effect on its relations with the more orthodox pact members became evident over succeeding days. The USSR, Bulgaria, Czechoslovakia, and the GDR, all of which had attacked the PRC for collusion with the U.S. imperialists earlier in the month, now found cause to express concern over Maurer's actions in Peking. Radio Sofia on 11 July quoted White House spokesperson George Christian as saying that President Johnson had asked Maurer to convey his views to the PRC leaders. On the same day, Radio Prague reported that the Middle East and Vietnam were high on the agenda of the secret Sino–Romanian talks. *Neues Deutschland* reported that in effect Johnson had asked Maurer to convey to the Chinese government his belief that one day the PRC would take a "respected seat" in the UN.[154]

The Romanians avoided a summit conference in Budapest on 11–12 July that was attended by all the other Warsaw Pact members and Yugoslavia. The 12 July communiqué, like the 9 June Moscow statement, included accusations of Israeli "aggression" and threats that the signatories "favored a still fuller use of appropriate means [of] meeting the interests of the struggle against aggression."[155] It was clear why the Romanians absented themselves.

The Budapest meeting aggravated the problems of Soviet–Romanian relations that had developed before and during the Middle East crisis. *Pravda* said on 14 July that the events in the Middle East gave "added urgency" to the need for unity of action by the communist parties.[156] Radio Moscow recommended broadcasts to Romania in Romanian that not only highlighted the theme of joint action and communist party conferences as contributing to the consolidation of communist unity but also explicitly warned against the pursuit of a policy of "optional or neutral internationalism."[157]

Romania's neutrality on the Sino–Soviet dispute, its relations with the FRG, its failure to attend international communist conferences, and its independent diplomacy in the Middle East crisis had finally caused the Soviets to break their silence and to openly attack Romania.

SUMMARY

The widely varying responses of the USSR and the other Warsaw Pact members to the events of June 1967 suggest that:

1) The Middle East war aggravated existing tensions within the pact.

2) The USSR had reason to doubt the reliability of some of the Warsaw Pact states as allies.

Bulgaria, Czechoslovakia, and East Germany remained the USSR's most reliable allies, never wavering in their support of Soviet policy during the Middle East crisis. The GDR's hatred of the FRG and publicly expressed disdain of Romania, however, began to strain internal Warsaw Pact relations and, in the long run, might have become a problem to the Soviet leadership, intent on maintaining communist unity.

Hungary and Poland probably caused the Soviets some immediate concern. In both countries, public opinion apparently had a moderating effect on official policy. Both diverged from the Soviet line in the timing and conditions of severing relations with Israel, in the emphasis their media put on Israel's right to exist, and in their reluctance—each for different reasons—to attack the PRC. The Hungarians, for a couple of weeks, even went so far as to support openly Romania's bid to act independently of the other pact members. Such behavior must have caused the Soviet leaders to begin to question the political reliability of these two allies in a crisis.

Romania continued to pursue its independent policy, challenging the USSR on the basic issue of the limits of Romania's military and political obligations to communist unity in general and to the Warsaw Pact in particular. Specific differences with the USSR involved Romania's refusal to attend international communist conferences, its failure to sign the statement of the 9 June Moscow emergency meeting on the Middle East, its independent diplomacy in seeking a solution to the Middle East crisis, its neutrality in the Sino–Soviet ideological dispute, and its trade and diplomatic relations with the FRG and Israel. But while the Romanians remained a Soviet problem, a new and far more urgent threat demanded immediate attention.

NOTES

1. See Agerpres, *Statement on the Stand of the Romanian Workers' Party Concerning Problems of the World Communist and Working Class Movement* (Bucharest: Agerpres, 1964), especially pp. 5–51.

2. A more detailed discussion of these events can be found in Fritz Ermarth, *Internationalism, Security, and Legitimacy: The Challenge to Soviet Interests in East Europe, 1964–1968*, The Rand Corporation, RM-5909-PR (March 1969), pp. 33–40; Thomas W. Wolfe, *Soviet Power and Europe, 1945–1970* (Baltimore: The Johns Hopkins Press, 1970), pp. 308–11; and A. Ross Johnson, *The Warsaw Pact's Campaign for "European Security,"* The Rand Corporation, R-565-PR (November 1970), pp. 8–12.

3. Willy Brandt claims that Romania, rather than the FRG, brought up the subject of diplomatic relations and pressed for their rapid establishment. See Willy Brandt, *People and Politics: The Years 1960–1975* (Boston: Little, Brown, 1976), p. 170.

4. Nicolae Ceausescu, *Scinteia*, May 7, 1967, in *Foreign Broadcast Information Service (FBIS), Daily Report (DR), USSR and Eastern Europe (USSR & EE)* (May 11, 1967), p. JJ2.

5. Ibid., p. JJ4.

6. Ibid., pp. JJ4–5.

7. The Washington–Moscow hot line, established by agreement in 1963, was inaugurated by the Soviet leadership during the early hours of 5 June, 1967. Lyndon Baines Johnson, *The Vantage Point: Perspectives of the Presidency, 1963–1969* (New York: Holt, Rinehart and Winston, 1971), p. 287.

8. Moscow Domestic Service, 1300 Greenwich Meantime (GMT), June 4, 1967, in *FBIS, DR, USSR & EE* (June 6, 1967), pp. BB12–14.

9. See, for example, Victor Mayevskiy, *Pravda*, June 4, 1967, in *FBIS, DR, USSR & EE* (June 5, 1967), pp. BB6–7.

10. Moscow Domestic Service, 1000 GMT, June 5, 1967, in *FBIS, DR, USSR & EE* (June 5, 1967), p. BB1.

11. Moscow TASS International Service, 1402 GMT, June 5, 1967, in *FBIS, DR, USSR & EE* (June 6, 1967), p. BB9.

12. *FBIS, DR, USSR & EE* (June 6, 1967), p. BB1.

13. Igor Belyayev, *Pravda*, June 6, 1967, in *FBIS, DR, USSR & EE* (June 6, 1967), p. BB10; Sergey Kondrashov, *Izvestiya*, June 6, 1967, in *FBIS, DR, USSR & EE* (June 8, 1967), p. BB4.

14. Moscow Domestic Service, 1300 GMT, June 6, 1967, reported: "The Arab Command said today that it has real proof of interference by U.S. and British aircraft, which are based on aircraft carriers, in military actions on the Israeli side," and noted that "on the eve of military hostilities, West Germany delivered to Israel several thousand gas masks." *FBIS, DR, USSR & EE* (June 8, 1967), pp. BB4–5. See also Yevgeniy Grigoryev, *Pravda*, June 10, 1967, in *FBIS, DR, USSR & EE* (June 12, 1967), p. BB29.

15. Moscow TASS International Service, 1138 GMT, June 6, 1967, in *FBIS, DR, USSR & EE* (June 6, 1967), p. BB5.

16. *FBIS, DR, USSR & EE* (June 7, 1967), p. BB17.

17. Although still a de jure member of the Warsaw Pact, Albania had not participated in pact affairs since the Twenty-second CPSU Congress in October 1961 and sent no delegate to the conference on the Middle East.

18. Moscow Domestic Service, 2130 GMT, June 9, 1967, noted that the conference had been held and listed eight participating states: Bulgaria, Hungary, GDR, Poland, Romania, USSR, Czechoslovakia, and Yugoslavia. Moscow TASS International Service, 2205 GMT, on the same day, carried the text of the statement, which excluded Romania from the list of the participants and excluded the names of the Romanian delegates from the list of signers. *FBIS, DR, USSR & EE* (June 12, 1967), pp. BB16–17.

19. Ibid., pp. BB17–18.

20. Commentary to Arab world, 1230 GMT, June 10, 1967, in *FBIS, DR, USSR & EE* (June 12, 1967), p. BB19. The same pattern was repeated in *Pravda*. See "The Aggressor Must Be Restrained," *Pravda*, June 11, 1967, in *FBIS, DR, USSR & EE* (June 12, 1967), p. BB22.

21. The entire text of the note can be found in ibid., p. BB24. Bulgaria and Czechoslovakia also immediately severed diplomatic relations with Israel on 10 June, Hungary and Poland on 12 June, and Yugoslavia on 14 June. The GDR did not have diplomatic relations with Israel to begin with. Only Romania among the participants maintained ties with Israel.

22. Lieutenant Colonel A. Leontyev and Yu. Dymov, *Krasnaya Zvezda*, June 9, 1967, in *FBIS, DR, USSR & EE* (June 16, 1967), p. BB17.

23. Vladimir Zhukov, "Review of the Foreign Press," *Krasnaya Zvezda*, June 21, 1967, in *FBIS, DR, USSR & EE* (June 23, 1967), p. BB3.

24. Moscow Domestic Service, 0530 GMT, June 7, 1967, in *FBIS, DR, USSR & EE* (June 8, 1967), p. BB17.

25. See V. Petrov, *Izvestiya*, June 12, 1967, in *FBIS, DR, USSR & EE* (June 13, 1967), p. BB6.

26. I. Aleksandrov, *Krasnaya Zvezda*, June 8, 1967, in *FBIS, DR, USSR & EE* (June 8, 1967), p. BB19.

27. Dmitriy Shevlyagin, *Pravda*, June 14, 1967, in *FBIS, DR, USSR & EE* (June 14, 1967), p. BB23.

28. The stress on Karlovy Vary is interesting in light of the fact that Romania refused to send a delegate to that conference. See Jean Riollot, "The Karlovy Vary Conference," CRD 223/67, *Radio Liberty* (April 20, 1967), pp. 1–4. Radio Liberty, an organization in Munich, Germany, broadcasts news to the Soviet Union and publishes a series of Research Reports and Situation Reports that are available to the public.

29. See, for example, V. Petrov, *Izvestiya*, June 12, 1967, in *FBIS, DR, USSR & EE* (June 13, 1967), p. BB7.

30. Moscow in Romanian to Romania, 1600 GMT and 1800 GMT, June 15, 1967, in *FBIS, DR, USSR & EE* (June 16, 1967), pp. BB22–23; 25.

31. Moscow in Romanian to Romania, 1800 GMT, June 21, 1967, and 1800 GMT, June 22, 1967, in *FBIS, DR, USSR & EE* (June 23, 1967), pp. BB4–8.

32. See Jeffrey Simon, *Comparative Communist Foreign Policy, 1965–1976*, The Rand Corporation, P-6067 (August 1977), pp. 54, 90.

33. Sofia Domestic Service, 1830 GMT, June 3, 1967, in *FBIS, DR, USSR & EE* (June 6, 1967), p. KK3.

34. Bulgarian Situation Report, *Radio Free Europe (RFE)* (June 8, 1967), p. 1. Radio Free Europe, an organization in Munich, Germany, that broadcasts news to Eastern Europe, also publishes a series of Research Reports and Situation Reports that are available to the public.

35. Sofia Domestic Service, 1400 GMT, June 6, 1967, in *FBIS, DR, USSR & EE* (June 7, 1967), p. KK1.

36. Goran Gotev in *Rabotnichesko Delo*, June 8, 1967, in *FBIS, DR, USSR & EE* (June 8, 1967), p. KK1. *Otechestven Front* on 6 June noted that "it is clear to the whole world that the plans for aggression were worked out in the secret offices of the Pentagon." Bulgarian Situation Report, *RFE* (June 8, 1967), p. 4.

37. "The Government of the Bulgarian People's Republic, taking into consideration the fact that the Israeli Government . . . is flagrantly violating the request of the United Nations by retaining the occupied Arab territories has decided to sever diplomatic relations with Israel." Sofia Domestic Service, 1030 GMT, June 11, 1967, in *FBIS, DR, USSR & EE* (June 12, 1967), p. KK1.

38. *Rabotnichesko Delo*, June 10, 1967, in *FBIS, DR, USSR & EE* (June 12, 1967), pp. KK2–3. Dobri Zhurov, Bulgarian minister of national defense, in an article published in *Krasnaya Zvezda* on 3 June also found cause to attack the Chinese. *FBIS, DR, USSR & EE* (June 6, 1967), p. BB22.

39. Bulgarian Situation Report, *RFE* (June 13, 1967), p. 4.

40. Anti-Soviet demonstrations were also held in Peking on the same days. *FBIS, DR, USSR & EE* (June 14, 1967), p. KK2.

41. BTA International Service, 1300 GMT, June 14, 1967, in *FBIS, DR, USSR & EE* (June 14, 1967), p. KK2.

42. Sofia Domestic Service, 1700 GMT, June 16, 1967, in *FBIS, DR, USSR & EE* (June 20, 1967), p. KK7.

43. Sofia Domestic Service, 1000 GMT, June 21, 1967, in *FBIS, DR, USSR & EE* (June 23, 1967), pp. KK6–7.

44. Czechoslovak Situation Report, *RFE* (June 7, 1967), p. 1.

45. Bratislava Domestic Service, 1800 GMT, June 4, 1967, in *FBIS, DR, USSR & EE* (June 9, 1967), p. GG3.

46. Novotny provided an authoritative elucidation of this position in a speech at Lidice on 11 June, published in *Rude Pravo*, June 12, 1967. In addition to discussing West German militarism and revanche, Novotny said: "Undoubtedly Israel would not have been able to undertake such a military campaign had it not been certain of the support of imperialist forces, particularly the United States." *FBIS, DR, USSR & EE* (June 15, 1967), p. GG3.

47. *Mlada Fronta*, June 6, 1967, in *FBIS, DR, USSR & EE* (June 9, 1967), p. GG9.

48. CTK International Service, 2035 GMT, June 5, 1967, in *FBIS, DR, USSR & EE* (June 7, 1967), p. GG4.

49. Prague Domestic Service, 1200 GMT, June 6, 1967, in *FBIS, DR, USSR & EE* (June 6, 1967), p. GG1.

50. Broadcast over Prague Domestic Service, 1200 GMT, June 8, 1967, in *FBIS, DR, USSR & EE* (June 9, 1967), p. GG1.

51. CTK International Service, 1810 GMT, June 10, 1967, in *FBIS, DR, USSR & EE* (June 12, 1967), p. GG1.

52. E. S. Rosian, *Praca* (Bratislava), June 13, 1967, in *FBIS, DR, USSR & EE* (June 16, 1967), p. GG1. See also Prague Domestic Service, 1200 GMT, June 18, 1967, in *FBIS, DR, USSR & EE* (June 19, 1967), pp. GG1-2.

53. *Rude Pravo*, June 11, 1967, in *FBIS, DR, USSR & EE* (June 13, 1967), p. GG2. Novotny also stressed the importance of Karlovy Vary in his Lidice speech that same day, published in *Rude Pravo* on 12 June, in *FBIS, DR, USSR & EE* (June 15, 1967), p. GG5.

54. CTK International Service, 1247 GMT, June 10, 1967, in *FBIS, DR, USSR & EE* (June 12, 1967), p. GG12.

55. *Rude Pravo*, June 12, 1967, in *FBIS, DR, USSR & EE* (June 15, 1967), p. GG4.

56. *Prace*, June 21, 1967, in *FBIS, DR, USSR & EE* (June 22, 1967), p. GG2.

57. The GDR had consulates general in Egypt, Burma, Ceylon, Indonesia, Iraq, Yemen, Cambodia, Syria, and Tanzania. See GDR: Foreign Relations, *RFE* (August 11, 1967), pp. 1-5.

58. See, for example, the June 1 Council of Ministers resolution, ADN Domestic Service, 1710 GMT, June 1, 1967, in *FBIS, DR, USSR & EE* (June 2, 1967), p. EE2.

59. See *Neues Deutschland*, May 31, 1967, in *FBIS, DR, USSR & EE*, p. EE2. Also see East Berlin Domestic Service, 1403 GMT, June 2, 1967; ADN Domestic Service, 1143 GMT, June 3, 1967, in *FBIS, DR, USSR & EE* (June 5, 1967), pp. EEE1-2.

60. *Saechsische Zeitung* (Dresden), June 6, 1967, in *FBIS, DR, USSR & EE* (June 9, 1967), p. EE3.

61. See, for example, Paul Fröhlich, *Sozialistische Demokratie* (East Berlin), June 9, 1967, p. 12, in *Joint Publications Research Service (JPRS)*, 41,777 (July 11, 1967), pp. 8-9. JPRS, like FBIS, translates foreign-language journal articles and reports. These, too, are on file for public reference at the Library of Congress and at many public and university libraries throughout the United States.

62. Walter Ulbricht, "Speech to Leipzig Voters, June 15," *Neues Deutschland*, June 16, 1967, in *FBIS, DR, USSR & EE* (June 19, 1967), especially pp. EE2-9; "Speech to Agriculture Workers in Markkleeberg, June 20," *Neues Deutschland*, June 21, 1967, in *FBIS, DR, USSR & EE* (June 22, 1967), especially pp. EE14-15; "Speech to Potsdam Voters, June 22," *Neues Deutschland*, June 23, 1967, in *FBIS, DR, USSR & EE* (June 26, 1967), especially pp. EE2 and 5.

63. See: *Neues Deutschland*, June 6, 1967, in *FBIS, DR, USSR & EE* (June 7, 1967), pp. EE4-5.

64. Ibid., pp. EE1-2; *Neues Deutschland*, June 10, 1967, in *FBIS, DR, USSR & EE* (June 12, 1967), p. EE2; *Neues Deutschland*, June 11, 1967, in *FBIS, DR, USSR & EE* (June 12, 1967), p. EE4.

65. ADN Domestic Service, 2038 GMT, June 6, 1967, in *FBIS, DR, USSR & EE* (June 7, 1967), p. EE4.

66. ADN Domestic Service, 1910 GMT, June 7, 1967, in *FBIS, DR, USSR & EE* (June 8, 1967), p. EE1.

67. *FBIS, DR, USSR & EE* (June 23, 1967), pp. EE3-4.

68. *FBIS, DR, USSR & EE* (June 26, 1967), p. EE2.

69. ADN Domestic Service, 1800 GMT, June 1, 1967, in *FBIS, DR, USSR & EE* (June 2, 1967), p. EE1.

70. East Berlin Domestic Service, 2110 GMT, June 13, 1967, in *FBIS, DR, USSR & EE* (June 14, 1967), p. EE1.

71. This criticism was not unprecedented. Relations between the two states had worsened after Romania established diplomatic relations with the FRG on 31 January 1967, and on 3 February *Neues Deutschland* had openly criticized Romania's action. East Germany: Foreign Relations, Warsaw Pact, *RFE* (February 3, 1967), pp. 1-6.

72. *Neues Deutschland*, June 12, 1967, in *FBIS, DR, USSR & EE* (June 13, 1967), p. EE1.

73. Heinz Kessler, "Military Aspects of European Security," *Einheit* (East Berlin), December 1967, pp. 1510-20, in *JPRS* 44,058 (January 18, 1968), p.10.

74. PAP International Service, 0715 GMT, June 2, 1967, in *FBIS, DR, USSR & EE* (June 2, 1967), p. FF1.

75. Polish Situation Report, *RFE* (June 5, 1967), p. 2.

76. *Le Monde*, June 3, 1967.

77. Polish Situation Report, *RFE* (June 8, 1967), p. 1.

78. *FBIS, DR, USSR & EE* (June 6, 1967), p. FF1.

79. See "A New Hotbed of War," *Zycie Warszawy*, June 6, 1967, in *FBIS, DR, USSR & EE* (June 7, 1967), p. FF2.

80. Bernard Margueritte, *Le Monde*, June 7, 1967.

81. Polish Situation Report, *RFE* (June 12, 1967), p. 1.

82. *FBIS, DR, USSR & EE* (June 12, 1967), p. FF1.

83. This motive was expressed in the 10 June resolution of a joint meeting of the Sejm Assembly of Seniors and the Sejm foreign relations committee, broadcast by PAP International Service, June 12, 1967. *FBIS, DR, USSR & EE* (June 13, 1967), p. FF4.

84. *Trybuna Ludu*, June 7, 1967, in *FBIS, DR, USSR & EE* (June 8, 1967), p. FF1; Maksimillian Berezowski, *Trybuna Ludu*, June 14, 1967, in *FBIS, DR, USSR & EE* (June 15, 1967), p. FF1.

85. After the 9 June Moscow meeting, the press made frequent reference to West German involvement in Israel. See, for example, "Amunition for Bonn's Claims," *Trybuna Ludu*, June 15, 1967, in *FBIS, DR, USSR & EE* (June 15, 1967), pp. FF1-2. The same linkage was established by Minister of National Defense Marian Spychalski on the occasion of Navy Day, 25 June. *FBIS, DR, USSR & EE* (June 27, 1967), p. FF6.

86. This distinction was carefully developed by Wladyslaw Gomulka in his 19 June speech to the Sixth Trade Union Congress. *FBIS, DR, USSR & EE* (June 20, 1967), p. FF3. The distinction was also emphasized by Cyrankiewicz on 23 June at the UN. *FBIS, DR, USSR & EE* (June 26, 1967), pp. FF3-4.

87. PAP International Service, June 12, 1967, in *FBIS, DR, USSR & EE* (June 13, 1967), p. FF1.

88. See, for example, "Cardinal Conditions for Peace," *Trybuna Ludu*, June 12, 1967, in *FBIS, DR, USSR & EE* (June 14, 1967), p. FF1.

89. Henry Kamm, The New York *Times*, June 13, 1967, p. 18.

90. PAP International Service, 2120 GMT, June 10, 1967, in *FBIS, DR, USSR & EE* (June 12, 1967), p. FF1. The only Polish protest meeting noted was that at the Steel Industry Design Bureau in Krakow.

91. Polish Situation Report, *RFE* (June 15, 1967), p. 2.

92. Bernard Margueritte, *Le Monde*, June 14, 1967, in Polish Situation Report, *RFE* (June 15, 1967), p. 2.

93. PAP International Service, 0715 GMT, June 12, 1967, in *FBIS, DR, USSR & EE* (June 13, 1967), p. FF4. Margueritte pointed out that the Sejm resolution had not been passed unanimously, since Lubienski abstained. Polish Situation Report, *RFE* (June 15, 1967), p. 2.

94. *FBIS, DR, USSR & EE* (June 20, 1967), p. FF4. Cyrankiewicz reiterated this theme in his 23 June address to the UN General Assembly. *FBIS, DR, USSR & EE* (June 26, 1967), especially p. FF3.

95. Ibid., pp. FF5-6.

96. In fact, the Chinese leaders were portrayed in one instance as acting in a rational and responsible fashion. Grzegorz Jaszunski, "The Battle of Hong Kong", *Zycie Warszawy*, June 9, 1967, in *FBIS, DR, USSR & EE* (June 9, 1967), p. FF2.

97. For example, although the USSR discussed at length the one hundred thirty-third meeting of the U.S. and Chinese ambassadors in Warsaw as evidence of USA-PRC collusion, the Poles noted only that the meeting had occurred, but made no comment on its significance. PAP International Service, 1820 GMT, June 14, 1967, in *FBIS, DR, USSR & EE* (June 15, 1967), p. FF2.

98. PAP International Service, 2114 GMT, June 29, 1967, in *FBIS, DR, USSR & EE* (June 30,

1967), p. FF1. Polish–Chinese trade did, in fact, increase during 1967. See Simon, *Comparative Communist Foreign Policy, 1965–1976*, p. 89.

99.   The Hungarian government statement on the Middle East on 6 June 1967, said: "On 5 June Israel committed aggression against the UAR. . . . Israel and the imperialist powers backing it . . . have driven the people of the Near East into another war." MTI Domestic Service, 1950 GMT, June 6, 1967, in *FBIS, DR, USSR & EE* (June 7, 1967), p. HH1. Arpad Pullai, a party secretary, said in a speech on 6 June in Budapest: "It is quite obvious that Israel would not have decided to attack the UAR and to provoke almost the entire Arab world without the support of American imperialism." *Nepszabadsag*, June 7, 1967, in *FBIS, DR, USSR & EE* (June 9, 1967), p. HH3.

100.   Hungarian Situation Report, *RFE* (June 9, 1967), p. 4; *Nepszabadsag*, June 7, 1967, in *FBIS, DR, USSR & EE* (June 9, 1967), pp. HH2–3.

101.   The text of the Hungarian statement can be found in *FBIS, DR, USSR & EE* (June 7, 1967), p. HH1.

102.   Hungarian Situation Report, *RFE* (June 13, 1967), pp. 2–4.

103.   Budapest Domestic Service, 1830 GMT, June 14, 1967, in *FBIS, DR, USSR & EE* (June 15, 1967), pp. HH4–5.

104.   See Brandt, *People and Politics*, p. 170.

105.   *FBIS, DR, USSR & EE* (June 28, 1967), p. HH2.

106.   MTI Domestic Service, 1933 GMT, June 10, 1967, in *FBIS, DR, USSR & EE* (June 12, 1967), p. HH1.

107.   Budapest Domestic Service, 1800 GMT, June 12, 1967, in *FBIS, DR, USSR & EE* (June 13, 1967), p. HH1.

108.   For example, officially organized demonstrations such as were held in the USSR and more orthodox states to protest the Israeli aggression were missing from Hungary.

109.   *FBIS, DR, USSR & EE* (June 16, 1967), pp. HH2–3.

110.   Budapest in Hungarian to Western Europe, 1900 GMT, May 29, 1967, in *FBIS, DR, USSR & EE* (June 1, 1967), p. HH2.

111.   Hungarian Situation Report, *RFE* (June 13, 1967), p. 2.

112.   Ibid.

113.   Bucharest Domestic Service, 1800 GMT, May 31, 1967, in *FBIS, DR, USSR & EE* (June 1, 1967), p. JJ1.

114.   Declaring "the strengthening of collaboration and friendship with all the socialist countries" to be "at the center of Romania's foreign policy," Ceausescu let it be known, however, that Romania was also interested in "developing relations with all states, regardless of their social order." Ibid., p. JJ3.

115.   Ibid.

116.   *FBIS, DR, USSR & EE* (June 6, 1967), p. JJ2.

117.   The full text of the Romanian government appeal was broadcast by Budapest Domestic Service, 2000 GMT, June 5, 1967, in *FBIS, DR, USSR & EE* (June 6, 1967), p. JJ1.

118.   Romanian Situation Report, *RFE* (June 9, 1967), p. 1.

119.   Romanian Situation Report, *RFE* (June 7, 1967), p. 1.

120.   Ibid.

121.   The full text of the statement was broadcast by Bucharest Domestic Service, 1400 GMT, June 10, 1967, in *FBIS, DR, USSR & EE* (June 12, 1967), p. JJ1.

122.   Bucharest Domestic Service, 1800 GMT, June 12, 1967, in *FBIS, DR, USSR & EE* (June 13, 1967), p. JJ1.

123.   *FBIS, DR, USSR & EE* (June 16, 1967), p. JJ6.

124.   Bucharest Domestic Service, 0500 GMT, June 17, 1967, in *FBIS, DR, USSR & EE* (June 19, 1967), p. JJ1.

125.   Radio Bucharest reported on 6 June that Brezhnev had received the Romanian ambassador in Moscow, Teodor Marinescu, for a "comradely talk"; on the same day, TASS called it a

"friendly conversation." The meeting took place the day after the Romanian government had handed appeals for the cessation of hostilities in the Middle East to the UAR and Israeli envoys in Bucharest. Romanian Situation Report, RFE (June 7, 1967), p. 2. Although we cannot know the substance of the Brezhnev–Marinescu discussion, we may assume that Brezhnev protested the Romanian stand.

126. See *Romania Libera*, June 15, 1967, in *FBIS, DR, USSR & EE* (June 16, 1967), p. JJ2.

127. Bucharest Domestic Service, 1400 GMT, June 13, 1967, in *FBIS, DR, USSR & EE* (June 14, 1967), pp. JJ4–5.

128. , On 15 June, Ceausescu spoke in Brasov, Tirgu Secuesc, and Sfintu Gheorghe; the next day to the staff of an institute in Brasov, as well as in Medias, Rupea, Sighisoara, and Blaj; and on 17 June, in Fagaras, Sibiu, and finally to the Brasov party organization. The texts of these speeches can be found in *FBIS, DR, USSR & EE* (June 16, 1967), pp. JJ2–6; (June 20, 1967), pp. JJ1–6; (June 22, 1967), pp. JJ1–5; (June 23, 1967), pp. JJ2–11; and (June 28, 1967), pp. JJ2–10.

129. "Ceausescu Speech to Brasov Party Organization, June 17," *Scinteia*, June 19, 1967, in *FBIS, DR, USSR & EE* (June 28, 1967), p. JJ10. Romanian Defense Minister Col. Gen. Ion Ionita had an interesting article, "Defending Peace and Socialism," in the Soviet military organ, *Krasnaya Zvezda*, June 24, 1967, in which he reiterated Romania's independent policy of maintaining fraternal collaboration with "all socialist countries" and "expanding and strengthening its relations with all states of the world, regardless of their social system." He also criticized U.S. policy in Vietnam and, significantly, omitted any reference to the Middle East. *FBIS, DR, USSR & EE* (June 29, 1967), p. BB30.

130. Ceausescu's attention to the relationship of the national armed forces to the Warsaw Pact (in his speeches of 7 and 31 May and 17 June) may have been related to the delay in appointing a successor to Marshal A. A. Grechko as commander of the Warsaw Pact forces. See also Romanian Situation Report, RFE (June 23, 1967), pp. 4–5. Within two weeks after Ceausescu demanded that "each country and each army possess its own command," the Romanians and Soviets evidently came to some agreement, and Marshal I. I. Yakubovskiy was named commander of the United Armed Forces. See Romanian Situation Report, RFE (July 12, 1967), p. 2. At the July session of the Romanian National Assembly, Colonel General Ionita alluded to a central committee decision providing for increased domestic production of relatively unsophisticated military goods so as to save currency resources for the purchase of more advanced equipment abroad. See Ermarth, *Internationalism, Security, and Legitimacy*, p. 52.

131. Bucharest Domestic Service, 1600 GMT, June 21, 1967, in *FBIS, DR, USSR & EE* (June 22, 1967), p. JJ2.

132. *FBIS, DR, USSR & EE* (June 28, 1967), p. JJ1.

133. On 19 June Radio Bucharest carried only a 15-line report on the speech by Kosygin. Romanian Situation Report, RFE (June 21, 1967), p. 2. Romania provided a marked contrast to the other states, which published the entire address along with lengthy commentaries.

134. Bucharest Domestic Service, 2100 GMT, June 19, 1967, in *FBIS, DR, USSR & EE* (June 20, 1967), p. JJ1.

135. Bucharest Domestic Service, 2100 GMT, June 21, 1967, in *FBIS, DR, USSR & EE* (June 21, 1967), p. JJ1. Soviet Foreign Minister Andrey Gromyko and Maurer were the only communist representatives to meet with the U.S. secretary of state.

136. Romanian Situation Report, RFE (June 21, 1967), p. 1.

137. Bucharest Domestic Service, 2000 GMT, June 21, 1967, in *FBIS, DR, USSR & EE* (June 23, 1967), p. JJ1.

138. Bucharest Domestic Service, 0900 GMT, June 22, 1967, in *FBIS, DR, USSR & EE* (June 22, 1967), p. JJ5.

139. The USSR and GDR were notably absent. A full list of the participants was broadcast by Bucharest International Service, 0925 GMT, June 23, 1967, in *FBIS, DR, USSR & EE* (June 23, 1967), p. JJ1.

140. The New York *Times Index* (1967), p. 678.

141. *FBIS, DR, USSR & EE* (June 26, 1967), p. JJ1.

142. Ibid., p. JJ3.

143. Ibid., pp. JJ4–5. The speech touched off new speculations at the UN regarding the possibility of a Maurer–Krag effort to mediate the Arab–Israeli dispute. Romanian Situation Report, *RFE* (June 30, 1967), pp. 2–3. The communist media gave the speech minimal coverage.

144. Bucharest Domestic Service, 1100 GMT, June 24, 1967, in *FBIS, DR, USSR & EE* (June 26, 1967), p. JJ6.

145. The New York *Times Index* (1967), p. 678.

146. Romanian Situation Report, *RFE* (June 28, 1967), p. 1.

147. Ibid., pp. 1–2.

148. De Gaulle had met with Kosygin on 16 June, when the Soviet premier stopped in Paris on his way to New York. *FBIS, DR, USSR & EE* (June 30, 1967), p. JJ1.

149. Romanian Situation Report, *RFE* (June 28, 1967), p. 2.

150. Romanian Situation Report, *RFE* (July 5, 1967), p. 1.

151. The Romanians subsequently admitted that "this attitude of finding political solutions and of not resorting to solutions based on force was adopted by this country in connection with the war in Vietnam and with the conflict in the Middle East." Military Publishing House, *National Defense: The Romanian View* (Bucharest: Military Publishing House, 1976), p. 67.

152. See Simon, *Comparative Communist Foreign Policy, 1965–1976*, pp. 90 and 93, for Romania's trade with China in comparison with that of the other Warsaw Pact states.

153. Romanian Situation Report, *RFE* (July 5, 1967), p. 2.

154. Romanian Situation Report, *RFE* (July 12, 1967), p. 1.

155. The full text of the communiqué can be found in *FBIS, DR, USSR & EE* (July 13, 1967), pp. AA1–2.

156. Romanian Situation Report, *RFE* (July 14, 1967), p. 2.

157. Romanian Situation Report, *RFE* (August 23, 1967), pp. 1–3.

3

The Invasion of Czechoslovakia, August 1968

DUBCEK'S CHALLENGE

Soviet efforts to restore communist unity began with the attempt in the fall of 1967 to convene a consultative meeting to prepare for a world communist party conference. After much negotiation, party leaders exacted a promise from the Soviets that they would not excommunicate any communist parties, and invitations were issued to a consultative meeting to be held in Budapest on 26 February 1968.

While these efforts were in progress, the USSR was challenged anew, this time by Czechoslovakia. The Czechoslovak Socialist Republic (CSSR), faced with economic problems and in need of reform, adopted a so-called new economic model, which, like its Yugoslav counterpart, combined a socialist and market economy and required the infusion of Western technological aid. Relations with the West (as witnessed by the Warsaw Pact's response to Romania's diplomatic recognition of the FRG in January 1967), coupled with domestic reforms and the attendant threat to the power of the party apparatus, caused immediate concern among conservatives in Czechoslovakia, the rest of Eastern Europe, and the USSR.[1]

Antonin Novotny, first secretary of the Czechoslovak Communist Party, challenged by liberals from within the CPCS and fearful of losing control, invited Brezhnev to Prague in mid-December 1967, without the approval of the CC CPCS, and appealed to him for support. Brezhnev apparently took a neutral position in the affair and returned to Moscow.

Alexander Dubcek replaced Novotny in early January 1968, promising "democratization" of Czechoslovak political life but professing loyalty to the

USSR.[2] Thereupon, an unprecedented public debate (including even noncommunist groups), joined in by the press and radio, revitalized political life in Czechoslovakia. Prague's new foreign policy became apparent soon afterward.

The Budapest consultative meeting, which opened on 26 February, revealed continuing but not inconsistent disunity. The Soviets, East Germans, and Poles issued hard-line, "centralist" position statements calling for binding political documents, warning against "dangerous nationalistic tendencies," and criticizing the PRC. The Bulgarians and Hungarians showed somewhat more restraint. The Romanians walked out on 29 February, claiming that the Soviets had reneged on their assurance that they would not criticize China.

The surprise came from Czechoslovakia, whose delegate, Vladimir Kouchy, argued against the binding political documents advocated by the centralists and for most of Romania's stands—and even approved some West German positions.[3] Czechoslovak foreign policy, orthodox during the Middle East war, seemed to have been immediately and significantly affected by the change in leadership.

Czechoslovak liberalism spread and, in early March, took on momentum of its own, proving once again the threat of liberal ideas to the communist system. Not only was there wider public expression of noncommunist views in Czechoslovakia, but student and intellectual unrest also appeared in the form of public disorders in Poland, contributing to a factional feud within the PUWP.[4] In East Germany, Ulbricht, like Gomulka in Poland, became increasingly concerned about the contagion of liberalism and apparently pressured the Soviets to contain Czechoslovakia.

The Warsaw Pact leaders, meeting in Dresden on 23 March, exacted assurances from Dubcek that his reform would not jeopardize "socialist construction" in the CSSR. Ulbricht censured the Czechoslovaks most vociferously. Poland (involved with its own domestic crisis), Bulgaria, and Hungary refrained from open criticism. The Romanians, who were not invited to Dresden, publicly denounced the deliberations.[5]

The Czechoslovak Communist party's adoption of an "Action Program" on 5 April challenged the system anew. A summary of the program, *Czechoslovakia's Road to Socialism*, published on 9 April, established as the party's goals greater independence in matters of military and foreign policy, including improved relations with Bonn, freedom of the press and assembly, and a role for noncommunist parties and organizations in a national front.[6] Brezhnev reported to the CC CPSU on the Eastern European problem on 9–10 April, following which the Soviet press began an exposé of the threats of subversion by Western (principally U.S. and West German) imperialism and the "rightist excesses" of Prague.

Dubcek went to Moscow on 4–5 May, apparently to convince the Soviet leaders that he retained control of the democratization process and to get a hard currency loan of $440 million to finance machinery imports to bolster the still sagging Czechoslovak economy. He failed on both counts. On 8 May, the hardcore pact members (again minus Romania) met in Moscow to discuss the Czechoslovak situation. At the meeting, Ulbricht and Gomulka pressed for strong measures against Czechoslovakia; the Bulgarians continued to mirror Soviet ambivalence; and Kadar argued against sanctions and for patience. Romania publicly protested the meeting, supported by Yugoslavia and the French, Italian, and Spanish communist parties.[7]

That the Soviets were still attempting to find a compromise solution was evident on 17 May when Aleksey Kosygin began a ten-day visit to Karlovy Vary while Marshal Grechko spent six days in Prague. At the end of May, it was announced that Warsaw Pact maneuvers (Code-named Sumava) would be held in Czechoslovakia in June under the command of Marshal Ivan Yakubovskiy. On 30 May, a plenum of the CPCS central committee first reiterated the party's commitment to the action program, although it now indicated that no opposition parties would be tolerated, and second endorsed an extraordinary party congress to be held in September.

Moscow feared that the Czechoslovaks would use the congress as the occasion to oust the remaining conservatives from the party. After hesitating for about two weeks, the Soviet press again attacked the Czechoslovak reformists. Then, on 27 June, the Czech newspaper *Mlada Fronta* carried a manifesto, "2000 Words," written by Ludvik Vaculik and signed by 70 prominent figures. The manifesto argued that the reform had not gone far enough and that popular action from below was needed to remove the conservatives, who were a stumbling block to democracy. Dubcek disavowed any connection with the manifesto, but the Soviets were clearly suspicious and kept the maneuvering Warsaw Pact troops in Czechoslovakia beyond their intended 30 June termination.

On 4–5 July, each of the Warsaw Pact party leaders (except Ceausescu) sent a letter to the CC CPCS calling the Czechoslovak leaders to a meeting to discuss Czechoslovak policies.[8] When the Czechoslovaks refused (although they offered to hold bilateral party meetings), the Soviet position hardened. On 11 July, *Pravda* for the first time linked the Czechoslovaks with the "counterrevolutionary elements in Hungary" that had led to the invasion of Hungary by the USSR in 1956.[9]

The Soviet, Bulgarian, East German, Hungarian, and Polish leaders met in Poland and issued a letter indicting and threatening the CC CPCS. On 18 July, the CPSU politburo demanded that the Czechoslovak presidium meet with them in the USSR. The Czechoslovaks refused to go to the USSR but arranged to meet the Soviets at Cierna nad Tisou, on the Soviet–Czechoslovak border, on 29 July–1 August. The Czechoslovaks and Soviets were able to reach an agreement, which was ratified by the six involved parties in Bratislava on 3 August.

The Bratislava agreement seemed to signify the end of the crisis and a Czechoslovak victory. The Soviet press ceased its criticism of the Czechoslovak leaders, and the Warsaw Pact troops withdrew.

Seventeen days later, the USSR invaded Czechoslovakia.

THE SOVIETS RESPOND

Walter Ulbricht, the most doctrinaire of the Warsaw Pact communist leaders, went to Czechoslovakia between the visits of Dubcek's supporters Tito and Ceausescu. (The latter was the only Warsaw Pact party chief to back Dubcek.) After bilateral meetings with the Czechoslovak leaders on 12–13 August, Ulbricht went on to Moscow, where he may have played a role in the subsequent Soviet decision to invade Czechoslovakia.[10]

Coincidentally, on 14 August, the Soviet polemic against the Czechoslovak reformers resumed.[11] The Soviet newspaper *Literaturnaya Gazeta* attacked the liberalism of the Czechoslovak press, particularly of *Literarny Listy.*[12] Over succeeding days, other Soviet newspapers added new charges. The theme of West German revanche was developed. The FRG was accused of seeking a new status quo in Eastern Europe, of having plans to invade the GDR and Czechoslovakia, and of maintaining links with "rightist" Yugoslavia and "leftist" China and Albania.[13] The Soviet press attacked the Czechoslovak leadership for, among other reasons, its failure to appreciate the dangers of revanche. It criticized the liberals who advocated a multiparty solution and those whose lack of vigilance permitted subversive activities by antisocialist forces and a "witch hunt against the [Czechoslovak] workers" who had written a letter to *Pravda* to complain about anti-Soviet and anti–Warsaw Pact activities at their plant.[14]

Warsaw Pact troops entered Czechoslovakia during the night of 20–21 August. Although this was a multilateral action (in contrast to the Soviet intervention in Hungary in 1956), the Soviets were the predominant force, contributing about 170,000 of the 225,000 troops.[15] From the beginning, the Soviets claimed that they were responding to an urgent request for aid, including military, from the Czechoslovak party and state leaders "to help in the struggle against counterrevolutionary forces."[16] The "Prague Spring" had ended.

A two-page editorial in *Pravda* on 22 August justified the intervention in terms of the "situation of disarray, vacillation, and uncertainty" in the Czechoslovak communist party, the "existence of reactionary, antisocialist forces which relied on world imperialism for support," the repeated calls by certain party leaders for "ending communist power monopoly," and finally, naming names, the "minority of the presidium members, with Alexander Dubcek at the head, [who] spoke from openly rightwing opportunist positions." The editorial concluded:

> Their wicked treacherous actions created a real threat to Czechoslovakia's socialist gains . . . and the republic itself [was] imperiled.
>
> In that situation it was necessary to act and act purposefully and resolutely without losing time. Therefore, the Soviet Union and other socialist states decided to meet the request of Czechoslovak party leaders and statesmen to render urgent assistance to the fraternal Czechoslovak people, including assistance with armed forces.[17]

Although TASS reported on the first day that many Czechoslovak citizens had expressed "their gratitude to soldiers of the allied armies for their timely arrival in Czechoslovakia to help in the struggle against counterrevolutionary forces,"[18] other reports indicated that the Warsaw Pact forces encountered hostility from the Czechoslovak populace and that a lengthy occupation would be likely.[19] At no time, however, did Czechoslovak forces engage the Warsaw Pact forces: The Czechoslovak government did not call out the army, and the military did not take any initiative in attempting to repel the invaders.[20]

Dubcek was taken forcibly to Moscow but was spared the fate of Imre Nagy, the Hungarian party leader who was tried and executed following the Hungarian uprising in 1956. On 26 August 1968, despite their having accused Dubcek of treachery, the Soviets concluded an agreement on Czechoslovakia's future with him and General Ludvik Svoboda, the Czechoslovak president, who had fought alongside the Soviets in World War II. The two returned to Prague on this date, still more or less in control. Dubcek's apparent success may have been due in part to the fact that the Czechoslovak party and populace united solidly behind him and the Romanian and Yugoslav leaders, as well as the French, Italian, and Spanish communist party heads, supported him.

The Soviet reaction, as reflected in the media, to the role of the other communist states during the crisis built up from indifference at the outset to explicit criticism, after the invasion, of those states and leaders who had remained neutral or opposed the Warsaw Pact action.

Although the Romanians had publicly criticized the Dresden and Moscow meetings of 23 March and 6 May (to which they had not been invited), the Soviets refrained from openly censuring them at the time.[21] As tension over the Czechoslovak situation continued to rise, however, the press emphasized the need for communist unity and criticized Chinese and Albanian "leftist" revisionism.[22] Later, but still before the invasion, it linked "rightist" Yugoslavia with the FRG.

After the invasion—condemned from the socialist side by the Romanians, Yugoslavs, Albanians, and Chinese, as well as by the French, Italian, and Spanish CPs—the Soviet press addressed itself to "rightist" revisionism. On 23 August, Yuriy Zhukov wrote in *Pravda*:

> During recent days some facts have come to light which are difficult to understand. This is, as I would put it, the inconsistent stand taken by leading members of some communist parties who mistrust the actions of the healthy forces of Czechoslovakia and fraternal countries.
>
> Does this not show that some of our friends abroad, obviously misled by imperialist propaganda, have failed to understand the essence of the prevailing situation and are hastily expressing their disagreement with the actions of the socialist countries which are fulfilling the commitments undertaken by them in Bratislava?[23]

The next day, *Izvestiya* named the "misled friends": Noting that the imperialists called the allied action in Czechoslovakia "intervention . . . it is strange, to say the least, to hear exactly the same formulations from the lips of Romanian and Yugoslav leaders."[24]

The "rightists" and "leftists" were linked on 25 August, when the Soviet press noted that Chou En-lai, speaking at the Romanian embassy in Peking, had called on the Czechoslovaks to revolt against the Warsaw Pact and had charged that the Soviets were preparing a similar intervention in Romania.[25] The speech, incidentally, marked the first time the Chinese used the term *social imperialists* in referring to the USSR.[26]

After the Soviets had come to terms with Dubcek and Svoboda, the press criticized the Romanian leaders, including Ceausescu and Maurer, for meeting with Czechoslovak reformers outside Czechoslovakia and reminded them that, were it not for the USSR, socialist Romania would not have survived to cele-brate its twenty-fourth anniversary.[27]

BULGARIA FOLLOWS

Bulgaria, of all the Warsaw Pact members, followed the USSR most closely in dealing with the 1968 Czechoslovak crisis. Between January and August, as the Soviets vacillated between adopting the hard line advocated by Ulbricht and Gomulka and seeking a settlement of the political differences with Czechoslova-kia, the Bulgarians did the same.[28]

A token force of Bulgarian troops invaded Czechoslovakia alongside Soviet forces, and Bulgarian leaders publicly justified the invasion in much the same terms as the Soviets used. General Dobri Dzhurov, Bulgaria's minister of na-tional defense, followed the Soviet line in condemning the continuing imperial-ist, primarily U.S., intervention in the affairs of other nations. He cited as evidence the war in Vietnam and the support of "aggressive circles in Israel" and of "former fascists" in the FRG. Explaining that in the case of Czechoslovakia the Bulgarians were responding to the request of the Czechoslovak leaders for aid, Dzhurov said:

> This decision was welcomed by the small nations and world progressive public opinion with satisfaction. We are actually fulfilling our international and allied duty. May the backward forces understand that counterrevolution cannot take place anywhere.[29]

Politburo member Boris Velchev, to justify the intervention, argued in the Defense Ministry newspaper *Narodna Armiya* that every concession made to antisocialist forces and revisionists threatened the working class. To Velchev, the invasion kept the Czechoslovak communist party from going the way of the revisionist League of Communists of Yugoslavia.[30] Another article in *Narodna Armiya* justified the invasion by linking Czechoslovak dissidence (that is, revisionism) with that in Hungary (which brought on the 1956 Soviet invasion) and in Poland (which led to the March 1968 disorders):

> This form of revisionism deserves our greatest attention, since the events in Hungary in 1956, in Poland in March of this year and in Czechoslovakia were its work. . . . Experience with the malignant spread of revisionism in the Czechoslovak communist party during the last several months teaches communists in socialist countries that antirevisionist therapy and prophylaxis represent an important problem affecting the basic interests of socialism.[31]

Bulgarian military reports from the field claimed that the FRG was directing the Czechoslovak counterrevolution and indicated that Bulgarian troops had encountered anti–Warsaw Pact violence.[32] And, like the Soviets, the Bulgarians predicted that: "The battle for normalization will be difficult and lengthy and will require considerable efforts within Czechoslovakia and outside its borders."[33]

The Bulgarian press reaction to the Czechoslovak crisis mirrored the Soviet but at the same time reflected traditional enmities between Bulgaria and its Balkan neighbors, who now opposed Soviet policy. Tensions between Albania and Bulgaria built up as the Czechoslovak crisis developed, and on 22 July, Bulgaria expelled the Albanian ambassador. The Albanians, in turn, spread reports— which the Bulgarians officially denied—that Soviet troops were massed in Bulgaria, preparing to invade Romania.[34]

The Bulgarians raised the Macedonian question in mid-August—as they tend to do when Soviet–Yugoslav tensions run high—and launched a vigorous press attack against the Yugoslav position on Macedonia, but not against Yugoslav support of Romania and Czechoslovakia (that is, revisionism). When the Yugoslav press condemned the invasion of Czechoslovakia, however, the Bulgarians fell in behind the Soviets in denouncing Yugoslav revisionism.[35]

Remaining silent on the matter of Romanian dissidence until the Soviets finally took it up on 24 August, the Bulgarian press published an article by Boris Petkov that named both leftists and rightists:

> Today again international reaction is spouting fire and brimstone against the joint action of the socialist countries in defense of Czechoslovakia. It is no wonder when this is done by the enemies of communism, socialism and progress. . . . What is really surprising is the fact that there were figures and leaderships of some communist parties who did not succeed in properly orienting themselves in this situation. The positions and the comportment of the Chinese, Albanian, Yugoslav, and Romanian parties appeared in a peculiar light.[36]

General Dzhurov reaffirmed the military and political alliance of Bulgaria and the USSR on 23 September at the anniversary celebration of the Bulgarian

People's Army.[37] The Czechoslovak crisis appeared to create no strain in the Soviet–Bulgarian relationship.

ULBRICHT PRODS BREZHNEV

East Germany adopted a hard line in dealing with the Czechoslovak reforms, as it had done in dealing with the Middle East crisis of 1967, again because of its continuing political isolation and animus against the FRG. In fact, Ulbricht's report on the Czechoslovak situation to the Soviet leaders may well have influenced the Soviet decision to invade. The GDR press, in accusing the FRG of directing the Czechoslovak counterrevolution, revealed the extent of the East Germans' paranoid fear of West German influence in Eastern Europe and lent credence to the hypothesis that Ulbricht was the catalyst of the intervention.[38] As might be expected under the circumstances, the GDR media followed the Soviet line in justifying the invasion.

Harry Czepuk, assistant editor of the party newspaper, *Neues Deutschland*, clarified East Germany's stake in a 1 September editorial. Reiterating the charge that the FRG was directing the Czechoslovak action, he cited as evidence an article in the West German trade journal *Handelsblatt* advising the Czechoslovaks to remain quiet until the occupation troops had departed, which advice he interpreted as instructions to the counterrevolutionaries to go underground and regroup. Czepuk concluded: "That is the very reason why socialist forces in the CSSR and their allies will remain watchful. One thing is clear: the whole iceberg must disappear so that the way might be cleared for good socialist development in our neighboring country."[39] Hence, the East German military establishment concluded that a lengthy occupation would be necessary.[40]

The East Germans stood firm on the issue of communist unity, accusing the PRC of pursuing a policy of splitting the communist movement and of collaborating with the imperialists, namely, the United States and the FRG.[41] During the first week following the invasion, the GDR media, without naming Romania or Yugoslavia, criticized those who did not see the situation from their perspective.[42] The position on unity hardened over the next two weeks. *Junge Welt*, on 6 September 1968, became the first official GDR organ specifically to attack Romania by name.[43]

The East German press concluded that the situation more than ever required proletarian internationalism (implying the hegemony of the USSR), not only to thwart the war plans of West German and American imperialism,[44] but also to promote the development of the socialist states. Referring to the Warsaw Pact invasion of Czechoslovakia as an example of proletarian internationalism in action, Ulbricht said: "There are people who maintain that this military aid action violates the sovereignty of the Czechoslovak Socialist Republic. This is an error."[45] In what was clearly an attack on the Romanian concept of internationalism and unity, politburo member Hermann Axen added an ominous warning:

The joint international interests of the community of socialist states by no means contradict the national interests of the various socialist countries; rather, they unite them. A contradiction can arise only—and this became obvious in connection with the Czechoslovak events—if the party and state management of one country tolerates the repudiation of Marxism–Leninism and socialist internationalism.[46]

Although the evidence remains inconclusive, the hypothesis that Ulbricht prodded the hesitant, if not unwilling, Soviet leaders into invading Czechoslovakia gains plausibility. If some Soviets afterward had second thoughts about the political costs and consequences of the invasion, they may also have had second thoughts about Ulbricht's credibility. Ulbricht's hatred of the FRG, distrust of Romania for recognizing the FRG, and fear of liberal contagion from Czechoslovakia may have coincided with Soviet interest in August 1968 but would become a source of tension with Soviet leaders later.

POLISH UNREST

Internal forces beyond the control of the PUWP leadership significantly affected Polish policy in the 1968 Czechoslovak crisis, as similar forces had affected it in the 1967 Middle East crisis. But whereas in 1967 those forces moderated Polish support of Soviet policy, in 1968 they contributed to it, indeed, probably to the extent of compelling Gomulka to urge the Soviets to invade.

Czechoslovak liberalism had spilled over into Poland and led to public protests in March 1968. The protesters included prominent writers, journalists, philosophers, economists, and sociologists whose liberalism combined Polish nationalism, resentment of Soviet hegemony, and the desire for political and economic reforms. These domestic events led, in turn, to factional feuding and a power struggle within the Polish party and forced Gomulka to seek Soviet support. To head off a possible coup by hardliners, Gomulka bolstered the power of the "technocrat" faction of regional party secretaries.[47]

One may speculate, in the absence of published confirmation, that internal troubles drove Gomulka to support the Soviet invasion, which he saw as a likely way to preserve the status quo in Eastern Europe and his own power in Poland. This assumption would explain Poland's contribution of 40,000 troops (second in size only to the USSR's) to the invasion force.

The Polish press, like the East German, justified the invasion primarily in terms of West German revanchist policy:

It is beyond any doubt that these [Czechoslovak] demands were dictated . . . by West German intelligence centers. . . . It is beyond any doubt that a Czechoslovakia torn away from the socialist community would turn into a bridgehead of West German revanchism.[48]

The orthodox reactions of the military press—from the home front and field—reflected solidarity with both the PUWP and the USSR. Lieutenant General Wojciech Jaruzelski, minister of national defense, claimed that the intervention and Polish participation in it prevented

> an attempt at penetration from the outside aimed at a profound intrusion of imperialist and West German militarism into the Warsaw Pact camp, an attempt to establish strategic pincers, and an attempt against the vital interests of the socialist countries, particularly against the security of Poland and the GDR.[49]

The army newspaper *Zolnierz Wolnosci* devoted considerable space to reports about the Polish troops stationed in Czechoslovakia. A 19 September article, "For Merit in Defense of the Country," described the "dangerous actions" undertaken by Polish soldiers to destroy "illegal underground stations which disseminated untrue, slanderous broadcasts, reviled socialist countries, and incited the population to resist what they called the forces of occupation."[50] The newspaper also indicated that Polish soldiers had faced danger on entering Czechoslovakia and that Polish army helicopters had been fired on. *Zolnierz Wolnosci* implied also that Polish troops were preparing for a long occupation of Czechoslovakia.[51]

Trybuna Ludu, following the lead of the Soviet press after the Soviets had worked out an agreement with Dubcek and Svoboda, devoted a lengthy editorial, "Nationalism Led Astray," to a denunciation of Romania's support of Czechoslovakia in defiance of its other Warsaw Pact allies:

> The stand adopted by the Romanian leaders, who came out against the unanimous action of the fraternal countries of the Warsaw Pact to defend socialist Czechoslovakia against the threat of counterrevolution, cannot be reconciled with this supreme dictate of the moment.[52]

The Polish press also criticized Yugoslavia. Henryk Korotynski, editor of *Zolnierz Wolnosci*, wrote on 5 September: "Yugoslavia not only does not observe the principle of solidarity, she also adds her voice to the anticommunist, antiSoviet chorus."[53] As during the 1967 Middle East war, the press evidenced a lack of concern for the dangers of leftist revisionism, neglecting to follow the orthodox line linking the Chinese with the FRG or with events in Czechoslovakia.

The Czechoslovak crisis seemed—at least superficially—to have the effect of returning Poland to the fold of orthodoxy. From the Soviet perspective, however, this crisis, like the one in 1967, demonstrated the effect of unpredictable and uncontrollable domestic pressures on Polish policy.

KADAR ATTEMPTS MEDIATION

Hungary participated only reluctantly in the invasion of Czechoslovakia. Its reluctance contrasted with the responses of the other Warsaw Pact members to the crisis—the vacillation of the USSR and Bulgaria and the apparent zeal of East Germany and Poland.

The Czechoslovak reforms, particularly the economic experiment, which closely resembled the so-called New Economic Mechanism that the Hungarians had launched in January 1968, elicited Hungarian support.[54] Between January and August 1968, the Hungarian leaders appeared to be walking a tightrope between interest in the Czechoslovak reforms and détente with the FRG on one side and loyalty to the USSR and the other pact members on the other side. In recognizing its responsibilities to the USSR and the more orthodox allies, the Hungarian leadership was doubtless motivated by the hope of preserving the benefits of the liberalization that had been allowed to develop in Hungary following the return to orthodoxy after the 1956 rebellion.[55]

The Hungarians demonstrated their solidarity with the Czechoslovaks in a number of ways. Immediately after the Dresden meeting in March, which had generated considerable tension among the Warsaw Pact members, General Lajos Czinege, the minister of defense, in an address to the Parliament, seemed to qualify Hungary's commitment to the Warsaw Pact organization when he said that Hungary and the other socialist countries would develop their own armies:

> Within the community of fraternal socialist countries the Soviet Union assumes the main burdens of the tasks deriving from this community—in accord with its logical internationalist policy. We and the other socialist countries will develop our armies and will participate in the destruction of the aggressor forces in proportion to our size, economic capacities, and obligations assumed within the Warsaw Pact.[56]

In June, the Hungarian leaders cordially welcomed Dubcek, who had come to Budapest to renew the Czechoslovak–Hungarian mutual defense treaty. And although in a major address during the visit Kadar warned against "antisocialist tendencies" and the danger of West German revanche, he reaffirmed Hungary's "full solidarity" with Prague.[57] Following the July summit meeting in Moscow (boycotted by both the Czechoslovaks and Romanians), the Hungarians published the July letter indicting the Czechoslovak party central committee—possibly without the consent of the other signers.[58]

The Hungarians tried to mediate between the Czechoslovaks and the other Warsaw Pact partners. Kadar, meeting with Dubcek in Komarno on 17 August, counseled caution and moderation. (Later Kadar said that Dubcek's unrealistic attitude had disappointed him.) Although the Hungarians reluctantly supported the decision to invade taken in Moscow on 18 August, Kadar tried to persuade the Warsaw Pact group (USSR, Bulgaria, GDR, and Poland) to reverse that decision. After the Moscow meeting, Kadar met Dubcek on the Czechoslovak–Hungarian border, but it was too late to stop the intervention, and he said nothing.[59] It was rumored, however, that the Czechoslovak ambassador in Budapest was informed of the imminent invasion, and he presumably passed the warning on to Dubcek.[60]

The Hungarian press, unlike the press in the other Warsaw Pact states, avoided personal attacks on the Czechoslovak leaders in the tense days before the invasion. Its approach continued to differ afterward as well. First, while the USSR and its other allies portrayed the Czechoslovak leadership, and especially Dubcek, as "treacherous" and "revisionist," the Hungarians refrained from comment.[61] Second, while the orthodox press suggested that the Warsaw Pact should be the instrument to correct the state of affairs in Czechoslovakia, the Hungarians expressed the view that it was up to the Czechoslovaks to solve their own problems. Lajos Feher, a politburo member and deputy premier, said of the role of the pact forces:

> The only task of these forces is to check counterrevolutionary forces and to give effective aid to the communist party, government, and people of Czechoslovakia in strengthening the socialist system and legality and in insuring the necessary consolidation. The allied forces did not want, and still do not want, to interfere in the solution of the internal affairs of our Czechoslovak friends.[62]

Third, while the Soviet press described open hostility on the part of the Czechoslovak populace and suggested that a long period of occupation would be required, the Hungarian press reported that the streets of Prague were returning to normal and that there were no incidents of violence, and Hungary began to withdraw its troops from Czechoslovakia.[63]

Romania's condemnation of the invasion generated considerable hostility among the pact members, except for Hungary, where criticism of the Romanian position was tempered. An editorial in the Hungarian newspaper *Magyar Hirlap* on 24 August 1968 expressed regret that the intervention had been condemned by leaders of "other socialist countries," and two days before the Soviets, the Hungarians specifically cited Ceausescu by name;[64] however, this criticism had no discernible effect on Hungarian–Romanian relations. While the Soviets and other pact members were openly criticizing Ceausescu, the Hungarian press reported that Ceausescu had met with politburo member Dezmo Nemes and that a discussion of "bilateral relations and problems of interest to the two parties" had taken place in a "warm comradely atmosphere."[65]

In line with the Hungarian sympathy for certain aspects of the Czechoslovak reforms and of the Romanian foreign policy, the Hungarian press criticized neither the rightist revisionism of Yugoslavia nor the leftist revisionism of the PRC.

Premier Jeno Fock, in a speech at the Miklos Zrinyi Military Academy on 25 September 1968, justified in retrospect Hungary's part in the invasion, but also revealed its reluctance:

In view of the events in Czechoslovakia, it was necessary for the socialist countries to take military measures. They were required by our proletarian internationalist duties. . . . We, on our part, did everything possible, also on our own,
to avoid this step.[66]

The Soviets were not unaware of Hungary's special relationship with
Czechoslovakia during this crisis (for example, the warning to the Czechoslovak
ambassador in Budapest that the Warsaw Pact forces were about to invade), nor
were they blind to Hungary's pursuit of relations with the FRG and support of
Romanian independence in 1967. In fact, there is reason to believe that they had
not completely trusted the Hungarians since the 1956 uprising, when the populace and the Hungarian People's Army played an important role in the resistance
against Soviet Troops.[67]

ROMANIA'S REFUSAL TO CENSURE
CZECHOSLOVAKIA

Romania's refusal to censure and invade Czechoslovakia evolved logically from
its April 1964 declaration of independence, its rapprochement with the FRG in
January 1967, and its diplomatic activity with Israel and the Arabs, the United
States, France, NATO, and the PRC during the 1967 Middle East war. The Romanians stood firm throughout the Czechoslovak crisis. In late February, when
the Soviets applied centralist pressure for communist unity at the Budapest consultative meeting, the Romanian press emphasized the important independent
role played by small and medium-sized states (including Romania) but indicated
that these states were "encountering some opposition from the powers accus-
tomed to decide alone in international affairs."[68]

Although the Romanians acceded to Soviet pressure to attend the Budapest
conference of communist parties, they walked out in protest on 29 February.
They were not invited to, and publicly criticized, the Dresden (March) and Moscow (May) pact meetings. And in contrast to the Soviet press, which criticized
the Czechoslovak experiment, the Romanian press stressed the solidarity and
friendship between the Romanian and Czechoslovak parties and people.[69]

In June and July, as the Warsaw Pact forces held maneuvers and tension
heightened, the Romanian press highlighted the historical futility of military
force in international affairs and criticized the role of military blocs in the contemporary world. While the Soviet and Eastern European press demanded military unity to counter the imperialist threat to Czechoslovakia, the Romanian
media saw danger in the failure to respect the basic principles of international
affairs:

Proceeding from the firm conviction that the breeding grounds of strife in any
portion of the globe . . . are generated by the failure to respect the principles

which must govern relations among states and by the brutal attempts of imperialist circles to interfere in the internal affairs of other peoples, Romania continually promotes the establishment of a climate of legality, equity, and respect on a mutual basis.[70]

Romania evidently opposed socialist as well as imperialist blocs.

In a major speech on 14 August, just one week before the invasion of Czechoslovakia, Ceausescu openly supported the Czechoslovak experiment and warned quite candidly that Romania's military obligation to the Warsaw Pact did not include support of intervention in the affairs of an ally. After carefully paying tribute to the USSR's role in the liberation of Romania from the Nazis in World War II, Ceausescu said:

> It is not a secret that in the course of the years some mistakes and unjust practices occurred in the relations among the socialist countries; hence it is necessary to act with great responsibility and determination to remove those mistakes and practices and to develop friendship and collaboration among the socialist countries on the basis of the Marxist–Leninist principles of respect for sovereignty, noninterference in internal affairs, and comradely mutual aid.[71]

Ceausescu described the functions of the Romanian army in the general context of the continuing existence of imperialism and the need therefore to maintain an army to defend socialism. His specific notions of the army's role, however, differed from those of the other Warsaw Pact members. First, he assigned the responsibility for the army to the Romanian party, government, and people:

> As a socialist country and as a member of the Warsaw Pact . . . we set out from the premise that the responsibility and obligation for endowing, instructing, and educating each national army belongs to—and cannot but belong to—the party and government of the respective country. . . . Each army is responsible to the peoples of its country . . . this is an essential and unalienable attribute of national sovereignty. . . . Hence, it follows with the utmost clarity that the command of the armed forces cannot be exercised by an outside organ: this is a sovereign attribute of the leadership of our party and state.[72]

Second, he sought to limit the Warsaw Pact's role and, implicitly, Romania's obligation to the pact:

> The military cooperation of the socialist countries has been and is directed against the danger of an imperialist aggression from outside. . . . There cannot exist any justification for admitting in any way the use of the armed forces in the internal affairs of a country which is a member of the Warsaw Pact. The solving of domestic problems belongs exclusively to the party and people of each country; any interference cannot but harm the cause of socialism.[73]

Repeating his advice to top Soviet and Warsaw Pact leaders for improving relations among the socialist states and restoring socialist unity, Ceausescu demanded (1) the right of each individual party to act independently and (2) noninterference in each party's internal affairs:

Respect for the independence of each party and noninterference in internal affairs is a fundamental condition for the building of relations of equality and mutual trust among the communist and workers' parties and among the socialist countries. Our party, which is consistently guided by these principles . . . has shown its confidence that the Czech and Slovak peoples . . . will consolidate and develop the revolutionary achievements obtained in the interests of their fatherland.[74]

Ceausescu immediately and unequivocally condemned the entry of Warsaw Pact troops into Czechoslovakia as "inconceivable and unjustified." In a brief address to a mass rally in Bucharest on 21 August, he expressed "complete solidarity" with the Czechoslovak party and people:

We know, comrades, that the entry of the forces of the five socialist countries into Czechoslovakia is a great error and a serious danger to peace in Europe and to the fate of socialism in the world. It is inconceivable in today's world, when the peoples are rising to the struggle to defend their national independence and for equality of rights, that a socialist state, that socialist states should violate the freedom and independence of another state.[75]

Although the Soviets withheld open criticism of Romania until they had concluded an agreement with the Czechoslovak leadership on 27 August,[76] tension reached such proportions that many believed an invasion of Romania to be imminent. Rumors circulating in Bucharest and in the West claimed that Soviet troops massed along the Romanian border were prepared to invade momentarily.[77]

The Romanian leadership apparently took the invasion rumors seriously. Ceausescu indicated to the 21 August rally in Bucharest Romania's determination to defend itself against attack and announced the establishment of the so-called Patriotic Guards:[78]

We have today decided to set up worker–peasant . . . guards. . . . We want our people to have their armed units in order to defend . . . the independence and sovereignty of our socialist fatherland. . . . It has been said that there was danger of counterrevolution in Czechoslovakia; perhaps tomorrow they will say that our meeting has mirrored counterrevolutionary tendencies. If so, we will declare to all that the entire Romanian people will not permit anybody to violate the territory of our fatherland.[79]

The press indicated that the armed forces general staff fully supported the Romanian party's condemnation of the inv⸱ ⸱n of Czechoslovakia and its determination to defend Romania against similar attack.[80] Patriotic Guards were set up in industrial and agricultural enterprises and institutions, and the Romanian armed forces remained in a state of military readiness for three months.[81]

These military preparations notwithstanding, the Romanians sought a political solution. On 21 August—the same day that Ceausescu vowed that nobody would be allowed to violate Romanian territory—the party central committee formulated a declaration of the basic principles of Romania's foreign policy, which a special session of the Grand National Assembly adopted the next day (22 August). An editorial in *Scinteia* on 26 August said: "The declaration adopted by. . . the Grand National Assembly gave the power of law to the policy directed toward the continuous strengthening of the friendship and alliance between Romania and the other socialist countries."[82] The thirteen other socialist countries with which Romania wanted to be friendly and allied, according to *Scinteia*, included the Warsaw Pact regulars—the USSR, Bulgaria, Poland, Hungary, and East Germany—as well as Albania, Yugoslavia, and the PRC, all three of which had condemned the incursion into Czechoslovakia.[83]

The declaration, despite Romania's condemnation of the invasion, reaffirmed that country's commitment to the Warsaw Pact:

> As a participant in the Warsaw Pact, Romania has fulfilled and is fulfilling its duties . . . tirelessly concerning itself with the strengthening of its defense capacity . . . so as to be ready at any time to defend . . . the gains of socialism against an imperialist aggression.[84]

But although the Romanians obviously were attempting to pacify the USSR, *Scinteia* refused to concede Romania's basic political principles:

> In no case can our party share the idea that differences of opinions which have arisen between communist parties . . . can be solved otherwise than by the tested paths of comradely discussion. . . . All the more so, it is inadmissible to resort to the path of military action.[85]

Scinteia added that, to avoid exacerbating the disagreement within the Warsaw Pact, Romania had refrained from responding to the criticism of its policies by the countries that had sent troops to Czechoslovakia and had published articles distorting the Romanian communist party's efforts to achieve a "constructive, principled solution of the crisis."[86]

Ceausescu's activities during this period suggest skillful political maneuvering. On 23 August, he met with Czechoslovak leaders Ota Sik and Frantisek Vlasek, who had been in Belgrade at the time of the Soviet invasion of Czechoslovakia and who had hastened to Bucharest to hold "warm, comradely" discussions.[87] Ceausescu held similar warm, comradely discussions with Tito in Vrsac on 24 August and Spanish communist party leader Santiago Carrillo in Bucharest on 27–28 August,[88] both of whom opposed the invasion, as well as with Dezmo Nemes of the HSWP politburo on 28–29 August.[89]

On 25 and 26 August, Ceausescu traveled about the country, as he had done during the June 1967 Middle East war, this time with Premier Maurer, to ensure popular support of Romanian policy. The RCP leader spoke at Brasov, Sfintu Gheorghe, Miercurea Ciuc, and finally, Odorhei Sacuesc, where he reaffirmed Romania's commitment to maintain both its Warsaw Pact obligations and its own sovereignty:

> We are members of the Warsaw Pact and we are determined to carry out our obligations . . . if some socialist country were to be attacked by the imperialists. . . . Our people are determined always to respect their obligations. But we are just as determined not to allow anyone under any pretext to infringe on our national sovereignty.[90]

The invasion of Czechoslovakia permanently altered Romania's military relationship with the Warsaw Pact generally and the USSR specifically. Although it remained committed to the pact, Romania enhanced its military self-defense force by retaining and expanding the Patriotic Guards.[91] Its military difficulties with the USSR continued even after the threat of a Soviet invasion of Romania appeared to have passed. The issue involved the Soviet demand that Romania, as a member of the Warsaw Pact, honor its obligations, including allowing joint maneuvers on its territory. Despite renewed Soviet pressures in September 1968, the Romanians refused.[92]

The Czechoslovak crisis drove the Romanians into closer political and economic ties with the West, with other socialist countries outside the Warsaw Pact, and especially with its Balkan neighbors (except Bulgaria). Romania found itself in the delicate position of seeking détente with the West and simultaneously reaffirming its adherence to the pact:

> The idea of constantly acting for the creation of a climate of détente, mutual trust, and cooperation between all states, irrespective of their social system, is deeply rooted in the conscience of the peoples of the European Continent. . . .
>
> We are linked to the socialist countries . . . for the defense against attack of imperialism and against any outside aggression. Romania faithfully fulfills its role of active member of the Warsaw Pact which, as long as NATO exists, will keep the mission for which it has been formed.[93]

The Romanian economy still depended on Soviet imports, especially for industrial products and some raw materials. Since the invasion, however, the Romanians have significantly expanded their trade with the West (the United States, FRG, France, the United Kingdom, and Italy), as well as with the PRC, Yugoslavia, and the nonaligned nations, clearly with the intention of reducing their economic and political dependence on the USSR.[94]

In sum, Romania pursued its own political, military, and economic policy during the Czechoslovak crisis, apparently with the full support of the Romanian armed forces. But despite its divergence from the orthodox party line, it continued to reaffirm its commitment to the Warsaw Pact and declined to engage in polemics with the USSR and other pact allies. In pursuit of these policies, Romania supported Dubcek and the Czechoslovak reforms and condemned the Warsaw Pact invasion; maintained friendly relations with all socialist states, including those that opposed the invasion, and developed new links with its Balkan neighbors; increased political and economic ties with the West while moving away from the USSR and CMEA; refused to allow Warsaw Pact maneuvers on Romanian soil; and established the Patriotic Guards to defend Romania against invasion.

A NEW ALLIANCE IN THE BALKANS

The Czechoslovak crisis reverberated in the Balkans. Yugoslavia and Albania, like Romania, supported the Czechoslovak reforms. Bulgaria exchanged heated polemics with Yugoslavia and Albania. Yugoslavia and Romania developed a close working relationship.

As Romania became estranged from its pact partners, its leaders turned increasingly toward the Yugoslavs. Ceausescu visited Tito in Belgrade on 3–4 January. At the time of the Dresden meeting, to which neither the Yugoslavs nor the Romanians were invited, Yugoslav Foreign Minsiter Marko Nikezic met with Ceausescu, Maurer, and Manescu in Bucharest (21–23 March). While the orthodox Warsaw Pact leaders met in Moscow on 8 May, Ceausescu held discussions with Vladimir Bakaric, the Croatian party leader. Ceausescu, together with Maurer and other Romanian officials, visited Yugoslavia again on 27 May–1 June. Tito, and then Ceausescu, went to Prague just before the invasion.

An editorial in the Yugoslav party newspaper *Borba* on 9 August 1968, the eve of Tito's departure for Prague, explained Yugoslav support of the Czechoslovak reforms, "which mean an important contribution to the richness of socialist paths, to the democratization and full equality of all nations."[95]

Tito condemned the Warsaw Pact invasion[96] and convened an emergency session of the presidium and the executive committee to discuss the emergency. The lead article in *Borba* on 22 August reiterated Yugoslav support for the Czechoslovaks,[97] and the emergency tenth plenum of the CC League of Communists Yugoslavia (LCY) on 23 August issued an official resolution on Czechoslovakia and the USSR, which said in part:

1) The Yugoslav League of Communists Central Committee expresses its protest against a violent action whose methods and aims are diametrically opposed to socialist principles. . . . Never before in the history of socialism has an act of hegemonism and bureaucratic despotism been so isolated and naked in opposing the historic interests of the working class and the anti-imperialist forces.

2) The occupation of Czechoslovakia is not an accidental mistake, but the consequence of the persistent efforts to settle contradictions and conflicts within socialism . . . by means of a growing use of force in order to maintain outdated relations and institutions. . . . The blow against the Czechoslovak CP does not amount to assistance, but strangles its development.

3) Communists should be in the van of this struggle to liberate people both ideologically and with action. The intervention of the five member countries of the Warsaw Pact in Czechoslovakia is in profound contradiction to these elementary requirements, demonstrating once again that bloc policy safeguards neither a just peace nor independence. Hence, the struggle to surmount the bloc division of the world is part and parcel of the struggle against imperialism, hegemonism, and war. The policy of nonalignment is the expression of resistance of peoples which feel threatened by this sort of practice in international relations.[98]

The Yugoslavs' opposition to the invasion and to the use of force to maintain outdated relations and institutions, as well as their preference for the political settlement of differences between socialist states, coincided with the Romanian positions.

The Warsaw Pact members attacked the Yugoslav protests and justified the intervention as a measure to keep the Czechoslovak communist party from going the way of the revisionist LCY. The Soviet media accused Yugoslavia of having joined the imperialist chorus. The Bulgarian, Polish, and East German newspapers echoed these accusations and claimed further that the Yugoslav system had failed and that the Yugoslav path to socialism was a false one. The Yugoslav press responded with further criticism of the invasion.[99]

Romania (and Hungary) remained aloof from the polemic between the orthodox Warsaw Pact states and Yugoslavia, and Romania continued to support the Yugoslav positions. At the height of the crisis (24 August), Tito and Ceausescu met in Vrsac, near the Romanian–Yugoslav border, where they held "warm, comradely" discussions "concerning bilateral relations and current international problems of interest to both countries."[100]

The Yugoslav people's army, like the Romanian army, fully approved its national leaders' stand on the invasion, including (in the case of the Yugoslav army) the 23 August resolution of the CC LCY.[101] As tension intensified, so did rumors of an impending invasion of Yugoslavia. The Yugoslavs, again like the Romanians, responded to the threat by expanding the people's defense system.[102] On 24 September, the Yugoslav Federal Assembly committee for social security and national defense established a state security control commission and an ad hoc territorial defense force. The secretary of state for defense, General Nikola Ljubicic, addressed the Federal Assembly on that date to request the measure's immediate passage.[103]

In his address, General Ljubicic explained the concept of an "all-people's defensive war," starting with the general premise that nuclear war was not unlikely and that local wars were a continuing phenomenon of the times.

In case of an aggression, the armed resistance of all the peoples will be raised and will prevent the aggressor from achieving quick success and will make his victory hopeless. . . . The realism of our concept rests on . . . readiness which all our working people have clearly and unequivocally shown in all circumstances whenever danger has arisen from any side threatening to endanger our independence and the achievement of our socialist and self-managing development.[104]

Although the USSR did not invade Yugoslavia, it continued its propaganda attack for the next six months, criticizing not only Yugoslavia's foreign policy (on Czechoslovakia specifically and nonalignment generally) but also its "rightist revisionist" domestic self-management policy. The Yugoslavs responded in kind to the Soviet censure. Following the Soviet condemnation of the Yugoslav doctrine on the rejection of force to solve political disagreements, one Yugoslav commentator said: "The fact remains that imperialism has been done a favor through a political aggression and not by Yugoslavia's struggle against force of any kind whatsoever. We may regret that in Moscow these two things are being confused."[105]

To conclude, the Czechoslovak crisis exacerbated Soviet–Yugoslav tensions. (The June 1967 war, in contrast, did not.) The Czechoslovak crisis, at the same time, drew Yugoslavia and Romania together. Since then, the two states have increasingly evidenced similar political, economic, and military responses toward the United States, Western Europe, the nonaligned nations, and other communist states in successive crises.

THE LEFTIST REVISIONIST CRITIQUE

The Czechoslovak crisis widened the rift between the orthodox communist Warsaw Pact states and the Albanian and Chinese "leftist revisionists." The rift had developed at the Twentieth CPSU Congress (1956), which began the "de-Stalinization" process. After Khrushchev condemned the revisionists at the Twenty-second CPSU Congress (1961), Albania stopped participating in Warsaw Pact activities, although it remained a member de jure, and the two sides began to exchange polemics and charges of revisionism. By the time the Czechoslovak crisis ended, Albania had formally withdrawn from the Warsaw Pact (13 September) and Chou En-lai had offered to aid the Romanians in the event of a Soviet invasion of their country.

Zeri i Popullit, the Albanian party organ, outlining the Albanian position just before the invasion of Czechoslovakia, characterized the Eastern European leaders as "revisionist renegades" who were following the lead of the "Brezhnev–Kosygin clique," exploiting their people, and repressing the "true Marxist–Leninist forces" within their respective parties.[106]

The party newspaper apparently considered Dubcek no better than his predecessor, Novotny, whom it dubbed "Khrushchev's beloved son." It characterized

Czechoslovakia under Dubcek as "a revisionist satellite of the Soviet revisionists . . . now striving to ally itself with the Americans and with western capitalism."[107]

The Albanian Democratic Front organ, *Bashkimi*, articulated the Albanian response to the invasion in an editorial accusing the Warsaw Pact of the oppression and murder of the Czechoslovak people. *Bashkimi* charged that the commander of the Soviet occupation forces in Brno had threatened to "raze the town if the resistance was not stopped." According to the editorial, the pact no longer served its purpose:

> The foul aggression against the Czechoslovak Socialist Republic and the Czechoslovak people substantiates once again what our party has said: that the Warsaw Pact has long since ceased to be a pact for the defense of the socialist countries; that it no longer serves the purpose for which it was created, that is, for defense against German revanchism.[108]

Bulgaria's expulsion of the Albanian ambassador in July led to a bitter polemic exchange, increased tensions among the Balkan countries,[109] and Bulgaria's ultimate isolation from its neighbors. Following the invasion, the Bulgarian press criticized the revisionist positions of the Albanians, Chinese, Romanians, and Yugoslavs alike,[110] while the Albanian press reported that the Soviets were massed in Bulgaria with the intention of invading Romania.[111]

The only Chinese reference to the crisis prior to the invasion took the form of a lengthy summary of the *Zeri i Popullit* article of 24 July,[112] which was carried by the New China News Agency (NCNA) on 9 August and by other Chinese news media the following day.[113] A month later, at the Romanian embassy's Romanian national day reception in Peking, Chou En-lai promised to support Romania in the event of a Soviet invasion.[114] Although this gesture was doubtless intended to be only symbolic in view of the limited Chinese capability to send military aid, it must have annoyed, if not threatened, the Soviets[115] and increased their doubts regarding Romania.

SUMMARY

The Czechoslovak crisis, unique among those studied here in that only Warsaw Pact members were directly involved, united the orthodox pact members in the short term but failed to reassure the USSR of the long-term reliability of its partners.

Of the USSR's staunchest allies in the 1967 Middle East crisis—Bulgaria, Czechoslovakia, and East Germany—Czechoslovakia became the cause of the 1968 imbroglio, while the other two continued to follow the Moscow line.

Poland's apparent support in the 1968 crisis, like its apparent divergence a year earlier, resulted from internal pressures beyond the control of either the

Polish or Soviet leaders. Hence, the Soviets again, if for the opposite reason, had cause to question Poland's reliability.

Both East German and Polish support appeared to depend on the Soviets' maintaining their temporarily frozen European policy, for the USSR obviously could not count on Ulbricht, and apparently not on Gomulka, to back détente and rapprochement with West Germany.

The Soviets probably had doubted Hungarian reliability since the 1956 uprising. Hungary's attempts in the 1968 crisis to mediate between Czechoslovakia and the Warsaw Pact states, its reluctance to participate in the invasion, and its sympathy for Romania's independent policy doubtless reinforced that Soviet evaluation of Hungary as an ally.

The Czechoslovak crisis fundamentally altered Romania's relationship with the Warsaw Pact, as well as relationships among other socialist states, especially the Balkans. The threat of a Soviet invasion nudged Romania, a Warsaw Pact member, and Yugoslavia, a "rightist revisionist," into a close and lasting relationship. The crisis also drew the PRC, a "leftist revisionist," into relations with pact member Romania and, ultimately, with "rightist revisionist" Yugoslavia. Finally, it caused Albania to withdraw from the Warsaw Pact, leaving Bulgaria isolated among varyingly hostile Balkan neighbors.

The developing relationships in the Balkans (in the Southern Tier) and possibly disintegrating relationships between the USSR and its closest allies, the Northern Tier Warsaw Pact countries, form the background against which we will analyze the next crisis—the clash between the USSR and the PRC on the Ussuri River in March 1969.

NOTES

1. R. V. Burks, *The Decline of Communism in Czechoslovakia*, The Rand Corporation, P-3939 (September 1968), pp. 1–8.

2. Pavel Tigrid, *Le Printemps de Prague* (Paris: Editions du Seuil, 1968), p. 141ff.

3. Thomas W. Wolfe, *Soviet Power and Europe, 1945–1970* (Baltimore, Md.: The Johns Hopkins Press, 1970), pp. 355–56.

4. A. Ross Johnson, *The Power Struggle in the Polish Communist Leadership: The "March Events"—End of an Era*, The Rand Corporation, P-4238 (November 1969), pp. 1–15.

5. Ceausescu told the Bucharest party organization on 26 April, "Our country was not invited to the Dresden meeting. We do not reproach anyone for that. But what struck our attention is the fact that at this meeting problems of CMEA activity and of the high command of the united armed forces of the Warsaw Pact were discussed. We hold that the discussion of such problems, referring to international bodies in whose founding Romania took part, cannot be carried out only by some member countries. We are astonished that the military command of the Warsaw Pact member states was discussed." *Scinteia*, April 28, 1968, pp. 1, 3, in *FBIS, DR, Eastern Europe (EE)* (May 3, 1968), p. H15.

6. Paul Ello, ed., *Czechoslovakia's Blueprint for "Freedom"* (Washington, D.C.: Acropolis Books, 1968), pp. 89–178.

7. Wolfe, *Soviet Power and Europe, 1945–1970*, p. 369.

8. *FBIS, DR, EE* (July 1, 1968), pp. D6–11. While all the letters were critical, they varied markedly in tone—Ulbricht's being the harshest, Kadar's the mildest.

9. I. Aleksandrov, "The Attack against the Socialist Foundations of Czechoslovakia," *Pravda*, July 11, 1968, in *FBIS, DR, Soviet Union (SU)* (July 11, 1968), pp. A1–5, especially p. A2.

10. Jiri Valenta, "The Bureaucratic Politics Paradigm and the Soviet Invasion of Czechoslovakia," *Political Science Quarterly*, 94 (Spring 1979): 56–76.

11. Galia Golan, *Reform Rule in Czechoslovakia: The Dubcek Era, 1968–1969* (Cambridge, England: Cambridge University Press, 1971), pp. 24–25.

12. "The Political Will of *Literarny Listy*," *Literaturnaya Gazeta*, August 14, 1968, in *FBIS, DR, SU* (August 15, 1968), p. A2.

13. "What New Policy Has Bonn Invented?" *Izvestiya*, August 15, 1968, in *FBIS, DR, SU* (August 20, 1968), pp. A14–15; V. Matveyev commentary, "Mao's Hope for Disunity" and Nina Vladimirova commentary, "What Is Shown by the Distortions of Albanian Propaganda Concerning the Bratislava Meeting," in *FBIS, DR, SU* (August 19, 1968), pp. A34–36.

14. Vsevolod Kurytsin, "The One Party System and Democracy," Moscow in Czech to Czechoslovakia, 1730 GMT, August 17, 1968, in *FBIS, DR, SU* (August 19, 1968), pp. A36–38; and I. Aleksandrov, "The Blatant Attacks of Reaction," *Pravda*, August 18, 1968, in *FBIS, DR, SU*, (August 19, 1968), pp. A6–7.

15. Poland contributed 40,000 troops; the GDR, Bulgaria, and Hungary each sent a token force of 5,000 to 10,000. Romania refused to participate. H. Gordon Skilling, *Czechoslovakia's Interrupted Revolution* (Princeton: Princeton University Press, 1976), p. 714.

16. Moscow TASS, 0450 GMT, August 21, 1968, in *FBIS, DR, SU* (August 22, 1968), p. A1. Anatoly Dobrynin, the Soviet ambassador to Washington, used the same argument to the U.S. president. See Lyndon Baines Johnson, *The Vantage Point: Perspectives of the Presidency, 1963–1969* (New York: Holt, Rinehart and Winston, 1971), p. 488.

17. *FBIS, DR, SU* (August 22, 1968), pp. A7–13.

18. Moscow TASS, August 21, 1968, in *FBIS, DR, SU* (August 22, 1968), p. A1.

19. Moscow TASS, 1649 GMT, August 24, 1968, in *FBIS, DR, SU* (August 27, 1968), p. A21; *Krasnaya Zvezda*, August 23, 1968, p. 1, in *FBIS, DR, SU* (August 27, 1968), p. A8.

20. The Soviets established headquarters at Milovice, near Prague, as the Central Group of Soviet Forces, thus becoming an occupation army to keep an eye on Czechoslovakia. Rudolf Woller, *Warsaw Pact Reserve Systems: A White Paper* (Munich: Bernard & Graefe Verlag, 1978), p. 29. On 16 October, a treaty on the temporary stationing of troops was signed between the USSR and Czechoslovakia, and some of the troops withdrew. Five Soviet divisions remain. Wolfe, *Soviet Power and Europe, 1945–1970*, p. 399. According to Woller, *Warsaw Pact Reserve Systems*, during the temporary command of the Main Political Administration of the Soviet Armed Forces, 9,000 officers were dismissed from the Czechoslovak armed service.

21. This did not mean that the Soviets did not privately criticize the Romanians. Ermarth noted that after both meetings *Pravda* (30 March and 15 May) reported that K. Katushev, the CC CPSU secretary in charge of relations with ruling parties, received the Romanian ambassador to Moscow, "at his [Katushev's] request and had with him a conversation"—not a "friendly," therefore, an unfriendly conversation. Fritz Ermarth, *Internationalism, Security, and Legitimacy: The Challenge to Soviet Interests in East Europe, 1963–1968*, The Rand Corporation, RM-5909-PR (March 1969), p. 82.

22. Vitaliy Korionov, "The Sacred Duty of All Communists," *Pravda*, August 12, 1968, in *FBIS, DR, SU* (August 15, 1968), pp. A2–3.

23. Yuriy Zhukov, "Who Are Their Protectors?" *Pravda*, August 23, 1968, in *FBIS, DR, SU* (August 26, 1968), pp. A10–11.

24. Vladimir Kudryavtsev, "Counterrevolution Disguised as 'Revival,' " *Izvestiya*, August 24, 1968, in *FBIS, DR, SU* (August 26, 1968), p. A3.

25. Moscow Domestic Service, 1530 GMT, August 25, 1968, in *FBIS, DR, SU* (August 26,

1968), pp. A12–13. See also Yuriy Mushkaterov, "Who Are Peking and Belgrade Echoing?" *Sovetskaya Rossiya*, September 12, 1968, in *FBIS, DR, SU* (September 13, 1968), p. A5.

26. See Thomas M. Gottlieb, *Chinese Foreign Policy and the Origins of the Strategic Triangle*, The Rand Corporation, R-1902-NA (November 1977), pp. 84–86.

27. See "An Unusual Attitude," *Izvestiya*, August 26, 1968, in *FBIS, DR, SU* (August 28, 1968), p. A10; Moscow Domestic Service, 1840 GMT, August 26, 1968, in *FBIS, DR, SU* (August 27, 1968), pp. A9–10.

28. The Bulgarians followed the Soviet line throughout, both in supporting Soviet positions at the meetings of the pact members before the invasion and in adopting Soviet press interpretations of the dangers of revisionism.

29. Speech at the commissioning of 1968 military school graduates, August 24, 1968, in *FBIS, DR, EE* (August 25, 1968), p. C7.

30. *FBIS, DR, EE* (September 5, 1968), p. C9.

31. Ivan Grigorov, *Narodna Armiya*, September 4, 1968, p. 3, in *JPRS*, 46,690 (October 17, 1968), pp. 15, 19.

32. Colonel Pyrban Pyrbanov, "We Are Fulfilling an International Duty," *Narodna Armiya*, August 30, 1968, p. 1, in *FBIS, DR, EE* (September 5, 1968), pp. C6–7; Colonel Stancho Mitev, "Vigilance Should Not Decrease," *Narodna Armiya*, September 12, 1968, in Bulgarian Situation Report/63, *RFE* (September 16, 1968), pp. 3–4.

33. Vladimir Kostov, "The Battle for Normalization in Czechoslovakia," *Literaturen Front*, No. 39 (September 19, 1968): 4, in *JPRS*, 46,866 (November 14, 1968), p. 9.

34. *FBIS, DR, EE* (September 23, 1968), pp. C1–2; and Bulgarian Situation Report/66, *RFE* (September 12, 1968).

35. "Who Distorts the Truth?" *Otechestven Front*, August 18, 1968, p. 3, in *JPRS*, 46,478 (September 20, 1968), pp. 14–24; "Do Not Throw a Boomerang, Because It Returns," *Rabotnichesko Delo* (August 21, 1968), in Bulgarian Press Survey/682, *RFE* (September 5, 1968).

36. Boris Petkov, "Internationalism in Action," *Rabotnichesko Delo* (September 3, 1968), p. 2, in *FBIS, DR, EE* (September 5, 1968), p. C9.

37. *FBIS, DR, EE* (September 26, 1968), p. C7.

38. In the Czechoslovak crisis as in the Middle East crisis, the East German press blamed, first, the FPG and, second, the United States for many of the world's ills; the other socialist media assessed the responsibility in the reverse order. See "Interview with Admiral Verner, GDR Deputy Defense Minister," *Deutsche Aussenpolitik*, March 1968, pp. 282–91, in *JPRS*, 45,534 (May 31, 1968), p. 13.

39. "New Directions from Bonn," *Neues Deutschland*, September 1, 1968, in GDR: Foreign Relations/11, *RFE* (September 2, 1968), p. 2.

40. See General Kessler, *Volksarmee*, September 3, 1968, pp. 2–3, in *JPRS*, 46,697 (October 18, 1968), p. 56; and Minister of National Defense Heinz Hoffmann, in a speech on September 13, in *FBIS, DR, EE* (September 16, 1968), p. E5.

41. Peter Burschik, "Change in Washington-Peking Relations," *Deutsche Aussenpolitik*, May 1968, pp. 569–77, in *JPRS*, 46,227 (August 19, 1968), pp. 29–45; Peter Burschik, "On the Development of West German–Chinese Relations," *Deutsche Aussenpolitik*, September 1968, pp. 1073–82, in *JPRS*, 46,866 (November 14, 1968), pp. 32–45.

42. "The Point of View of the GDR," *Neues Deutschland*, August 30, 1968, in *FBIS, DR, EE* (August 30, 1968), p. E2.

43. GDR: Foreign Relations/13, *RFE* (September 9, 1968), p. 1.

44. Heinz Niemann, *Neuer Weg*, October 1968, pp. 972–75, in *JPRS*, 46,939 (November 25, 1968), pp. 31–36.

45. "Our United Defense Strength Bridles Every Aggressor," *Volksarmee*, No. 43 (October 1968): 2–5, in *JPRS*, 47,679 (March 19, 1969), pp. 135–36.

46. "Proletarian Internationalism in Our Time," *Einheit*, No. 10 (October 1968): 1203–19, in *JPRS*, 46,866 (November 14, 1968), p. 62.

47. A. Ross Johnson, *The Polish Riots and Gomulka's Fall*, The Rand Corporation, P-4615 (April 1971), pp. 12–13.

48. "One Must Not Have Waited," *Zolnierz Wolnosci*, August 29, 1968, in *FBIS, DR, EE* (August 29, 1968), pp. G5–6. See also General Roman Paszkowski, *Trybuna Ludu*, August 23, 1968, p. 5, in *JPRS*, 46,478 (September 20, 1968), pp. 84–85.

49. Speech in *Zolnierz Wolnosci*, September 2, 1968, p. 2, in *FBIS, DR, EE* (September 6, 1968), p. G5.

50. Polish Situation Report/69, *RFE* (September 27, 1968), p. 3.

51. "In the Brotherly Republic," *Zolnierz Wolnosci*, September 21–22 1968, ibid.

52. Editorial, *Trybuna Ludu*, August 29, 1968, in *FBIS, DR, EE* (August 29, 1968), p. G6.

53. Polish Situation Report/63, *RFE* (September 6, 1968), p. 3.

54. Harry Schwartz, *Prague's 200 Days: The Struggle for Democracy in Czechoslovakia* (New York: Praeger, 1969), p. 122.

55. *Pravda* had already linked the Czechoslovaks wth the "counterrevolutionary elements in Hungary," as a result of which the USSR had invaded that country in 1956. *FBIS, DR, SU* (July 11, 1968), p. A2.

56. *Polgari Vedelem*, March 30, 1968 (Supplement), pp. 1–4, in *JPRS*, 45,352 (May 13, 1968), p. 5.

57. Ermarth, *Internationalism, Security, and Legitimacy*, p. 81.

58. Ibid., p. 89.

59. Jean Audie Basset, a French correspondent in Budapest, provided this account of Kadar's attempts at mediation. Paris AFP in English, 1953 GMT, September 6, 1968, in *FBIS, DR, EE* (September 10, 1968), pp. F1–2. Richard Lowenthal supported the account. "The Sparrow in the Cage," *Problems of Communism*, 17 (November–December 1968): 21.

60. Ladislav Bittman, *The Deception Game: Czechoslovak Intelligence in Soviet Political Warfare* (Syracuse, N.Y.: Syracuse University Press, 1972), p. 198.

61. Extensive radio and press summaries of the *Pravda* editorial of 22 August 1968 denouncing Dubcek immediately appeared in Bulgaria, East Germany, and Poland; the Hungarian coverage omitted all of the Soviet accusations against Dubcek and the other Czechoslovak leaders. See East Europe Situation Report/30, *RFE* (August 28, 1968), pp. 3–4.

62. *FBIS, DR, EE* (September 10, 1968), p. F2. Istvan Szirmai, another politburo member, added that the Hungarian army units were supporting "the political solution that was desired at the very beginning. . . . Now it depends on the Czechoslovak communists to bring order. . . ." East Europe Situation Report/28, *RFE* (August 28, 1968), pp. 4–5.

63. "There Is No Overt Objection," *Magyar Hirlap*, September 4, 1968, p. 3, in *FBIS, DR, EE* (September 10, 1968), p. F2. See also L. Szabo, "Among Our Soldiers in Slovakia," *Nepszabadsag*, September 8, 1968, in Hungarian Press Survey, No. 1948, *RFE* (September 16, 1968), pp. 1–4.

64. Hungarian Press Survey, No. 1949, *RFE* (September 18, 1968), pp. 2–4.

65. East Europe Situation Report/29, *RFE* (September 1, 1968), p. 7. See Ermarth's analysis of the meetings between Katushev and the Romanian ambassador in Moscow, about which *Pravda* did not use the word "friendly" and which Ermarth therefore assumed to have been unfriendly. Ermarth, *Internationalism, Security, and Legitimacy*, p. 82.

66. *FBIS, DR, EE* (September 26, 1968), p. F3.

67. As a consequence, the Soviet leaders doubted the loyalty of the Hungarian military, and "the reconstruction and modernization of the Hungarian People's Army [HPA] was begun only after a period of years and after systematic preparations. . . . Proof of the fact that the Soviets do not have unlimited trust in the 'new HPA' is the relatively large numbers of Soviet 'advisers' in the units of the forces." Woller, *Warsaw Pact Reserve Systems*, p. 75.

68. Mircea Malita, "Small and Medium States in International Relations," *Lupta de Clasa*, February 1968, pp. 44–56, in *JPRS*, 45,745 (June 20, 1968), p. 114.

69. Corneliu Vlad, *Lumea*, No. 20 (May 9, 1968): 16–17, in *JPRS*, 45,784 (June 25, 1968), p. 67.

70. Mircea Predescu and Traian Chebelu, *Lumea* (June 27, 1968): 13–15, in *JPRS*, 46,123 (August 7, 1968), p. 98. Also see Dan Ciobanu, "Military Blocs in Contemporary Relations," *Revista Romana de Drept*, July 1968, pp. 41–51, in *JPRS*, 46,603 (October 7, 1968), pp. 60–72.

71. "Speech at the Graduation of Cadets from the General Military Academy, Bucharest," *Scinteia*, August 15, 1968, pp. 1, 3, in *FBIS, DR, EE* (August 20, 1968), p. H3.

72. Ibid., p. H5.

73. Ibid., p. H6.

74. Ibid., pp. H12–13.

75. Bucharest Domestic Service, 1113 GMT, August 21, 1968, in *FBIS, DR, EE* (August 21, 1968), p. H4.

76. See above, note 27.

77. See: E. J. Czerwinski and Jaroslav Piekalkiewicz, eds., *The Soviet Invasion of Czechoslovakia: Its Effects on Eastern Europe* (New York: Praeger, 1973), pp. 164–66.

78. The Patriotic Guards, established by Decree No. 765 of the Romanian State Council, September 4, 1968 (see *Bulletinul Oficial Al Republicii Socialiste Romania*, September 5, 1968, pp. 1133–34), have remained a permanent feature of Romanian defense. The earlier, anti-Nazi Guard of Patriotic Defense, set up by General Emil Bodnaras in 1944, had been disbanded in January 1949. Stephen Fischer-Galati, *Romania* (New York: Praeger, 1957), pp. 122–24.

79. *FBIS, DR, EE* (August 21, 1968), p. H5.

80. Colonel General Ion Ionita, minister of national defense, said: "Inspired by the successes obtained along the road of completing socialist construction, deeply devoted to the state, the people, and the party, the members of the armed forces are devoting all their energy to perfecting their battle and political training, to raising the combat readiness of units." *FBIS, DR, EE* (August 30, 1968), pp. H9–10. Major General Constantin Sociu said: "The countries whose armed forces have unleashed the aggression against Czechoslovakia have brutally violated the provisions of the Warsaw Pact and the principles of this important document." *FBIS, DR, EE* (August 25, 1968), p. H4. General Emil Lepure said: "This intervention cannot have any justification whatsoever." Ibid.

81. Woller, *Warsaw Pact Reserve Systems*, p. 113.

82. Bucharest Agerpres International Service in English, 0905 GMT, August 26, 1968, in *FBIS, DR, EE* (August 26, 1968), p. H1.

83. Ibid. The other socialist countries named were Czechoslovakia, the Democratic Republic of Vietnam, People's Democratic Republic of Korea, Mongolia, and Cuba.

84. Ibid., p. H2.

85. Ibid., pp. H2–3.

86. Ibid., p. H4.

87. Bucharest Domestic Service, 1700 GMT, August 23, 1968, in *FBIS, DR, EE* (August 25, 1968), p. H1.

88. Bucharest Domestic Service, 1400 GMT, August 27, 1968, in *FBIS, DR, EE* (August 30, 1968), p. H3.

89. Bucharest Agerpres International Service, 1949 GMT, August 28, 1968, in *FBIS, DR, EE* (August 29, 1968), p. H2.

90. Bucharest Agerpres International Service, 2130 GMT, August 26, 1968, in *FBIS, DR, EE* (August 28, 1968), p. H13. For Ceausescu's other speeches on 26 August, see *FBIS, DR, EE* (August 27, 1968), pp. H1–9.

91. The size of this force grew from 50,000 in 1968 to 125,000 in 1969. See International Institute for Strategic Studies, *The Military Balance: 1969–1970; 1970–1971*; (London: International Institute for Strategic Studies, 1969; 1970).

92. D. Hanekovic, "Romanian Concerns and Dilemmas," *Vjesnik* (Zagreb), September 22, 1968, p. 5.

93. A. Cimpeanu, "Through Unrelenting Efforts Toward International Détente," *Scinteia*, September 14, 1968, in *FBIS, DR, EE* (September 17, 1968), p. H3.

94. See Jeffrey Simon, *Comparative Communist Foreign Policy, 1965–1976*, The Rand Corporation, P-6067 (August 1977), especially Chapter 7.

95. *Joint Translation Service* (Belgrade), No. 5091 (August 9, 1968): p. 22.

96. Radio Belgrade (August 21, 1968), in Yugoslavia: Foreign Relations, *RFE* (August 22, 1968), p. 1.

97. *Joint Translation Service* (Belgrade), No. 5102 (August 22, 1968): p. 22.

98. Text of resolution of tenth plenum of the CC LCY, in *FBIS, DR, EE* (August 26, 1968), pp. I1–4.

99. C. Zakret, "Escalation Is a Threat to Peace," *Narodna Armija*, August 30, 1968, p. 12, in *JPRS*, 46,589 (October 3, 1968), pp. 1–2.

100. East European Situation Report/25, *RFE* (August 25, 1968), p. 5.

101. *FBIS, DR, EE* (August 25, 1968), p. 15.

102. Immediately before the Middle East war, the Yugoslavs had established the Council of National Defense. See *Sluzheni List SFRJ*, No. 18 (April 26, 1967): 486, in *JPRS*, 41,145 (May 24, 1967), pp. 2–3; General Ivan Gosnjak, "Basic Concepts of Yugoslav National Defense in Case of War," *Narodna Armija*, December 1, 1967, p. 3, in *JPRS*, 44,242 (January 5, 1968), pp. 9–17. See also A. Ross Johnson, *Total National Defense in Yugoslavia*, The Rand Corporation, P-4746 (December 1971).

103. *FBIS, DR, EE* (September 18, 1968), p. I1. The size of the territorial defense force jumped from 19,000 in 1968 to 1,019,000 in 1969. International Institute for Strategic Studies, *The Military Balance: 1969–1970; 1970–1971*.

104. *FBIS, DR, EE* (September 18, 1968), p. I4.

105. "Milika Sundic Commentary," in *FBIS, DR, EE* (August 26, 1968), p. I7.

106. "Soviet Revisionism and Czechoslovakia," *Zeri i Popullit*, July 24, 1968, in *FBIS, DR, EE* (July 25, 1968), p. B1.

107. Ibid., p. B2.

108. "The Warsaw Pact Has Been Turned into a Pact for Wars of Enslavement in the Hands of the Soviet Revisionists," *Bashkimi*, August 27, 1968, in *FBIS, DR, EE* (September 6, 1968), pp. B2–3.

109. See note 34.

110. See note 36.

111. "The Presence of Soviet Troops in Bulgaria," in *FBIS, DR, EE* (September 24, 1968), pp. B1–3.

112. See note 107.

113. See New China News Agency, August 23, 1968, in China: Foreign Relations/2, *RFE* (August 27, 1968), p. 2.

114. Ibid., p. 1. Also see note 25.

115. See Gottlieb, *Chinese Foreign Policy*, pp. 84–86.

4

The Ussuri Incident,
March 1969

UNEASY CALM

Soviet policy toward Western Europe remained quiescent during the fall of 1968; the press continued to hammer away at the themes of the Czechoslovak crisis—counterrevolution, (limited) sovereignty,[1] and revisionism—and the Soviet leaders formalized the arrangements to maintain troops in Czechoslovakia.

Relations with the United States may have caused the Soviets some concern at this time. First, the invasion of Czechoslovakia had prompted Secretary of State Dean Rusk to cancel a joint announcement, which was to have been made on 21 August, of a USA–Soviet agreement to begin SALT discussions on 30 September.[2] Second, Richard Nixon's election to the presidency in November undoubtedly suggested to the Soviets that the United States might be moving in new directions, including that of a change in policy toward the PRC.[3]

Early in 1969, the Soviets turned again toward Europe and, along with the Romanians and Poles, renewed their long-standing appeals for a European security conference.[4] The Warsaw Pact Political Consultative Committee (PCC), meeting in Budapest on 17 March 1969, issued the most conciliatory proposal for a European security conference to that time. What came to be known as the Budapest appeal presented "a concrete program" for "ensuring European security through joint efforts, taking into account the interests of all countries and peoples of Europe."[5]

Two other issues introduced by the Soviets at the Budapest PCC meeting appeared to meet considerable delegate resistance. The first confrontation allegedly arose over the military measures adopted at the session. The second involved the unsuccessful Soviet attempt to have the PCC condemn China following the Soviet–Chinese clashes on Damanskiy Island in the Ussuri River on 2 and 15 March 1969.

This section describes the reactions of the USSR and the other Warsaw Pact members to the interconnected issues raised by the Ussuri incident, the Budapest PCC meeting, and the activities of the Yugoslav revisionists. These reactions provide further evidence of the erosion of both Warsaw Pact cohesiveness and the reliability of some of its members as Soviet allies.

SHATTERED PEACE

The growing number of Chinese-initiated incidents—2,000, according to the Soviet side[6]—along the USSR–PRC boundary since 1959 had concerned the Soviets increasingly.[7] The first serious clash took place on Sunday, 2 March 1969, when Chinese troops attacked Soviet-held Damanskiy Island in the Ussuri River. More than 30 Soviet border guards died in the fighting.[8]

The incident involved the Soviet leadership in a new crisis. Their tension was immediately evident in two actions. First, in what was to this point unprecedented in their diplomatic practice, Soviet envoys called on NATO leaders to discuss the incident and their concerns about the Chinese threat. Second, the Soviets tried to get their Warsaw Pact allies to condemn China's Ussuri attack. In failing, they created new tensions within the pact.[9]

The Soviets showed deliberate restraint during the first four or five days after the attack. On the day of the incident, the Soviet government sent a protest note to the Chinese government accusing Chinese troops of "crossing the Soviet state border and moving on Damanskiy Island." The note demanded the immediate punishment of those responsible (but no compensation) and warned that further provocation would be "rebuffed."[10]

TASS broke the news of the incident about 12 hours after it happened. On 3 March, the press reported protest meetings in the Soviet Far East—in Khabarovsk, Vladivostok, and Blagoveshchensk.[11] Although TASS on 4 March accused Mao of provoking the USSR to gain support for his nationalistic policies on the eve of the Chinese party congress[12] and Moscow radio called the attack "premeditated,"[13] Soviet exploitation of the incident for propaganda was limited at this time. A Czechoslovak correspondent in Moscow said of the situation: "If my assessment is correct, . . . there is an interest in not allowing emotions to be whipped up."[14] On 5 March, Moscow radio made a brief, low-key statement to the effect that China's "impudent claims to Soviet territory . . . show that the incident was not a chance occurrence but premeditated."[15]

The anti-Chinese propaganda barrage began in earnest on 7 March. Speaking in Vladivostok at the funeral of the border guards killed on Damanskiy Island, Colonel General Zakharov, first deputy chairman of the Committee of State Security (KGB), said:

The perfidious intrusion into Soviet territory on March 2 is not a chance or isolated happening. Provocations on the border and insolent claims to Soviet territory have intensified after the PRC leaders began to promote their adventuristic course directed at aggravating Chinese–Soviet relations.[16]

At a press conference in Moscow that same day, Leonid Zamyatin, head of the press department, USSR Ministry of Foreign Affairs, showed photographs of mutilated bodies, charged the Chinese with bayoneting the wounded Soviets to death, and implied that the Chinese were drunk at the time of the attack. Crowds gathered around the Chinese Embassy in Moscow "to express their indignation at the provocation."[17]

The Soviet line accused Mao of collaborating with the United States and West Germany. Viktor Vasilyev, for example, said on 10 March:

The Mao group is now forcing through a radical reorientation of its foreign policy. Acting on a broad front against the Soviet Union and the other socialist countries, it is indulging in an unprincipled political flirtation with the imperialist states, primarily with the United States and West Germany. It was not by chance that the Maoists arranged their bandit raid on the Soviet border guards to coincide with Bonn's provocative act of holding presidential elections in West Berlin.[18]

Despite these accusations of Chinese collusion with the United States and West Germany, evidently intended for domestic consumption, the Soviets did not hesitate, in a bid for foreign sympathy, to have their ambassador to Bonn deliver a government statement on the Ussuri incident to Chancellor Kiesinger. Claiming that there had been 2,000 border incidents since 1960, the Soviet ambassador described China's foreign policy as a threat to "all Asiatic peoples." The other major NATO powers were similarly informed.[19]

More lives were lost and further tension aroused when "a group of armed Chinese soldiers made another attempt to invade . . . Damanskiy Island" on 14 and 15 March.[20] The Soviet propaganda line continued, first, to link the clashes to the "cultural revolution" and the forthcoming (ninth) Chinese party congress, claiming, as it did after the 2 March attack, that the purpose of the provocation was to distract the Chinese people and to create support for Mao and his "military–bureaucratic regime" and, second, to link China with U.S. and West German "imperialism."[21] The Soviets saw Chinese "anti-Sovietism" as a betrayal of socialism.[22]

The 17 March PCC session in Budapest—attended by Bulgaria, Czechoslovakia, East Germany, Poland, Romania, and the USSR—opened five hours late and lasted only two hours. The Soviet attempt (and failure) to convince its Warsaw Pact partners to condemn China's attacks on Damanskiy Island may well have caused the delay;[23] certainly it aggravated tensions within the alliance.

The military measures introduced by the Soviets and adopted by the PCC may also have met with resistance.[24] Nevertheless, the Budapest communiqué on the military reorganization (which was probably aimed at greater military integration) created the impression that the measures had been adopted unanimously:

> The participating states at the meeting examined in detail and unanimously approved the provisions concerning the committee of the Defense Ministers of the Warsaw Pact member states, the new proposal on joint armed forces and a joint command, and other documents aimed at further improving the structure and control organs of the Warsaw Pact defense organization. The commander in chief of the joint armed forces has been entrusted with ensuring implementation of the decisions adopted in accordance with established procedures.[25]

The Budapest appeal—the PCC proposal for a European security conference—listed among the prerequisites of European security: the inviolability of existing boundaries, including the Oder–Neisse and that between East and West Germany; recognition of the existence of the GDR and the FRG; and the FRG's renunciation of nuclear weapons. Soviet media coverage of the appeal focused generally on achieving security and cooperation in Europe:

> The countries participating in the meeting consider it their duty to do everything necessary to guard Europe from new armed conflicts and to develop cooperation between all European countries, regardless of their social system, on the basis of the principles of peaceful coexistence.[26]

The Soviet media failed, however, to separate the West Germany with whom the USSR sought rapprochement from the West Germany of the "imperialists" and "revanchists" with whom the Maoists were conniving. A 19 March editorial in *Krasnaya Zvezda* directly linked, and rejected outright, both Chinese and West German territorial claims:[27]

> The provocative policy of the Peking adventurists is obviously to the liking of the Rhine enemies of a European settlement, enemies who rave about reshaping postwar borders.
> The Budapest appeal has blown away the chimera of the militarists and revanchists. . . . It is not by chance that the appeal stresses that one of the basic preconditions for ensuring European security is the inviolability of existing borders in Europe, including the Oder–Neisse border and also the border between the GDR and the German Federal Republic; an end to the German Federal Republic's claim to represent all German people; a rejection of their ownership of any form of nuclear weapons; and also recognition of the fact that West Berlin does not belong to West Germany but has a special status of its own.[28]

Although the PCC had refused to condemn the Chinese territorial claim (to Damanskiy Island), its rejection of West German territorial claims was stated unequivocally in the Budapest appeal.

The Soviets had vacillated and then decided against attending the Ninth LCY Congress, which opened in Belgrade on 11 March. The Bulgarian and Mongolian parties on 5 March accepted invitations to the congress but withdrew their acceptances two days later, presumably at Moscow's insistence.[29] The Soviet press criticized Tito's 11 March report to the central committee (in which he reiterated Yugoslavia's condemnation of the invasion of Czechoslovakia), as well as the Yugoslav press coverage of the Ussuri incident.

In summary, the Soviets responded to the Ussuri crisis by:

- Charging China with aggression and collusion with U.S. and West German imperialism.
- Linking Chinese and West German territorial claims.
- Threatening to rebuff any further Chinese provocation.
- Attempting to gain the sympathy of NATO powers.
- Accusing China, after the second Ussuri attack, of betraying socialism.
- Prompting the Warsaw Pact countries to condemn China and, failing in that effort, denying that they had asked.

BULGARIA'S TRIAL BALLOON

The Bulgarian media took the initiative, two days after the 2 March Ussuri incident, in linking the Chinese and West Germans.[30] The media of other Warsaw Pact members later picked up this line, including the Soviets on 10 March.

Ivan Peev, writing in the defense ministry newspaper, *Narodna Armiya*, accused West Germany, first, of counting on "a military clash between China and the Soviet Union" to further its Eastern European territorial claims, which he compared to "Chinese territorial claims against the Mongolian People's Republic and certain southeastern areas of the USSR."[31] He justified this accusation by claiming that Willy Brandt said: "China is far away, but despite this the German Federal Republic may hold a Chinese card in the political game which must not be neglected."[32] Second, Peev accused West Germany of planning to develop a joint Sino–German nuclear program. Pointing out that according to the Brussels and Paris postwar agreements West Germany has no right to manufacture nuclear weapons on its territory, Peev wrote: "An important point of contact in the foreign political position of the two countries is their negative attitude toward the treaty on nonproliferation of nuclear weapons."[33] Peev noted that West Germany had sent a well-known medium-range missile specialist and other technical personnel to China, in addition to the "equipment and instruments for missile construction."[34] He also pointed out that, although some Western diplomats had suffered during the excesses of the cultural revolution in China, the West German specialists had not, and concluded that "the Bonn–Peking axis is already in existence."[35]

Rabotnichesko Delo, the party organ, noted on 11 March that the "special symbiosis between the West German monopolistic and revanchist circles and Maoist anti-Sovietism . . . developed . . . as a new Bonn–Peking axis,"[36] and then, in a new twist, linked the Chinese escalation of anti-Sovietism to the U.S. escalation of the Vietnam war:

> The present new anti-Soviet provocation of Mao's group aims to affect again the Paris talks and to impede the settlement of the Vietnamese question. Facts so far unequivocally show that there exists a strange interrelation between Peking's escalation of anti-Sovietism and American escalation of the war in Vietnam.[37]

In the days following the Ussuri incident, the Bulgarians organized mass protests against the Chinese and expressed their solidarity with the Soviets. Meetings and rallies were held in Sofia, Plovdiv, Ruse, Sopot, and other towns.[38] At the same time, the media praised the Soviet border guards who fell victim to Mao Tse-tung's "bandits," concluding that: "We [Bulgarians] believe in the just cause and might of the Soviet Union. As always, we are now shoulder to shoulder with our Soviet brothers and sisters from Kaliningrad to Vladivostok."[39]

Kosta Andreev, writing in *Trud* (Sofia) on 14 March, charged that the Ussuri provocation had been intentional. He cited four " 'quite accidental' coincidences" in support of this charge:

1) Lin Piao visited Damanskiy Island on the day of the incident.
2) The Chinese troops had received anti-Soviet banners from their headquarters.
3) The invaders were " 'immunized' with a certain amount of alcohol."
4) The "Bonn parliament was due to assemble illegally in West Berlin" two days later.[40]

Andreev also mirrored the Soviet accusation that the Chinese had betrayed socialism. Analyzing the degeneration of the PRC, he blamed the cultural revolution for destroying the Chinese party, government, and trade unions and for creating a "military–bureaucratic regime . . . which has nothing in common with the dictatorship of the proletariat and the ideals of socialism."[41] He also cited the preponderance of China's trade with the capitalist countries—including the United States, but especially the FRG—and its "almost nonexisting" trade with the socialist countries. Finally, he drew the conclusion that China considered the USSR, rather than imperialism, its worst enemy.[42]

The Bulgarian media, like the Soviet, laid the blame for Mao's anti-Soviet provocations on his need to unite the Chinese people for the Ninth CCP Congress. Dimiter Peichinov said of that congress in the 17 March issue of the weekly *Pogled*:

> It would be a sacrilege with Marxism–Leninism and proletarian international-ism if we used the concept of congress for the Ninth "congress" of the Chinese

Communist Party, preparations for which are now being made, because the true communist party has ceased to exist both ideologically and organizationally as a result of the outrages of the so-called "cultural revolution."[43]

The press implicitly criticized Ceausescu and the Romanian party for sending a congratulatory telegram to the Chinese on the occasion of the congress: "It was not attended by a single foreign delegation. Only some congratulatory telegrams were sent to the congress, mainly by parties and groups which have proclaimed themselves "Marxist–Leninist" parties of the Maoist type."[44] Bulgarian reporting on the 17 March Political Consultative Committee meeting in Budapest, like the Soviet coverage, ignored the disagreements among the members and claimed that the session "was held in a spirit of fraternal friendliness and cooperation."[45] The Budapest appeal for a European Security Conference (ESC) was explained in terms of the desirability of détente.

The Bulgarian press stressed the need to preserve socialist unity as a barrier against anti-Sovietism (that is, revisionism) and imperialism. Vladimir Kostov articulated this position in the 24 March issue of the weekly *Pogled*:

> The struggle for peace and socialism . . . is based on the cohesion and unity of action of the socialist countries and the Soviet Union. The upbuilding of this unity of the anti-imperialist forces cannot be achieved without exposing and isolating the *leftist and rightist revisionists* and, in particular, without defeating those of them who are pursuing a political line in which anti-Sovietism takes up a most important place and which has turned them into direct helpers of imperialism [emphasis added].[46]

This warning suggests that (1) the Sino–Soviet clash and Soviet demands at the PCC meeting had increased the tensions within the socialist camp and (2) the Yugoslav (and Romanian) dissidence continued to plague the orthodox Warsaw Pact members.

Bulgaria's relations with "rightist revisionist" Yugoslavia were again strained over Macedonia. The USSR and the other Warsaw Pact countries (except Romania) had refused to attend the Ninth LCY Congress, which opened in Belgrade on 11 March. The boycott resulted, in part, from Tito's reiteration of the Yugoslav condemnation of the invasion of Czechoslovakia. Then, in his report to the party congress, Tito took specific note of the Yugoslav–Bulgarian dispute stemming from the latter's claims to Macedonia.[47] (Bulgaria had raised the Macedonian issue during the Czechoslovak crisis.) *Rabotnichesko Delo*, in its 12 March coverage of Tito's report, highlighted what he had said about Yugoslavia's unsolved economic problems but ignored what he had said about the Macedonian problem.[48]

Bulgaria apparently remained a faithful and dependable Soviet ally.

ULBRICHT BALKS AT BUDAPEST

Continuing political isolation, hatred for the FRG, and dependence on Soviet power for its international status motivated the GDR's reactions to the Ussuri crisis. The East Germans, who had singled out West German "aggressiveness" as the root of the June 1967 Middle East war and the 1968 attempted counterrevolution in Czechoslovakia,[49] repeated that accusation in response to the Ussuri incident, likening Chinese territorial claims against the USSR to West German revanchist claims against Eastern Europe.

The East German press unswervingly followed the Soviet line on the Ussuri incident, branding the Chinese a military-bureaucratic regime whose chief foreign policy aim was "to continue the disruptive activity in the international communist movement [and] to sow mistrust of the Soviet Union and the CPSU."[50] The press blamed Mao and his associates for China's "adventurous course" and warned that "only imperialist reaction benefits from the military provocations against the Soviet Union."[51]

The bulk of the GDR media coverage focused on the linkage of Chinese and West German imperialism, suggested first by the Bulgarian press. *Neues Deutschland* picked up (without attribution) *Narodna Armiya*'s accusation that the West Germans—including Willy Brandt and Franz-Josef Strauss—considered the border conflict between the USSR and the PRC to be to the FRG's advantage:

> Willy Brandt expressed his hope that the Chinese people will play an important role in the coming decades not only in Asia but elsewhere in the world. . . . Strauss states openly that West Germany is interested in a stronger engagement of the Soviet Union on its Asian Eastern frontier. . . . Brandt presently praises the good relations between West Germany and the CPR. . . . Apparently the Bonn rulers by this praise want to thank the Mao group for having committed the border violation against the USSR at the very time when the West German Government on its part carried out the West Berlin provocation.[52]

An article in *Neue Zeit* went so far as to imply that the FRG had made use of its "Chinese lever" to *initiate* the Ussuri incident.[53]

The East German radio told its listeners that "the border provocations must be seen as direct components of the preparations for the [Ninth Chinese Communist] Party Congress."[54] The congress itself was criticized because, first, "anti-Sovietism and reckless opportunism in foreign policy were elevated to the rank of official procedure,"[55] and second, "the splitter course of the Maoists was legalized, confirming the reality of the Bonn–Peking axis."[56]

At the same time that it was loyally supporting the USSR against China, East Germany was trying to balk the Soviet efforts to organize a European security conference. The GDR leaders feared that a European security conference would place them at a disadvantage unless all of the GDR's demands on the FRG were met beforehand. Speaking to the National Front congress on 22 March, Ulbricht demanded that West Germany make the first concessions:

The essential contribution to . . . the preparation of a conference on European security . . . would have to come from the leadership of the country which is the only one in Europe so far to raise and to maintain demands for border alterations.[57]

Although, after a secret meeting with Brezhnev in late March, Ulbricht modified East German opposition to a European security conference, there is reason to believe that the East Germans remained unenthusiastic in the absence of advance guarantees. On the other hand, they appeared to accept the military reorganization demanded by the Soviets at the Budapest PCC meeting.[58]

East Germany, in compliance with the orthodox position on rightist revisionism, did not send a delegation to the Yugoslav party congress. Although the GDR press did not openly engage in polemics with Yugoslavia, the SED reportedly criticized the LCY leadership, congress, and policies.[59]

In sum, East Germany faithfully supported the USSR in the Sino–Soviet conflict over the Ussuri incident, acceded to the Soviet-inspired Warsaw Pact military reorganization, and followed the Soviet line in avoiding the LCY congress. But it attempted to balk the Budapest appeal for a European security conference, as it had opposed earlier attempts at rapprochement with its archenemy, West Germany.

WARSAW'S SURPRISE

The unpredictability of Polish official and popular support of Soviet policy in the Middle East and Czechoslovak crises carried over to the issues related to the Ussuri incident. While the Polish media sided with the USSR against the Chinese, the moderation of their response, noted in the earlier crises, was again apparent.

In the context of Soviet policy in Europe, unresolved territorial issues with the FRG had brought Poland and East Germany together in the Czechoslovak crisis, and one might have expected Gomulka—like Ulbricht—to oppose the 1969 appeal for a European security conference. This was not the case. In January 1969, simultaneously with domestically initiated changes in its foreign ministry, Poland's European policy was revitalized,[60] and Stefan Jedrychowski, the new foreign minister, called for a European security conference and the resumption of political dialogues with Western Europe.[61]

Pursuing these new foreign policy initiatives, Poland supported the USSR in the Ussuri crisis to the extent that Polish and Soviet foreign policy objectives coincided. The Polish media, like the Soviet, Bulgarian, and East German, portrayed the Damanskiy Island attack as premeditated and "an attempt to win the masses for Mao's thought"[62] in connection with the Ninth CCP Congress. In this context, the Maoists were linked to West German imperialism: "It is no accident that the incident . . . took place at the moment when the imperialist and in particular . . . [FRG] forces were winding up the spiral of provocation in West Berlin."[63]

The press also linked the Chinese to U.S. imperialism. According to one commentator, when the "Peking politicians stepped up their attacks against the Soviet Union . . . this was understood by Washington as an overture to a 'thaw' on the Peking–Washington line."[64] The semi-official Warsaw daily *Zycie Warszawy* called "Soviet–Chinese friction and the impossibility of coordinating the assistance by socialist countries to the attacked Vietnam" a factor in President Johnson's decision to escalate the war in Vietnam.[65]

Nevertheless, Polish reaction to the Chinese positions appeared somewhat more moderate than that of the orthodox Warsaw Pact members. The Polish media did not refer to a "Bonn–Peking axis," nor did they call the PRC a military–bureaucratic regime that had rejected the dictatorship of the proletariat and betrayed the cause of socialism. In fact, *Trybuna Ludu*, the party organ, obviously still looked on the Chinese as fellow socialists; after linking the CPR's provocation on the Ussuri River to the FRG's provocation in West Berlin, the newspaper said: "It is axiomatic . . . that . . . only imperialism . . . benefits from conflicts between *socialist* states" (emphasis added).[66]

The media coverage of the 17 March PCC session indicated Poland's support of the Budapest appeal. *Trybuna Ludu* called it a historic document but also noted the disagreement at the Budapest meeting:

> Attentive reading of the appeal proves that it is a political document of great significance. . . . The Budapest appeal has been worked out and signed by all the seven Warsaw Pact member states.
> Within the socialist bloc there were and are differences of opinion or evaluation of some aspects of the international situation, of the roads of a further development of socialism and [the] international working class movement.[67]

The openness of the Polish press in regard to the dissension proved a marked contrast to the attempt of the Soviet press to convey the impression of unanimity at the meeting. Polish enthusiasm for the appeal manifested itself also in the Polish press calls for support of the appeal as a sign of socialist unity and in the castigation of those—that is, the Yugoslavs—who claimed that nothing important had occurred in Budapest.[68]

The Polish military translated the need for maintaining socialist unity into the need for combat readiness. General Jozef Urbanowicz, deputy minister of national defense, in a speech to the Polish Army General Staff Academy on 18 March, reiterated Polish military concerns in terms of West German revanche:

> The importance of combat readiness of the Polish Armed Forces is all the greater in the present international situation, and particularly in view of the growing revisionist and revenge-seeking anti-Polish aspirations of the FRG.[69]

Although the media continued to criticize West German imperialism, noting the dangers that it posed specifically for Poland, they, unlike the Bulgarian and East German media, refrained from raising the specter of Nazism by referring to a "Bonn–Peking axis."

The Polish press condemnation of Yugoslavia, however, was unusually harsh, and Poland, like the USSR, did not send a delegation to the LCY Congress. *Zycie Warszawy* launched the attack on 19 March, arguing that LCY opposition to the Warsaw Pact intervention in Czechoslovakia was a deviation as significant as the American aggression in Vietnam and the Israeli aggression in the Middle East.[70]

Such media attacks may have been provoked by Tito's continuing condemnation of the invasion of Czechoslovakia, in which Poland was the major Soviet ally, and by the Yugoslav media's denigration of the Budapest appeal's importance. In fact, before these events there had been evidence of a Polish softening toward Yugoslavia.

In summary, while the Polish press supported the USSR in response to the Ussuri incident, it never suggested support for the Soviet move to condemn the PRC or to expel it from the communist movement. Media interpretations of the Budapest appeal, in addition to indicating agreement with the USSR, displayed clear national initiative and enthusiasm; and, in contrast to the USSR, noted differences of opinion. Polish condemnation of Yugoslavia, however, matched that of the most orthodox Warsaw Pact members.

HUNGARY ISOLATES BONN FROM PEKING

Janos Kadar, who had tried to mediate between Czechoslovakia and the other Warsaw Pact partners to forestall the invasion of that country in 1968, may have felt the need in 1969 to demonstrate his loyalty to the Soviets, at least to the extent that Soviet positions did not conflict with Hungary's own. To this end, Hungarian reports of the Ussuri incident branded China the aggressor and attributed the attack to Mao's domestic problems. What distinguished the Hungarian reports of these events from those of the USSR, Bulgaria, East Germany, and Poland was that the Hungarians omitted linking China and West Germany and branding the Mao regime a military-bureaucratic betrayer of socialism.

The Hungarians were quick to side with the Soviets after the 2 March skirmish. The media reported anti-Soviet demonstrations at the Soviet embassy in Peking,[71] and during the next ten days, the party newspaper, *Nepszabadsag* editorialized on the causes of the conflict. On 4 March, for example, the party organ blamed the Ussuri provocation on Mao's desire for unity before the party congress.[72] *Nepszabadsag* wrote on 16 March that the provocations of 2 and 15 March made it clear that the leaders of China are aiming at the methodical smashing of interstate relations between the Soviet Union and China. The border provocations [and] the armed assaults planned well in advance . . . have become everyday policy of the Peking leaders. . . . Every honest person, every sincere believer in socialism . . . feels complete and clear solidarity with the Soviet Union.[73]

A 20 March editorial in *Magyar Hirlap* accused the Chinese of collusion with imperialism:

It is worthwhile noting that China has not taken any wild and furious actions against either Taiwan or Hong Kong, which truly belong to her, such as the kind she has taken against the Soviet Union. . . . [The Chinese] wish to weaken the Soviet Union, the socialist world. They want to divide its forces. . . . And all this in an international situation when the unity of the socialist system in an anti-imperialist world front is more important than it has ever been before.[74]

The Hungarian media, by criticizing the Chinese but not linking them to the West Germans, were able to demonstrate their support of the Soviets and, at the same time, to preserve Hungary's developing relations with Western Europe, especially the FRG.

Hungarian foreign policy intentions were also apparent in the optimistic press coverage of the 17 March session of the Warsaw Pact Political Consultative Committee in Budapest. The media commented enthusiastically on the Budapest appeal, emphasizing such aspects as the socialist initiative in suggesting concrete measures in the interest of peace:

[The appeal] points up positive possibilities by speaking of necessary and possible joint action in European cooperation in the field of power resources, communications, or more comprehensively, for the sake of the welfare of the people of the continent as a whole.[75]

An outspoken commentary by Magda Halasz, broadcast on 18 March, discussed not only what the appeal included but also what it omitted—specifically, the appeal made no mention of the Vietnam war, Middle East tension, U.S. imperialism, or NATO threat.[76] By comparison, when the Soviet, Bulgarian, and East German media appealed for European cooperation, their concomitant accusations of a "Bonn–Peking axis"—or at least an "imperialist PRC–FRG tie"—in the context of the Ussuri provocation made their appeal seem less credible and raised some doubt as to the sincerity of their intentions.

Although Hungary, like most of the Warsaw Pact states, did not send a delegation to the Yugoslav party congress, its press coverage of the event, despite the indication of policy differences, was considerably less hostile. On 9 March, before the congress began, *Nepszabadsag* discussed without bitterness or polemic the LCY congress draft resolution containing the criticism of the Warsaw Pact intervention in Czechoslovakia.[77] Hungarian commentaries on the congress itself consistently stressed the positive aspects of Yugoslav policy and indicated the desire for better Hungarian–Yugoslav relations: "We are delighted to acknowledge the fact that a number of speakers at the congress stressed the importance of further development of economic and cultural cooperation with our country."[78]

The Hungarian public reaction to the events connected with the Ussuri incident and the Budapest PCC meeting of 17 March reflected Hungary's earlier rapprochement with the FRG and a more sincere commitment to European détente (including with Yugoslavia) than that of its more orthodox Warsaw Pact partners.[79] At the same time, Hungary always decoupled the FRG from its condemnation of the Ussuri provocation.

DUBCEK FAILS THE SOVIET TEST

The Czechoslovak responses to events connected with the Ussuri incident failed to meet Soviet expectations and may well have contributed to Dubcek's ouster in April 1969. Demonstrating that their relations with the USSR were still not normalized, the Czechoslovaks refused at first to blame the Chinese. Even when they admitted that the Chinese had initiated the attack, their criticism showed a moderation that annoyed the Soviets.

Although *Rude Pravo* wrote on 6 March that Czechoslovakia could not remain impartial to the Ussuri conflict "because it undoubtedly weakens the whole world anti-imperialist front and can serve only the forces which speculate with a tragic split within the socialist community," the party organ failed to take sides, saying only that information on the conflict was "incomplete and does not allow wide-ranging conclusions."[80] Only after the second Chinese attack on Damanskiy Island on 15 March[81]—and undoubtedly as a result of Soviet pressure[82]—did the Czechoslovak press blame the Chinese for firing into Soviet territory and for conducting an anti-Soviet campaign.[83]

The Czechoslovaks continued to regard the PRC as a member of the socialist community. Recalling that a year earlier the Chinese had criticized Czechoslovakia's ultrarevisionism, *Rude Pravo* said that, although Czechoslovakia resented the present Chinese attempt to sow dissent between it and the USSR, it still considered the Chinese to be socialists:

> We admired the heroism of the Chinese communists in the "long march" and the Chinese revolution. . . . Even today we see in the Chinese Republic the fruit of the anticolonial and anti-imperialist revolution. We consider her to be a part of the socialist community, from which it should not be expelled, but from which she should not even expel herself.[84]

Czechoslovak Foreign Minister Marko admitted at a press conference on 15 March that the Chinese had "organized" border clashes along the Indian as well as the Soviet border and that the USSR "most certainly was not interested in provoking" the Ussuri incident.[85] Then Marko contradicted the Moscow line linking the Ussuri provocation to Chinese internal politics: "It can be regarded as an error if somebody thinks that Mao Tse-tung needs an aggravation of anti-Soviet moods to support his policy, which he has submitted for approval by the approaching CCP Congress."[86] Similarly, a radio commentary by Jiri Hromadka criticized the Chinese aggression on the Ussuri, but then singled out the "unequal treaties" imposed on China by the Russians in 1868 and 1870 as the cause.[87]

In light of the Warsaw Pact invasion of Czechoslovakia only seven months earlier and the continuing Soviet occupation, Czechoslovakia's independent position on West Germany and China was quite extraordinary. The Soviets had warned at the time of the Czechoslovak invasion that West German revanchist policy threatened Czechoslovakia, and the East Germans had accused the FRG of having directed the Czechoslovak counterrevolution. Nevertheless, in early 1969, noting the existence of "positive forces in the West German society," *Rude Pravo* called for a European security conference, saying that Czechoslovakia "must continue to maintain contact with these forces, for it is in our interest and in the interest of Europe."[88]

After the Ussuri provocation, the Czechoslovak media did not link the PRC and FRG, ignored the coincidence of the West Berlin elections and the Chinese attack on Damanskiy Island, and avoided any reference to a Bonn–Peking axis.

Czechoslovakia's position on the Warsaw Pact PCC session in Budapest, like its position on the Ussuri incident, differed from that of most of the other pact members. Rather than calling on the spirit of "fraternal friendship and cooperation" in preparation for the meeting, Czechoslovak commentaries speculated on what would be discussed and what problems and disagreements might arise. Significant military issues were examined obliquely in terms of how Romania might react to the military reorganization of the Warsaw Pact and to pact maneuvers on its territory.[89]

The Czechoslovak press reported the Romanian positions straightforwardly, uncritically, and sympathetically, quoting at length from various Romanian policy statements. Included among the quotations was Ceausescu's 14 August 1968 military academy speech, in which he had said that "the command of the armed forces cannot be exercised by an outside organ: this is a sovereign attribute of the leadership of our party and state." On the subject of military maneuvers, Ceausescu was reported to have said: "Romania believes that the European states would do a great service if they would decide that they would give up military maneuvers and other manifestations of force on the territories or frontiers of other states."[90]

On his return from Budapest, Dubcek indicated that there had been disagreements. In an interview with Jiri Sekera, the chief editor of *Rude Pravo*, Dubcek outlined the results of the PCC session, including the planned military reorganization of the Warsaw Pact, in terms that, for the most part, conformed with the Soviet positions. He also reiterated the Soviet statement that relations with the PRC had not been discussed at the meeting. However, despite Soviet attempts to convey the impression of unanimity at the Budapest meeting, Dubcek admitted not only that military problems had existed, but that some remained unsolved: "The adopted [military reorganization] documents will contribute to improving existing conditions, especially by further clarifying and defining some problems in this sphere that have not been completely solved."[91]

The Czechoslovak media reported after the Budapest meeting that "unity of opinion does not exist, at least not in the old sense enforced at one time by the Comintern."[92] Despite the official denials, the press assumed that the Sino–Soviet disagreement had been discussed[93] and credited the Romanian delegation with keeping an indictment of China out of the final documents of the session:

It appears that there were no doubts about the wish of the Soviet Union to mention China in a certain way. Similarly one knows, on the other hand, the position of the Romanian politicians, according to whom no conference in which a socialist country does not participate (and China after all is still a socialist country) can be allowed to assess and condemn the internal or foreign policy of the absent country. If the documents of Budapest are clearly confined to the European range of problems (not even Vietnam is mentioned in them) this delegation also exerted its influence.[94]

The Romanian argument to prevent the Warsaw Pact condemnation of China sought by the USSR—namely, the argument that the Warsaw Pact sphere of influence should be limited to Europe—was adopted by the Czechoslovaks:

The scope of the Warsaw Pact . . . is limited to Europe, not only in respect to the geographical location of the member states, but also as regards fulfillment of obligations. . . . [The] new measures also increased the share of the individual socialist states in the solution of tasks and the command of the Warsaw Pact.[95]

The Czechoslovaks supported the Budapest appeal unequivocally, not because the Soviets proposed it, or for the same reasons that the Soviets proposed it, but because they believed that an agreement on European security "might mean that there would be fewer tanks in Europe."[96] The presence of Soviet occupation forces in Czechoslovakia suggests that the Czechoslovaks probably meant that there would be fewer Soviet tanks in Czechoslovakia.

The appeal found favor with the Czechoslovaks also because (still not according to the Soviet line) "it is directed against the division of the world into military blocs, against vigorous armaments, and the threats which these raise for the peace and security of nations."[97]

The Czechoslovak position on the dangers of rightist and leftist revisionism also differed from the Soviet positions. Regarding the Chinese, the Czechoslovaks did not interpret the Ninth CCP Congress as deviating from the socialist path and destroying the "true" party. Czechoslovak commentaries made no references to the excesses of the cultural revolution and the replacement of the dictatorship of the proletariat with a military–bureaucratic regime. And the Czechoslovaks continued to consider China a member of the socialist community.

Regarding relations with the rightist revisionists, the Czechoslovaks made it quite clear that their decision not to attend the Ninth LCY Congress, where Tito again condemned the Soviet-led invasion of Czechoslovakia, had been forced on them. Josef Smrkovsky told a group of workers that the decision had been reached "at the last minute," as a result of the August 1968 events, and under Soviet pressure.[98]

The sympathetic Czechoslovak press coverage of the Yugoslav party congress referred to the tradition of friendship between the two countries. An article in *Prace* praised the Yugoslavs for having "enriched socialist practice and theory with many ideas" (in contrast to the criticism of Yugoslav self-management by the USSR, Bulgaria, Poland, and East Germany) and for fighting "for the rights of nations, for human freedom" and against "fascism, imperialism, and *great-power arrogance*" (emphasis added).[99] Public sentiment manifested itself in expressions of support for the Yugoslavs in the Bulgarian–Yugoslav debate over Macedonia[100] and in Czechoslovak student demonstrations outside Charles University and the Yugoslav embassy in Prague in which the students hailed Yugoslavia and the party congress and chanted anti-Soviet slogans.[101]

Czechoslovak reactions to the crisis of March 1969 must have confirmed continuing Soviet doubts as to the reliability of their ally. In every area where the Soviets desired Warsaw Pact support, the Czechoslovaks failed to meet Soviet wishes. Whether the issue involved interpreting the Budapest appeal and communiqué on military reorganization in light of West German revanche, recognizing the dangers of rightist and leftist revisionism, or supporting the USSR against China in the Ussuri conflict, the Czechoslovaks exhibited a surprising degree of independence.[102]

This show of independence, added to the tensions remaining between the leaders of the two countries as a result of the August 1968 invasion and continued Soviet occupation of Czechoslovakia,[103] probably led to the Soviet decision to remove Dubcek in April 1969.

ROMANIA REMAINS NEUTRAL

Romania's independent foreign policy toward Israel and the FRG in 1967 and toward Yugoslavia and the PRC in 1968 continued into the 1969 crisis following the Ussuri provocation. The Romanian press virtually ignored the Damanskiy Island attack. On 4 March, *Scinteia*[104] published without comment the TASS and New China News Agency announcements of the incident. At no time did the press carry commentaries, as the Soviet press had, for example, blaming the Chinese for provoking the incident, condemning the Chinese cultural revolution and ninth party congress, and linking the Maoist imperialists and West German revanchists.

In defense of Romania's independent policy, Deputy Foreign Minister Vasile Gliga had explained earlier that Romania was pursuing relations with nonsocialist states so as "to solve the most urgent problems in international life." At the same time he stressed the importance of Romania's socialist relations, repeating Ceausescu's reassurance that "Romania . . . centers its foreign policy on friendship, alliances, and collaboration with all socialist countries." Gliga concluded, however, that despite the importance of socialist unity, "every party has the right to work out its own political line independently, taking account of the practical historical, social, and economic conditions of the country."[105]

Ceausescu went further than Gliga and rejected the recently enunciated Brezhnev doctrine of limited sovereignty:

> The thesis—and attempts have been made recently to have it accepted—that the common defense of the socialist countries against an imperialist attack presupposes the limitation or renunciation of the sovereignty of a member state of the pact does not correspond to the principles of the relations among the socialist countries and cannot be accepted under any form whatsoever.[106]

Scinteia's comments on 11 March in connection with the Comintern's fiftieth anniversary were also intended to convey a message to Moscow. In recalling the errors that had been made during the Comintern's existence because the leadership ignored the internal conditions of the various member countries, the Romanian party organ was obviously reminding the Soviets once again that they should not interfere in the internal affairs of other communist parties.[107]

Romania's need to safeguard its independence dominated both its internal and its foreign policy. On 14 March, Maurer told the Grand National Assembly in connection with the establishment of the Romanian defense council that the fundamental aim of the party during the 25 years since Romania's liberation had been

> the combination of . . . building the new social system with . . . consolidating the great revolutionary conquests of the Romanian people who, for the first time in the course of their stormy history, *have become the only master of their own fate.* . . . The circumstances in which we are completing socialist construction and the realities of the contemporary world force us to persist in increasing the military potential of the fatherland [emphasis added].[108]

The Budapest appeal for a European security conference received the Romanians' full support because they saw in it the possibility for ending the great-power bipolarization of Europe (and for the concomitant relaxation of Soviet control over Eastern Europe): "Such a conference would give the possibility of finding, by the contribution of *all the European states—big and small*—the ways and means for the liquidation of Europe's division into military groupings" (emphasis added).[109]

Romania argued in favor of limiting the Warsaw Pact's sphere of influence to Europe. Pursuant to its policy of remaining on good terms with all socialist states, Romania, as a pact member, did not want to have to support a future Soviet action (political or military) against China. A joint session of the Romanian State Council and the Council of Ministers on 10 April, convoked to ratify the Budapest PCC decisions of 17 March, instructed the minister of armed forces to: "Adopt the necessary measures so that the armed forces can fulfill their obligations within the Warsaw Pact in case of an armed attack *in Europe* against a Warsaw Pact member state" (emphasis added).[110]

In his speech to the 10 April joint government session, Ceausescu said—reassuring the Romanians and warning the Soviets—that the agreements reached in Budapest would not derogate Romania's sovereignty and that no Warsaw Pact military decisions involving Romanian forces could be implemented without the approval of the Romanian constitutional organs:

> I wish to stress once again, comrades, that in accordance with the constitution and the laws of our country, our army cannot be engaged in action except by the constitutional organs. Furthermore, only these organs can approve the presence on our territory, in any situation, of foreign troops.[111]

The Romanian leadership and press considered Romania's independent military policy—the limitation of its obligations to the Warsaw Pact and the separation of its military obligations to the pact from obligations to the other socialist countries—a Romanian success of the Budapest PCC session.[112]

Romania apparently was not forced to make any military or political concessions to the USSR as a result of the Ussuri incident or the Budapest PCC session. Romania continued to pursue European détente on its own terms and to maintain its cordial relationship with China. Its spokespersons made clear Romania's qualified acceptance of "internationalist obligations" to the pact and its resolve to let nothing endanger its developing relations with the western capitalist states.[113]

Relations with the leftist and rightist revisionists also did not follow the Moscow line. The Romanians had developed close political (and apparently military) relations with the Yugoslavs at the time of the invasion of Czechoslovakia. Unlike the USSR and the other Warsaw Pact states, Romania sent a delegation to the Ninth LCY Congress in Belgrade. Emil Bodnaras, the head of the delegation, told the Yugoslav congress that any form of interference in the domestic affairs of other states, or any attempt to limit the sovereignty of the socialist countries, harmed the cause of socialism. In addition, Bodnaras said again that Romanian foreign policy was based on friendship and alliance with all socialist countries and on the strict observance of the principles of equality, independence, sovereignty, and noninterference. He added that the Romanians had resolved to try to end the problems of the international communist movement and to work for "normalization and consolidation of relations among socialist countries."[114] Although Bodnaras did not refer specifically to Czechoslovakia, his rejection of the concept of limited sovereignty as interference in domestic affairs applied unmistakably to the Brezhnev doctrine and the Soviet role in Czechoslovakia.[115]

In defiance of the USSR and the orthodox Warsaw Pact states, the Romanian CP Central Committee sent a message to the Ninth CCP Congress and to the "fraternal" Chinese people, expressing the conviction that relations and cooperation between Romania and China would continue to develop in many areas.[116] Romanian press coverage of the congress was limited to a discussion of the election of Mao Tse-tung as party chairman, Lin Piao as deputy chairman, and other members of the new standing presidium.[117] The Romanian coverage contained no criticism of the PRC.

To conclude, Romania's position toward both China and Yugoslavia continued to differ fundamentally from the positions of the other Warsaw Pact allies. Romania seemed unconcerned over the alleged dangers of revisionism on communist unity. Romania's neutrality toward the Ussuri conflict, its notions of qualified and conditional obligation to the Warsaw Pact, and its support of the Budapest appeal were consistent with its détente initiative toward the West and its policy of remaining friendly with all socialist states.

THE BALKAN ALLIANCE DEVELOPS

The Yugoslav–Romanian friendship continued to be reflected in the two countries' political and military policies. Like the Romanians, the Yugoslavs rejected the Brezhnev doctrine of limited sovereignty, maintained close relations with the Italian communists, and passed a new defense law, based on a "new concept of security."

The Yugoslav and Romanian responses to the Ussuri conflict differed, however, to the extent that the two countries' relations with both the USSR and PRC differed. Romania was caught between its Warsaw Pact obligation to maintain working relations with the USSR and its national aspiration for better relations with China; Yugoslavia had poor relations with both. The Yugoslavs could therefore afford to be less restrained than the Romanians.

The Yugoslav interpretation of the incident was consistent with its policy of political nonalignment. The press speculated on whether the USSR or PRC had initiated the provocation, but it did not take sides. Yugoslav spokespersons saw in the conflict only the dangers of bloc and superpower actions.

Zagreb Domestic Service reported the incident on 3 March, the day after it happened. Finding the Soviet account somewhat more plausible than the Chinese, the report concluded that the Chinese had started the fighting. Nevetheless, it neither condemned the PRC nor supported the USSR:

> Foreign observers believe the USSR would find a conflict on its Far Eastern border less useful than China because Soviet policy has gotten bogged down in its European mistakes. This fact as well as the frequent consultations with the Warsaw Pact allies, who keep arriving in Moscow suddenly and unannounced, show that their problems are both urgent and difficult and that nervousness is their constant companion.[118]

On 8 March, a *Borba* editorial by Andro Gabelic analyzed the military implications of the Ussuri incident in terms of China's drive for superpower status. Without condemning the Chinese aggression, Gabelic contemplated Chinese intentions toward the United States and USSR:

> China is tying up 30 Soviet divisions, and according to some opinions, even up to 40. By just as many divisions the USSR is weaker in Europe. The PRC essentially wants to make the superpowers realize (not only the USSR but to a certain extent also the United States) that bipolar calculations in the solution of world problems are tantamount to reckoning without one's host.[119]

Before the Warsaw Pact PCC session in Budapest, Yugoslav commentaries took it for granted that the meeting had been called to deal with the Sino-Soviet conflict. Milos Corovic, the Tanjug correspondent, theorized that the Soviets would try to involve the entire Warsaw Pact in the dispute and foresaw that the Romanians would resist.[120]

Yugoslavia did not attend the meeting because it was not a Warsaw Pact member. The Yugoslav press obviously knew what went on there, however, and supported the positions that the Romanians had taken, for example, the refusal to condemn China and the demand for national sovereignty for individual Warsaw Pact states. Bozidar Kicevic said:

> It is believed that the so-called Chinese problem was raised at the conference with the intention to condemn China and its policy, both toward the Soviet Union as well as toward the international workers movement. As has been learned certain parties already opposed in Budapest the intention to make the conference a holy council, which would pronounce anathemas and carry out excommunications of unbelievers.[121]

The media also supported the positions of Czechoslovakia and Hungary, the other Warsaw Pact partners who had opposed the Soviets in Budapest. Aleksandar Nenadovic, the New York correspondent for *Politika*, quoted the *Washington Post's* Budapest correspondent to the effect that the Soviet demands for mobilization against China had met with the firm resistance of the Romanian delegation and tacit disapproval on the part of Czechoslovaks and Hungarians.[122] Otta Sik's economic ideas were compared to Yugoslavia's self-management system; and the invasion of Czechoslovakia was condemned again:

> The decision by the office of the president of the Czechoslovak Communist Party by a vote of nine to three (Dubcek, Cernik, and Smrkovsky) not to send its delegation to the congress of Yugoslav Communists only confirmed the observation according to which the invasion had been and remained what it actually was, an invasion.[123]

Yugoslav spokespersons considered Soviet hegemony, bipolarization, and the derogation of the sovereignty of individual states to be major problems in socialist relations. The Tanjug correspondent in Bucharest said that Romania had made no concessions to the USSR in Budapest and that the USSR should have learned the lesson that democratization is the only way to end the Warsaw Pact's difficulties.[124] A 19 March *Borba* editorial stated:

> If there is a genuine desire to overcome the division into blocs—with the concrete goal of disbanding all military blocs on European territory—the sovereignty and independence of individual states within military-political formations must also become a reality. . . . Yugoslavia's position on these fundamental questions of cooperation based on equality have always been crystal clear. Nobody has ever had cause to accuse us of disharmony between words and deeds.[125]

Revisionism, on the other hand, was not seen as a threat to socialist unity. Although they sent neither a delegation nor a message to the Ninth CCP Congress, the Yugoslavs did not regard the conduct of the congress as a deviation from socialism. Branko Bogunovic, formerly a correspondent in Peking, analyzed the congress in terms of Chinese foreign policy ambitions. He wrote in *Politika* on 13 April that China would do everything it could to strengthen its position in the Moscow–Peking–Washington triangle.[126]

Yugoslavia's independent interpretation of the March 1969 crisis conformed to its nonaligned and antibloc positions. The press spoke openly of the tensions among the Warsaw Pact allies at the Budapest PCC meeting, demanded greater independence for pact members, and called for an end to great-power military blocs—essentially the positions taken at the meeting by Romania and Czechoslovakia. Yugoslavia's position with regard to China indicated the beginning of an improvement of the poor relationship between the two up to that point. Yugoslav reluctance to condemn the PRC provided evidence of the developing thaw, which was motivated by the perception of a common threat from the USSR,[127] especially since the invasion of Czechoslovakia in August 1968. The

Yugoslav–Chinese rapprochement probably benefitted from the good offices of the Romanians, who enjoyed good relations with both Yugoslavia and China.

TIRANA SUPPORTS PEKING

The Albanian press accepted the Chinese version of the Ussuri incident, charged the USSR with the aggression, and linked Soviet revisionism to U.S. and West German imperialism. The title of a *Zeri i Popullit* editorial expressed Albania's hope: "The anti-China provocations and plots of the Soviet revisionists will always fail shamefully." The editorial itself indicated some of the fears:

> The criminal provocation of the Soviet revisionists against the People's Republic of China is a bandit-like act carried out with premeditation, with definite aims.... The events ... clearly show that the main sword-edge of the Soviet–U.S. counterrevolutionary alliance is spearheaded against great people's China, the most resolute fighter for the cause of revolution and socialism.[128]

Bashkimi the Democratic Front daily, linked the Soviet aggression with the FRG as well.[129] When the Soviet ambassador in Bonn saw Chancellor Kiesinger to discuss the Ussuri incident, *Zeri i Popullit* interpreted the meeting as evidence of collusion between NATO imperialism and Warsaw Pact revisionism.[130]

After the 15 March fighting on Damanskiy Island, *Luftetari*, the newspaper of the Albanian defense ministry, accused the Soviets of provoking the Ussuri incident to unite the Warsaw Pact countries—just as the USSR and some of its pact partners had accused the Maoists of provoking the incident to unite the Chinese people behind Mao before the party congress.[131]

Zeri i Popullit called the PCC session a "comprehensive failure," and quoted "press organs, close to the Budapest revisionist circles, which said that the Moscow chiefs asked the Warsaw Treaty member countries to send some contingents of military units to the Far East."[132]

According to the party organ, "Soviet–U.S. collaboration dominated the Budapest meeting."[133] The USSR was accused of rejecting socialist ideals in seeking closer ties with the West through the Budapest appeal.[134] Romania, however, was separated from the "aggressive pact": "Now, with the exception of Romania, all of the other member nations of this pact are under the control of the armed forces of Soviet revisionism."[135]

The Albanian party organ saw the issue of Yugoslavia and the Ninth LCY Congress also as a Soviet defeat at the Budapest meeting:

> Thus, on the issue of the attitude towards Yugoslavia, likewise, the Soviet leaders suffered another defeat in Budapest. They could not impose on the other partners a common line. The Romanians, for instance, went to Belgrade and occupied there a place of greatest honor among foreign guests. The Czecho-

slovaks did not go there, for as it seems they did not succeed in obtaining the permission from Moscow; but the Czechoslovak press extensively wrote about it and in a quite warm tone.[136]

SUMMARY

The Ussuri incident of March 1969 became a Warsaw Pact crisis when the USSR sought to involve its allies in the dispute at the 17 March session of the Warsaw Pact PCC in Budapest. What exactly the USSR wanted of the other pact members in regard to China remains obscure; the Soviet demands, according to speculations in the less orthodox Eastern European media, ranged from censure of China for the Ussuri attack to condemnation of Chinese revisionism to sending Warsaw Pact troops to the Sino–Soviet border to expulsion of China from the international communist movement.[137] Unable to obtain agreement from its allies on any kind of action, the Soviets denied that they had raised the issue at the Budapest meeting.[138]

The PCC succeeded, apparently after hard-fought negotiation, in arriving at a consensus on a second major issue, the Soviet-proposed Warsaw Pact military reorganization. The communiqué issued after the Budapest meeting stated (at Soviet insistence) that the proposal for a Warsaw Pact joint armed forces and joint command had been approved unanimously.

Only the Budapest appeal for a European security conference (ESC), the most conciliatory of many such proposals and the third major issue of the session, seemed to generate enthusiasm among most of the delegates. The broad support notwithstanding, each Warsaw Pact member country supported the appeal in pursuit of its own national interests.

The Soviet press described the Budapest meeting as having been marked by "friendship and unity" and said that only European issues had been discussed. The Bulgarian media echoed the Soviet. The Hungarians said nothing. The East German, Polish, Czechoslovak, and Romanian press referred openly to political differences and/or unresolved issues.[139]

Which of the other countries attending the Budapest PCC meeting— Bulgaria, Czechoslovakia, East Germany, Hungary, Poland, and Romania— supported the USSR, and on which of the three major issues?

On the condemnation of China:

The Bulgarians and East Germans publicly condemned the Chinese aggression, compared Chinese territorial claims against the USSR to West German revanchist claims against Eastern Europe, referred to a Bonn–Peking axis (even the Soviets had not raised the specter of Nazism), and branded the Chinese a military–bureaucratic regime that had rejected the dictatorship of the proletariat and betrayed the cause of socialism. The harshness of their criticism indicates that they supported the Soviet position on an official Warsaw Pact condemnation and may even have agreed to an alleged Soviet demand for the PRC's expulsion from the communist movement.

Although the Poles and Hungarians blamed the Chinese for initiating the Ussuri attack, their more moderate criticism of the PRC and their omission of references to a military–bureaucratic regime and a Bonn–Peking axis suggests that they did not support the Soviet demand.

The Czechoslovaks admitted reluctantly that the Chinese had been the aggressors; the Romanians remained neutral. Both continued to regard China as a member of the socialist community and argued that the pact's obligations should be limited to Europe; such a limitation would, of course, have ruled out the possibility of a pact condemnation of the PRC or of sending pact forces to the Sino–Soviet border.

On the Warsaw Pact military reorganization:

The Bulgarian, East German, and Polish media created the impression, in support of the Soviet line, that the reorganization had been agreed on unanimously and that its purpose was to increase pact unity and combat efficiency in case of imperialist aggression. Again, the Hungarian press remained silent. The Czechoslovak and Romanian (as well as the Yugoslav) press, in contrast, described the purpose as being to increase national participation in the pact's command structure. After the Budapest meeting, Dubcek noted that some military problems remained, and Ceausescu claimed that the reorganization did not derogate Romania's sovereignty.

On the Budapest appeal for a European security conference:

The Bulgarians, as always, adopted the Soviet position and supported the appeal for a European security conference. However, the Bulgarian and East German media were the only ones to use the World War II axis symbolism, and the Bulgarians were the first to link Chinese and West German imperialism, suggesting Bulgarian sympathy, if not support, for East Germany's opposition to a European security conference. (Brezhnev had to pressure Ulbricht into accepting the idea of a European security conference on Soviet terms.)

The other Warsaw Pact members readily supported the appeal because it coincided with their own national foreign policy objectives. Poland, as a result of changes in its top political leadership, in January 1969 had initiated an independent European policy, including overtures for a European security conference. Hungary had sought relations with Western Europe, especially the FRG, and backed the appeal enthusiastically. Czechoslovakia's support of a European security conference reflected national and anti-Soviet motivations, that is, to eliminate military blocs and to get (Soviet) tanks out of (Eastern) Europe. Romania, whose recognition of the FRG in January 1967 drew open criticism from fellow pact members, had continued to seek wider relations with West Germany and the rest of Europe.

Yugoslavia's rightist revisionism also continued to trouble Warsaw Pact relations. The Soviet media's criticism of Yugoslav economic self-management, foreign policy, and party congress was echoed in Bulgaria, East Germany, and Poland. In contrast, the Hungarian, Czechoslovak, and Romanian media expressed support for Yugoslavia, and Romania, in defiance of Soviet orders, sent a delegation to the party congress.

Warsaw Pact public support of Soviet policies in the Ussuri crisis of March 1969 varied widely in degree, by country, and by specific issue. If this analysis of pact responses to Soviet policies reflects what Soviet leaders perceived about the political reliability of their allies during this period, the Soviets probably were reassured by the overall support of Bulgaria and East Germany (although differences had developed with the GDR over European policy). Poland and Hungary generally supported Soviet policies, but the Soviet leaders may well have questioned their motives on specific issues. Polish inconsistency may have added to Soviet concern. The Czechoslovaks and Romanians openly opposed the Soviets; in the matter of European policy, on which they appeared to support the USSR, their motivations were clearly anti-Soviet. That the Soviets perceived the Czechoslovaks as unreliable was confirmed by Dubcek's ouster in April 1969. They would undoubtedly have liked to remove Ceausescu also, but were afraid or unable to do so.

After five years in power, Brezhnev and Kosygin had been unable to restore socialist unity. The crisis caused by Nixon's visit to Peking in February 1972 contributed further to that disunity.

NOTES

1. Brezhnev's justification of limited sovereignty (that is, intervention in states where socialism was threatened) at the Polish fifth party congress became known as the Brezhnev doctrine.

2. John Newhouse, *Cold Dawn: The Story of SALT* (New York: Holt, Rinehart and Winston, 1973), pp. 130–31.

3. For example, Nixon had written before his election of the need to "come to grips" with the reality of China. "Asia after Vietnam," *Foreign Affairs*, 46 (October 1967):111–25.

4. The Soviets first proposed an all-European conference on security arrangements for Europe in 1954 as part of an unsuccessful diplomatic effort to block the rearmament of West Germany.

5. Editorial in *Trud*, March 19, 1969, p. 1, in *FBIS, DR, SU* (March 21, 1969), p. A42.

6. *Sueddeutsche Zeitung*, March 12, 1969, in USSR: Sino–Soviet Report/42, *RFE* (March 12, 1969), p. 6.

7. Nevertheless, only in 1965 did the USSR begin gradually to build up troop strength east of Lake Baykal. By 1967, the Soviets had 14–16 divisions in that area, as well as tank and missile forces in Mongolia. During this period, the USSR also increased its border guard strength by about 20,000. See Thomas W. Robinson, *The Sino-Soviet Border Dispute: Background, Development, and the March 1969 Clashes*, The Rand Corporation, RM-6171-PR (August 1970), pp. 27–29.

8. This information was "leaked" to Western news agencies on 4 March. USSR: Sino–Soviet Report/42, *RFE* (March 12, 1969), p. 3.

9. Ultimately, the most important effect of the crisis was that it altered the Soviets' perceptions of their Asian security requirements. By mid-1969, the USSR increased its military force east of Lake Baykal to 25–27 divisions. This force represented 300,000 troops and their supporting air and missile elements. Thomas W. Wolfe, *Soviet Power and Europe, 1945–1970* (Baltimore, Md.: The Johns Hopkins Press, 1970), p. 467.

10. The PRC sent a similar protest to the USSR in which it claimed the island and demanded compensation for its losses; it also rejected the Soviet note. USSR: Sino–Soviet Report/42, *RFE* (March 12, 1969), p. 2. Of a grand total of about 115 army divisions, the Chinese normally deployed about 32 in the three northern military regions: four in the Inner Mongolian region, and a total of 28 in the Manchurian and Peking regions. In addition to the army the Chinese have border-guard troops, and there were probably also two or three divisions of border guards in the Inner Mongolian region. See Institute for Strategic Studies, *The Military Balance, 1968–1969* (London: Institute for Strategic Studies, 1968), pp. 6, 10–11.

11. *FBIS, DR, SU* (March 4, 1969), p. A16; and *FBIS, DR, SU* (March 5, 1969), p. A2.

12. Ibid., p. A1.

13. Moscow Domestic Service, March 5, 1969, in *FBIS, DR, SU* (March 6, 1969), p. A2.

14. Report of Antonin Kostka, Prague Domestic Service in Czech, 1730 GMT, March 3, 1969, in *FBIS, DR, SU* (March 4, 1969), p. A18.

15. *FBIS, DR, SU* (March 6, 1969), p. A2.

16. Telegraph Agency of the Soviet Union (TASS), March 7, 1969, in *FBIS, DR, SU* (March 10, 1969), p. A5.

17. TASS, March 7, 1969, in *FBIS, DR, SU* (March 7, 1969), p. A1.

18. Viktor Vasilyev, Moscow Domestic Service, 1500 GMT, March 10, 1969, in *FBIS, DR, SU* (March 11, 1969), p. A8.

19. *Sueddeutsche Zeitung*, March 12, 1969, in USSR: Sino–Soviet Report/42, *RFE* (March 12, 1969), p. 6.

20. TASS, March 15, 1969, in *FBIS, DR, SU* (March 17, 1969), pp. A1–3.

21. A. Grigoryants, "Whom is Peking Playing Up To?" *Trud*, March 11, 1969, p. 1, in *FBIS, DR, SU* (March 18, 1969), pp. A41–43.

22. See, for example, Yu. Mushkaterov, "Merely Coincidences?" *Sovyetskaya Rossiya*, March 15, 1969, p. 3, in *FBIS, DR, SU* (March 18, 1969), p. A32. See also: A. Mirnov and Ya. Mikhaylov, "The Maoist Course—Military Bureaucratic Dictatorship," *Krasnaya Zvezda*, March 22, 1969, p. 5, in *FBIS, DR, SU* (March 26, 1969), pp. A16–22.

23. The Soviets, to save face, later claimed that they had not raised the issue, but Ulbricht, who attended, said: "In the framework of the Budapest conference, the military provocations of the Mao Tse-tung group, directed against the borders of the USSR, were frequently discussed." *Neues Deutschland*, March 23, 1969, in *FBIS, DR, EE* (March 28, 1969), p. E4.

24. The measures, under discussion since the March 1968 PCC session, included the establishment of a committee of defense ministers and reorganization of the Warsaw Pact joint armed forces and command. See Malcolm Mackintosh, "The Evolution of the Warsaw Pact," *Adelphi Papers*, No. 58 (June 1969); and Malcolm Mackintosh, "The Warsaw Pact Today," *Survival*, 16 (May–June 1974): 122–26.

25. The texts of the Budapest military communiqué and appeal may be found in *FBIS, DR, EE* (March 18, 1969), pp. F2–7.

26. Editorial in *Trud*, March 19, 1969, p. 1, in *FBIS, DR, SU* (March 21, 1969), p. A42.

27. Nine days earlier, Moscow radio had tied the first Damanskiy Island raid to "Bonn's provocative act of holding presidential elections in West Berlin." See note 18.

28. *Krasnaya Zvezda*, March 19, 1969, p. 1, in *FBIS, DR, EE* (March 21, 1969), p. A40.

29. Yugoslavia: Party/31, *RFE* (March 11, 1969), p. 2.

30. Bulgarian Situation Report/19, *RFE* (March 12, 1969), p. 3. Bulgaria's usually close adherence to the Moscow line suggests that this linkage may have been a Soviet trial balloon.

31. Ivan Peev, "The Invisible Axis," *Narodna Armiya*, March 6, 1969, p. 3, in *FBIS, DR, EE* (March 11, 1969), pp. C2–3.

32. Ibid., p. C2.

33. Ibid.

34. Ibid., p. C3.

35. Ibid., p. C4. The Soviet media did not use the term "Bonn–Peking axis."

36. Dimiter Peichinov, "PRC 'Provocation' Purposes," *Rabotnichesko Delo*, March 11, 1969, in *FBIS, DR, EE* (March 11, 1969), p. C1.

37. Ibid. The USA–PRC linkage was further developed in Boris Petkov, "Escalation of Anti-Sovietism by the Mao Tse-tung Group," *Novo Vreme*, No. 5 (May 1969): 100–07, in *JPRS*, 48,518 (July 30, 1969), p. 12.

38. Sofia Bulgarian Telegraph Agency (BTA), March 12, 1969, in *FBIS, DR, EE* (March 14, 1969), p. C1.

39. *FBIS, DR, EE* (March 18, 1969), p. C1

40. Kosta Andreev, "The Sinister Shadow of 'the Reddest Sun,' " *Trud*, March 14, 1969, pp. 1, 3, in *FBIS, DR, EE* (March 20, 1969), p. C2. The Soviets had offered similar evidence. See note 22.

41. Ibid., p. C4; and Boris Petkov, *Narodna Armiya*, July 17, 1969, pp. 2–3, in *JPRS*, 48,776 (September 9, 1969), pp. 12–13.

42. Andreev, "The Sinister Shadow of the 'Reddest Sun,' " pp. C3, C5.

43. *FBIS, DR, EE* (March 19, 1969), p. C2.

44. Yordan Bozhilov, "The Congress of Maoists—Elimination of the Chinese Communist Party," *Novo Vreme*, No. 5 (May 1969): 108–14, in *JPRS*, 48,518 (July 30, 1969), p. 17.

45. Sofia Domestic Service, March 18, 1969, in *FBIS, DR, EE* (March 19, 1969), p. C1.

46. *FBIS, DR, EE* (March 25, 1969), p. C2.

47. See Jeffrey Simon, *Ruling Communist Parties and Détente: A Documentary History* (Washington, D.C.: American Enterprise Institute, 1975), p. 211.

48. Bulgarian Situation Report/20, *RFE* (March 17, 1969), p. 3.

49. See particularly the speech by Walter Ulbricht in *Volksarmee*, No. 3 (January 1969): 2–5, in *JPRS*, 47,585 (March 6, 1969), pp. 84–99.

50. "Mao Group Helps the Imperialists," *Neues Deutschland*, March 11, 1969, in *FBIS, DR, EE* (March 11, 1969), p. E1.

51. "On an Adventurous Course," *Neues Deutschland*, March 19, 1969, p. 2, in *FBIS, DR, EE* (March 25, 1969), pp. E11–12.

52. *Neues Deutschland*, March 15, 1969, p. 2, in *FBIS, DR, EE* (March 19, 1969), p. E1. Compare Ivan Peev's accusations in *Narodna Armiya*, March 6, 1969, p. 3.

53. "Flirting with the Mao Group," *Neue Zeit*, March 30 1969, p. 3, in *JPRS*, 48,020 (May 12, 1969), pp. 34–36.

54. East Berlin Domestic Service, March 24, 1969, in *FBIS, DR, EE* (March 25, 1969), p. E13.

55. Ch'uan Li-chiao article, *Horizont*, No. 19 (May 1969): 19, in *JPRS*, 48,228 (June 13, 1969), p. 91.

56. Wilfried Weber, *Einheit* (May 1969): 592–604, in *JPRS*, 48,474 (July 23, 1969), pp. 28–29.

57. *Neues Deutschland*, March 23, 1969, pp. 3–6, in *FBIS, DR, EE* (March 28, 1969), p. E4.

58. General Heinz Kessler, Deputy Minister of National Defense, in *Horizont*, No. 19 (May 1969): 5–6, in *JPRS*, 48,228 (June 13, 1969), p. 127.

59. See " 'SED Attacks Yugoslav Communists'—From a Confidential Report to SED Cadres," *Frankfurter Allgemeine Zeitung*, September 26, 1969, pp. 9–10, in *JPRS*, 49,296 (November 24, 1969), pp. 1–8.

60. Ross Johnson attributed this revitalization to the 1968 party crisis in which Gomulka thwarted a challenge from hardliners by allowing younger leaders to rise to important positions. These younger leaders, concerned with internal economic problems and Poland's loss of international prestige because of (1) anti-Semitic overtones in the purge following the Middle East war and (2) Poland's role in the Czechoslovak crisis, initiated the new policy. A. Ross Johnson, *The Warsaw Pact's Campaign for "European Security,"* The Rand Corporation, R-565-PR (November 1970), pp. 57–58.

61. On May 17, 1969, Gomulka proposed a border treaty with the FRG that embodied recognition of the Oder–Neisse boundary but not Ulbricht's demands for the FRG's recognition of the GDR. This decoupling represented a Polish national initiative in the guise of support of the European security conference proposal. Ibid., pp. 55–57.

62. Jerzy Nocun, "Shots Over the Ussuri," *Zolnierz Wolnosci*, March 8, 1969, in *FBIS, DR, EE* (March 10, 1969), p. G1.

63. *Trybuna Ludu*, March 10, 1969, in *FBIS, DR, EE* (March 11, 1969), pp. G7–8.

64. Grzegorz Jaszunski, *Zycie Warszawy*, March 7, 1969, in *FBIS, DR, EE* (March 7, 1969), p. G5.

65. PAP International Service in English, 0630 GMT, March 18, 1969, in *FBIS, DR, EE* (March 18, 1969), p. G2.

66. "Logic of Facts and Responsibility," *Trybuna Ludu*, March 18, 1969, in *FBIS, DR, EE* (March 18, 1969), p. G2. We noted a similar moderation in Poland's attitude toward the PRC in the two preceding crises.

67. K. Malcuzynski, "Historical Appeal," *Trybuna Ludu*, March 19, 1969, in *FBIS, DR, EE* (March 19, 1969), p. G1.

68. This was particularly the position of *Borba* of Yugoslavia. Polish Situation Report/22, RFE (March 19, 1969), p. 1.

69. *FBIS, DR, EE* (March 21, 1969), p. G7.

70. "Significant Coincidence," *Zycie Warszawy*, March 19, 1969, in *FBIS, DR, EE* (March 19, 1969), p. G2.

71. *FBIS, DR, EE* (March 5, 1969), p. F5.

72. *FBIS, DR, EE* (March 12, 1969), p. F1.

73. *FBIS, DR, EE* (March 17, 1969), p. F5.

74. *FBIS, DR, EE* (March 21, 1969), pp. F17–18.

75. Budapest Domestic Service, March 18, 1969, in *FBIS, DR, EE* (March 19, 1969), p. F2.

76. *FBIS, DR, EE* (March 19, 1969), p. F3.

77. F. Varnai, "Unfortunate Development," *Nepszabadsag*, March 9, 1969, in Hungarian Press Survey No. 1990, RFE (March 11, 1969), pp. 1–3.

78. Istvan Perenyi, "Yugoslavia after the Party Congress," *Csongrad Megyei Hirlap*, March 20, 1969, in Hungarian Press Survey No. 2000, RFE (April 9, 1969), p. 6.

79. Hungary's moderation was noted by the Italian Communists. See *L'Unita*, February 2, 1969, p. 6, in *JPRS*, 47,447 (February 19, 1969), pp. 74–77.

80. *Rude Pravo*, March 6, 1969, in *FBIS, DR, EE* (March 6, 1969), p. D7.

81. As late as March 13, *Politika* continued to present a balanced account of the Sino–Soviet incident and even so far as to quote a "revisionist" Yugoslav view of the possibility of armed conflict between socialist states. Vaclav Horak, "Is Only a Border Involved?" *Politika*, March 13, 1969, pp. 39–40, in *JPRS*, 47,858 (April 15, 1969), p. 23.

82. The Soviets indicated their displeasure with the Czechoslovak media coverage of the Ussuri incident in a 12 March editorial, "Where Is *Mlada Fronta* Going?" in *Literaturnaya Gazeta*, in *FBIS, DR, SU* (March 18, 1969), p. A11.

83. "We and China," *Rude Pravo*, March 15, 1969, in *FBIS, DR, EE* (March 17, 1969), p. D6.

84. Ibid., pp. D6-7. This was written after the Soviet media had linked the PRC with U.S. and West German imperialism and accused the Maoists of betraying socialism. See also, Stanislav Budin, "Ice on the Ussuri," *Zemedelske Noviny*, March 25, 1969, p. 2, in *FBIS, DR, EE* (March 28, 1969), p. D11.

85. *Pravda* (Bratislava), March 15, 1969, pp. 1-2, in *FBIS, DR, EE* (March 21, 1969), p. D10. Stanislav Budin, in "The Conflict on the Ussuri River" [*Reporter*, No. 13 (April 3, 1969)], was slower to blame the Chinese in the incident because "there are too few facts by which to determine who took the initiative and for what reason." Czechoslovak Press Survey No. 2208, *RFE* (April 21, 1969), p. 5.

86. J. Marko, "Answering the Journalists," *Pravda* (Bratislava), March 15, 1969, pp. 1-2, in *FBIS, DR, EE* (March 21, 1969) p. D10.

87. Jiri Hromadka, March 25, 1969, in *FBIS, DR, EE* (March 27, 1969), pp. D12-14.

88. Antonin Snejdarek, "Czechoslovakia in the Modern World," *Rude Pravo*, February 7-8, 1969, p. 7, in *JPRS*, 47,652 (March 17, 1969), p. 5.

89. See *Lidova Demokracie*, March 17, 1969, p. 2, in *FBIS, DR, EE* (March 21, 1969), p. D16.

90. Ibid.

91. "Dubcek Interview with Jiri Sekera," *Rude Pravo*, March 19, 1969, pp. 1-2, in *FBIS, DR, EE*, No. 56 (March 24, 1969), p. D8.

92. Vera Stovickova, *Politika*, March 20, 1969, pp. 3-4, in *JPRS*, 47,914 (April 24, 1969), p. 15.

93. See: L. K., "From the Official and the Unofficial Angle: After Budapest," *Pravda* (Bratislava), March 19, 1969, p. 3, in *FBIS, DR, EE* (March 25, 1969), p. D12.

94. Miroslav Pavel, "Security Requires Deeds," *Mlada Fronta*, March 20, 1969, p. 5, in *FBIS, DR, EE* (March 25, 1969), p. D13.

95. Lieutenant Colonel Miroslav Linha, *Atom*, No. 5 (1969): 132-33, in *JPRS*, 48,310 (June 27, 1969), p. 37.

96. Pavel, "Security Requires Deeds," p. D13.

97. Linha, *Atom*, p. 37.

98. *Svet Prace*, March 26, 1969, in Czechoslovak Situation Report/25, *RFE* (March 28, 1969), p. 4.

99. Z. Jiricek, *Prace*, March 11, 1969, in *FBIS, DR, EE* (March 11, 1969), p. D1.

100. *FBIS, DR, EE* (March 11, 1969), p. D2.

101. Budapest Domestic Service, March 14, 1969, in *FBIS, DR, EE* (March 17, 1969), p. F5.

102. An example of Soviet sensitivity to Czechoslovakia's dissidence was the specific omission of Czechoslovakia (and Romania) from a list of Soviet supporters in the Ussuri conflict. See O. B. Borisov and V. T. Koloskov, *Sino-Soviet Relations, 1945-1973: A Brief History* (Moscow: Progress Publishers, 1975), p. 311.

103. Martin Dzur, the Czechoslovak minister of defense, after visiting Brezhnev in February 1969, admitted that some members of his delegation had "doubts" and that the Soviet military were "very sensitive" about developments in Czechoslovakia. Czechoslovak Situation Report/20, *RFE* (March 3, 1969), pp. 3-4.

104. *Scinteia*, March 4, 1969, p. 6, in *FBIS, DR, EE* (March 20, 1969), p. H2.

105. Vasile Gliga article, *Politique Etrangere* (Paris), 33 (1968): 315-30, in *JPRS*, 47,339 (January 29, 1969), pp. 101-02.

106. Speech on 29 November in *Scinteia*, November 30, 1968, pp. 1, 4, in *FBIS, DR, EE* (December 4, 1968), p. H22.

107. V. Iliescu, "The Communists, an Invincible Political Force in Today's World," *Scinteia*, March 11, 1969, in *FBIS, DR, EE* (March 12, 1969), pp. H5-9. V. Iliescu is a pseudonym used to sign important articles in *Scinteia* (as is I. Aleksandrov in *Pravda*)

108. Ion Gheorghe Maurer, "Report on Draft Bill," *Scinteia*, March 15, 1969, p. 3, in *FBIS, DR, EE* (March 19, 1969), p. H3.

109. Constantin Mitea, "For Security in Europe," *Scinteia*, March 20, 1969, in *FBIS, DR, EE* (March 21, 1969), p. H1.

110. "Decision Approving the Documents on Perfecting the Structure and the Leadership Organs of the Warsaw Pact," April 10, 1969, Bucharest Domestic Service, in *FBIS, DR, EE* (April 11, 1969), pp. H3–4. The Czechoslovak media also stressed the European focus.

111. Nicolae Ceausescu speech, Bucharest Domestic Service, April 10, 1969, in *FBIS, DR, EE* (April 11, 1969), p. H2.

112. "Our Country will continue developing its collaboration with the armies of the Warsaw Pact and all the socialist countries." Nicolae Ceausescu, "Letter to Military Academy Graduates," *Scinteia*, August 19, 1969, p. 1, in *JPRS*, 48,811 (September 15, 1969), p. 91; and Ceausescu's speech on Armed Forces Day, *Scinteia*, October 25, 1969, pp. 1, 3, in *JPRS*, 49,251 (November 14, 1969), pp. 204–5.

113. For example, at a war crimes conference in Moscow in March 1969, the USSR attempted to pass a resolution condemning the FRG (for revanchist and neo-Nazi designs), the United States (for the war in Vietnam), Israel, and Greece. Romania refused to sign the condemnation. TASS, March 28, 1969, in *FBIS, DR, SU* (April 1, 1969), p. A19.

114. Romanian Situation Report/25, *RFE* (March 13, 1969), p. 3.

115. Paul Niculescu-Mizil, the Romanian delegate to the Twelfth Italian Communist Party Congress (8–15 February 1969), did specifically mention Czechoslovakia on that occasion. The Italian communist party's message to the Yugoslav party congress not only explicitly condemned the invasion of Czechoslovakia but also rejected "any theory of a guiding state or party." *L'Unita*, March 14, 1969, in Non-Ruling CPs Situation Report/6, *RFE* (March 17, 1969), pp. 1–3. The positions of the Yugoslav, Romanian, and Italian parties were strikingly similar at this time.

116. Hsinhua and Radio Bucharest, April 4, 1969, in Romanian Situation Report/34, *RFE* (April 8, 1969), p. 1.

117. Romanian Situation Report/42, *RFE* (April 29, 1969), pp. 1–2.

118. *FBIS, DR, EE* (March 4, 1969), p. I2.

119. Andro Gabelic, "What is China Trying to Say?" *Borba*, March 8, 1969, in *FBIS, DR, EE* (March 11, 1969), p. I26.

120. *FBIS, DR, EE* (March 17, 1969), pp. I15–16.

121. Belgrade Domestic Service, March 19, 1969, in *FBIS, DR, EE* (March 20, 1969), p. I2.

122. *FBIS, DR, EE* (March 21, 1969), p. I1.

123. Frane Barbieri article, *Politique Aujourd'hui* (Paris), May 1969, pp. 89–102, in *JPRS*, 48,394 (July 10, 1969), p. 39.

124. Stjepan Vukusic, Tanjug correspondent in Bucharest, in *FBIS, DR, EE* (March 24, 1969), p. I5.

125. Risto Bajaloki, "The Budapest Meetings," *Borba*, March 19, 1969, in *FBIS, DR, EE* (March 24, 1969), p. I6.

126. *FBIS, DR, EE* (April 15, 1969), p. I4. The Ussuri provocation had also been analyzed in terms of Chinese foreign policy.

127. One example involved Macedonia. Josip Djerdja stated openly that the USSR had directed the recent Bulgarian campaigns to raise the Macedonian issue with Yugoslavia. *FBIS, DR, EE* (March 26, 1969), p. I1. The Romanians and Czechoslovaks had sided with Yugoslavia on the Macedonian issue.

128. *Zeri i Popullit*, March 5, 1969, in *FBIS, DR, EE* (March 5, 1969), p. B1.

129. "Notes on International Events," *Bashkimi*, March 9, 1969, p. 3, in *JPRS*, 47,740 (March 28, 1969), p. 2.

130. "The Aggressive Actions of the Soviet Revisionists," *Zeri i Popullit*, March 14, 1969, in *FBIS, DR, EE* (March 17, 1969), pp. B2–3.

131. "Anti-China Provocations," *Luftetari*, March 17, 1969, in *FBIS, DR, EE* (March 17, 1969), p. B1.

132. "Soviet-U.S. Collaboration," *Zeri i Popullit*, March 22, 1969, in *FBIS, DR, EE* (March 24, 1969), p. B3.

133. Ibid., p. B1.

134. Tirana Domestic Service, March 24, 1969, in *FBIS, DR, EE* (March 27, 1969), p. B1.

135. Arben Puto, "Socialist Principles of Foreign Policy and the Soviet Revisionists' Shift to Social-Imperialist Policy," *Ruga e Partise*, March 1969, pp. 99–108, in *JPRS*, 48,403 (July 11, 1969), p. 9.

136. *Zeri i Popullit*, March 22, 1969, in *FBIS, DR, EE* (March 24, 1969), p. B5.

137. The Soviets continued to pursue a dual strategy of threats of violence and offers of compromise. Although on 8 August the Soviets and Chinese signed a protocol on the improvement of navigation on boundary rivers, according to Henry Kissinger, "far from easing tensions, this seemed to spur them." Henry Kissinger, *White House Years* (Boston: Little, Brown, 1979), p. 183.

138. Ulbricht, who attended the session, said afterward that China had been discussed.

139. Ulbricht and Dubcek, both participants in the PCC session, confirmed the existence of differences in regard to a European security conference and to the Warsaw Pact reorganization, respectively.

5

Nixon's Visit to Peking, February 1972

CEAUSESCU HELPS LINK WASHINGTON TO PEKING

The developing USA–PRC relationship manifest in the Shanghai communiqué of February 1972 compounded the USSR's China problem. Since the Sino–Soviet rift in October 1961, the Soviets had felt threatened by China's increasingly active political role in the communist world (especially in Eastern Europe), as well as in the international arena following its admission to the United Nations in October 1971. More important, the Soviets had come to consider the PRC a serious military threat.[1] They indicated the extent of their fear by (1) warning the United States against any attempt to profit from Sino–Soviet tensions and (2) attempting to draw the United States into an anti-PRC alignment.[2]

Meanwhile, the Soviets were pursuing a policy of détente in Europe—possibly influenced by the burden of increased military assistance to the Middle East since 1967, of maintaining five divisions in Czechoslovakia since 1968, and of building up their forces in the Far East since 1969. The March 1969 Budapest appeal for a European security conference was followed by the signing of a treaty with the FRG on 12 August 1970 in Moscow. Most of the USSR's Warsaw Pact allies welcomed the USSR–FRG rapprochement, and Poland signed a similar treaty with the FRG on 7 December 1970.

The ouster of two troublesome Eastern European leaders also contributed to European détente. Following the spontaneous eruption of riots in Poland at the end of December, Edward Gierek succeeded Gomulka as PUWP first secretary. In May 1971, Erich Honecker replaced Ulbricht (who had opposed a European security conference) as SED leader. The eased tension in Europe, as expressed in the Soviet and Polish treaties with the FRG, and the changes in the Polish and East German political leaderships seemed to moderate the responses of the USSR and the orthodox pact members to Nixon's visit to China.

The Romanian problem, however, continued to plague the Soviet leadership. Romania's reaction to Nixon's China visit appeared to be influenced by (1) Romania's developing military relations with China and Yugoslavia and (2) Romania's instrumental role in establishing relations between the United States and the PRC.

Following the Ussuri incident, Romania's close political relations with China, which had taken on military overtones during the invasion of Czechoslovakia, continued to evolve and thus to exacerbate relations with the USSR. Although after prolonged hesitation Romania renewed its friendship pact with Moscow in July 1970, it refused to agree to compulsory military assistance to Moscow or to consult with the USSR before making foreign policy decisions. Two weeks later, Minister of Defense Ion Ionita led a military delegation to Peking, where the Chinese promised the Romanians "fraternal help in the defense of Romanian sovereignty" and allegedly offered to deliver nuclear warheads for Romanian medium-range rockets should the USSR threaten Romania.[3]

Romania's military ties with Yugoslavia involved a joint fighter aircraft project, begun in early 1971.[4] Although still a Warsaw Pact member, Romania based its military relationships with Yugoslavia and China on its announced doctrine of maintaining friendly relations with both its "Warsaw Pact partners *and all socialist countries*" (emphasis added).[5]

Its long-standing relationship with China led to Romania's role in the Nixon administration's moves toward diplomatic recognition of the PRC and the resolution of the Vietnam war. In 1967—before his election—Nixon had discussed with Ceausescu the normalization of relations with Peking. Nixon later wrote of their meeting in Bucharest:

> We had a long talk. . . . I said that I thought the United States could do little to establish effective communications with China until the Vietnam war ended. After that, however, I thought we could take steps to normalize relations with Peking. *Ceausescu was guarded in his reaction, but I could tell that he was interested to hear me talking in this way, and that he agreed with what I said* [emphasis added].[6]

At the time of Nixon's election, however, U.S. relations with the PRC remained practically nonexistent. The sporadic talks between U.S. and Chinese representatives at the Polish foreign ministry in Warsaw did not constitute a readily available channel of communication.[7]

Although the main purpose of Nixon's trip around the world in July–August 1969 was to end the Vietnam war, the new president also hoped to open communications with China. In Romania on 2–3 August—the first visit to a communist state by a U.S. president since Roosevelt had attended the Yalta conference in 1945[8]—Nixon discussed with Ceausescu "the need for a new Chinese–American relationship."[9] It is not known whether the Soviets knew at that time of Nixon's remarks regarding China; however, on 8 August, Konstantin Katushev, then CC CPSU secretary in charge of ruling communist parties, addressing the Tenth Congress of the Romanian communist party, referred to the "perfidious imperialist tactics of bridge-building . . . to undermine the unity of the socialist countries."[10]

The Romanians had ample opportunity to convey Nixon's message to Peking. In September, Premier Maurer attended the funeral of Ho Chi Minh in Hanoi. En route to and from the funeral, he stopped in Peking for talks with Chou En-lai. Whether Maurer discussed Nixon's visit is unknown; however, on 12 December U.S. and PRC representatives met unofficially in the Chinese embassy in Warsaw, presumably at the request of the United States. As a result of this meeting, the official talks were scheduled to reopen on 20 January 1970.[11]

Although Romania's influence in bringing about the unofficial USA–PRC meeting in December 1969 remains obscure,[12] Ceausescu played an important role in 1970 in getting the Chinese to invite Nixon to Peking. Nixon wrote of his 26 October 1970 meeting with Ceausescu in Washington:

> I said that, even short of the ultimate ideal of re-establishing full diplomatic relations with China, there could be an exchange of high-level personal representatives. He agreed to pass this word along to Peking, and this was the beginning of the "Romanian channel."[13]

On returning home from Washington, Ceausescu sent his vice premier, Corneliu Bogdan, to Peking. Chou responded with a message for President Nixon to the effect that the PRC was prepared to receive a U.S. special envoy in Peking and that in view of Nixon's visits to Bucharest in 1969 and Belgrade in 1970, Nixon himself would be welcome in Peking.[14]

Ceausescu went to China in June 1971, the first visit of a Warsaw Pact party leader to the PRC since the Sino–Soviet rift ten years earlier. The Romanian press coverage highlighted the Chinese recognition, in the joint communiqué, of the Romanian concept of the special role of small and medium-sized states in determining international policies.[15]

During Ceausescu's visit to Peking, the Soviets strongly criticized the CCP's foreign policy, citing specifically the dangers of a USA–PRC rapprochement and the military–bureaucratic nature of China's regime.[16] Although the Soviet media did not openly attack Ceausescu, broadcasts to Romania warned that Peking's policies undermined communist unity.[17] The West German magazine *Spiegel* alleged that, while Ceausescu was in Peking, "Warsaw Pact troops moved into maneuver positions [code-named Yug] near the Romanian border" in anticipation of an "officers' putsch," which failed.[18] The Romanians reacted to Soviet pressure by labeling Soviet anti-Chinese opinions "clumsy, if not ridiculous,"[19] and beginning a large-scale military mobilization that included the Patriotic Guards.[20]

Romania was the only Warsaw Pact member to react favorably[21] to Nixon's 15 July 1971 public acceptance of Chou En-lai's invitation to visit China before May 1972 (the scheduled date of Nixon's Moscow summit meeting).[22] The Romanian press stated that an improvement in USA–PRC relations would benefit all countries and that no major international problems could be solved without China. On 21 July, *Scinteia* wrote that in Romania, "the news about the development of Sino–American contacts has been welcomed with satisfaction and approval."[23]

Romania's good offices in bringing the United States and PRC together and the increasing convergence of its foreign policy with China's Asian policy[24] caused considerable anxiety and irritation in Moscow. Ceausescu's absence from the traditional July meeting of communist party secretaries in the Crimea, which occurred simultaneously with the public announcement of Nixon's intended visit to Peking and two Soviet-led exercises (code-named Opal and Preslav) directed toward the Southern Tier, provided indications of the tension beween Romania and the USSR. Ceausescu responded by delivering a frantic series of speeches throughout Romania and mobilizing the Patriotic Guards.[25] (Tito also mobilized the Territorial Defense Forces in Yugoslavia.)

The Soviets indicated their apprehensions concerning U.S. foreign policy in their coverage of Nixon's 9 February 1972 report to the Congress and his visit to Peking. Soviet and other socialist media coverage of these events are compared below as a basis for further evaluation of Warsaw Pact unity.

A TAIWAN-FOR-PEKING DEAL?

On 9 February 1972, Richard Nixon addressed the Congress on the issues confronting U.S. foreign policy worldwide.[26] The report received especially broad international coverage because it was delivered on the eve of the president's trip to China.

After a week of massive Soviet press and radio commentary, *Pravda* published a comprehensive critique of the Nixon report. The commentator, Yuriy Zhukov, maintained that Nixon's desire to dramatize his statesmanship before the upcoming presidential elections had inspired the report. Zhukov also claimed that the United States was reasserting a "position of strength" policy and that the only innovation was the pursuit of a China course:

> The only more or less new element in this relapse into the "from a position of
> strength" policy is the reference in the report to the fact that the United States

had decided to initiate a "dialog" with China proceeding from the fact that "China and the United States have many parallel interests."[27]

Charging that Washington wanted to develop Sino–American contacts to the detriment of the socialist community's interests and of international détente in general, he cautioned that U.S. actions would be monitored quite closely in this regard.

Zhukov gave several examples of what he considered to be U.S. recalcitrance in international affairs. First, he interpreted the goal of Nixon's new plan for Vietnam to be a military victory rather than a negotiated peace. Second, he alleged that, while Nixon was advising the Soviets to decrease arms deliveries to Egypt, the United States was increasing its arms sales to Israel. Finally, he criticized China and the United States—but not Romania—for supporting Pakistan rather than India in the United Nations.[28]

An *Izvestiya* article by V. Petrusenko the next day essentially reiterated Zhukov's charges; however, Petrusenko interpreted Nixon's report as a preelection tactic to deflect American public opinion from the Republican Party's domestic program failures to its foreign policy successes. Then Petrusenko cited the failures of U.S. foreign policies in Vietnam, the Middle East, and the India–Pakistan subcontinent. He especially criticized the U.S. report's harsh tone regarding the USSR as opposed to the restrained tone regarding the PRC:

> International commentators do not disregard the very striking difference of tone in the approach to Sino–American relations on the one hand and to Soviet–American relations on the other. Even the Washington journalists drew attention to the restrained tone of the message regarding the PRC and the harshness in the approach to the problems concerning relations with the Soviet Union. When they decided to verify how true this judgment of theirs is, such an authoritative representative of the administration as H. Kissinger by no means began trying to change their minds but merely observed that "almost everything is written for a deliberate purpose" in the foreign policy message.[29]

Regarding Europe, Petrusenko merely noted that the sections of Nixon's report concerning European peace and security were "amorphous and vague."[30] At no time did any commentary link Bonn with Peking, perhaps reflecting the softened stance toward the FRG since the March 1969 Budapest appeal and the August 1970 USSR–FRG treaty.

The Soviet media stressed three themes concerning China during the period between Nixon's 9 February message and his arrival in Peking on 21 February: the PRC's possible role in a Vietnam settlement, its divisive role in the Third World, and its repression at home of intellectuals and national minorities. First, despite reports that the Chinese did not intend to discuss Vietnam with the president, the Soviets remained unconvinced of Chinese neutrality and feared that the Chinese might act in collusion with the United States against the interests of North Vietnam.[31] On 14 February, Viktor Lyubovtsev commented that: "The U.S. Government felt a certain relief when renewed bombings of North Vietnam in December 1971, which had continued into 1972, elicited a comparatively mild reaction from Peking."[32] Another broadcast several days later also hinted at USA–PRC collusion:

> U.S. military authorities announced in Saigon today that President Nixon will issue an order for intensifying mass bombings of South Vietnam if the National Liberation Front of South Vietnam (NLFSV) does not discontinue military actions. . . . To make such a statement on the eve of departure for talks with the Peking leaders would be extremely careless on the part of the White House if the President were not confident that Peking will in no way react to his new threats addressed to the peoples of Indochina.[33]

Second, the Soviets alleged Chinese betrayal of the national liberation movement. Emphasizing the USSR's continuing commitment to the movement, the Soviets assailed Peking's divisive actions in the Third World. For example, *Pravda* wrote:

> The successes of the national liberation movement could have been more considerable had it not been for the Maoist leadership's position, which is treacherous in its attitude. Despite its vociferous revolutionary utterances about support for the national liberation movement and its verbal denunciations of imperialism, recent facts, and particularly the Indo–Pakistan conflict, leave no doubt that in practice the Maoist leadership is encouraging reactionary regimes in the Third World, undermining the unity and cohesion of progressive and democratic forces and fomenting nationalism and anti-Sovietism.[34]

Third, the Soviets charged the Chinese with internal repression of national minorities and intellectuals.[35] The Soviet implication was clear: China had lost its revolutionary zeal.

During Nixon's trip to China,[36] the Soviet media again referred to Nixon's reelection campaign maneuvers and U.S. policy "failures" in Vietnam and Bangladesh; however, the media addressed mainly the intensified American bombing in Vietnam. The Soviets charged that Chinese silence regarding the bombing constituted a betrayal of Vietnam. On 23 February, Moscow Domestic Service concluded that Nixon's presence in Peking during the intensified bombing indicated that "the actions of U.S. aircraft in Vietnam are in actual fact coordinated and directed from Peking."[37] This view was reiterated on the radio and in the press.

On the day after Nixon's departure from China, a commentary in *Trud* warily assessed the implications of his journey and of the Shanghai communiqué:

> We still have insufficient information to speak of the full results of this noisily publicized trip. The talks took place in the strictest secrecy, behind tightly

closed doors. The only things which are known more or less positively are the details of the deliberately magnificent ceremonies, the statistics of the length of the talks, and the timing of the trips.[38]

The article speculated also that China's sellout of Vietnam could be the beginning of a USA–PRC pattern of cooperation:

> Time will show how far Peking's and Washington's "parallel interests" . . . have gone. . . . The U.S. side undoubtedly counted on obtaining support from Peking for Nixon's "Guam Doctrine" in exchange for certain actions. . . . The Peking ruling circles . . . are avoiding everything which might look like criticism of the United States.[39]

An extensive 4 March analysis of the Shanghai communiqué in *Izvestiya* led the author, Kondrashov, to conclude that the "communiqué is only the tip of an iceberg called 'normalization of American–Chinese relations' "[40]—relations motivated by anti-Sovietism. Kondrashov cited the following evidence of Peking's "increasingly obvious split with the international communist movement": First, Peking's silence regarding U.S. policy in Vietnam; second, the "parallel interests" of the United States and China in Indian–Pakistani relations; third, the communiqué's failure to refer either to Middle East problems or to the socialist system even though, in Kondrashov's words, "the communiqué was compiled according to the principle that each side should include in it everything it considered important."[41]

The following day *Pravda* charged that the United States had colluded with the PRC in an anti–Soviet course and in a Taiwan-for-Vietnam deal:

> Following "agonizing reappraisals of values," disputes, and probings, Washington decided in a presidential election year to revise only a single element of its overall Asian and Far Eastern policy which has existed since the time of General MacArthur—that is, to "build a bridge" in relations with China. Insofar as all other elements of the chain (the aggression in Indochina, occupation of South Korea, military bases along the entire periphery of the Far East and Southeast Asia) have remained unaltered.
>
> The United States is still holding on to Taiwan with a stubbornness which makes one prick up one's ears. . . . The United States will gradually reduce the number of its armed forces and military bases on Taiwan "as tension in this region is relaxed." . . . [This] is a "Taiwan-for-Vietnam" deal. Thus, Washington has struck a bargain with Peking behind the backs of the Vietnamese people and the other Asian peoples.[42]

In summary, the Soviets:

- Charged that Nixon's *U.S. Foreign Policy for the 1970s* merely reasserted the United States's "position of strength" policy and provided the president a means to divert voter attention from domestic problems.

- Refrained from criticizing Romania, either for its instrumental role in arranging Nixon's China visit or for its support of Pakistan in the conflict with India.
- Attacked the PRC for collusion with the United States on issues involving Vietnam, India–Pakistan, and the Middle East.
- Characterized the Shanghai communiqué as anti-Soviet and accused the United States and China of an unwritten agreement to exchange Taiwan for Vietnam.
- Charged the Chinese with betraying the revolution and socialism.

BULGARIA INDIRECTLY ATTACKS ROMANIA

The Bulgarian media adopted the Soviet interpretation of Nixon's foreign policy address but concentrated primarily on the USA–USSR relationship. Stressing the anti-Soviet aspects of U.S. policy enabled the Bulgarians at the same time to reiterate their support of the Soviet position.

The newspaper *Otechestven Front*,[43] in analyzing the Nixon address, speculated at length on the impending (May 1972) USA–USSR summit talks but took little note of Nixon's planned visit to the PRC. The article outlined the inconsistencies of U.S. policy in terms that accorded with the Soviet critique of the U.S. stand on a European security conference, Vietnam, and the Middle East.

A *Trud* (the Bulgarian trade union organ) analysis of Nixon's speech, ignoring Romania's role in the USA–PRC rapprochement, echoed the Soviet perception of collusive secrecy in the Sino–American relationship: "Nixon pointed out that the change of U.S. policies toward China had been accomplished after almost three years of patient, meticulous, and *necessarily secret preparations.*"[44]

In a minor departure from the Soviet interpretation, the Bulgarians did not draw attention to Nixon's election needs or domestic problems. They did, however, reflect the Soviet stance in not linking Bonn with Peking (in effect, decoupling Europe from Asia).

Turning from Nixon's address to the Congress to his planned trip to China, the Bulgarians linked U.S. and Chinese anti-Sovietism. They charged the Chinese with betraying socialism and colluding with imperialism. One article cited the two-superpower theory (which the Chinese used to connect Soviet and U.S. imperialism) as evidence of Chinese anti-Sovietism:

> The struggle against the "two superpowers" proclaimed by the Chinese leaders is in fact a struggle only against the Soviet Union. The threats against imperialism . . . are empty incantations to camouflage Peking's collusion with Washington.[45]

The same article, without naming Romania or mentioning its role in establishing Washington–Peking relations, linked the Romanian concept of the role of small and medium states and the Chinese two-superpower theory:

Blinded by anti-Sovietism, . . . the Chinese leaders do not hesitate to use the feelings of some of the most backward strata in "third world" countries, . . . as well as the saccharine nationalistic dreams and groundless claims of some politicians regarding the "special role of medium and small states" in determining international policies.[46]

Criticizing the two-superpower theory as a classless concept that exemplified class treason, another commentator wrote: "The main clash on the international arena is not between "small" and "large" [states], but between the two social systems in the world—socialism and capitalism."[47]

That the Chinese had betrayed socialism in collusion with American imperialists was the explicit conclusion of a six-article series by Ivan Peev in *Narodna Armiya*, the Bulgarian military organ. In the final article, Peev argued that Maoism was essentially anti-Sovietism and that, in pursuing its anti-Soviet course, the PRC was acting "in collusion with the U.S., the citadel of capitalism." The author concluded that Chou and Mao not only "desire to weaken the world socialist system, but their diplomacy is infected with the 'Munich spirit of 1938.' "[48]

Bulgarian commentaries paralleled Soviet analyses of the Shanghai communiqué. Colonel Ivan Vandev, writing in *Narodna Armiya*, upheld the Soviet charge of anti-Sovietism:

There is only one truth: The United States is interested in a strong China which it would like, at a given moment, to push into a prolonged and tiring war against the Soviet Union. In pursuit of this goal, U.S. diplomacy launched lively activity along two fronts: alignment with China *and breakup of the unity between socialist countries* [emphasis added].[49]

Vandev said also that, despite the secrecy surrounding the talks in Peking, the Shanghai communiqué provided evidence "of the alignment between U.S. imperialists and Peking 'ultrarevolutionaries.' "[50] The Bulgarians noted, as had the Soviets, that the communiqué failed to mention the Vietnam war, India–Pakistan conflict, Middle East crisis, and socialist relations.[51]

On 1 March, Bulgarian party leader Todor Zhivkov described the USSR as the embodiment of socialism and warned unnamed socialist countries that persisting nationalistic trends threatened the socialist system:

Above all, the Soviet Union is the embodiment of socialism and communism for hundreds of millions of people, for the friends of peace and its enemies. *The belonging of one or another country to the world of socialism is measured by its proximity to the social order, the home and foreign policy of the Soviet Union.* It is no secret to anybody that some serious nationalistic trends existed and exist in some socialist countries. These trends are not only a favorable ground for the flourishing of right-wing and left-wing revisionism and place under threat the socialist acquisitions of the working people and the socialist road of development of these countries, but also grow into anti-Sovietism and undermine the unity and cohesion of the world socialist system. . . . The example of the Mao Tse-tung group shows how far one may go by following the road of opposing the Communist Party of the Soviet Union [emphasis added].[52]

In conclusion, the Bulgarians, seconding the Soviets:

- Emphasized the unchanged nature of U.S. imperialist policies.
- Charged the Chinese with anti-Sovietism, betraying socialism, and collusion with the United States on issues involving Vietnam, India and Pakistan, and the Middle East.
- Attacked indirectly Romania's views on the equality of large and small states by criticizing China's two-superpower theory.

EAST GERMANY'S REVERSAL

Willy Brandt's election to the chancellorship of the FRG exacerbated the Soviet–East German tensions generated in March 1969 by Ulbricht's opposition to a European security conference. Brandt's *Ostpolitik* to improve relations with Eastern Europe elicited a ready response from the Soviet (and Polish) leadership. Despite Ulbricht's demand that the FRG recognize de jure the GDR's borders before any of the Warsaw Pact allies concluded treaties with the FRG, in August 1970 the Soviets and West Germans signed a treaty without such recognition, and the Poles and West Germans signed in December.

Ulbricht's perceptions of East Germany's national interests led to divergence from the Soviet line.[53] His intransigence and obstruction of Soviet policy finally resulted in his forced (tactfully and ceremoniously) retirement on 5 May 1971, immediately preceding the Eighth SED Congress. Erich Honecker's succession was orderly—and prearranged with the Soviets.[54]

Détente (and SED leadership changes) apparently modified the GDR's behavior. Although Bonn had been the East Germans' major propaganda target in the 1967, 1968, and 1969 crises, not once during Nixon's 1972 visit to China did the GDR media link U.S. and PRC actions with those of West Germany.

East German coverage of Nixon's foreign policy and the USA–PRC rapprochement essentially followed the Soviet line. *Neues Deutschland*, like the Soviet press, adduced proof of the United States's continuing aggressive course from its Vietnam and Middle East policies. And like the Soviets, the East Germans repeated Nixon's description of evolving USA–PRC relations without revealing Romania's involvement:

Speaking about his forthcoming visit to China, he [Nixon] said that no foreign political step of the United States has ever been so meticulously prepared as the approach to Peking. After a period of cautious probing and growing trust a *reliable means of communication* has been created between Washington and Peking [emphasis added].[55]

GDR press coverage of Nixon's trip to China, also following the orthodox line, described the visit as a reelection campaign maneuver:

To insure that the voters back in the United States can watch the historical events live and in color, in addition to the two planeloads of journalists, Nixon has even taken a complete ground satellite station with him behind the Bamboo Curtain.[56]

Horizont attributed the USA–PRC rapprochement to anti-Sovietism: "Peking became interesting for Washington only when the Mao Tse-tung group had led China out of the socialist community and onto an anti-Soviet course. For Washington and Peking this is the foundation of the joint field of interests."[57]

Other themes evident in the Soviet coverage were also highlighted in the East German reports. For instance, citing the scarcity of Chinese verbal attacks against the increased bombings in Vietnam on the eve of Nixon's departure, an East German commentator predicted: "Nixon . . . will probably attempt to come to terms with the Maoist leaders in Peking on an 'arrangement for Indochina' behind the backs of the peoples concerned."[58]

An article in *Einheit* charged China with betraying the Bangladesh national liberation struggle by supporting "American imperialist policy" in the United Nations.[59] The same article criticized the "misuse of concepts by the Maoists," the "classlessness" of the two-superpower theory, and China's attempt "to join with the revisionist forces in Czechoslovakia," citing specifically Chou En-lai's speech at the 23 August 1968 reception at the Romanian embassy in Peking as proof of the last charge.[60]

The East German analysis of the Shanghai communiqué highlighted the secrecy and supported the Soviet hypothesis of USA–PRC conspiracy:

The pronounced secretiveness resembled a conspiracy rather than necessary diplomatic discretion—an impression which the concluding communiqué reinforced. . . . Nixon himself said agreement extended far beyond this communiqué. Obviously, it was agreed to keep secret the actual content of the negotiations.[61]

Claiming that Nixon's trip had been accompanied by a tremendous escalation of the U.S. bombing of South Vietnam, North Vietnam, and Cambodia, another commentator pointed to China's silence regarding U.S. policy: "In the communiqué, the PRC reiterates its position on Indochina, [but] there is not a single word mentioning that it is the United States that is waging a dirty war . . . nor is there any talk of aggression, nor is it condemned."[62] The author added that the Chinese were less reluctant to condemn the USSR. Finally, he endorsed the Soviet acccusation of USA–PRC collusion, quoting from *Trud:*

> It was precisely the policy of "Vietnamization" announced by Nixon in 1969 which prompted the Maoists to invite the President to Peking. This policy suits the Chinese leaders. . . . They want to utilize the American policy of pitting Asians against Asians for their great-power goals.[63]

The East Germans, like the Bulgarians, sang a paean of support to the USSR:

> It is certain that Nixon's euphoric outburst that his days of Peking have "changed the world" constitutes nonsensical, ostentatious boasting. The peoples have known for a long time which ten days changed the world, and the source of the world-changing force of our age in the future also is the Soviet Union, the great socialist power of peace, with its allies, the socialist community of states, that is, the communist parties, and the national liberation movement.[64]

In sum, the East Germans accepted the Soviet interpretations of Nixon's foreign policy address, his China trip, and the Shanghai communiqué. The most significant aspect of East Germany's reaction to events in China—its decoupling of European (specifically, West German) from Asian problems—constituted a reversal of its behavior in earlier crises. The change apparently reflected, first, the Eastern European–West German rapprochement culminating in the USSR–FRG treaty of August 1970 and, second, the changes the following year in the East German party's top leadership.

CZECHOSLOVAKIA "NORMALIZED"

Gustav Husak's replacement of Alexander Dubcek as party first secretary in April 1969 marked the normalization of Czechoslovakia's internal situation and its return to the Soviet fold. Husak told the fourteenth party congress on 25 May 1971:

> Today we can responsibly declare that the advance of counterrevolutionary forces has been repelled, the socialist system defended. Since April 1969 the Central Committee has taken a firm course to overcome the crises in the party and society.[65]

In March 1969, despite the continued presence of Warsaw Pact occupation troops, the Czechoslovaks had exhibited independent positions on "rightist and leftist revisionism" by their support of the Yugoslav ninth party congress and their neutrality on the Chinese ninth party congress. In marked contrast, Husak warned in May 1971 that: "Right-wing opportunism and international revisionism . . . must necessarily merge into open betrayal of socialism . . . and anti-communist and anti-Soviet positions."[66]

The Czechoslovak response to Nixon's February 1972 foreign policy speech, although sparser than that of the other Warsaw Pact states, confirmed the turnabout under Husak's leadership. The Czechoslovak media, following the Soviet line, analyzed the speech in terms of Nixon's reelection strategy and the unresolved problems in the Middle East, Vietnam, and Western Europe. But in contrast to the Soviets, Bulgarians, and East Germans, the Czechoslovaks did not fault Nixon for stressing the seriousness of USA–USSR problems while indicating optimism that U.S. difficulties with the Chinese could be resolved. Nor did the Czechoslovaks note, in this context, the anti-Soviet aspects of the USA–PRC rapprochement. They did, however, express the hope that existing disagreements between the United States and USSR would be worked out at the May 1972 summit meeting.[67]

Czechoslovak coverage of Nixon's China trip accorded with the Soviet. Accusations of USA–PRC collusion and anti-Sovietism dominated. In making the trip, the media said, Nixon sought to enhance his popularity with the American electorate and to weaken the international position of the USSR. *Rude Pravo*, for example, charged the United States with attempting to weaken the USSR's position by exploiting the differences in the international communist movement:

> The U.S. Government is looking for ways leading to a rapprochement with Peking at a time when the PRC is already quite openly pursuing a policy aimed at breaking up the unity of the socialist community and betraying the national liberation movement. Surely it is no coincidence that the Nixon administration is . . . increasing the barbarous attacks against the Vietnamese people. . . . Backstage the United States is doing everything it can to create an anti-Soviet front.[68]

Another *Rude Pravo* commentary, by Zdenek Horeni, condemned the Chinese for their negative attitude toward the USSR and the other socialist countries and for their rapprochement with the United States.[69] Horeni also attributed to Melvin Laird the statement, "Chinese guided missiles are threatening the majority of cities and other targets in the area of South and East Asia and a substantial part of the Soviet Union."[70] Horeni concluded that the statement was calculated to "provoke and intrigue, to set one country against another."[71] Another commentator, reporting on the president's departure, found evidence of USA–PRC collusion in (1) the United States's reversal of its China policy, (2) the United States's continued bombing of North Vietnam, (3) the similarity of U.S. and Chinese positions on the India–Pakistan conflict, (4) China's anti-Sovietism, and (5) China's desire to emulate Japanese postwar successes through U.S. economic aid.[72]

The Czechoslovaks, like the Bulgarians, contrived to link the Romanian concept of the rights of small and medium-sized nations (still without naming Romania) and the Chinese two-superpower theory to prove Chinese anti-Sovietism. Accusing the Chinese of "chauvinist ambitions and sinocentrism," a Bratislava commentator said:

> Not only the theory of the "small and medium countries" is to serve this [chauvinist and sinocentrist] purpose, but also the concept of "super powers." . . . In this way the Chinese leadership tries to introduce a split into the anti-imperialist front, to separate the national-liberation movement in the developing countries from the Soviet Union and the other socialist countries.[73]

The same commentator saw evidence of collusion in the coincidence of U.S. and PRC policy on the India–Pakistan conflict and intimated the possibility of further USA–PRC intrigues.

Czechoslovak accusations of USA–PRC collusion culminated in analyses of the Shanghai communiqué. Radio Prague editor Josef Hora noted the secrecy of the meetings and implications of the communiqué:

> On more closely studying the communiqué, it might seem that it was Nixon who gave and China who took. However, this would be unrealistic at the very least, because those things which are absent from the communiqué, which have remained only between Chou En-lai, Nixon, and their advisers, will be far more important for Sino–American relations and for the world situation.[74]

Writing in *Rude Pravo*, Zdenek Horeni used the imagery of Canossa[75] to show that the real purpose of Nixon's journey to Peking was to strengthen "the tactical and strategic positions of American imperialism."[76] Nixon, he claimed, wanted to suppress the national liberation movement in Southeast Asia, to acquire a foothold in China so as to counter the increasingly competitive influence of Japan and Western Europe, and to ensure his own reelection. In return, Horeni speculated, Nixon guaranteed U.S. noninterference in China and support for anti-Soviet aims.

Other commentaries, accusing the Chinese of Munich-like appeasement, concluded that the Chinese had rejected socialism:

> Now the PRC is calling the Soviet Union its main enemy. . . . As though only a few kilometers from the Chinese borders American bombs were not falling in Indochinese villages and cities! All these facts tell us that the policy of the Chinese leadership no longer proceeds from solidarity with the policy pursued by the socialist countries, and not even with the policy of the international communist movement.[77]

The reversal of its sympathies in the Sino–Soviet dispute proved the turnabout of Czechoslovak foreign policy. Reluctance to condemn the Chinese and to support the Soviet side in the Ussuri incident in 1969 turned into complete defense of the Soviet and rejection of the Chinese position at the time of the USA–PRC rapprochement in 1972. In sum, Czechoslovakia, returning to Soviet socialist orthodoxy:

- Charged the Chinese with anti-Sovietism, betraying socialism, and collusion with the United States on issues involving Vietnam, India and Pakistan, and the Middle East.
- Condemned the Chinese two-superpower theory and attacked Romania indirectly by linking the Romanian concept of the equality of large and small states to the two-superpower theory.

POLAND VACILLATES

Three major factors influenced Poland's relationship with the USSR and its reaction to the USA–PRC rapprochement. First, the Polish media had consistently taken a moderate position regarding China's foreign policies. At the time of the 1967 Middle East war and the 1968 invasion of Czechoslovakia, the Poles did not repeat the Soviets' criticisms of China, possibly because U.S. and PRC representatives were then meeting unofficially in Poland. And although the Poles blamed the Chinese for the 1969 Ussuri provocation, Polish commentaries continued to characterize China as socialist and never echoed the Soviet reference to China as a military-bureaucratic regime.[78] During July 1971, when the Soviets criticized the PRC's rapprochement with the United States, the Polish press noted favorably the "process of normalization of relations between the government of the PRC and those of the socialist nations."[79] In particular the Poles approved China's friendly relations with Romania and Yugoslavia.

Second, resuming a policy of détente with Western Europe, Poland and West Germany signed a treaty in December 1970 in which the FRG accepted the Oder–Neisse as Poland's frontier but did not, however, recognize the GDR. For Poland, the treaty effectively ended the bogey of German revanche and, in so doing, greatly reduced Polish dependence on the guarantee of Soviet power. Polish acceptance of the treaty, however, strained Polish–East German relations.

Third, Gomulka lost control following riots in late December 1970 protesting sharply increased food and fuel prices.[80] Gierek, who came to power committed to raising the Polish standard of living, turned to the Soviets to assure them of his loyalty and to obtain a long-term loan to enable him to roll back domestic prices.[81]

The Polish press coverage of events connected with the USA–PRC rapprochement in most particulars followed the Soviet interpretation. An article in *Zycie Warszawy* analyzing Nixon's foreign policy address to the U.S. Congress cited his "wholly disappointing" comments on Vietnam, his omission of any reference to Bangladesh, his "irreconcilable position" on the Middle East, and his scanty attention to the issue of a European cooperation and security conference as evidence of U.S. policy failures. The article reiterated the Soviet claim that Nixon, to win votes in the next election, sought to minimize those foreign policy failures by diverting U.S. public attention to the negotiations with China.[82]

Trybuna Ludu's commentator faulted Nixon for stressing the "real and considerable" ideological and political differences between the United States and USSR and at the same time overdramatizing his forthcoming trip to China as "historic," "unprecedented," and ending a 25-year period of "inexorable hostility." He, too, attributed Nixon's excesses to reelection rhetoric. However, where the Soviets had ignored the president's references to Eastern Europe, the *Trybuna Ludu* writer, reflecting the Polish national interest in broadening economic and cultural ties with the United States, added: "The President believes that there are great possibilities for developing U.S. economic, technical, and cultural cooperation with the Eastern European countries."[83]

The Polish media, like the Soviet, Bulgarian, and East German, refrained from linking Bonn with Peking's allegedly anti-Soviet intrigues.

Press coverage of Nixon's trip for the most part adhered to the Soviet line. Fear that the USA–PRC rapprochement would be made at Soviet and North Vietnamese expense emerged as a major theme. The week before Nixon arrived in Peking, *Kultura* accused the United States and China of seeking to undermine the influence and prestige of the USSR and the entire socialist community and implied that the two countries might enter into a "guarantee of limited cooperation in case of a 'threat' to the interests of the two powers on the part of a third power, that is, the Soviet Union."[84]

Grzegorz Jaszunski suggested that the United States and China had come to an agreement on Vietnam.[85] The Polish radio said two weeks later: "The present Chinese leadership is ready to settle Asian problems behind the backs of the nations concerned, while sitting at the table with the American aggressors."[86]

The Polish radio also faulted the Chinese for remaining silent when the United States stepped up the bombing at the time of the trip: "Chinese leaders could have prevented the new escalation of military actions in Vietnam . . . had they but indicated to Nixon that [escalation] would bring about a cancellation of the visit."[87]

However, instead of charging, as the Soviets had, that Chinese silence represented collusion, another commentator posited that: "For the Americans, the Peking attitude toward the Vietnam conflict is a complete mystery."[88]

The Polish press coverage of Nixon's trip diverged from the orthodox in several other minor respects. Before Nixon arrived in Peking, the press apparently continued to regard the Chinese as socialists.[89] Moreover, it did not comment on China's two-superpower theory and espousal of the Romanian theory of the role of small and medium states in determining international policies.[90] Finally, the Polish press did not accuse the Chinese, as *Pravda* did in its analysis of the Shanghai communiqué, of colluding with the United States in a Taiwan-for-Vietnam deal.

Gierek himself, however, dispelled any uncertainties regarding Poland's China policy: On 21 February, Nixon's first day in Peking, the new Polish party leader told a Sejm preelection rally that the Chinese leaders had replaced Marxist–Leninist principles with "Maoist ideology," based on nationalism and great-power chauvinism, with the result that China was turning

> against its natural and reliable allies—the socialist countries. The anti-Soviet, disruptive course of the Chinese leadership is aimed against the interests of the whole socialist community, including the vital interests of Poland.[91]

Gierek, however, held out the hope that the Chinese would "find sufficient strength within themselves to reject the dangerous Maoist course and to restore socialist principles to the policy of their state."[92]

The Polish press followed the Soviet line also on the Shanghai communiqué. *Zycie Warszawy*, for example, analyzed it in terms of what had been omitted—namely, all reference to the USSR, to the establishment of diplomatic relations between the United States and China, and to U.S. aggression in Vietnam. And like the Soviet media, *Zycie Warszawy* found the communiqué suspiciously secretive: "It is very probable that Nixon's talks with Chou En-lai have produced a certain number of agreements and settlements which the two sides have found advisable to keep secret."[93]

Trybuna Ludu charged that anti-Sovietism motivated the USA–PRC talks, that bilateral relations were developing "at the expense of vital interests of other peoples," that the United States continued to bomb Vietnam, Laos, and Cambodia while the talks were being held, and that in opposing "the hegemony of any country or group of countries in the region of Asia and the Pacific, . . . Mao and Chou gave an official permission to the United States to co-decide on the main problems in that region." Finally, the party organ warned: "It is impossible today to act in favour of world peace and at the same time to be against the Soviet Union and the socialist commonwealth. All attempts to create any 'axis' are doomed to failure."[94]

Poland's moderate policy regarding China continued through Nixon's visit. Following Gierek's 21 February speech, in which he accused China of acting against Poland's "vital interests," Polish commentaries toed the Soviet line. Like the Soviets, the Poles never linked China to Europe. Unlike the Soviets, the Poles looked favorably on Nixon's East European policy as enunciated in his foreign policy address to the Congress. A vice foreign minister's acceptance (in October 1971) of the Romanian position on small and medium-sized states seemed to be reconfirmed during this period by the absence of any Polish condemnation of China's two-superpower theory. In sum, the volatility and uncertainty of Polish domestic politics, coupled with the national orientation of the media, may have raised further questions about Poland's reliability in the minds of Soviet leaders.

KADAR WALKS A TIGHTROPE

Hungary's political course remained relatively independent of the USSR's. The Budapest appeal had revitalized Hungary's desire, frustrated by its Warsaw Pact allies in 1967, to expand relations with Western Europe and the FRG. The Hungarians advocated a European security conference, as they had been doing since March 1969. Their natural sympathies for "rightist" revisionism (in part because of its tolerance of a less rigid economic system, such as their New Economic Mechanism), evident toward Czechoslovakia in 1968 and Yugoslavia in 1969, continued. Their apparent insensitivity to the dangers of "leftist" revisionism softened their responses to Nixon's message to the Congress of February 1972 and his subsequent visit to China.

The Hungarian coverage, in contrast to that of the orthodox states, made no reference to the president's unequal treatment of the USSR and China or of his favoring China. Nor did it refer to secrecy or a conspiracy against the USSR. The first report of the speech, on Budapest radio, evenhandedly discussed Nixon's forthcoming trips to both Moscow and Peking, stressing the balance of his approach. The reporter, Tibor Koeves, quoted Nixon as saying:

> The "positive steps toward peace" made a meeting with Soviet leaders at the highest level timely, particularly regarding arms limitations and economic cooperation. That is why, for the first time, an American President will visit Moscow. I am not going to the meeting in May with any naive illusions, but with some reasonable expectations.[95]

Koeves continued:

> Nixon said that within two weeks he would set out on his "peace journey" to Peking. He said that "the agreement on the meeting and the mutual trust required for organizing the first visit of an American head of state to the PRC has been a very important breakthrough."[96]

By ignoring the possibility of collusion between the United States and China, the Hungarians may have been signaling the desire to expand relations with both countries.[97] Where *Pravda* saw a Taiwan-for-Vietnam deal, *Nepszabadsag* quoted Nixon as saying that relations between the PRC and Taiwan would have to be settled by the two parties concerned "by peaceful means . . . but we do not urge either party to follow any particular course."[98]

Hungarian attention to Nixon's discussion of Europe reflected Hungary's interest in its European relations. During the Ussuri crisis in 1969, the Hungarian press had not linked West German and Chinese territorial claims but had focused on the Budapest appeal, noting specific areas for achieving European cooperation. Vajda, in *Nepszabadsag*, noted with apparent concern that Nixon's address to the Congress did "*not* contain a positive reply to the Warsaw Pact socialist countries' appeal concerning European peace and security" (emphasis added).[99] He wondered also whether the apparent U.S. desire to expand trade with East European countries would lead to easing trade restrictions.

Hungary differed also in its coverage of Nixon's trip. While the orthodox Warsaw Pact media published extensive, critical reports of Nixon's activities, Hungarian radio and press coverage remained relatively sparse and low-keyed. The restraint may be explained in part by the Hungarians' desire to avoid articulating the Soviet line during Janos Kadar's visit to Bucharest on 24–26 February 1972[100] to sign a friendship treaty with the Romanians.

Hungarian interests outside the Warsaw Pact appear also to have contributed to the Hungarian reluctance to criticize the United States. Hungary had developed a close relationship with the Italian communist party (CPI), which had actively opposed the invasion of Czechoslovakia and which now supported USA–PRC rapprochement.[101]

The frequent and cordial contacts between the Hungarian and Italian parties had intensified after August 1968. Giancarlo Pajetta, a member of the CPI politburo, visited Hungary on 11 September 1968 to explain the CPI's position to Hungarian party leaders; Hungary, of course, had sided with the Czechoslovaks and had only reluctantly contributed a negligible force to the invasion. Rezso Nyers, Hungarian politburo member and CC secretary, had delivered a friendly speech at the CPI Congress in February 1969. Zoltan Komocsin visited Italy twice that year, meeting with Enrico Berlinguer (deputy secretary-general of the CPI and virtual party leader owing to Longo's poor health) and Pajetta, with whom he had a cordial relationship.

Contacts between the Hungarian and Italian parties continued through 1970 and 1971. In fact, just before the Nixon trip, these contacts again intensified. Komocsin went to Rome on 19–20 November 1971, and Pajetta visited Hungary between 27 December 1971 and 3 January 1972. In Budapest, Pajetta met with Janos Kadar to discuss questions of interest to the two parties, including foreign policy.[102]

The relatively straightforward Hungarian position on Vietnam also diverged from the orthodox. Budapest radio noted that: "In the text of the communiqué, American and Chinese views differ on Indochina and Korea. Only in their evaluation of the relations between India and Pakistan is there agreement."[103]

The press took the same position. Ferenc Varnai, *Napszabadsag* commentator, whose articles generally reflect the party's foreign policy line, wrote: "The joint communiqué mentions Vietnam and both sides reiterate their known positions on it."[104]

The media did not call Taiwan a bargaining chip to be used in exchange for Vietnam, nor did they hint at a Munich-style sellout. In fact, Janos Nemes, writing in the party daily, seemed puzzled by the modification of the U.S. position on Taiwan (the U.S. recognition of only one China): "Still, it is not clear why Nixon has yielded on an issue which is not easily acceptable either in the United States or on Taiwan itself, or even in South Korea and among its own allies and puppets in Southeast Asia generally."[105]

Although the Hungarian press did not accuse the Chinese (as did the more orthodox Warsaw Pact media) of having strayed from the socialist fold, Ferenc Varnai warned that, if the Chinese continued to pursue a policy of anti-Sovietism, they could in the future alienate themselves from the communist movement.[106]

In conclusion, the Hungarian critique of Nixon's address to the Congress did not contain charges of U.S. anti-Sovietism or collusion with the PRC; instead, it emphasized the United States's future role in Europe. Hungary's long-standing relationship with the Italian communist party, whose views on Nixon's China trip conflicted with those of the USSR, may have contributed to Hungary's restraint in criticizing Nixon's visit. The Hungarians did not see evidence of USA–PRC collusion in the Shanghai communiqué, nor did they accuse China of no longer being socialist. By their moderate course, the Hungarians hoped to maintain cordial relations with the United States and with the Romanian and Italian communist parties and to avoid straining relations with the USSR.

ROMANIA APPLAUDS NIXON'S JOURNEY

Romania's coverage of Nixon's foreign policy address and visit to China was even less orthodox than Hungary's. Because Ceausescu had helped Nixon establish contact with the Chinese, it was to be expected that the Romanians would approve the visit and the events surrounding it. Their reactions indicated the extent of USA–Romanian cooperation.

The Romanian interpretation of Nixon's address to Congress differed fundamentally from that of the USSR, Bulgaria, Poland, East Germany, and Czechoslovakia. Where the more orthodox pact members saw an imbalance in Nixon's treatment of the USSR and China, indicating the potential dangers of USA–PRC collusion based on a common policy of anti-Sovietism, the Romanians saw only statesmanlike motives:

> Nixon mentioned that "some have suggested that the United States could use the opening toward Peking to exploit Sino–Soviet tension. I have explained to all sides," he said, "that we will not try to proceed in this manner, because this would be damaging and dangerous. We will try to have better relations with both countries."[107]

Where the more orthodox Warsaw Pact press criticized Nixon's unyielding stand regarding Middle East issues, the Romanian press sought to justify U.S. military aid to Israel:[108]

Speaking of the situation in the Middle East, the President pointed out that the Security Council resolution of November 1967 remains the accepted framework for the solution of the conflict. He tried to justify the decision of the United States to intensify the granting of American arms to Israel, although he stressed that the choice of political solutions instead of the military ones must be stimulated.[109]

The Romanian press highlighted the apparent U.S. policy shift toward improved relations with Eastern Europe. Like the Poles, Hungarians, and Yugoslavs, the Romanians wanted to increase trade with the United States:[110]

Concerning relations with the countries of East Europe, the President pointed out the existence of certain broad possibilities for economic, technical and cultural cooperation on the basis of reciprocity. "I was the first American President who had ever visited Romania and Yugoslavia," Richard Nixon said. "We have with these countries ties based on mutual respect, independence, equality and sovereignty. We share the conviction that this must stand at the basis of relations among nations, regardless of differences or similarities in social, economic and political systems."[111]

Following their initial favorable reaction to the announcement of Nixon's China visit, the Romanians abstained from further comments until 21 February, after which they reported and commented extensively.[112] Ignoring completely the Soviet critical themes—the dangers of USA–PRC collusion, anti-Sovietism, the degeneration of the Maoist regime, the Chinese repression of minorities and intellectuals, the Chinese betrayal of socialism and national liberation movements, the classlessness of the two-superpower theory, and the U.S. escalation of the bombing of Vietnam—the Romanians declared that "the first contacts are proof of a realistic stand."[113]

V. Iliescu, *Scinteia*'s political commentator, described Nixon's negotiating style as appropriate to the goals of his discussions with both the Chinese and Soviets:

In our days the method of negotiations and direct contacts is most pregnantly asserting itself as a rational way of tackling the outstanding issues, of promoting détente in inter-state relations, irrespective of their social system. In this framework President Nixon's visit to the People's Republic of China, as well as the visit he is to undertake in the Soviet Union in May, are fresh proof of the universal validity of this method.[114]

Unlike Zhukov in *Pravda*,[115] Iliescu did not accuse the United States of following a "position of strength" policy and saw the PRC as playing a positive international role.

The Romanian media covered the Shanghai communiqué straightforwardly and factually. On 27 February, Radio Bucharest broadcast excerpts, including all the essential points,[116] and *Scinteia* published a summary, including extensive excerpts, on 28 February.[117] On 1 March, Iliescu, in an article prominently displayed on the front page of *Scinteia*, described the USA–PRC talks as "one of the historical events of international life. . . . [It] can be assessed as a positive act, as a demonstration of a realistic spirit . . . [which] will positively influence international life, the process of détente."[118]

Iliescu praised the Chinese for supporting national liberation movements and, in direct opposition to the Soviet line, argued that the PRC remained "firm" in its commitment to Vietnam:

> The People's Republic of China expressed most resolutely its firm support for the peoples of Vietnam, Laos and Cambodia in their efforts to attain their national objectives. . . . It also firmly supports the eight-point program for Korea's peaceful unification.[119]

Where the Soviets had seen a Taiwan-for-Vietnam deal, Iliescu rationalized that the United States had taken a positive step in recognizing that there is but one China:

> The whole of mankind knows that Taiwan is an ancient province and an integral part of China, that the Government of the People's Republic of China is the sole legal government of China, Taiwan's liberation being an internal question of the country. Any formula that disregards this reality is inevitably doomed to failure. Of course, one cannot say that a full recognition of this reality by the American side has been reached, a positive element is, however, the fact that the USA recognizes—as asserted by it in the communiqué—that there is but one China and that Taiwan is part of China.[120]

Significantly, the Romanian press also highlighted another aspect of the Shanghai communiqué: the PRC's continuing commitment to the principles enunciated in the June 1971 Sino–Romanian communiqué. According to the Chinese part of the Shanghai communiqué: "All nations, large or small, must be equal; large nations must not tyrannize small ones, and powerful nations must not tyrannize weak ones."[121] And, "all nations . . . have . . . the obligation to refrain from any act encroaching upon the corresponding right of other states . . . and to take an active part in the discussion and solution of international problems."[122]

Iliescu summed up the Romanian position on China as follows:

> In Romania, the positive results of the Sino–American talks are hailed with justified satisfaction. The Romanian people welcomes the firm, consistent position of the People's Republic of China in support of the aspirations for liberty and progress of the nations, in the assertion of the basic principles of international relations, in solving the international issues in conformity with the general interests of the peoples of the cause of détente and peace.[123]

Thus, the Romanian interpretation of Nixon's address differed fundamentally from that of the USSR and its orthodox allies. The Romanians did not consider Nixon's policy toward China to be imbalanced or rooted in anti-Sovietism. They did not criticize Nixon's Mideast policy. Ignoring the Soviet charge of "imperialist bridge-building to undermine the unity of the socialist countries,"[124] the Romanians welcomed the United States' changing relationship with Eastern Europe. Regarding Nixon's China trip and the Shanghai communiqué, the Romanians perceived neither collusion nor secrecy. They did not accuse China of betraying Vietnam or socialism. On the contrary, Romanian treatment of USA–PRC negotiations emphasized the benefit to be gained from personal contacts among world leaders. Romania had, after all, assisted Nixon in his efforts to go to Peking.

BELGRADE–BUCHAREST CONSENSUS

The Yugoslavs' response to the USA–PRC rapprochement of February 1972 remained consistent with both the Romanian reaction and their own and Romania's positions in the March 1969 Ussuri crisis. In 1969, however, Romania had been caught between its need to maintain good relations with the USSR and its national aspiration for better relations with China; Yugoslavia had poor relations with both.

Yugoslavia's relations with the USSR and China began to improve after the Ussuri incident. Although Yugoslavia had avoided the June 1969 conference of communist and workers' parties in Moscow, it sent a delegation to the Twenty-fourth CPSU Congress in March 1971. Trade with both the USSR and PRC rose slightly.[125]

The Yugoslavs initially saw the U.S. president's February 1972 message to Congress not as a continuation of the U.S. "position of strength" policy, but as a "new philosophical approach to the world."[126]

> The president noted that the postwar bipolar division of the world into exclusive blocs has vanished and a multipolar world entity of nations and states with strong tendencies towards independence has appeared; that foes are not given for all time but are also convertible and that, owing to this, foreign policy should display more restraint, more preparedness to solve contradictory national interests by negotiation and not by confrontation.[127]

Like the Hungarians and Romanians, the Yugoslavs inferred no anti-Soviet imbalance in Nixon's policies toward the two communist superpowers. Milika Sundic argued that:

> Nixon's report pays main attention to the relations with China and the Soviet Union. We think that he dealt with both countries in a way which can satisfy

them in spite of the reproaches at the expense of the Soviet Union, which Moscow will not like.[128]

The Yugoslavs, again like the Hungarians and Romanians, approved of Nixon's policy toward Eastern Europe in general. They were particularly pleased by his endorsement of Yugoslav nonalignment:

> For us it is also no less important that the head of the White House speaks about Yugoslavia as a non-aligned country, *in which we see a U.S. interest that we remain as such* and that it is possible to reckon with such a Yugoslavia today and in the future [emphasis added].[129]

The Yugoslav media, in contrast to the Romanian, noted the escalation of the U.S. bombing of Vietnam but did not interpret it, as did the Soviet media, as evidence of Sino–American collusion. On the contrary, Sundic feared that it might affect the talks negatively:

> The latest American actions in Southeast Asia are not at all a good omen for the talks with the Chinese leaders. It can even be said that they are offensive to them and provocative and can have negative consequences for the relations between China and the Southeast Asian countries, especially Vietnam.[130]

Indeed, several days later, Sundic said: "On the day before Nixon's arrival in Peking, *China condemned U.S. foreign policy and particularly U.S. aggression in Southeast Asia in very severe terms*" (emphasis added).[131] The implication here is that Sundic, unlike the Soviets and their orthodox partners, did *not* question China's commitment to Vietnam, its revolutionary zeal, or its devotion to socialism.

The Yugoslavs, like the Romanians, saw no evidence of anti-Soviet collusion between the United States and China; they were neither as optimistic about the outcome of the trip as the Romanians[132] were nor as pessimistic as the Soviets were. *Borba*, attributing Nixon's diplomatic overtures to China to the U.S. realization "that it is no longer able to 'contain' China directly along its land borders,"[133] welcomed the U.S. willingness to negotiate.

The Soviet charge that the Shanghai communiqué concealed an anti-Soviet course and a Taiwan-for-Vietnam deal[134] failed to convince the Yugoslavs, who read no hidden meanings into the communiqué. In fact, there was surprise at the communiqué's openness. Sundic commented: "We are surprised by the content of the Sino–American communiqué because *more is said in it than could have been expected*" (emphasis added).[135] He admitted, however, that "it must be noted that such documents do not provide a true picture of all matters discussed."[136]

The Soviets blamed the Chinese for compromising their socialist principles in allowing a Taiwan-for-Vietnam deal. In contrast, the Yugoslavs, like the Romanians, argued that the United States, rather than the PRC, had made most of the concessions. Sundic noted that Nixon had made the major concession in Peking when he "admitted that Taiwan represented a part of China's indivisible territory."[137] Then Sundic refuted the Soviet charge that the Chinese had conceded Vietnam as follows:

> The communiqué also notes, probably on China's insistence, on what matters accord was not reached. This is the problem of Southeast Asia. True, China stated earlier that it did not wish to negotiate on behalf of people of Indochina, and it has now reiterated that it will unreservedly support their struggle until complete victory has been achieved. Thus Peking has insured itself against possible speculation in various quarters, speculation which the opponents of the American–Chinese dialog have not hesitated to engage in.[138]

Other commentators reiterated the view that if concessions were to be made, the United States, not China, would make them.[139]

Yugoslavia's independent interpretation of the events of February 1972 remained consistent with its and Romania's nonalignment policy. The media praised Nixon's address to the Congress for reflecting the changed world order and highlighted particularly his comments on U.S. relations with Yugoslavia (and Romania) as a model for relations between states of different social systems. The Yugoslavs viewed the visit to China with optimism,[140] seeing in it concessions on the part of the United States, not China. Nixon's willingness to negotiate with the Chinese, according to the Yugoslav media, reflected not anti-Sovietism, but U.S. recognition of the PRC's superpower status, not collusion on a Taiwan-for-Vietnam deal, but U.S. willingness to concede Taiwan's links to the mainland.

ALBANIA'S ISOLATION

China's negotiations with the imperialist United States embarrassed the Albanians, who had heretofore supported Chinese positions, and set Albania on a course of increasing isolation. The Albanian coverage of Nixon's address to the Congress and trip to China indicated distrust of both the United States and the USSR, which were said to be planning to share world power. But it did not comment on China.

The Albanians adopted the Soviet line that Nixon's address reiterated the U.S. "position of strength" policy:

> The U.S. President formulated the continuation of the existing policy on the position of strength. . . . Nixon has openly proclaimed his administration's future intention to increase and strengthen the military potential of the aggressive NATO.[141]

And like the Soviets, they interpreted Nixon's address as an election campaign ploy to divert attention from U.S. economic problems and foreign policy failures.[142]

However, whereas the Soviets and their orthodox allies charged USA–PRC collusion against the USSR, the Albanians claimed USA–USSR collusion against the true Marxist–Leninist revolutionaries. The Albanians charged that Nixon's call for increased U.S. military strength and his projected talks with the Soviets were intended to ensure USA–USSR domination of the world power balance.[143]

But neither did the Albanians support the Chinese. Apparently nonplussed by the U.S. overtures to China, the Albanian media commented neither on what Nixon said about China in his address to the Congress nor on the results of his visit to China. Only the facts of the trip were reported, belatedly.[144]

The Albanians had indirectly indicated their disapproval of USA–PRC relations soon after the visit was announced; they did so by criticizing Santiago Carrillo, the Spanish communist party chief.

Carrillo represented an anti-Soviet bloc (consisting of the Italian, Spanish, Yugoslav, and Romanian parties) that emphasized independence of Moscow, spoke out against normalization in Czechoslovakia, and remained neutral in the Sino–Soviet Ussuri conflict. During a September 1971 visit to Romania, Carrillo had indicated his approval of Ceausescu's trip to Peking and his concept of, in Carrillo's words, "unity which recognizes the right of each party to determine its line independently, without outside interference."[145] This concept was, of course, shared by the Romanians and Chinese.

Yet despite Carrillo's pro-Chinese, anti-Soviet credentials, the Albanians considered him a revisionist. In November 1971, after Nixon had announced his intention to go to China, and at the same time that Carrillo was visiting Peking, the Albanian sixth party congress hosted a secessionist Spanish Marxist–Leninist party, which attacked the Chinese policy of the "renegade" Carrillo.[146]

On 13 February, *Zeri i Popullit* sharply attacked the Italian party's ideological line, but obviously the criticism was again aimed at the Chinese:

Albanian communists will not be taken in by the fallacious anti-social imperialism of the Togliattists[147] and their friends, just as they will not be taken in by the demagogic anti-imperialism of other revisionists.

The AWP [Albanian Workers' Party] has rigorously adhered to the Marxist–Leninist principle that has stood the test of time and according to which one cannot have contacts and discussions with some revisionists just because differences and contradictions exist between them and other revisionists. *Just as one cannot side with one imperialist to oppose another, one cannot side with some revisionists in order to oppose others* [emphasis added].[148]

On succeeding days, the press continued to indicate the Albanian concern over China's opening to the United States, but without ever explicitly criticizing the Chinese. The party organ condemned the United States (and the USSR) after Nixon had left China:

> People are now accustomed to see Nixon swinging the olive branch, prattling about peace and the security of the peoples and at the same time sabrerattling. Precisely for this reason the peoples do not allow themselves to be deceived, but they bear in mind the indisputable truth that U.S. imperialism, jointly with the Soviet revisionist one, represents the most savage, the most perfidious and consistent enemy of socialism, of their freedom and independence and constitutes the main danger for the encroachment of world peace.[149]

Perhaps attempting to convince the Chinese of their political error in negotiating with the United States, the article frequently reiterated the idea that U.S. imperialism is the greatest enemy of true socialism.

The events of February 1972 put great strain on Albanian–PRC relations. Long estranged from the USSR and its orthodox allies, Albania now isolated itself from the European anti-Soviet bloc (the Italian, Spanish, Yugoslav, and Romanian communist parties), from its Balkan neighbor, Yugoslavia, and most unexpectedly, from its patron, China.

SUMMARY

The foregoing analysis of the Warsaw Pact states' reaction to the USA–PRC rapprochement and Nixon's visit to China in February 1972 suggests that, although the USSR had consolidated its hold over Czechoslovakia and solved its East German problem, dissension in Eastern Europe continued.

The analysis indicates, coincidentally, that relations between Eastern and Western Europe had improved significantly since the March 1969 conflict with China over the Ussuri incident. In 1969, the Soviets and their orthodox allies had linked Chinese and West German territorial aggression, and the Bulgarians and East Germans had raised the specter of Nazism by referring to a Bonn–Peking axis. In contrast, even those who in 1972 accused the United States and China of collusion and secret deals avoided implicating West Germany (or the other Western European "imperialist" states and NATO) in those anti-Soviet plots. This moderation undoubtedly stemmed from (1) the Budapest appeal for a European security conference and the subsequent Soviet and Polish treaties with West Germany in 1970 and (2) the party leadership changes in Czechoslovakia (1969), Poland (1970), and East Germany (1971).

The analysis of the 1972 events reveals that, as in the past, Bulgaria and East Germany did not waver in their support of the USSR. The tension that had developed between the GDR and USSR over the rapprochement with the FRG apparently had been resolved with Walter Ulbricht's removal in May 1971.

Czechoslovakia turned about and supported the Soviets. In 1969, Czechoslovakia initially had taken no position on the Ussuri conflict, refused to address the issue of whether or not China was a socialist state, and remained neutral on the meaning of the Chinese ninth party congress. After Husak's succession to party leadership in April 1969, the country had made great strides toward "normalization." By February 1972, in linking China with imperialism and arguing that it was no longer socialist, the Czechoslovaks were writing the Chinese out of the communist movement. It is likely that Soviet leaders now perceived Czechoslovakia to be quite reliable. Bulgaria, the GDR, and Czechoslovakia were the Soviet successes.

Polish unpredictability continued. Domestically inspired initiatives toward the FRG culminated in a treaty in December 1970. Also in December, spontaneous popular riots led to the ouster of party leader Gomulka. His successor, Gierek, needing Soviet economic assistance, was anxious to prove his loyalty to Soviet leaders. Although the Polish media in most particulars followed the Soviet line on the USA–PRC rapprochement, they continued to exhibit a distinct national orientation during 1972. This independence was apparent in Polish support of Nixon's offer to increase economic and cultural links with Eastern Europe and in the continued Polish softness on the China issue. Even after Gierek accused the Chinese of replacing Marxist–Leninist principles with Maoist ideology, the Polish media continued to ignore the "classlessness" of China's two-superpower theory, a position consistent with, and apparently influenced by, Poland's sympathy for Romania's small and medium-sized states thesis. From the Soviet perspective, the volatility and uncertainty of Polish domestic politics, coupled with the apparent national orientation of its media, likely raised further questions about Poland's political reliability.

Hungary also continued to concern the Soviets, although it showed consistency where Poland exhibited volatility. In 1969, the Hungarians had diverged from the Soviet line in not coupling the FRG with the Chinese provocation, in stresssing European cooperation at the March 1969 Budapest PCC session, and in qualifying its criticism of the Ninth Chinese CP Congress. The relatively soft position carried over to the 1972 USA–PRC détente: The Hungarians did not interpret Nixon's foreign policy report as being anti-Soviet, and they tempered their criticism of China. They interpreted the Shanghai communiqué as indicating that the PRC remained principled and socialist. Their positive evaluation of Nixon's offer to expand contacts with Eastern Europe, as well as their open and cordial relations with both the Romanian and Italian Communist parties, indicated an independence that distinguished Hungary from the more orthodox Warsaw Pact members.

Romania's response during February 1972 remained consistent with its foreign policy principles formulated since April 1964 and tested in subsequent crises. The principle involving the responsibility of small and medium-sized states to help resolve international conflicts was tested in 1967; that of noninterference in the affairs of other socialist states, in 1968; and that of maintaining friendship with the armies of the Warsaw Pact and with all socialist states, in 1969. Consistent with these principles—but in direct opposition to Soviet policy—Ceausescu helped bring the United States and China together.

In fact, the Romanians opposed the Soviet line on nearly every issue involved. Where the Soviets saw in Nixon's address to the Congress a continuation of the U.S. position of strength policy, an imbalance in his treatment of the USSR and China, and the desire to undermine communist unity by expanding trade with Eastern Europe, the Romanians saw a U.S. policy based on negotiations rather than confrontations, a balance in Nixon's treatment of the two communist superpowers, and the call for increased trade with Eastern Europe as a manifestation of détente. Where the Soviets saw in the Shanghai communiqué collusion and secrecy cloaking parallel USA–PRC interests in a Munich-like Vietnam-for-Taiwan deal, as well as China's betrayal of socialism, the Romanians saw no secrecy, no collusion, no deals, and no Chinese betrayal of socialism. Moreover, the Romanians considered the United States to have taken a positive step to further the cause of détente and peace.

From the Soviet perspective, although the 1970s had brought détente in Europe and some successes in relations with their Warsaw Pact allies (notably the normalization of Czechoslovakia and the elimination of tension with the GDR), socialist disunity continued. First, the Soviet eastern frontier, which had been a military concern since before 1969, was now further threatened by the possibility of USA–PRC cooperation. Second, the Warsaw Pact's Southern Tier continued to erode. Romania and Yugoslavia had moved closer together, and their similar political and economic policies toward Western Europe, the United States, the Italian and Spanish communist parties, and the PRC had begun to influence Hungary and, to a limited degree, Poland. These Soviet concerns became apparent immediately preceding and during the next crisis, the October 1973 Middle East war.

NOTES

1. At the time of the March 1969 Ussuri incident, only 14–16 Soviet divisions manned the long frontier east of Lake Baykal. Within three years, the Soviets had increased this force to 45 divisions of improved quality. See International Institute for Strategic Studies, *The Military Balance, 1969–1970; 1970–1971; 1971–1972; 1972–1973* (London: International Institute for Strategic Studies, 1969; 1970; 1971; 1972), pp. 6; 6; 7; 7.

The appointment of General Tolubko, first deputy commander of the Strategic Rocket Forces, as commander of the Far East Military District (August 1969–May 1972) indicated that the Soviets considered ICBMs to be a relevant factor in a Sino–Soviet war. See Kenneth G. Lieberthal,

Sino–Soviet Conflict in the 1970s: Its Evolution and Implications for the Strategic Triangle, The Rand Corporation, R-2342-NA (July 1978), pp. 22–24.

2. In August 1969, a Soviet embassy official in Washington asked a middle-level State Department specialist in Soviet affairs, out of the blue, what the U.S. reaction would be to a Soviet attack on Chinese nuclear facilities. Henry Kissinger, *White House Years* (Boston: Little, Brown, 1979), p. 183. During the Vienna SALT in 1970, the Soviets approached the United States on the possibility of establishing an alliance against other nuclear power (read PRC) planning a "provocative" action or attack. John Newhouse, *Cold Dawn: The Story of SALT* (New York: Holt, Rinehart and Winston, 1973), pp. 188–89.

3. *Der Spiegel*, March 6, 1972, pp. 100, 102, in JPRS, 55,539 (March 24, 1972), p. 18.

4. *International Defense Review*, No. 2 (1975): 106–8.

5. Ion Ionita, *Krasnaya Zvezda*, January 15, 1970, p. 3, in JPRS, 49,848 (February 16, 1970), p. 40.

6. Richard Nixon, *RN: The Memoirs of Richard Nixon* (New York: Grosset & Dunlap, 1978), pp. 281–82.

7. The one hundred thirty-fourth session had occurred in January 1968; the one hundred thirty-fifth, which was scheduled for February 1969, was called off by the Chinese at the last minute. Hoover Institution Press, *Yearbook on International Communist Affairs, 1970* (Stanford: Hoover Institution Press, 1971), pp. 562–63.

8. The visit to Romania provided an opportunity for Nixon to request Romania's intercession with Hanoi on behalf of the United States; it also provided a cover for Henry Kissinger's secret meeting in Paris with Xuan Thuy, the North Vietnamese representative. Nixon, *RN*, pp. 393–96.

9. Nixon, *RN*, p. 545.

10. "Speech of Comrade K. F. Katushev, Head of the CPSU Delegation to the Tenth Congress of the Romanian CP," *Pravda*, August 8, 1969, p. 4.

11. *Yearbook on International Communist Affairs*, p. 563.

12. Nixon noted only that "during 1969, the Chinese ignored the few low-level signals of interest we sent them." Nixon, *RN*, p. 545.

13. Ibid., p. 546. Kissinger said, however, that "Contrary to our expectations, the Romanian channel turned out to be one-way. We had thought that the Chinese might prefer to deal with us through Communist intermediaries. In fact, they proved too wary for that, perhaps fearful of Soviet penetration of even a country as fiercely independent as Romania." Kissinger, *White House Years*, p. 181. On 25 October, Nixon also established the "Yahya [Pakistan] channel."

14. Nixon, *RN*, p. 547.

15. Joint communiqué, *Lupta de Clasa*, No. 7 (July 1971): 43–51, in JPRS, 53,970 (September 2, 1971), p. 42.

16. For example, A. Nadezhdin, "The Metamorphoses of Peking Diplomacy," *New Times* (Moscow), No. 22 (May 28, 1971).

17. Vladimir Polyanskiy commentary (in Romanian), June 6, 1971, in FBIS, DR, SU (June 10, 1971), pp. D6–7.

18. *Der Spiegel*, March 6, 1972, p. 19. As in previous instances of tension between Romania and the USSR, similar tensions developed between Yugoslavia and Bulgaria.

19. Militiade Filipescu, *Informatia Bucurestiului*, June 29, 1971, p. 4, in JPRS, 55,804 (August 12, 1971), p. 55.

20. Rudolf Woller, *Warsaw Pact Reserve Systems: A White Paper* (Munich: Bernard & Graefe Verlag, 1978), p. 113.

21. Romanian Situation Report/28, RFE (July 26, 1971), pp. 14–15.

22. Although Nixon had met with Ceausescu in 1967, 1969, and 1970, he had yet to meet officially with Brezhnev.

23. Romulus Caplescu and Ion Fintinaru, "The Prospect of Normalizing Relations Between the USA and PRC," *Scinteia*, July 21, 1971, in FBIS, DR, EE (July 21, 1971), p. H4.

24. The first similarity between Romanian and Chinese policy in Asia became apparent in May 1970 when Norodom Sihanouk formed a Cambodian government in exile in Peking. On 6 May, the PRC, Romania, and Yugoslavia recognized the new government; the USSR and the other pact countries continued to recognize Lon Nol.

The second similarity involved the India–Pakistan crisis of November–December 1971, just before Nixon's visit to China. The USSR and other pact members supported India in the United Nations (India and the USSR had signed a 20-year military agreement on 9 August, 1971); the PRC, Romania, and United States supported Pakistan.

25. Romanian Situation Report/14, *RFE* (April 20, 1972), p. 15. Ceausescu did, however, attend these meetings in 1972 and 1973. For Ceausescu's six speeches of 14 August 1971, see Nicolae Ceausescu, *Romania on the Way of Building Up the Multilaterally Developed Socialist Society*, 6 (Bucharest: Meridiane Publishing House, 1972), pp. 271–302.

26. The address summarized *U.S. Foreign Policy for the 1970's: The Emerging Structure of Peace*, Report to the Congress by Richard Nixon, February 9, 1972.

27. Yuriy Zhukov, "In Defiance of Reality," *Pravda*, February 17, 1972, in *FBIS, DR, SU* (February 23, 1972), p. A2.

28. The USSR regarded the uprising in Bangladesh as a national liberation struggle that the Chinese had betrayed by supporting Pakistan.

29. V. Petrusenko, "A Prisoner of the Past," *Izvestiya*, February 18, 1972, in *FBIS, DR, SU* (February 24, 1972), p. A3.

30. Ibid., p. A4.

31. On 12 February, Moscow Domestic Service reported that the United States was not only stepping up the bombing strikes against Vietnam but was also reinforcing its air force throughout Indochina. *FBIS, DR, SU* (February 14, 1972), pp. AA2–3.

32. Viktor Lyubovtsev commentary, Moscow Domestic Service, February 14, 1972, in *FBIS, DR, SU* (February 15, 1972), p. AA1.

33. Moscow Domestic Service, February 17, 1972, in *FBIS, DR, SU* (February 17, 1972), p. AA1.

34. A. Iskenderov, "The Unity of National and Social Tasks," *Pravda*, February 10, 1972, in *FBIS, DR, SU* (February 15, 1972), p. A12.

35. A. Slavin, *Pravda*, February 11, 1972, in *FBIS, DR, SU* (February 16, 1972), pp. D5–6; A. Rashin, *Sovetskaya Rossiya*, February 20, 1972, in *FBIS, DR, SU* (February 24, 1972), pp. D7–10.

36. From 17 February, when he left the United States to 28 February, when he left China.

37. Moscow Domestic Service, February 23, 1972, in *FBIS, DR, SU* (February 24, 1972), p. AA2.

38. A. Repin and B. Stolpovskiy, "International Review," *Trud*, February 29, 1972, in *FBIS, DR, SU* (March 3, 1972), p. AA1.

39. Ibid., p. AA2.

40. S. Kondrashov, "After the Visit to Peking," *Izvestiya*, March 4, 1972, in *FBIS, DR, SU* (March 6, 1972), p. AA3.

41. Ibid.

42. G. Ratiani, "Old and New in World Politics," *Pravda*, March 5, 1972, in *FBIS, DR, SU* (March 6, 1972), pp. AA6 and AA7.

43. February 10, 1972, in *FBIS, DR, EE* (February 11, 1972), p. C2.

44. G. Todorchev, *Trud*, February 10, 1972, in *FBIS, DR, EE* (February 11, 1972), p. C3.

45. Dimitur Mitev, "Blinded by Anti-Sovietism," *Zemedelsko Zname*, February 9, 1972, in *FBIS, DR, EE* (February 11, 1972), p. C4.

46. Ibid.

47. Rosev Konstantinov, "The Role of Peking's Leaders," *Otechestven Front*, February 11, 1972, in *FBIS, DR, EE* (February 15, 1972), p. C5.

48. Ivan Peev, "From the Ping-Pong Table to the Negotiating Table," *Narodna Armiya*, February 15, 1972, in *FBIS, DR, EE* (February 18, 1972), p. C2.

49. Colonel Ivan Vandev, "A Dangerous Collusion," *Narodna Armiya*, March 3, 1972, in *FBIS, DR, EE* (March 7, 1972), p. C2.

50. Ibid., p. C3.

51. Mikhail Ninkov, "The Parallel Communiqué," *Otechestven Front*, February 29, 1972, in *FBIS, DR, EE* (March 2, 1972), pp. C2–3.

52. Todor Zhivkov, *Problems of Peace and Socialism*, March 1, 1972, in *FBIS, DR, EE* (March 2, 1972), p. C1.

53. Ulbricht's fear of the FRG and distrust of Romania had coincided with Soviet interests in the Middle East in 1967 and in Czechoslovakia in 1968. But Ulbricht could not accept the Soviet policy of rapprochement with the FRG initiated in March 1969 at the Warsaw Pact PCC meeting in Budapest.

54. Myron Rush, *How Communist States Change Their Leaders* (Ithaca, N.Y.: Cornell University Press, 1974), pp. 190–219.

55. *Neues Deutschland*, February 10, 1972, in *FBIS, DR, EE* (February 14, 1972), p. E1.

56. Karl Thomas, "Nixon in Peking," *Horizont*, No. 7 (February 1972): 19, in *FBIS, DR, EE* (February 28, 1972), p. E1.

57. Ibid. The theme of Chinese anti-Sovietism received wide coverage in East Germany during February.

58. Edward Reiche, *Horizont*, No. 8 (February 1972): 19, in *JPRS*, 55,488 (March 20, 1972), p. 3.

59. Genia Nobel article, *Einheit* (February 1972): 198–210, in *JPRS*: 55,749 (April 18, 1972), p. 32.

60. Ibid., p. 30.

61. Max Kahane, "Conspiracy in Peking," *Horizont*, No. 10 (March 1972): 5, in *FBIS, DR, EE* (March 6, 1972), p. E1.

62. Klaus Wilczynski, "Nixon's China Trip," *Berliner Zeitung*, March 2, 1972, in *FBIS, DR, EE* (March 6, 1972), p. E3.

63. Ibid.

64. Kahane, "Conspiracy in Peking." Genia Nobel called Maoism "one of the most dangerous enemies in the history of the communist and the entire anti-imperialist movement," *Einheit*, 33.

65. CTK International Service in English, 1500 GMT, May 25, 1971, in *FBIS, DR, EE* (May 25, 1971), p. D16.

66. Ibid.

67. See: Prague Domestic Service, 0830 GMT, February 10, 1972, in *FBIS, DR, EE* (February 10, 1972), p. D1.

68. Stanislav Robert, "Discrepancies in the New U.S. Concepts," *Rude Pravo*, February 7, 1972, in *FBIS, DR, EE* (February 9, 1972), p. D1.

69. Zdenek Horeni, "One Reader's Error," *Rude Pravo*, February 12, 1972, in Czechoslovak Situation Report/8, *RFE* (March 2, 1972), p. 3.

70. Zdenek Horeni, "What They Are Taking into Account," *Rude Pravo*, February 17, 1972, in *FBIS, DR, EE* (February 22, 1972), p. D6.

71. Ibid.

72. J. Hoda, "Nixon to Peking," *Lidova Demokracie*, February 18, 1972, in *FBIS, DR, EE* (February 22, 1972), p. D1.

73. Julius P. Lorincz, *Pravda* (Bratislava), February 21, 1972, in *FBIS, DR, EE* (February 25, 1972), pp. D2–3.

74. Josef Hora, Prague Domestic Service, 1730 GMT, February 22, 1972, in *FBIS, DR, EE* (February 28, 1972), p. D5.

75. To end a dispute with Pope Gregory VII, the Holy Roman Emperor Henry IV went to Canossa to do penance in 1077. Horeni commented that Henry knew very well what he was doing and that the dispute was resolved in Henry's favor.

76. Zdenek Horeni, "Behind the Words," *Rude Pravo*, February 28, 1972, in *FBIS, DR, EE* (March 2, 1972), p. D2.

77. Michael Havran, *Smena*, February 29, 1972, in *FBIS, DR, EE* (March 6, 1972), pp. D4–5.

78. The Poles also appeared to evidence a tolerance for Romania's policies, including its doctrine on the role of small and medium-sized states, and for Hungary's economic experiment.

79. Andrej Janicki, "China and the World," *Tygodnik Demokratyczny*, July 11, 1971, pp. 1, 4, 5, in *JPRS*: 53,891 (August 24, 1971), pp. 6–7.

80. "Bread-and-freedom" riots in Poznan had returned Gomulka to the leadership of the PUWP in October 1956 (following the Twentieth CPSU "de-Stalinization" Congress). He had previously been ousted in 1948 and imprisoned for refusing to support certain Stalinist policies.

81. A. Ross Johnson, *The Polish Riots and Gomulka's Fall*, The Rand Corporation, P-4615 (April 1971), pp. 13–15.

82. G. J., "Nixon Is Packing His Bags," *Zycie Warszawy*, February 13–14, 1972, in *FBIS, DR, EE* (February 16, 1972), pp. G1–3.

83. M. Berezowski, "Nixon's Address on Foreign Policy," *Trybuna Ludu*, February 10, 1972, in *FBIS, DR, EE* (February 16, 1972), pp. G3–4.

84. Stanislaw Glabinski, "From Peking with Love," *Kultura*, February 16, 1972; and *FBIS, DR, EE* (February 17, 1972), p. G2.

85. Grzegorz Jaszunski, *Zycie Warszawy*, February 4, 1972, in *FBIS, DR, EE* (February 10, 1972), pp. G13–15.

86. Warsaw Domestic Service, February 17, 1972, in *FBIS, DR, EE* (February 18, 1972), p. G2.

87. Ibid.

88. Stanislaw Glabinski article, *Argumenty*, February 20, 1972, pp. 5, 7, in *JPRS*, 55,994 (May 15, 1972), p. 3.

89. Glabinski, for example, wrote that *if* the United States and the PRC reached an agreement on Vietnam, then for China "it would mean drawing away from the basic principles of socialist policy." Ibid.

90. Josef Czyrek, vice-minister of foreign affairs, appeared to endorse the idea (without naming Romania), when he said: "I believe that every community, regardless of size and position, can make positive contributions in many areas of contemporary life." Interview in *Kultura*, October 30, 1971, p. 2, in *JPRS*, 54,338 (October 28, 1971), pp. 67–68.

91. Polish Situation Report/8, *RFE* (February 25, 1972), p. 4.

92. Ibid.

93. *Zycie Warszawy*, February 29, 1972, in *FBIS, DR, EE* (March 1, 1972), p. G1.

94. Daniel Lulinski commentary, *Trybuna Ludu*, March 1, 1972, in *FBIS, DR, EE* (March 2, 1972), p. G1.

95. Tibor Koeves, Budapest MTI Domestic Service, 1920 GMT, February 9, 1972, in *FBIS, DR, EE* (February 10, 1972), p. F1.

96. Ibid.

97. Janos Avar, "Nixon's Foreign Policy Message," *Magyar Nemzet*, February 10, 1972, in *FBIS, DR, EE* (February 14, 1972), p. F6.

98. Peter Vajda, *Nepszabadsag*, February 10, 1972, in *FBIS, DR, EE* (February 14, 1972), p. F5.

99. Ibid.

100. During this period, the Romanians' abundant and analytical coverage of Nixon's activities indicated only approval.

101. After Nixon's China trip was announced, Luigi Longo, CPI secretary-general, declared support for USA–PRC détente (*L'Unita*, July 17, 1971).

102. Hungarian Situation Report/2, *RFE* (January 11, 1972), pp. 11–12.

103. Budapest Domestic Service, 1605 GMT, February 28, 1972, in *FBIS, DR, EE* (February 29, 1972), p. F2.

104. Ferenc Varnai, "Peking—In Nixon's Wake," *Nepszabadsag*, March 5, 1972, in *FBIS, DR, EE* (March 8, 1972), p. F1.

105. Janos Nemes, "After the Peking Visit," *Nepszabadsag*, February 29, 1972, in *FBIS, DR, EE* (March 2, 1972), p. F2.

106. *FBIS, DR, EE* (March 8, 1972), pp. F3–4.

107. *Scinteia*, February 11, 1972, in *FBIS, DR, EE* (February 15, 1972), p. H10.

108. Romania was the only Warsaw Pact state that did not sever diplomatic relations with Israel at the time of the June 1967 war. As will be shown in Chapter 6, the Romanians had been mediating between Israel and the United States on the one hand and the Arab states on the other.

109. *Scinteia*, February 11, 1972, in *FBIS, DR, EE* (February 15, 1972), p. H11.

110. These countries wanted also to increase trade with Western Europe. In fall 1971, Cornel Burtica, Romanian minister of foreign trade, sought customs relief from the European Economic Community (EEC), despite the USSR's refusal to deal with the EEC as a political institution. *Der Spiegel*, March 6, 1972, in *JPRS*, 55,539 (March 24, 1972), p. 18. Yugoslavia, which already enjoyed preferential treatment by the EEC, supported the Romanian bid. *Vjesnik u Srijedu*, March 22, 1972, pp. 21–22, in *JPRS*, 55,733 (April 17, 1972), pp. 52–53.

111. *Scinteia*, February 11, 1972, in *FBIS, DR, EE* (February 15, 1972), p. H11.

112. Romanian Situation Report/9, *RFE* (March 1, 1972), p. 12.

113. V. Iliescu, "A Positive Event of International Life," *Scinteia*, February 23, 1972, in *FBIS, DR, EE* (February 23, 1972), p. H1.

114. Ibid.

115. See note 27.

116. Bucharest Domestic Service; *FBIS, DR, EE* (February 29, 1972), pp. H1–3.

117. Romanian Situation Report/9, *RFE* (March 1, 1972), p. 13

118. "In the Interest of Normal Bilateral Relations and of International Détente," *Scinteia*, March 1, 1972, in *FBIS, DR, EE* (March 2, 1972), p. H2.

119. Ibid., p. H2. Iliescu made no mention of the U.S. escalation of bombing in Vietnam, nor did he point out that the Chinese had failed to support the national liberation movement in Bangladesh.

120. Ibid., p. H3.

121. Dr. Edwin Glasser article, *Lumea*, March 30, 1972, pp. 17–19, in *JPRS*, 55,852 (May 1, 1972), p. 57.

122. Nicolae Ecobescu and Edwin Glasser, *Lupta de Clasa*, March 1972, pp. 51–62, in *JPRS*, 55,958 (May 10, 1972), p. 52.

123. Iliescu, "A Positive Event of International Life," p. H4.

124. See notes 10 and 42.

125. See Jeffrey Simon, *Comparative Communist Foreign Policy, 1965-1976*. The Rand Corporation, P-6067 (August 1977), Table 13 (p. 50) and Table 21 (p. 90).

126. Tanjug, February 9, 1972, in *FBIS, DR, EE* (February 10, 1972), p. I1.

127. Ibid.

128. Milika Sundic, Zagreb Domestic Service, 1400 GMT, February 10, 1972, in *FBIS, DR, EE* (February 11, 1972), p. I19.

129. Ibid.

130. Milika Sundic commentary, Zagreb Domestic Service, 1830 GMT, February 17, 1972, in *FBIS, DR, EE* (February 18, 1972), p. I11.

131. Milika Sundic commentary, Zagreb Domestic Service, 1830 GMT, February 20, 1972, in *FBIS, DR, EE* (February 22, 1972), p. I5.

132. Romanian optimism may have reflected Ceausescu's good offices in bringing the United States and China together.

133. Vlado Teslic, "A New Era?" *Borba*, February 21, 1972, in *FBIS, DR, EE* (February 24, 1972), p. I2.

134. See notes 39 and 42.

135. Milika Sundic commentary, Zagreb Domestic Service, 1830 GMT, February 27, 1972, in *FBIS, DR, EE* (February 28, 1972), p. I3.

136. Ibid.

137. Ibid.

138. Ibid., p. 14.

139. Compare Andro Gabelic, "The Sides of the Triangle and Their Dimensions," *Borba*, February 27, 1972; and Zvinimir Kristl, "The Giant Who Does Not Sit Still," *Vjesnik*, February 26, 1972, both in *FBIS, DR, EE* (March 1, 1972), pp. 13-4.

140. The Yugoslavs, like the Romanians, maintained close ties with the Italian communist party, which took a similar position on Nixon's visit to China.

141. Thimi Collaku commentary, "Nixon's Difficulties," Tirana Domestic Service, February 10, 1972, in *FBIS, DR, EE* (February 11, 1972), p. B3.

142. Cako Dango, *Zeri i Popullit*, February 16, 1972, in *FBIS, DR, EE* (February 16, 1972), p. B2.

143. *Luftetari*, February 20, 1972, in *FBIS, DR, EE* (February 25, 1972), pp. B1-2.

144. Albania: Foreign Relations/1319, *RFE* (March 8, 1972), p. 2.

145. See Santiago Carrillo speech, *Scinteia*, September 4, 1971, pp. 1, 4, in *JPRS*, 54,061 (September 15, 1971), pp. 39-40.

146. Albania: Foreign Affairs/1303, *RFE* (February 28, 1972), p. 2.

147. The Chinese had applied the epithet "social imperialists" to the Soviets (see note 26 in Chapter 3); the Albanians were referring here to the anti-Soviet stand of the Italian communist party, headed by Palmiro Togliatti.

148. *FBIS, DR, EE* (February 14, 1972), p. B7. The Albanians isolated themselves still further by refusing to attend the March 1972 Italian communist party congress, which lionized Carrillo.

149. "U.S. Imperialism, Enemy of Peace and Security of the Peoples," *Zeri i Popullit*, March 7, 1972, in *FBIS, DR, EE* (March 8, 1972), p. B1.

6

The Middle East War, October 1973

PREPARATIONS FOR WAR

The Soviets started to rebuild the Egyptian armed forces immediately following the 1967 Arab defeat and also to provide military aid to Syria.[1] Armed with Soviet weapons, Egyptian President Nasser began a "war of attrition" against Israel. By the end of 1969, however, the Israelis had destroyed most of the Egyptian interceptor air force and SAM-2 antiaircraft defenses. Faced with another defeat, Nasser secretly visited Moscow in January 1970. The resulting Soviet–Egyptian agreement sharply upgraded the quality of Soviet weapons and introduced Soviet combat personnel into a noncommunist country for the first time since World War II.[2]

The massive Soviet military aid prompted Anwar Sadat, who became president after Nasser's death, to label 1971 the "year of decision" and to press the Soviets for even more military aid. The USSR hesitated, however, weighing its commitment to help the Arabs retake Israeli-occupied lands against its "peace program," initiated at the Twenty-fourth CPSU Congress, which became the basis for improving Soviet–American relations. In May 1971, fearing Egyptian–Syrian military unpreparedness and a USA–USSR confrontation, the Soviets advised Syrian communist party leaders against another Middle East war.[3]

Although the continuing Soviet reluctance to deliver offensive weapons irritated Sadat[4] and although the pro-Soviet Egyptian vice-president, Ali Sabry, had attempted a coup against him early in the month, Sadat nevertheless signed a Treaty of Friendship and Cooperation with Podgorny in May 1971. Article 8 of the treaty promised Egypt Soviet military support to "liquidate the consequences of aggression" (that is, to end Israeli occupation of Egyptian territory).[5] Article 7 bound Egypt to consult with the USSR if hostilities threatened. According to Sadat, the plan to attack Israel before the year of decision ended was postponed because of the outbreak of the November 1971 Indo–Pakistani war.[6]

Already dissatisfied with dwindling Soviet aid, Sadat claims to have been "violently shocked" by the May 1972 Soviet–American summit, which, in his words, advocated "military relaxation in the Middle East."[7] Regarding the summit as a superpower attempt to stabilize the status quo,[8] Sadat reacted by expelling all but 100 to 200 Soviet military advisers in July.

Relations began to improve only in October 1972, after which the Soviets became more amenable to Egyptian demands. A joint communiqué following national security adviser Hafez Ismail's visit to Moscow on 7–10 February 1973 proclaimed the Arabs' right to use "any form of struggle in liberating their occupied territories" and reiterated the USSR's intention to strengthen Egypt's "military capabilities."[9] Egyptian Defense Minister General Ahmed Ismail Ali's trip to the USSR on 26 February–2 March, resulted in a dramatic increase in Soviet arms deliveries.[10]

In late April 1973, Sadat and Syrian President Assad agreed on three possible dates for the attack on Israel.[11] The Soviets probably were told these dates when Assad secretly visited Moscow on 2–3 May 1973.[12] Brezhnev began to refer publicly to the Middle East as a "serious hotbed of war."[13] Nixon noted that, during his June 1973 meeting with Brezhnev, the Soviet leader seemed especially concerned with preventing the outbreak of war in the Middle East. According to Nixon, Brezhnev

> kept hammering away at what he described as the need for the two of us to agree, even if only privately, on a set of "principles" to govern a Middle East settlement. . . . Brezhnev was blunt and adamant. He said that without at least an informal agreement on such principles he would be leaving this summit empty-handed. He even hinted that without such an agreement on principles he could not guarantee that war would not resume.[14]

The apparent contradictions in the USSR's foreign policy in mid-1973 reflected its leadership's concerns. On one hand, as champion of the Third World and nonaligned nations, the Soviets supplied the Arabs substantial arms[15] and reaffirmed the Arabs' right to regain lost territory. On the other hand, with an eye to détente and improved relations with the United States, the Soviets voiced hopes for a political solution of the Middle East crisis.

Soviet support for a political solution drew criticism from Arab states skeptical of Soviet intentions. The small mention accorded Middle East problems in the joint statement that followed the Nixon–Brezhnev summit[16] again triggered Arab fears of a Soviet sellout. Sadat dispatched Hafez Ismail to Moscow to assess the Soviet mood. Ismail reported that the Soviets had promised "to provide all forms of aid" and that he and the Soviets had "found complete agreement in our evaluation of the situation in the Middle East and on the step which we may take in the future."[17]

Sadat and Assad, meeting secretly in Alexandria in late August to prepare a war strategy, chose 6 October as the attack date.[18] Arab war plans were morally bolstered by the fourth nonaligned conference held in September 1973 in Algiers. Addressing the conference, Tito obliquely endorsed Arab belligerence:

> The basic prerequisites of a peaceful and just solution remain, of course, a complete withdrawal of Israel from all the occupied territories as well as respect for the legitimate rights of the Arab people of Palestine to a free national life. . . . Yugoslavia has pledged itself in favour of imposing sanctions and taking other effective measures in order to compel Israel to respect these decisions.[19]

Immediately following the Algiers conference, Sadat, Assad, and King Hussein met in Cairo to sign battle plans.[20]

Events preceding the 1973 war indicate that the Soviets were sufficiently forewarned to prepare their Warsaw Pact allies and to seek Yugoslav support.[21] Without advance announcement, Brezhnev visited Bulgaria on 18–21 September 1973, ostensibly to receive the Hero of the Bulgarian People's Republic decoration.[22] The real reason for Brezhnev's visit, however, may have been to promote Warsaw Pact unity. A joint communiqué noted that the Soviet and Bulgarian leaders discussed the nonaligned nations and the Middle East situation.[23] Quite possibly Brezhnev was seeking assurance from Zhivkov that Bulgaria would not, in light of the coming Middle East conflict, alienate Yugoslavia by raising the Macedonian issue.[24] Another reason for the visit may have been to enable Brezhnev to rendezvous with Sadat.[25] Whether or not Sadat was there,[26] he is reported to have informed Brezhnev at this time of the 6 October attack date.[27]

Warsaw Pact unity was also being strengthened during mid-September by Hungarian–Soviet military exercises, code-named Vertes 73, in the Bakony and Vertes Mountains.[28] Several high-ranking Soviet officers[29] observed the exercises, which took place in Veszprem County, over which the Soviets would later fly their Middle East airlift.

Kosygin went to Yugoslavia (24 September–1 October) "to discuss questions of bilateral relations and exchange opinions on current international issues."[30] Assuming that Kosygin was aware of the impending attack on Israel, this statement can be interpreted to mean that he wanted to neutralize the Macedonian issue[31] and to obtain overflight rights for the anticipated Middle East airlift to resupply the Arabs.[32] While in Yugoslavia, Kosygin visited both Skoplje, the Macedonian capital, and the Mostar and Pula airfields, used later by the Soviets for the airlift.[33]

Kosygin's toast at a luncheon following the first morning's talks indicated the Soviet desire for better relations with (and support from) Yugoslavia and implied that Middle East problems had been broached:

The very identity of the socialist setup in both countries creates the conditions that enable the Soviet Union and Yugoslavia to act as *comrades-in-arms* in the struggle for peace and relaxation of international tension. . . . Peace in the world is indivisible and therefore the concern about preserving and consolidating peace is the right and the duty of all countries without any exception whatever. Indeed, *firm peace can be built only through the collective efforts of the countries throughout the world. This thought was clearly expressed at the recent Algiers Conference of Nonaligned Countries* [emphasis added].[34]

Kosygin referred several times to the "*monolithic structure* of the socialist and world's progressive forces" (emphasis added).[35] This relatively new phrase reflected Soviet concern with coordinating a unified response to the coming conflict. At dinner that evening, Yugoslav President Bijedic noted that Israeli aggression and occupation of Arab lands "continues presenting a serious threat to peace not only in the Middle East and the Mediterranean."[36]

Kosygin was apparently extremely pleased with the course of the talks:

The interesting and constructive talks with Comrade Bijedic and other Yugoslav leaders arouse our profound gratification. The friendship between the peoples of the Soviet Union and Yugoslavia is historic in the full meaning of this word.[37]

A joint Yugoslav–Soviet communiqué reaffirmed the Arab right to Israeli-occupied territory:

Liberation of all Arab territories occupied by Israel in 1967 and ensurance of the legitimate rights and interests of all countries and peoples of the area, including the Arab people of Palestine, are the main condition for establishing a stable and fair peace in the Middle East.[38]

The Soviets had assured themselves of strong support in the Balkans.

MAINTAINING A DELICATE BALANCE

Egypt and Syria attacked Israel on 6 October at 2:00 PM. The Soviet radio and press, using only Arab news agency statements[39] to report the outbreak of war, claimed that Israel had attacked Egyptian and Syrian positions.

The official Soviet reaction to the hostilities was restrained: The government did not issue a statement until 7 October, the one-day delay suggesting a desire to gauge the international impact of the Soviet role in the conflict.[40] Although the statement claimed that Israeli aggression and occupation of Arab lands had caused the war, it neither specifically accused Israel of firing the first shot nor accused the United States and its allies of providing support. The Soviets, as they had done since 1967, called for Israel to withdraw completely from Arab territory:

> The responsibility [for war] falls wholly and entirely on Israel and those external reactionary circles which constantly encourage Israel in its aggressive ambitions.
> Condemning the expansionist policy of Israel, the Soviet Union resolutely supports the legitimate demands of the Arab states for relinquishing all Arab territories occupied by Israel in 1967.[41]

On 7 October, *Pravda* also charged Israel with aggression: "Yesterday, after careful preparation of the mobilization of their reserve soldiers, Israeli troops attacked Egypt and Syria. . . . The hawks from Tel Aviv have thus carried out a new act of aggression."[42] On 9 October, *Izvestiya* reiterated the charge that "Israel deliberately was preparing for aggression."[43]

The Soviets took a number of measures to ensure that their Middle East commitments would not endanger relations with the United States. First, they made three early attempts to obtain an Egyptian cease-fire.[44] Second, Brezhnev directed several exchanges with Nixon at avoiding confrontation, and Soviet Ambassador Dobrynin kept in daily contact with Kissinger.[45] Third, although the Soviets charged Israel with aggression, they were at first restrained in their allegations of U.S. involvement, and such allegations were confined to English and Arabic broadcasts aimed at undermining African and Arab support for U.S. policy.[46]

The Soviets' caution was evident also in their resistance to Arab demands for greater Soviet commitment. In response to Algerian President Boumediene's call for support, Brezhnev suggested greater Arab involvement:

> Comrade President, I believe that you agree that the struggle waged at present against the Israeli aggressor for the liberation of Arab territories occupied since 1967 and the safeguarding of the legitimate rights of the people of Palestine affects the vital interests of all Arab countries. In our view, there must be fraternal Arab solidarity today more than ever. *Syria and Egypt must not remain alone in the struggle* against a treacherous enemy [emphasis added].[47]

The USSR further tempered its Arab commitments by recognizing publicly Israel's right to exist. When the ambassadors of Syria, Egypt, Iraq, Algeria, and Jordan called on Gromyko in Moscow on 11 October to convey thanks for Soviet aid,[48] the foreign minister reportedly reaffirmed the USSR's intention to support the Arabs against Israel, but was said to have nonplussed the ambassadors by declaring that the USSR was determined "to pursue every effort to obtain a just peace that would guarantee the security of *all* states in the Middle East" (emphasis added).[49] Brezhnev also sent messages to Nixon, Pompidou, and Brandt on 13 October affirming the USSR's support of Israel's right to exist.[50]

The Israelis' sinking of the Soviet freighter *Ilya Menchikov* in the port of Tartus (Syria) on 12 October, however, led the Soviets to issue a stern warning to Israel[51] and, for the first time, to accuse the United States of direct involvement in the war. Soviet reports charged the United States with sending American pilots, volunteers, and military supplies[52] to Israel. Apparently with détente still in mind, however, the Soviets mitigated their criticism of the United States by blaming international Zionism rather than the U.S. government directly[53] for aid to Israel. And whereas in the 1967 Middle East war the Soviets described Israel's aggression as furthering U.S. objectives, in 1973 they attributed to it (1) Israel's desire to annex territory occupied since the 1967 war, (2) its need to relieve the pressures of its militarized economy, and (3) its fear of the increasing political leverage of Arab oil monopolies.[54]

A week later, the Soviets initiated a new propaganda line supporting the Arabs' use of oil as a weapon. The Soviets' silence on this subject during the first ten days of the war was surprising in light of their support of Arab oil manipulations both in 1967[55] and immediately preceding the 1973 war.[56] Beginning on 18 October, however, the Soviet media lauded the decision of the Arab petroleum exporting countries[57] to raise prices, reduce production, and boycott states aiding Israel and predicted that it would have disruptive effects on the West.[58]

As the Arab military situation deteriorated, diplomatic activity increased, and a cease-fire was finally negotiated. Boumediene went to Moscow on 14–15 October to seek more aid.[59] Then Kosygin, equipped with satellite photographs indicating an imminent Egyptian military disaster,[60] went to Cairo on 16–19 October to pressure Sadat to negotiate a settlement.[61] Finally, on 20 October, Kissinger arrived in Moscow to work out a cease-fire agreement with Brezhnev.[62] On 22 October, the United Nations approved this agreement as Resolution 338.[63]

The cease-fire was immediately broken. The Soviets alleged Israeli violations and threatened Israel with "the gravest consequences" if its aggressive actions against Egypt and Syria continued.[64] Although the Soviets had made empty threats to intervene on the Arabs' behalf following both the 1956[65] and 1967 cease-fires, the fact that the Soviets were sending arms in 1973 may have given the threat credibility.

Nixon, perceiving the possibility of unilateral Soviet intervention, ordered a worldwide U.S. military alert (Defcon 3).[66] Less than 15 hours after the alert, Soviet policy abruptly shifted,[67] suggesting Brezhnev may not have been seeking confrontation and may have been surprised by the American reaction.[68] On 25 October, the two superpowers agreed on another UN Security Council cease-fire resolution, which ended the crisis.

Addressing the World Peace Congress in Moscow on 26 October, Brezhnev again called for détente but implicitly blamed the United States for supporting Israel's alleged aggression and for alerting U.S. forces:

What are the fundamental reasons for military conflicts emerging periodically in this region, including the latest war? In our view, the answer is clear. It is the seizure by Israel of Arab lands as a result of the aggression it has committed, the stubborn unwillingness of Tel Aviv to have regard for the legitimate rights of the Arab peoples, *and the support given to this aggressive policy by those forces in the capitalist world* which strive to impede the free and independent development of the progressive Arab states.

In the cause of normalizing the situation in the Near East, the Soviet Union is prepared to cooperate with *all* countries concerned. But such cooperation of course cannot be furthered by such actions, undertaken *in some NATO countries in the last few days, as the artificial fanning of passions by disseminating all sorts of fantastic speculations about the intentions of the Soviet Union in the Near East* [emphasis added].[69]

The same day, Nixon defended the U.S. alert at a press conference, citing the threat of Soviet intervention.[70] TASS denied the charges, alleging that the president's actions had been aimed at intimidating the Soviets.[71] In an attempt to sow dissension in NATO, the Soviet media claimed that the United States had ignored its allies in making the decision to alert its forces, some of which were stationed at allied bases.[72]

Although the Soviets had come to terms with rightist revisionist Yugoslavia in anticipation of the Middle East war, relations with the leftist revisionist PRC remained strained. The Soviet media charged the Chinese with attempting to undermine Soviet–Arab unity,[73] taking an anti-Arab position in the UN,[74] failing to express sympathy for the Arab victims of Israeli aggression,[75] and refusing to participate in UN disarmament measures.[76] The Soviets also scored the Chinese for the policies formulated at the Tenth CCP Congress in August.[77] Brezhnev later repeated these criticisms in his 26 October speech to the World Peace Congress.[78]

To summarize, in contrast to their reaction to the 1967 war, in 1973 the Soviets:

- Planned their response and coordinated it with their Warsaw Pact allies and Yugoslavia before the war broke out.
- Accused Israel, but not the United States, of aggression, but not of firing the first shot.
- Publicly recognized Israel's right to exist.
- Supplied Egypt and Syria with arms and advisers during the war.
- Balanced their political commitments to the Arabs against their commitment to détente with the United States.

ZHIVKOV SEEKS BALKAN DÉTENTE

Bulgaria consistently upheld Soviet positions on the Middle East. Brezhnev had visited Sofia from 18–21 September 1973, among other reasons to promote Warsaw Pact unity in anticipation of a Middle East war.[79] Foreign Minister Petur

Mladenov indicated Bulgaria's adherence to Soviet policy in a speech to the UN General Assembly on 27 September, in which he also stressed the importance of Bulgarian relations "with neighboring countries . . . of the Balkan Peninsula."[80] A plenum of the Bulgarian party central committee, convened on 3–4 October to discuss Brezhnev's September visit, reaffirmed Bulgarian support:

> These talks are a great new contribution to the further expansion and intensification of unity and cooperation between the BCP and the CPSU. . . . The talks . . . confirmed the correctness of the Leninist foreign policy, . . . a policy of a just and final solution of the most important topical problems in international relations.[81]

With the outbreak of war on 6 October, Bulgarian radio and press reports, using only Radio Cairo, MENA, and Syrian armed forces communiqués,[82] portrayed Israel as the aggressor. Like the Soviets, the Bulgarians did not accuse Israel of firing the first shot and blamed the war solely on "Israeli ruling circles."[83] The government's official reaction also restrained allegations of Western complicity and focused blame on Israel's alleged aggression:

> Backed by certain imperialist and Zionist circles, they [the Israelis] grossly violate the generally known norms of international law and the UN Charter.
> The Government of the People's Republic of Bulgaria and the entire Bulgarian people sharply condemn the new Israeli aggression against the Arab Republic of Egypt and the Syrian Arab Republic and declare that if the government and the ruling circles of Israel continue their aggressive policy, all the responsibility for the consequences of this unreasonable course fall on them and may cost the Israeli people dearly.[84]

The Bulgarians demanded the return of Arab territories but not the creation of a Palestinian state.

Following the 12 October sinking of the Soviet freighter *Ilya Menchikov*, Bulgarian criticism of the West stiffened. Radio Sofia reports on 12–13 October accused the United States of supplying Israel with arms and volunteers. *Narodna Armiya* alleged that "considerable American forces" were concentrating along the coasts of the belligerents.[85] Zhivkov, however, mitigated the criticism of Israeli aggression and U.S. involvement by recognizing Israel's right to exist: "We condemn the aggressive actions of Israel. . . . A lasting and just peace can only be guaranteed . . . if the legitimate rights of all peoples in that region of the world are guaranteed."[86]

Like the Soviets, the Bulgarians referred to oil as a political weapon only after the 17 October session of the Arab oil exporting countries in Kuwait[87] and predicted that procurement problems would erode Western unity.[88] The Bulgarian media relied on TASS reports to describe U.S. and Soviet diplomatic efforts to solve the Middle East crisis and attributed the 22 October UN resolution solely to "Soviet initiative."[89] When the first cease-fire failed, the Bulgarians followed the Soviet lead in blaming the breakdown on Israel:

> The Arab Republic of Egypt and the Syrian Arab Republic accepted the resolution of the Security Council and halted military actions. Israel also declared itself ready to stop these actions, but in reality continued military operations with even greater intensity. . . . The Israeli Government bears full responsibility for these actions.[90]

Party Secretary Zhivkov's activities during October suggest that he considered the military situation to be under control. When he visited Vienna, as scheduled, on 9–13 October, the Bulgarian press devoted more space to his activities than to the Middle East fighting.[91] He paid an unscheduled visit to Prague (19–20 October), which led to speculation that the Macedonian issue was involved, because Czechoslovak Party Secretary Husak was scheduled to visit Yugoslavia on 23 October.[92] Zhivkov then flew as planned to Korea (23 October) and Mongolia (29 October), and returned home via Moscow (2–3 November).

Although Bulgaria, following the Soviet lead, attempted to smooth relations with Yugoslavia, reports issued during and after Yugoslav Foreign Minister Milos Minic's visit to Sofia on 4–6 November indicate that the Macedonian issue remained unresolved.[93]

The Bulgarians supported the Soviets in accusing the Chinese of anti-Sovietism, attempting to drive a wedge between the USSR and the Arabs, and failing to support a UN cease-fire.[94]

To summarize, the Bulgarians:

- Paralleled the Soviet propaganda regarding the Arab–Israeli war, U.S. involvement, and Israel's right to exist.
- Played down the Macedonian issue throughout the war.
- Criticized China's stand on Arab issues.

STRIDENT PRAGUE

Its reaction to the October 1973 Middle East war proved Czechoslovakia's normalization and return to Soviet orthodoxy. Immediately prior to the hostilities, Czechoslovak Foreign Minister Bohuslav Chnoupek, addressing the UN General Assembly, declared his country's support of the Arab claims against Israel.[95] The official Czechoslovak government statement of 8 October, showing the same restraint as the 7 October Soviet statement, did not specifically accuse Israel of firing the first shot but blamed its expansionist policies and other "reactionary" forces for the war:

The crisis in the Middle East . . . is a direct result of Israel's historic aggression against Egypt, Syria and the other Arab countries. . . . Israeli ruling circles, supported by the world reactionary forces, bear full responsibility for the present development of events in the Middle East and their possible consequences. The CPCS Central Committee Presidium and the Czechoslovak Government condemn the expansionist policy of Israel.[96]

Early Czechoslovak media criticism went further than the mild government reaction and the Soviet official and press response. Using only Arab sources at first, the Czechoslovaks accused Israel of attacking Egypt.[97] On 8 October, however, Prague radio accused the United States of supporting Israel's aggression to further its own policy:

Israel . . . is a fist always ready to strike against the Arab states, which are rich in oil. That is why the U.S. is so conscientiously and unreservedly supporting Israel in a policy which has openly ridiculed all international customs and standards during the past 6 years.[98]

Rude Pravo charged that Tel Aviv was "fully dependent, both economically and militarily, on Washington" and that the "United States has multiplied the offensive military potential of Israel, fully aware that Tel Aviv is continuing its aggression."[99]

Following the sinking of the *Ilya Menchikov*, the Czechoslovak press developed its own strident themes. Where the Soviets blamed "Zionism," the Czechoslovaks charged that "U.S. imperialism" had caused the 1973 war. Bratislava *Pravda* cited the presence of the U.S. 6th Fleet in the Eastern Mediterranean as evidence of U.S. aggressive intentions:

The movements of U.S. armed forces in the area are both dangerous and ominous. With its systematic military, political, economic and financial assistance to Israel, the United States bears a large share of responsibility for the audacity of the Israeli aggressor.

In this way, the Middle East crisis may very rapidly grow into an uncontrollable war conflagration, caused by Israel and by the U.S. policy in this area.[100]

Rude Pravo portrayed the Israeli–Arab struggle and American assistance in ideological terms reminiscent of the Cold War: "The Mideast crisis is a class conflict. The front of a militarized Israel and of the reactionary forces of American imperialism stands against the progressive Arab world."[101] On 19 October, Czechoslovak radio announced that a "limited number" of U.S. military personnel accompanying arms supplies had been sent to Israel. The next day, it reported that U.S. military assistance was substantially increasing.[102] Hewing to a harsher line than had the Soviets, the Czechoslovaks failed to assert Israel's right to exist. They also suggested—even prior to the Kuwait OPEC meeting—that the Arabs use oil as a means of furthering their own interests and dividing NATO.[103]

Zhivkov's sudden unofficial visit on 20 October to Prague may have had as its purpose the moderation of the Czechoslovak position.[104] Following his visit, Czechoslovak allegations of the United States's governing role in the war were suspended. The Czechoslovaks, like the Soviets and Bulgarians, now blamed only Israel (not the United States) for the cease-fire breakdown: "The Israeli Government bears full responsibility for this unheard of violation."[105] Czechoslovak media, paralleling the Bulgarian, attributed the initiative for the UN cease-fire resolution to the Soviets.[106]

Following Soviet policy, the Czechoslovaks tried to improve relations with the Yugoslavs but were unable to come to terms with the latters' rightist revisionism. Husak met with Tito in Belgrade on 23–26 October.[107] Returning home, Husak said: "We visited Macedonia and heard about a lot of other areas. . . . I think we have put the past behind us and shall now develop all-round relations."[108] Nevertheless, an article in *Rude Pravo* several weeks later blamed Yugoslavia's fuel crisis, which occurred despite good relations with Arab countries, on its decentralized economy.[109]

The Czechoslovaks outdid the Soviets in their criticism of China's leftist revisionist policies. Charging Chinese anti-Sovietism, the Czechoslovaks scored China's disarmament policy and UN voting record during the Middle East war.[110] Furthermore, they blamed China's internal disintegration on collusion with U.S. and NATO imperialists.[111]

After the Middle East crisis subsided, the Czechoslovaks resumed their vehement criticism of the United States, attributing the U.S. military alert to Nixon's instability brought about by the political pressures engendered by the Watergate investigation.[112]

To summarize, the Czechoslovaks:

- Intensified the Soviet criticism of Israel, the United States, and China.
- Attempted to resolve tensions with Yugoslavia.
- Failed to acknowledge Israel's right to exist, but, possibly reflecting Zhivkov's advice, followed the orthodox line in blaming Israel, not the United States, for the first cease-fire violations.

EAST GERMANY'S RESTRAINT

The June 1973 treaty between East and West Germany and the admission of both to the United Nations on 18 September marked the end of the GDR's political isolation and its integration into the world diplomatic community.[113] The move toward rapprochement had gained impetus with Honecker's replacement of Ulbricht in 1971; as early as February 1972, when Nixon visited China, the FRG had ceased to be the GDR's major propaganda target.

The East Germans supported the Arab cause in 1973, as they had done in 1967; in 1973, however, they did not link West Germany with Israel.[114] The official party and government statement on the Middle East conflict was as restrained as the Soviet statement had been in allocating blame for the war, neither accusing Israel of firing the first shot, nor the United States and its allies of providing aid:

> Since 6 October a military conflict has been taking place again in the Middle East, bringing untold suffering and misery to the people.
>   Israel and those imperialist forces which for years have supported its policy of aggression thus bear the full responsibility for the present dangerous situation and all consequences deriving from it.[115]

The next day, Minister of Defense Heinz Hoffmann expressed shock at the way "Israeli leaders are justifying their aggression."[116]

The East Germans at first blamed Israel alone for the aggression[117] but later implicated the United States.[118] Like the Soviets, they attributed the war to Israel's desire to annex territory: "Today Tel Aviv is no longer solely concerned with keeping the stolen territories. Today the war aim is, as Mrs. Meir said, to go beyond the armistice lines of 1967."[119]

While the East German press went further than the Soviet and Bulgarian media in blaming the United States for Israel's aggression, it did not go as far as the Czechoslovak, which accused the United States of inspiring the conflict: "The United States' dilemma as has become quite clear consists of the compulsion to support Israel on the one hand, and to consider the foreseeable difficulties in its oil supply . . . on the other."[120]

Following the sinking of the *Ilya Menchikov*, the GDR's position exhibited the same hardening as the USSR's. The East German media criticized U.S. military aid to Israel, but affirmed Israel's right to exist:

> President Nixon . . . thought that an increased arms supply was required to secure Israel's right of existence. But who questions this right of existence? The Arab side is, after all, prepared to recognize Israel's independence and sovereignty within the boundaries of June 1967.[121]

Although the East Germans preceded the Soviets in discussing the West's vulnerability to Arab oil policies,[122] they did not highlight the disruptive effects of oil procurement difficulties on NATO unity. They argued instead that a boycott would contribute to Arab unity and erode imperialist support of Israel.[123] This emphasis may have reflected East Germany's emerging interest in fostering relations with Western Europe.

As had Bulgaria and Czechoslovakia, East Germany ascribed the implementation of a cease-fire solely to Soviet efforts:

That instructions were given to cease fire is primarily due to the most powerful state of peace in the world, the Soviet Union, which took the initiative for a peaceful, political solution of the conflict. Once more it is clear to the world that socialism is the peace-maker.[124]

Following the cease-fire breakdown, the East Germans issued a joint party and government declaration which paralleled those of the USSR, Bulgaria, and Czechoslovakia. The declaration blamed the violation on Israel alone, implicating neither the United States nor other NATO members;

The dangerous policy of Israel, which hypocritically accepted the Security Council resolution on a cease-fire in the Middle East and yet at the same time cynically allows its troops to continue the war of aggression against the Arab Republic of Egypt, fills us with deep concern. This violation of the resolution of the Security Council, which contravenes international law, exposes the aggressive character of the ruling circles in Israel, who have the audacity to provoke the peace-loving peoples of the world.[125]

Although the East Germans did not credit the United States with playing a positive role during the crisis, their negative criticism showed moderation. Their single reference to the U.S. worldwide military alert noted only that it was "groundless . . . and a move which did not contribute toward détente."[126] Unlike the Soviets, they did not suggest that the U.S. alert was an affront to the NATO allies. As in the case of the Arab oil boycott, the East Germans seemed reluctant to say anything to offend the Western Europeans.

Like Zhivkov and Husak, for whom the war proved no impediment to official travels, SED Secretary Erich Honecker and Premier Horst Sindermann also demonstrated a business-as-usual approach to the 1973 Middle East war by fulfilling a previously scheduled visit to Mongolia (9–14 October).[127]

The Soviet–Yugoslav rapprochement eradicated, for the moment, the problem of "rightist" revisionism for the East Germans. Honecker met with Yugoslav Presidium member Stane Dolanc, who, on returning to Belgrade, said of the talks: "Our visit is a success. . . . To our thinking, there are all possibilities for our two countries' political, economic, and cultural cooperation."[128]

The East Germans also followed the Soviet line on leftist revisionism, criticizing China's Tenth CCP Congress policies and Chiao Kuan-hua's UN speech on disarmament and Chile.[129] After the outbreak of war, Defense Minister Hoffmann and Honecker accused China of colluding with imperialism,[130] although, again, neither the FRG nor other NATO members were specifically named.

To summarize, the East Germans:

- Repeated Soviet criticisms of Israel, China, and the United States and, like the Soviets, affirmed Israel's right to exist.

- Refrained from alleging FRG and NATO involvement in the conflict in the interest of fostering détente and their new relationship with the West Germans.
- Cultivated relations with Yugoslavia.

BUDAPEST'S BALANCED APPROACH

Pursuing its own national interests as it had done in earlier crises, Hungary diverged in small but meaningful ways from the Soviet position on the 1973 Middle East war. During the early days of the war, however, the Hungarian reaction resembled the reactions of the more orthodox Warsaw Pact states. The media supported the Arab side and accused Israel of attacking Egypt and Syria.[131] The official government statement condemned Israel and indirectly accused the United States of involvement:

> Israel's Government, which in 1967 unleashed its aggressive war against the progressive Arab countries, since that time has been occupying Arab territories and continuously fomenting tension. On 6 October it again set the Middle East area afire. It is well known that lurking behind the martial attitude of the Israeli aggressors lies the most reactionary circles of imperialism, the very ones who, in various areas of the world—yesterday in Chile, today in the Middle East—are attempting to stop the process of international détente. Encouraged by these circles the Israeli leaders have rejected every rational proposal for a just and peaceful solution to the crisis.[132]

Although the press blamed the war on Israel and the United States,[133] Hungarian criticism of the United States differed somewhat from the orthodox line. First, Foreign Minister Janos Peter, speaking to the UN General Assembly on 8 October, credited the United States with an interest in resolving the Middle East crisis: "Israel is becoming increasingly isolated with its unrealistic policy; attempts are being made to try out several new ways to approach the problem, including U.S. interest in trying to find a possible solution."[134]

Second, following the sinking of the *Ilya Menchikov*, the Hungarians, as had the Soviets, sharpened their criticism to include attacks on U.S. shipments of arms, aid, and volunteers to Israel,[135] but again the Hungarian media publicized the U.S. efforts to resolve the crisis:

> One knows about an exchange of messages on the highest Soviet–American level and about some foreign ministerial meetings, such as the talks between Kissinger and France's Jobert in New York. This . . . was the first indication that Kissinger, the leader of U.S. diplomacy, was throwing himself into the efforts to resolve the Middle East problems.[136]

Kissinger's diplomatic efforts received more media coverage than Kosygin's[137] and equal coverage with Brezhnev's.

Third, while other Warsaw Pact media attributed the UN cease-fire resolution to Soviet initiative, the Hungarian media cited the efforts of both the Soviet Union and the United States within the framework of détente:

> The UN resolution based on a joint Soviet–U.S. proposal also expresses . . . the fact that the trend of détente is stronger than the efforts of the adherents of war. . . . We also have no reason to leave the fact unsaid that the responsible attitude of the leaders of the Soviet Union and the United States and their consultations with each other and the parties concerned have played a very great role in this.[138]

The Hungarians followed the Soviet line both in accepting Israel's right to exist and in placing responsibility for the cease-fire breakdown solely on Israel.[139] A government declaration on 25 October noted:

> The Government of the Hungarian People's Republic declares that full responsibility rests on the Israeli Government for the grave situation which has thus evolved, for the crude violation of the Security Council's resolution and for every subsequent consequence.[140]

Unlike the USSR, however, which attempted to use the U.S. military alert to sow dissension in NATO,[141] Hungary postponed mention of the American military alert until 27 October, when it was reported without comment.[142]

As in past crises, Kadar remained relatively isolated during the 1973 Middle East war, neither traveling nor receiving other Warsaw Pact leaders. Going on public record only once during the hostilities—in an interview with a Moscow radio correspondent—Kadar did not mention the war. He did, however, indirectly criticize the USSR by implying that Hungary's military obligations constrained the solution of its domestic problems and suggested that peace, rather than military might, offered the best means for Hungary to achieve socialism:

> We Hungarians used to jokingly say, that if we were left alone to work calmly on our own we would not be daunted by our tasks. . . . The Hungarian people need a great deal to build socialism, but the requirement first and foremost is for peace. . . . Recently I took part in a joint military exercise, where I saw the most modern weapons. I spoke appreciatively about them, because I believe they serve our security and the prospect of peace. But what I said there was that our most modern and powerful weapon is our unity, and that is what will make us triumph.[143]

In the same interview, Kadar's expressed preference for achieving socialist unity through informal meetings seemed a veiled criticism of the more formal conferences (notably the Warsaw Pact PCC sessions) where international obligations were likely to be imposed:[144]

> I consider the informal character of the Crimea meetings [July 1973] to be very effective and fortunate, since after all, we do meet under different circumstances, like the conferences of the Warsaw Treaty Political Consultative Committee, where we usually make decisions. This free and informal exchange of views is not a bad means of coordinating ideas and opinions, of assessing a situation, of jointly discussing what is useful and purposeful, of supporting a given situation now or in the immediate future.[145]

The Hungarian press, again diverging from the Soviet line, noted the breakdown of Arab unity:

> Why is Jordan's King Hussein trying to keep out of the fighting, having only 6 weeks ago made peace with President as-Sadat of Egypt and Al-Assad of Syria? Why does Colonel al-Qaddafi's Libya not help Egypt after so many agreements binding the two in closest unity? Why does the head of Libya "disagree" with President as-Sadat's "strategy"?
> . . . King Feisal of Saudi Arabia is also idle: He is sending neither troops, aircraft or armour for the disposal of the joint Arab command, but at least he is rattling the sabre of oil.[146]

The Hungarians supported the Arab countries' 17 October decision to withhold oil and raise prices not because the decision contributed to Western disunity (as the Soviets noted)[147] but because it contributed to Arab unity:

> A new important element of the current Middle East situation is the solidarity of the Arab states to such a measure as has been unprecedented in the history of the Arab league. One of the characteristic signs of this solidarity is manifest in the Kuwait resolution.[148]

The Hungarian press also hinted at Warsaw Pact disunity by implicitly criticizing Romania's independent Middle East policy. As in 1967, Hungary was the only Warsaw Pact state to publicize Romania's failure to side unequivocally with the Arabs against Israel.[149]

Kadar did not need a Soviet push to solidify relations with Yugoslavia: he visited Tito in July. (Kosygin visited in September.)

The Hungarian criticism of China was sparser and milder than the Soviet. Kadar said on 14 October: "We can see that the most obstinate reactionary circles have not given up the idea of flirting with Peking, which at present—regretfully—is working against general socialist endeavors."[150] In reference to the 22 October cease-fire, Budapest radio reported only that "*Nepszabadsag* considers the attitude of the Chinese delegate in the Security Council to be regretful, stating that with this step 'China further on deepens the gap around itself.' "[151]

To summarize, in contrast to the more orthodox Warsaw Pact states, Hungary:

- Credited the United States (as well as the USSR) with attempting to resolve the Middle East crisis.
- Played down the U.S. worldwide military alert.
- Hinted at Arab and Warsaw Pact disunity.
- Preceded the USSR in rapprochement with Yugoslavia.
- Played down criticism of China.

POLAND EXHIBITS MORE CONCERN FOR DÉTENTE

Poland's foreign and domestic policy acquired an increasingly national orientation as its contacts outside the Warsaw Pact increased. In 1973, as in 1967, Poland sided with the Arabs in the war against Israel, but with noticeably greater moderation than its more orthodox Warsaw Pact allies. Polish Foreign Minister Stefan Olszowski, addressing the UN General Assembly on 27 September 1973, spoke at length on the importance of détente and Poland's relations with the West but limited his remarks on the Middle East to the following:

> The Near East situation is pregnant with a threat of an armed conflict. The Near East truce should not lull us, because Israel continues to ignore the Security Council decisions and follows a policy of aggression and terror toward its Arab neighbors. It is Poland's unchangeable position that Security Council resolution No 242 should be implemented as rapidly as possible. The occupied Arab lands should be returned immediately to the rightful owners.[152]

Only the initial Polish radio broadcasts accused Israel of attacking Egypt and Syria. Subsequent reports merely noted that "fighting erupted" again.[153] The official Polish statement of 8 October mentioned neither the "external reactionary circles" which the Soviets accused of encouraging Israel's "aggressive ambitions" nor the "imperialist and Zionist circles"[154] cited by the Bulgarians:

> The resumption of armed struggle is caused by the fact that the *ruling circles* of Israel . . . are stubbornly blocking all peaceful initiatives and render impossible a political settlement of the conflict.
>
> An urgent solution of the crisis in keeping with the resolutions of the UN Security Council is needed not only by nations in the Middle East but also *serves detente*, security and peace in Europe and in the whole world [emphasis added].[155]

The Polish press based its reports on diverse news sources, including Israeli, emphasized détente rather than Israel's alleged aggression,[156] and avoided the references that the other Warsaw Pact media made to imperialists arming and backing the Israelis. Apparently aware of the Poles' reticence, the Soviets aimed a number of Polish-language broadcasts at correcting the Polish omissions.[157]

Following the sinking of the *Ilya Menchikov*, the Polish press reported that the United States was supplying aircraft and rockets to Israel; the press did not, however, hold the United States responsible for the war or the participation of U.S. volunteers and pilots. Responding to Israel's bombing civilian targets in Syria and Egypt, the Polish Committee of Solidarity with Asian and African Nations blamed Israel alone: "Israel is solely responsible for these acts of terror and demonstrates her disregard for world public opinion, as well as the decisions and resolutions of the United Nations."[158]

The Poles did not address Arab use of oil as a potential weapon or mention the 17 October Kuwait meeting. After the war, treatment of the Arab oil issue was low key and occasionally critical of the Arabs: "Takeover of oil industry and the incomes it gives offers the Arab countries chances of considerable acceleration of economic development. . . . Not all Arab countries, however, use their oil properly."[159]

Like the Hungarians, the Poles attributed the 22 October UN cease-fire initiative to the efforts of both the USSR and the United States within the framework of détente: "The joint Soviet–American action to extinguish the flames of war in the Middle East is an unprecedented phenomenon."[160] Also like the Hungarians, the Poles devoted more media coverage to U.S. than to Soviet negotiation efforts. Kosygin's 16–19 October visit to Cairo merited only one brief comment; in contrast, Kissinger's negotiations with Brezhnev in Moscow received extensive coverage.[161]

The 25 October Polish government declaration held Israel alone responsible for the cease-fire breakdown:

> In spite of the Security Council's repeated call of October 23rd, the cease-fire in the Middle East is not being observed. The responsibility for the prolongation of this state of affairs and its consequences falls on the Israeli Government.[162]

The Polish media did not, however, report the U.S. worldwide military alert until a week after it happened,[163] and then made only one further reference, on 8 November: "At the forum of the NATO nuclear planning group . . . Schlesinger had to face embarrassing questions about absence of consultations with U.S. NATO allies in the 'period of crisis.' "[164]

Throughout the 1973 crisis, Polish economic expansion and détente, rather than the Middle East war, dominated Polish policy. PUWP First Secretary Edward Gierek, speaking to the party central committee on 11 October, highlighted Polish social and economic development but ignored the Middle East.[165] In a major address to the First National Party Conference on 22 October,

Gierek concentrated on Polish economic growth since December 1970 (when he became first secretary), alluding only briefly to the Middle East.[166] Emphasizing economic development, he again did not mention the Middle East in a 26 October speech to Warsaw industrial workers.[167] To Sosnowiec workers, Gierek stressed Poland's economic development and also détente and peace. Referring briefly to the Middle East crisis, he said: "On the motion of the Soviet Union and the United States, the Security Council has now adopted three resolutions whose complete implementation would help liquidate the hotbeds of war and tension in the Middle East."[168]

Poland pursued its active economic relations with the West during the crisis. In a two-week period, trade talks were held with the United States, Belgium, West Germany, and Italy. Secretary of Commerce Frederick Dent visited Poland.[169] A Polish delegation went to Brussels. West German Foreign Minister Walter Scheel and French Minister of Finance Valery Giscard d'Estaing visited Warsaw. Polish Foreign Minister Olszowski visited Rome and the Vatican.[170]

Poland maintained a closer relationship with Yugoslavia than did the other Warsaw Pact states, except Romania. *Zycie Warszawy* praised the role of Tito and Yugoslavia among both the nonaligned and socialist states:

> When a few weeks ago the conference of nonaligned states was in progress in Algiers, the Yugoslav delegation headed by President Tito played a great role there.
>
> It is a fact, however, that Yugoslavia occupies a special place in the family of socialist states. It does not belong to the Warsaw Pact and is not a member of CMEA. Its system is not basically different from, say, that of Poland or Hungary, but on some questions—such as economic policy, for example—it has its own position.
>
> Friendly cooperation between Yugoslavia and the other members of the socialist community has been developing since 1955.[171]

Poland had cooperation and coproduction arrangements with Yugoslavia in the automobile, shipbuilding, electronic, and agricultural machine industries. These economic agreements constituted the highest percentage (25) share in this type of arrangement with any of Poland's trade partners, including the Warsaw Pact countries.[172]

Unlike the other Warsaw Pact countries, Poland refrained from criticizing China during the first two weeks of the war. Finally, Gierek criticized China's failure to support the 22 October UN Security Council resolution, initiating an anti-Chinese tirade in the Polish press.[173] The tirade did not seem to be Soviet inspired. Rather, the Poles apparently viewed Chinese policies to be inimical to Poland's support for détente.

Trybuna Ludu summed up the interrelationship of Polish foreign policy, economic development, and détente as follows:

The effectiveness of the newly emerging system of peaceful coexistence is to a great extent measured by the results of the economic cooperation in the world. Autarky is no longer a feasible proposition.

We are for establishing and expanding constructive cooperation with all states, and we want this cooperation to be comprehensive and universal because peace is indivisible. . . . Making détente irreversible is a raison d'être of socialist Poland.[174]

The presence in Warsaw of two high-ranking Soviet military and political leaders during the critical period of the war suggests the possibility that the Soviets may have been concerned with Poland's reliability. On 11 October, Marshal Grechko, the Soviet defense minister, and General Yepishev, chief of the main political administration of the Soviet army and navy, attended the thirtieth anniversary celebration of the Polish People's Army.[175] In light of Soviet concerns over Polish media treatment of the Middle East War[176] and reports of economic problems between the two states,[177] Grechko's visit takes on potential significance beyond the formality of celebrating the Polish anniversary.

To summarize, the Poles:

- Appeared less concerned with the Middle East war than with their own national interests, including détente and economic ties with the West.
- Maintained cordial relations with Yugoslavia.

ROMANIA'S MEDIATION EFFORTS

Romania's diplomatic initiatives following the 1967 Middle East war reflected the Romanian principle that "the vocation of a country is not limited by any consideration of size or economic and military power."[178] Although early attempts to mediate between Egypt and Israel were frustrated by Nasser's determination in 1968 to pursue a war of attrition,[179] the Romanians kept up their contacts with both sides. Deputy Foreign Minister Gheorghe Macovescu met with Gideon Raphael of the Israeli foreign ministry in Rome in April 1970, and Ceausescu met with Prime Minister Golda Meir in the United States in October.[180] In July 1971, Macovescu conferred with Meir and Foreign Minister Abba Eban in Tel Aviv.[181]

Ceausescu visited Egypt on 2–6 April 1972, the last stop on a tour of Africa to increase trade and ideological ties with the Third World[182] and to continue the search for a Middle East solution. According to the joint Romanian–Egyptian statement, Ceausescu and Sadat reaffirmed their support of Security Council Resolution 242 of 22 November 1967 and called for the settlement of the Palestinian problem.[183]

Returning to Bucharest, Ceausescu announced Romania's willingness "to do everything to contribute to solving the Middle East problem as soon as possible."[184] The following week (14–15 April), Macovescu went to Israel, apparently to invite Meir to Romania.[185] Her visit to Bucharest in May 1972, the first by an Israeli prime minister to an Eastern European state, enhanced Romania's role as a center through which various sides in the Middle East dispute—the USSR and Israel, Egypt and Israel, the United States and Egypt—could communicate.

Ceausescu's message of greeting to the fourth nonaligned conference in Algiers on 5 September 1973 first, reiterated the principle that small and medium-sized countries have a role to play in the peaceful solution of international disputes, second, elucidated Romania's conciliatory position on a Middle East settlement, and third, by referring to Romania as a "socialist developing country,"[186] linked it to the nonaligned movement:

> The liquidation of underdevelopment is one of the cardinal problems of the contemporary world. As a socialist developing country, Romania considers that narrowing the gaps separating the world countries is of fundamental importance for strengthening international peace and security.
>
> Life demonstrates that a durable and equitable solution to the problems facing mankind today . . . can be found in present-day conditions only with the active participa[tion] of all countries, be they big, medium-sized or small. Romania campaigns for the solving of all disputed issues among states by political means and not by armed confrontations.[187]

Romania's reporting of the October war reflected its conciliatory diplomacy. On 6 October, Bucharest radio cited Egyptian, Syrian, and Israeli reports in which each side blamed the other for initiating the attack. On 8–9 October, Bucharest radio summarized without commentary the activities of the Syrian, Egyptian, Israeli, U.S., Soviet, and Chinese representatives at the United Nations.[188]

Romania's neutrality was evident also in its official statement, which differed radically from those of the other Warsaw Pact states. The statement referred neither to Israeli aggression and expansionist policies nor to imperialist and Zionist circles. It criticized, but with moderation, Israel's continued occupation of Arab territories, which it said constituted a source of permanent tension in the region. The statement reasserted the right of all Middle Eastern states to existence and the obligation of all nations (including Romania) to help end the conflict:

> In the spirit of its consistent policy, the Socialist Republic of Romania speaks out for finding a political solution to the Middle East conflict on the basis of the November 1967 Security Council resolution so as to bring about the withdrawal of the Israeli troops from the occupied Arab territories and the establishment of a just and equitable peace, insuring the recognition of the right to an independent and sovereign existence by all states in that area.
>
> The Romanian Government speaks out for solving the problem of the Palestinian population in accordance with its national interests and aspirations.

The Romanian Government considers that all nations have the highly responsible obligation to resolutely act to extinguish the hotbed of tension in the Middle East.[189]

Furthermore, upholding its policy of neutrality, Romania, in contrast to other pact members, did not mention the Middle East resupply efforts of either the United States or the Soviet Union.[190]

During the war, Foreign Minister Macovescu continued diplomatic efforts at the United Nations to settle the Middle East conflict. Macovescu's far-ranging intermediary role in 1973 was similar to Maurer's in 1967, as the following sequence of events suggests: Macovescu met with the Syrian deputy foreign minister at the United Nations on 11 October. The next day, in Bucharest, Ceausescu received the Syrian ambassador, who delivered a message from Assad.[191] Early Saturday morning, 13 October, Macovescu conferred with Kissinger in Washington.[192] The fact that Kissinger interrupted a busy schedule[193] to receive Macovescu suggests that the latter may have brought a message from the Syrians. Subsequent events substantiated the possibility that the message indicated a softening in the Syrian negotiating position.[194] First, after a lapse of four days, Ceausescu again referred to the Middle East crisis, noting: "We are firmly determined to do everything to contribute . . . to restoring peace in the Middle East."[195] Second, Romania was the only East European country not to evacuate families living in Cairo on 13 October.[196]

After meeting with Kissinger, Macovescu returned to New York, where his activities continued to suggest a broad diplomatic interest transcending the bounds of alliance obligations. On 16 October, he met with the Soviet and Chinese delegates; on 17 October, with the Albanian delegate and with Israeli Foreign Minister Eban; on 18 October, with the French and British delegates; and on 20 October, immediately before returning to Bucharest, with John Scali of the U.S. delegation.[197] That day, *Scinteia* carried an unsigned article calling on all states, including small and medium sized, to participate in a Middle East settlement:

An international conference under UN aegis, with the participation of all the states implicated in the conflict, as also of other states of the world—big, medium-sized and small—would most favourably bear on the developments on the line of promoting international détente and cooperation. . . . Socialist Romania is convinced that of special importance would be for all states to contact the countries implicated in the conflict for the cessation of the war and the speediest possible settlement of the Near East situation.[198]

The Romanians appeared unconcerned about Soviet reprisals for their independent policies. Ceausescu made fewer speeches over a longer period of time in 1973 than he had made in 1967, when he nervously barnstormed the country to muster popular support for Romania's independent stance.[199] The eight speeches delivered in October 1973 dealt primarily with the economic development of the locale of the speech.[200]

Romania supported the UN cease-fire resolution but, unlike the other Warsaw Pact states, gave neither the United States nor the USSR credit for arranging it. Instead, the party organ noted Romania's "intense political activity" at the UN and elsewhere and emphasized the intermediary role to be played by small and medium-sized states:

> Romania has carried on intense political activity . . . during the session of the United Nations Organisation as also in other circumstances. In this respect, Romania nurtures the conviction that the holding of an international peace conference within the UN or under UN auspices with the participation of all states engaged in the conflict, as well as of other states of the world—big, medium-sized, and small—would influence most favorably the progress and efficiency of the negotiations for turning the cease-fire into a lasting peace.[201]

Also in contrast to its Warsaw Pact allies, Romania did not condemn Israel for violating the cease-fire. The 25 October government declaration instead offered a proposal to end the violence:

> The Romanian government considers necessary the immediate establishment of an area separating the armies in the conflict, which, in our opinion, could be at least 5 km wide. Setting out from the fact that Israel has occupied following the 1967 war some areas of Arab territories, we consider that it could be envisaged that this zone be realized first of all through the withdrawal of the Israeli troops at least five kilometers back. In the opinion of our government, UN observers or peace-keeping forces, formed of the contingents supplied by the UN member-states, could be sent to this area, free from any military forces of the sides involved in the conflict.[202]

After the cease-fire took effect, Romania continued to act as an intermediary. Eban visited Romania from 4 to 7 November, meeting with Macovescu, Maurer, and Ceausescu—and possibly with Soviet officials.[203] Although the 8 November joint Romanian–Israeli communiqué indicated that a breakthrough had not been achieved, it referred to the positive spirit of the negotiations and—again—the desirability of small and medium-sized states participating in the search for a peaceful solution of the Middle East conflict.[204] The day after Eban left, it was announced that Ceausescu would visit Nixon on 4–8 December.[205] The USA–Romanian joint declaration of 5 December 1973 stated that both sides "understood the necessity of immediately beginning the negotiations envisaged by the Security Council resolution of 22 October 1973 and convening the peace conference."[206]

Romania had declared its intention in 1968 to strengthen its friendship and alliances with all socialist states, including Yugoslavia and the PRC.[207] Although tensions had developed between Romania and Yugoslavia as a result of Romania's position on the 1967 Middle East war,[208] the 1968, 1969, and 1972 crises, during which Romania had perceived varying degrees of Soviet threat, had edged Romania into closer political, economic, and military ties with both Yugoslavia and China. To indicate the close relationship between Romania and Yugoslavia, Manescu said that Ceausescu and Tito had met a dozen times between 1968 and 1973 and that

> throughout the centuries Yugoslavia and Romania continued to build and strengthen their traditional friendship, which has been further fortified by their suffering and struggles—frequently joint struggles—for the defense of their peoples and national existence and for the fulfillment of the ideals of freedom and national independence.[209]

Romania and Yugoslavia pursued parallel policies in the Middle East, and the Yugoslavs may have played an intermediary role between the USSR and the Arabs. Unlike the Warsaw Pact leaders, whose subordinate roles allowed them to follow previously established schedules, Tito on 11 October abruptly cancelled a scheduled visit to Denmark; on 15 October, he received Sadat's special envoy; on 16 October, he met Algerian President Boumediene, who apparently sought reassurance from the Yugoslav leader after particularly difficult dealings with Moscow.[210] Concurrently, Yugoslav Foreign Minister Minic may have been called upon to mediate between Sadat and Kosygin during the latter's 16–19 October stormy visit to Cairo.[211]

Romania and Yugoslavia pursued parallel policies also in relations with the nonaligned nations. The Yugoslavs helped the Romanians to develop contacts, in return for which Romania nurtured the Yugoslavs' rapprochement with the Chinese.[212]

Romania continued to maintain close relations with China in 1973. On 1 September, Ceausescu congratulated Mao Tse-tung on his reelection by the Tenth CCP Congress.[213] During the war, Romania did not criticize China's Middle East policy. Immediately following the war, the two countries signed a trade protocol that substantially increased commercial relations.[214] Military delegation exchanges, begun in 1970 with Defense Minister Ionita's visit to Peking,[215] and military cooperation also increased. The Romanians began to produce Chinese naval vessels and by 1975 had deployed one Hu Chwan-class hydrofoil and ten Shanghai-class motor gunboats.[216]

To summarize, the Romanians:

- Pursued a policy of neutrality and active diplomacy in the Middle East, thus playing the role of a small or medium-sized state participating in the peaceful solution of an international conflict.
- Cooperated with the Yugoslavs in a policy of nonalignment.
- Maintained close ties with and refrained from criticizing the Chinese.

SUMMARY

The USSR and its Warsaw Pact allies exhibited greater restraint in reacting to the October 1973 Middle East war than they had shown at the time of the June 1967 war. Several factors contributed to the change. First, thanks to ample warning, the Soviets were able to prepare themselves and their allies for the 1973 Middle East conflict. Second, in the interest of preserving USA–USSR détente, the USSR wanted to avoid a confrontation with the United States over the Arab–Israeli hostilities. Third, as a result of European détente, the USSR's Warsaw Pact allies were reluctant to blame the United States and its Western European allies for the Middle East war.

Balancing their political commitments to the Arabs against their commitment to détente with the United States, the Soviets planned their response to the 1973 war and coordinated it with the Warsaw Pact states and Yugoslavia before the fighting began. The Soviets accused Israel, but not the United States, of aggression, but not of firing the first shot. Finally, the USSR recognized Israel's right to exist.

Bulgaria, the acquiescent ally, adopted the Soviet line on the war, the U.S. involvement, and Israel's right to exist. Czechoslovakia may have worried the Soviets enough to make them send Zhivkov, the reliable Bulgarian leader, to Prague to moderate the Czechoslovaks' overly zealous criticism of the United States, Israel, and China and to encourage the Czechoslovaks to seek rapprochement with Yugoslavia. In the end, Czechoslovakia failed to resolve tensions with Yugoslavia and never acknowledged Israel's right to exist.

The GDR, because of its 1973 peace treaty with the FRG and its newly acquired legitimacy as a member of the United Nations, reacted with restraint to the Middle East crisis. The East Germans repeated Soviet criticism of the United States, Israel, and China, supported Israel's right to exist, and cultivated relations with Yugoslavia.

Pursuing its own national interests in 1973 as it had in earlier crises, Hungary responded with moderation to the Middle East war, credited the United States (as well as the USSR) with trying to end the war, hinted at Arab and Warsaw Pact disunity (and as in 1967, blamed the pact's troubles on Romania's independent Middle East policy), and minimized criticism of China. These deviations from the Soviet positions, because they were consistent with previous Hungarian behavior, probably did not surprise or especially trouble the USSR.

Poland appeared less concerned with the Middle East war and communist unity than with détente and economic relations with the West. The Poles showed greater restraint than the Hungarians in their criticism of Israel and less restraint than the Hungarians in their recognition of the U.S. peacemaking role. Poland maintained better relations with Yugoslavia than did any other Warsaw Pact country except Romania. The Soviets betrayed some concern regarding Poland's moderation. They beamed a number of Polish-language broadcasts to that country to correct the Polish interpretation of events in the Middle East and, perhaps more significantly, sent Marshal Grechko and another high-ranking political–military officer to Warsaw during the critical period of the war to attend the thirtieth anniversary celebration of the Polish People's Army.

Romania's fundamental divergence from Soviet policy was manifest again in the 1973 Middle East crisis. Following its own principle regarding the responsibility of small and medium-sized states to participate in the peaceful resolution of international conflicts, Romania played an active intermediary role in negotiations with Egypt and Israel before the war, the United States and Syria during the war, and Israel and the USSR after the war. Romanian diplomacy, because it was consistent with Romanian behavior in earlier crises and because it sought some of the same goals as Soviet diplomacy in 1973 (an end to the Middle East fighting and, most important, détente with the West), probably did not unduly concern the Soviets. Nor, apparently, did Ceausescu fear Soviet reprisals in 1973.

NOTES

1. Jon D. Glassman, *Arms for the Arabs: The Soviet Union and the War in the Middle East* (Baltimore, Md.: The Johns Hopkins University Press, 1975), pp. 66–67; and Mohamed Heikal, *The Road to Ramadan* (New York: Quadrangle Books, 1975), pp. 50–51.

2. The Soviets agreed to supply SAM-3s and the crews to run them. By December 1970, the Soviets had sent Egypt more than 200 pilots to operate 150 aircraft, 4,000 military advisers, and 12,000 to 15,000 missile operators at 75–80 SAM sites. See International Institute for Strategic Studies, *Strategic Survey, 1970* (London: International Institute for Strategic Studies, 1971), p. 47.

The Soviets were aware of the gravity of their action. Heikal, who was present with Nasser at the 22 January meeting in Moscow, claims that the Politburo consulted twelve Soviet marshals before making the decision. Heikal, *The Road to Ramadan*, pp. 83–89.

3. Glassman, *Arms for the Arabs*, p. 87.

4. Anwar el-Sadat, *In Search of Identity* (New York: Harper & Row, 1978), pp. 219–21.

5. Supposedly Podgorny promised immediate delivery of MIG-23s. Sadat interview, *Newsweek*, August 7, 1972.

6. Sadat speech to Arab Socialist Union Central Committee, July 23, 1973, in *FBIS, DR, Middle East-Africa (ME-A)* (July 24, 1973), p. G20.

7. Sadat, *In Search of Identity*, p. 229–30.

8. Kissinger claims he arranged that the Middle East general working principles be vague in order to "raise additional questions in Sadat's mind." Henry Kissinger, *White House Years* (Boston: Little, Brown, 1979), p. 1294.

9. Text of Egyptian–Soviet statement of February 10, in *FBIS, DR, SU* (February 12, 1973), p. B4.

10. *FBIS, DR, ME-A* (April 4, 1973), p. D7; and Sadat, *In Search of Identity*, p. 238.

11. Sadat, *In Search of Identity*, p. 241.

12. Assad returned to Syria accompanied by Marshal Kutakhov, Soviet Air Force commander-in-chief, who was apparently sent to shore up Syria's air defense. Galia Golan, *Yom Kippur and After: The Soviet Union and the Middle East Crisis* (Cambridge: Cambridge University Press, 1977), p. 57.

13. See, for example, Moscow TASS, 1715 GMT, May 21, 1973, and June 24, 1973; and *Pravda*, July 12, 1973, p. 1.

14. Richard Nixon, *RN: The Memoirs of Richard Nixon* (New York: Grosset & Dunlap, 1978), p. 885.

15. The Soviets supplied the Arabs with weapons previously confined to the Warsaw Pact: the Samlet and Scud missiles, SAM-7s, and the Sukhoi-20 ground attack aircraft. Glassman, *Arms for the Arabs*, pp. 112–16.

16. The communiqué stated simply that "each of the parties set forth its position on this problem." Nixon, *RN*, p. 886.

17. *FBIS, DR, SU* (July 16, 1973), pp. B4–6. The step was obviously war.

18. Sadat, *In Search of Identity*, p. 242. In Heikal's account, Sadat and Assad agreed to an attack between 5 and 10 October. Heikal, *The Road to Ramadan*, p. 14.

19. Josip Broz Tito, "It Is the Right of the Non-Aligned to Participate in the Solution of International Problems," *Socialist Thought and Practice*, No. 56 (September 1973): 9–10.

20. William B. Quandt, *Soviet Policy in the October 1973 War*, The Rand Corporation, R-1864-ISA (May 1976), p. 9. See also Michael I. Handel, "Perception, Deception and Surprise: The Yom Kippur War," *Jerusalem Papers on Peace Problems* (Hebrew University of Jerusalem, 1976), p. 31.

21. The outbreak of Arab–Israeli hostilities in 1967 apparently surprised the Soviets, as evidenced by the hastily called Moscow conference.

22. Moscow Domestic Service, 0700 GMT, September 18, 1973, in *FBIS, DR, SU* (September 18, 1973), p. D1.

23. Moscow TASS, 1801 GMT, September 21, 1973, in *FBIS, DR, SU* (September 24, 1973), p. D4.

24. Paul Lendvai, *Financial Times* (London), September 19, 1973, p. 7.

25. The Beirut newspaper *Al-Hayah* reported that Sadat disappeared on 18 September to meet secretly with Brezhnev. Concurrently, the Egyptians announced officially that Sadat was "outside Cairo" and would "postpone his engagements until his return." Cairo, Middle East News Agency, (MENA), September 18, 1973, in *FBIS, DR, ME-A* (September 20, 1973), p. G1. *L'Unita* also claimed that Sadat had secretly visited Bulgaria during this period. See Quandt, *Soviet Policy in the October 1973 War*, p. 11.

26. Sadat and Heikal do not refer to a September meeting with Brezhnev.

27. Marvin Kalb and Bernard Kalb, *Kissinger* (Boston: Little, Brown, 1974), p. 453.

28. Moscow Domestic Service, 1730 GMT, September 17, 1973, in *FBIS, DR, SU* (September 18, 1973), p. D7.

29. Marshal Grechko (Soviet defense minister), Marshal Kutakhov (Air Force commander-in-chief), General Pavlovsky (Ground Forces commander-in-chief), and General Yepishev (chief of the Main Political Administration of the Soviet Armed Forces). *FBIS, DR, SU* (October 20, 1973), p. D6.

30. Moscow TASS, 0908 GMT, September 24, 1973, in *FBIS, DR, SU* (September 24, 1973), p. D1.

31. Ironically, during the Czechoslovak (1968) and Ussuri (1969) crises, the USSR had purposely aggravated the Macedonian issue by supporting Bulgaria.

32. In an emergency, the Soviets would likely have overflown Yugoslavia without permission (as they did Turkey). However, overflight without permission would have antagonized the Yugoslavs, whose influence in the nonaligned movement the Soviets may have wanted to exploit.

33. *Krasnaya Zvezda*, September 29–30, 1973, p. 1. During the war, 90 percent of the Soviet flights were over Yugoslavia (10 percent over Turkey). Soviet equipment was flown from Budapest to Yugoslav air bases to the Middle East. See John C. Campbell, "Soviet Strategy in the Balkans," *Problems of Communism*, 23 (July–August 1974): 6–7; and *Aviation Week and Space Technology*, November 19, 1973, pp. 14–15.

34. Belgrade Domestic Service, Tanjug, 1326 GMT, September 24, 1973, in *FBIS, DR, SU* (September 25, 1973), p. D4.

35. Ibid., p. D5. A similar phrase, "monolithic cohesion," had appeared in reference to Hungary during the Vertes maneuvers. See Colonel Korolkov, "Combat Brotherhood," *Krasnaya Zvezda*, September 27, 1973, p. 1, in *FBIS, DR, SU* (October 2, 1973), p. D6.

36. Moscow TASS, 1806 GMT, September 24, 1973, in *FBIS, DR, SU* (September 25, 1973), p. D2.

37. Moscow TASS, 1045 GMT, September 27, 1973, in *FBIS, DR, SU* (September 27, 1973), pp. D1–2.

38. Moscow TASS, 1506 GMT, October 1, 1973, in *FBIS, DR, SU* (October 2, 1973), p. D2.

39. Moscow Domestic Service, 1300 GMT, October 6, 1973, in *FBIS, DR, SU* (October 9, 1973), pp. F5–7.

40. In 1967, with no foreknowledge of the war, the Soviets nevertheless issued an official statement the day the war broke out.

41. The text of the Soviet government statement was broadcast by Moscow TASS, 1659 GMT, October 7, 1973 and published in *Pravda* (p. 1) the same day. *FBIS, DR, SU* (October 9, 1973), pp. F1–2.

By contrast, at the 9 June 1967, Moscow conference, the Soviets threatened to "do everything necessary to help the peoples of Arab countries to administer a resolute rebuff to the aggressor."

42. Vladimir Yermakov, "The International Week," *Pravda*, October 7, 1973, pp. 1 and 4, in *FBIS, DR, SU* (October 11, 1973), p. A10.

43. See: L. Koryavin, "Tel Aviv Is Playing with Fire," *Izvestiya*, October 9, 1973, p. 4, in *FBIS, DR, SU* (October 12, 1973), p. F9.

44. Soviet ambassador to Egypt, Vinogradov, contacted Sadat only six hours after the war broke out, and on 7 and 9 October. Sadat spurned all three overtures. See Sadat, *In Search of Identity*, pp. 252–54; Heikal, *The Road to Ramadan*, pp. 208–17; and "The Vinogradov Papers," *Journal of Palestinian Studies*, 3 (Summer 1974): 161–64. Tension existed between Sadat and Brezhnev following Brezhnev's request on 4 October to evacuate Soviet advisers' families from Egypt. Sadat was "dumbfounded" by the request, which he felt, if implemented, could alert Israeli and American intelligence. Sadat, *In Search of Identity*, p. 247.

45. Kalb and Kalb, *Kissinger*, p. 463.

46. For example, one broadcast drew attention "to the suspicious movement of the U.S. 6th Fleet to the battle zone." Moscow in Arabic, 1600 GMT, October 9, 1973, in *FBIS, DR, SU* (October 10, 1973), p. F3.

47. The text of Brezhnev's cable to Boumediene was broadcast and commented on by Paris Domestic Service, 1200 GMT, October 9, 1973, in *FBIS, DR, SU* (October 10, 1973), p. F3. The Soviets remained sensitive, however, to the problem of balancing their concessions and commitments to each side.

48. The Soviet air and sea arms deliveries were the first to warring noncommunist countries. The air deliveries arrived 10 October. See Golan, *Yom Kippur and After*, p. 85; Glassman, *Arms for the Arabs*, p. 130; and for the timing and inventory, Quandt, *Soviet Policy in the October 1973 War*, pp. 23–26.

49. "From Our Correspondent," The *Times* (London), October 12, 1973, p. 10.

50. Hamburg DPA, 1637 GMT, October 13, 1973, in *FBIS, DR, SU* (October 15, 1973), p. A7.

51. Moscow Domestic Service, 1737 GMT and Moscow TASS, 1757 GMT, October 12, 1973, in *FBIS, DR, SU* (October 15, 1973), pp. F1–2.

52. Moscow TASS, 1841 GMT, October 13, 1973, in *FBIS, DR, SU* (October 15, 1973), pp. F15–16. Moscow TASS, 2204 GMT, October 15, 1973, noted "that some 30,000 American 'volunteers' are waiting for transportation from the United States to Israel." *FBIS, DR, SU* (October 15, 1973), p. B2. Moscow Domestic Service, 1730 GMT, October 15, 1973, noted that: "The United States has decided to replace in part losses in aircraft and other military equipment suffered by Israel." *FBIS, DR, SU* (October 15, 1973), p. B1.

53. See Lev Korneyev commentary, Moscow Domestic Service, 2030 GMT, October 12, 1973, in *FBIS, DR, SU* (October 15, 1973), p. F10.

54. Koryavin, "Tel Aviv Is Playing with Fire," *Izvestiya*, October 9, 1973, p. 4, in *FBIS, DR, SU* (October 12, 1973), pp. F9–11; Vikentiy Matveyev, "The Price of Recklessness," *Izvestiya*, October 11, 1973, p. 2, in *FBIS, DR, SU* (October 12, 1973), pp. F13–15; and Viktor Mayevskiy, *Pravda*, October 14, 1973, p. 4, in *FBIS, DR, SU* (October 17, 1973), p. A3.

55. During the 1967 war, the Soviets called on the Arabs to embargo oil to the West. See Arthur Jay Klinghoffer, *The Soviet Union and International Oil Politics* (New York: Columbia University Press, 1977), p. 159.

56. See Soviet commentaries supporting the OPEC meetings on 5–6 September in Kuwait, which discussed the coordination of oil policy to promote Arab interests. *FBIS, DR, SU* (September 7, 1973), pp. F1–3.

57. The decision was taken on 17 October at an emergency session in Kuwait.

58. Moscow Domestic Service, 2130 GMT, October 18, 1973, in *FBIS, DR, SU* (October 19, 1973), pp. F3–4; B. Rachkov, "Oil Is a Weapon for the Arab Peoples," *Moskovskaya Pravda*, October 21, 1973, p. 3, in *FBIS, DR, SU* (October 25, 1973), p. F5; and V. Osipov, "The West and Arab Oil," *Izvestiya*, October 20, 1973, p. 4. Citing from *Newsweek*, Osipov notes: "If competition for petroleum begins, then it will be virtually impossible to keep it from turning into a political and diplomatic war. In that case the whole postwar system of U.S. alliances with West Europe and Japan could be shattered." *FBIS, DR, SU* (October 24, 1973), p. F8.

59. Moscow Domestic Service, 1800 GMT, October 15, 1973, in *FBIS, DR, SU* (October 16, 1973), pp. F1–2. He got the aid, but Quandt claims that "the Soviets were quite tough in the bargaining over aid until Boumediene offered to pay for the arms in cash." Quandt, *Soviet Policy in the October 1973 War*, p. 24.

60. Heikal, *The Road to Ramadan*, p. 235.

61. Sadat described Kosygin as "vicious" and "aggressive." Sadat, *In Search of Identity*, p. 258.

62. For the Soviet coverage of Kissinger's visit, see *FBIS, DR, SU* (October 23, 1973), pp. B1–4. For the U.S. versions, see Kalb and Kalb, *Kissinger*, pp. 481–84; and Nixon, *RN*, p. 933.

63. The UN Resolution 338 stated that "The Security Council: 1. Calls upon all parties to the present fighting to cease all firing and terminate all military activity immediately, no later than 12 hours after the moment of the adoption of this decision, in the positions they now occupy; 2. Calls upon the parties concerned to start immediately after the ceasefire the implementation of Security Council Resolution 242 in all of its parts; 3. Decides that, immediately and concurrently with the ceasefire, negotiations will start between the parties concerned under appropriate auspices aimed at establishing a just and durable peace in the Middle East."

64. Moscow TASS, 1810 GMT, October 23, 1973. The full text of the Soviet government's statement can be found in *FBIS, DR, SU* (October 24, 1973), p. F2.

65. The Soviet proposal of a joint Soviet–American military force to enforce the peace in November 1956 was clearly a bluff. Khrushchev knew that Eisenhower would never join forces against England, France, and Israel. Nevertheless, he made the proposal so that "by putting him [Eisenhower] in the position of having to refuse, we'll expose the hypocrisy of his public statement condemning the attack against Egypt. We'll make him put his money where his mouth is." Nikita Khrushchev, *Khrushchev Remembers*, Vol. 1 (Boston: Little, Brown, 1970), p. 434.

66. Nixon characterized the threat as "perhaps the most serious threat to U.S.–Soviet relations since the Cuban missile crisis eleven years before." Nixon, *RN*, p. 938.

67. Quandt holds that the Soviets never contemplated a massive military intervention to save the Egyptian Third Army. He suggests the threat was an attempt to convince the United States to restrain Israel. Quandt, *Soviet Policy in the October 1973 War*, p. 33.

68. A Hungarian reporter, Pal Ipper, said that Brezhnev, about to speak at the World Peace Congress in Moscow on 25 October, received a telex (apparently Nixon's reply to the Soviets' intervention threat) and abruptly left the hall with Gromyko. Brezhnev's speech was postponed until the next day. *FBIS, DR, EE* (November 2, 1973), p. F1.

69. *FBIS, DR, SU*, Supplement 40 (October 29, 1973), pp. 5 and 7. At no time, however, did Brezhnev make any negative references specifically to the United States, nor did he refer to the alert.

70. For the transcript of the press conference, see *The New York Times*, October 27, 1973, p. 14.

71. Moscow Domestic Service, 0300 GMT, and Moscow TASS, 0326 GMT, October 27, 1973, in *FBIS, DR, SU* (October 29, 1973), pp. B3–4. Because the TASS release was issued at an unusual hour (6:30 AM, Moscow time) within four hours of Nixon's conference, Hedrick Smith has hypothesized it was authorized, if not composed, by Brezhnev himself. *The New York Times*, October 28, 1973, p. 1.

72. See "Disappointment and Dissatisfaction," *Pravda*, October 30, 1973, p. 5, in *FBIS, DR, SU* (October 31, 1973), p. A4.

73. Yuriy Kornilov, "Peking's Words and Deeds," Moscow TASS, 1224 GMT, October 19, 1973, in *FBIS, DR, SU* (October 23, 1973), pp. C1–2.

74. *Pravda* and Moscow TASS on 19 October noted that "China refused to support the United Nations resolution condemning Israel and thereby joined the positions of the United States." *FBIS, DR, SU* (October 25, 1973), p. C4. Referring to the Security Council's 24 October emergency resolution, the Soviets noted: "The Chinese representative not only refused to take part in the voting but also tried to prevent the adoption of the important resolution, in fact playing into the hands of the Tel Aviv aggressors." Yuriy Kornilov, "Peking's 'Special Tactics,' " *Sovetskaya Rossiya*, October 25, 1973, p. 3, in *FBIS, DR, SU* (October 30, 1973), pp. C3–4.

75. Moscow TASS, 0538 GMT, October 10, 1973, in *FBIS, DR, SU* (October 10, 1973), p. A7.

76. See "The General Political Discussion Continues," *Pravda*, October 4, 1973, p. 5, in *FBIS, DR, SU* (October 11, 1973), pp. A12–13 and V. Kalinin, "A Valuable Contribution," *Sovetskaya Rossiya*, October 15, 1973, p. 3, in *FBIS, DR, SU* (October 17, 1973), pp. A5–6.

77. See the editorial, "On the 10th CCP Congress," *Pravda*, October 16, 1973, pp. 4–6, in *FBIS, DR, SU* (October 18, 1973), pp. C1–10.

78. *FBIS, DR, SU*, Supplement 40 (October 29, 1973), pp. 11–12.

79. See notes 22–25. Galia Golan contends that some Soviet war materiel was flown out of Bulgarian air bases during the war. Golan, *Yom Kippur and After*, p. 87.

80. "Peace and International Security Will Continue to Strengthen," *Rabotnichesko Delo*, September 28, 1973, p. 5, in *FBIS, DR, EE* (October 5, 1973), p. C3. This undoubtedly referred to Brezhnev's newly improved relations with Yugoslavia.

81. The 4 October decision of the plenum was broadcast by Sofia Domestic Service, 1830 GMT, October 4, 1973, in *FBIS, DR, EE* (October 5, 1973), p. C2.

82. Bulgarian Situation Report/36, RFE (October 12, 1973), p. 2.

83. Zhivko Kefalov, "Dangerous Provocation," *Trud*, October 8, 1973, p. 1, in *FBIS, DR, EE* (October 10, 1973), pp. C2–3; Vladimir Topencharov, "The Way Out," *Otechestven Front*, October 11, 1973, pp. 1, 3, in *FBIS, DR, EE* (October 15, 1973), p. C1.

84. Sofia BTA, 1324 GMT, October 8, 1973, in *FBIS, DR, EE* (October 9, 1973), p. C2.

85. Bulgarian Situation Report/37, RFE (October 19, 1973), pp. 8–9.

86. Address to the Eighth Congress of the World Federation of Trade Unions, Sofia Domestic Service, 0840 GMT, October 15, 1973, in *FBIS, DR, EE* (October 16, 1973), p. C7.

87. Radio Sofia hailed the Arab decision as an effective political weapon on 18 October. Bulgarian Situation Report/38, RFE (October 25, 1973), p. 12.

88. *Vecherni Novini*, October 29 and 30, and November 1, *Otechestven Front*, October 30, and *Rabotnichesko Delo*, November 1 and 3, in Bulgarian Situation Report/39, RFE (November 9, 1973), p. 15.

89. Radio Sofia on October 22 and 23, in Bulgarian Situation Report/39, RFE (November 9, 1973), p. 13. For excerpts from the 23 October issues of *Rabotnichesko Delo*, *Zemedelsko Zname*, *Otechestven Front*, and *Trud*, see *FBIS, DR, EE* (October 24, 1973), p. C2.

90. Sofia Domestic Service, 1830 GMT, October 25, 1973, in *FBIS, DR, EE* (October 26, 1973), p. C1.

91. See Bulgarian Situation Report/37, *RFE* (October 19, 1973), pp. 3–6; and *FBIS, DR, EE* for the period of the visit. In 1967, the outbreak of war had caused Zhivkov to cut short his state visit to Yugoslavia.

92. Macedonia had become an issue again in March 1973, when, during Czechoslovak Foreign Secretary Bohuslav Chnoupek's visit to Belgrade, the Czechoslovak party organ *Rude Pravo* (March 3) published an article supporting the Bulgarian claim to Macedonia. Chnoupek reportedly apologized to the Yugoslavs for the article. See Bulgarian Situation Report/10, *RFE* (March 8, 1973), pp. 5–7; and Bulgarian Situation Report/37, *RFE* (October 19, 1973), pp. 1–2.

93. Minic admitted problems with Bulgaria in his opening toast at dinner on November 4, 1973. Sofia BTA, 0807 GMT, November 5, 1973, in *FBIS, DR, EE* (November 8, 1973), p. C2. Returning to Belgrade, Minic said: "There are still open problems . . . mainly the nonrecognition of the Macedonian nationality in Bulgaria," Tanjug (November 6). Bulgarian Situation Report/39, *RFE* (November 9, 1973), p. 7.

94. See, for example, Eugeni Alexandrov, "Chinese Policy and the 10th Congress of the CCP," *Anteni*, November 3, 1973, in *FBIS, DR, EE* (November 6, 1973), p. C3; Colonel Anastas Anastassov, "The Nuclear Ambitions of the Maoists," *Narodna Armiya*, November 9, 1973, p. 1, in *FBIS, DR, EE* (November 13, 1973), p. C8. Bulgarian relations with "leftist-revisionist" Albania improved, however. Sofia BTA, 1430 GMT, October 27, announced that the two countries signed a protocol to increase trade in 1974. *FBIS, DR, EE* (October 29, 1973), p. C1. See also the editorial calling for better ties with Albania: "29 November, the National Holiday of Albania," *Otechestven Front*, November 28, 1973, p. 3, in *FBIS, DR, EE* (November 30, 1973), pp. C6–7.

95. See *Pravda* (Bratislava), October 6, 1973, pp. 2, 7, in *FBIS, DR, EE* (October 10, 1973), pp. 4–9.

96. Prague Domestic Service, 1730 GMT, October 8, 1973, in *FBIS, DR, EE* (October 9, 1973), p. D1.

97. Czechoslovak Situation Report/36, *RFE* (October 10, 1973), pp. 10–13.

98. Prague Domestic Service, October 8, 1973, in *FBIS, DR, EE* (October 9, 1973), p. D2. Another broadcast argued that: "Israel is not alone in being responsible. . . . Clearly responsible here are those imperialist and Zionist circles in the West, in particular the United States." Ibid., pp. D2–3.

99. Milan Jelinek, "Israel's Playing with Fire," *Rude Pravo*, October 9, 1973, p. 7, in *FBIS, DR, EE* (October 12, 1973), p. D6.

100. Jul, "Playing with Fire," *Pravda* (Bratislava), October 13, 1973, p. 7, in *FBIS, DR, EE* (October 17, 1973, p. D1.

101. Milan Jelinek, "The World and the Times: The Mercenaries," *Rude Pravo*, October 18, 1973, p. 7, in *FBIS, DR, EE* (October 24, 1973), pp. D1–2.

102. CTK, 1901 GMT, October 19, 1973; Prague Domestic Service, 1230 GMT, October 20, 1973, in *FBIS, DR, EE* (October 23, 1973), pp. D1–2.

103. Czechoslovak Situation Report/37, *RFE* (October 17, 1973), p. 6; "U.S.–European Disagreements," *Rude Pravo*, October 31, 1973, in *FBIS, DR, EE* (October 31, 1973), pp. D5–7.

104. The Soviets, occupied elsewhere (Kosygin with Sadat, Brezhnev and Gromyko with Kissinger), may have called on the politically reliable Zhivkov to convey Soviet apprehensions lest the Czechoslovaks' strident ideological tone foment the Macedonian issue. Still fresh in the Soviet leaders' minds may have been the March 1973 Czechoslovak ideological provocation of the Yugoslavs over the Macedonian issue. See note 92.

105. Prague Domestic Service, 0400 GMT, October 25, 1973, in *FBIS, DR, EE* (October 30, 1973), p. D5.

106. Milan Jelinek, "An Irrevocable Fact," *Rude Pravo*, October 23, 1973, p. 7, in *FBIS, DR, EE* (October 26, 1973), p. D2.

107. This marked the first meeting between Tito and a Czechoslovak leader since the 1968 invasion of Czechoslovakia.

108. Jan Zelenko interview with Gustav Husak, Prague Domestic Service, 2030 GMT, October 26, 1973, in *FBIS, DR, EE* (October 29, 1973), pp. D3–4.

109. Jan Hrobar, "Emphasis on the Necessity of Adriatic Pipeline," *Rude Pravo*, November 17, 1973, p. 6, in *FBIS, DR, EE* (November 20, 1973), pp. D1–2.

110. See, for example, Jozef Lenart, First Secretary of the Slovak communist party, *Pravda* (Bratislava), October 8, 1973, p. 3, in *FBIS, DR, EE* (October 19, 1973), p. D7; and interview with Foreign Minister Chnoupek at the United Nations on October 10, 1973, in *FBIS, DR, EE* (October 11, 1973), p. D2.

111. Prague Domestic Service, 1545 GMT, October 8, 1973, in *FBIS, DR, EE* (October 17, 1973), pp. D4–5; and *Rude Pravo*, October 25, 1973; *FBIS, DR, EE* (October 26, 1973), pp. D3–4.

112. Prague Domestic Service, 1730 GMT, October 27, 1973, in *FBIS, DR, EE* (October 29, 1973), pp. D1–2. See also Milos Krejci, "Pressure Against Nixon: The Watergate Affair Is Becoming More Acute," *Rude Pravo*, November 6, 1973, p. 7, in *FBIS, DR, EE* (November 8, 1973), pp. D1–2.

113. In a 5 October 1973 interview, Herbert Kalikowski, the East German ambassador to Czechoslovakia, said: "Last year, the GDR had normal diplomatic relations with 31 states; this year, it maintains diplomatic contacts with 96 states." Prague CTK, 2030 GMT, October 5, 1973, in *FBIS, DR, EE* (October 9, 1973), p. E14. At the time of the 1967 Middle East war, the GDR had full diplomatic relations only with other communist states.

114. From 1967 through 1971, the East Germans had portrayed West Germany as a major cause of the war. See the interview with Defense Minister Heinz Hoffmann on his return from Egypt, Syria, and Iraq. *Horizont*, No. 47, November 1971, pp. 3–4, in JPRS: 54,868 (January 6, 1972), p. 5.

115. The full text of the 7 October official statement can be found in *FBIS, DR, EE* (October 10, 1973), pp. E1–2.

116. *FBIS, DR, EE* (October 9, 1973), p. E4.

117. GDR Domestic Service, 1705 GMT, October 6, 1973, in *FBIS, DR, EE* (October 9, 1973), p. E1.

118. "The imperialist bridgehead, Israel, could not continue its dangerous game without the 'benevolent' attitude of the United States." Klaus Wilczynski, "Aimed Shots against Détente," *Berliner Zeitung*, October 8, 1973, p. 2, in *FBIS, DR, EE* (October 10, 1973), p. E5.

119. Wielard Weber commentary, GDR Domestic Service, 1705 GMT, October 12, 1973, in *FBIS, DR, EE* (October 15, 1973), p. E1.

120. Albert Reisz commentary, East Berlin Domestic Service, 2120 GMT, October 9, 1973, in *FBIS, DR, EE* (October 10, 1973), p. E3.

121. GDR Domestic Service, 1765 GMT, October 16, 1973, in *FBIS, DR, EE* (October 17, 1973), p. E1.

122. Albert Reisz, 9 October commentary, in *FBIS, DR, EE* (October 10, 1973), p. E3.

123. See, for example, Klaus Olizeg commentary, GDR Domestic Service, 1705 GMT, October 18, 1973, in *FBIS, DR, EE* (October 19, 1973), pp. E1–2; Horst Kaeubler commentary, GDR Domestic Service, 1705 GMT, November 5, 1973, in *FBIS, DR, EE* (November 6, 1973), pp. E1–2.

124. Speech by politburo member Albert Norden, ADN International Service, 0932 GMT, October 23, 1973, in *FBIS, DR, EE* (October 23, 1973), p. E16. See also Foreign Minister Otto Winzer: ADN International Service, 1939 GMT, October 23, 1973, in *FBIS, DR, EE* (October 23, 1973), p. E5.

125. The full text of the declaration is in *FBIS, DR, EE* (October 25, 1973), p. E1.

126. ADN International service, 2152 GMT, October 31, 1973, in *FBIS, DR, EE* (November 1, 1973), p. E1.

127. *FBIS, DR, EE* (October 10, 1973), pp. E6–7; and (October 15, 1973), p. E4.

128. Tanjug, 1759 GMT, November 1, 1973, in *FBIS, DR, EE* (November 2, 1973), p. I5.

129. Albert Norden's 2 October report to the SED Central Committee, *Neues Deutschland*, October 3, 1973, pp. 3–5, in *FBIS, DR, EE*, Supplement 39 (October 15, 1973), p. 15.

130. Hoffmann noted in a speech to military academy graduates: "[Imperialism] uses Maoism as an obedient tool to split the international communist movement and to create a 'Far Eastern pressure' on the Soviet Union." *Neues Deutschland*, October 16, 1973, p. 5, in *FBIS, DR, EE* (October 19, 1973), p. E9. Honecker said: "The Chinese leaders are trying in Europe to thwart the process of détente." *Neues Deutschland*, November 1, 1973, pp. 3–5, in *FBIS, DR, EE* (November 7, 1973). Interestingly, Honecker ascribed the aggressive initiative to the Chinese; Hoffmann, to the Western imperialists. However, East German relations with Albania, like Bulgarian, appeared to improve. See *Neues Deutschland*, November 17, 1973, in *FBIS, DR, EE* (November 20, 1973), p. E6.

131. Budapest Domestic Service, 1500 GMT, October 6, 1973, quoted a TASS report that Israel had attacked Egypt and Syria. Hungarian Situation Report/35, *RFE* (October 9, 1973), p. 17.

132. See Budapest Domestic Service for the full text of the statement: 1315 GMT, October 8, 1973, in *FBIS, DR, EE* (October 9, 1973), p. F1.

133. On 9 October, *Nepszabadsag* wrote that the present conflict "is nothing else but the continuation of the war of 1967. The responsibility of it falls on Israel," and that behind the Israel militarists are "American imperialists arming and financing them." *FBIS, DR, EE* (October 10, 1973), p. F1.

134. Budapest Domestic Service, 1900 GMT, October 9, 1973, in *FBIS, DR, EE* (October 12, 1973), p. F2.

135. Peter Vajda, "The Middle East: The Responsibility and the Way Out," *Nepszabadsag*, October 14, 1973, in *FBIS, DR, EE* (October 16, 1973), p. F1.

136. Jozsef Palfy commentary, Budapest Domestic Service, 1335 GMT, October 13, 1973, in *FBIS, DR, EE* (October 15, 1973), p. F2. Henry Kissinger also received positive coverage over Budapest Domestic Television Service, 1830 GMT, October 16, 1973, in *FBIS, DR, EE* (October 17, 1973), p. F1.

137. Radio Budapest reported Kosygin's visit to Cairo (16–18 October) in a two-line news item after the visit had ended. The press did not cover the results of the talks. Hungarian Situation Report/37, *RFE* (October 23, 1973), p. 14.

138. Ferenc Varnai, "The Security Council Cease-Fire Appeal," *Nepszabadsag*, October 23, 1973, p. 3, in *FBIS, DR, EE* (October 25, 1973), p. F2.

139. See Otto Kovacs commentary, Budapest, 1900 GMT, October 17, 1973, in *FBIS, DR, EE* (October 18, 1973), p. F1; and Andras Kereszty commentary, Budapest Domestic Service, 1630 GMT, October 25, 1973, in *FBIS, DR, EE* (October 26, 1973), pp. F2–3.

140. Budapest Domestic Service, 1400 GMT, October 25, 1973, in *FBIS, DR, EE* (October 29, 1973), p. F3.

141. See note 72.

142. Hungarian Situation Report/38, *RFE* (October 30, 1973), pp. 13–14.

143. Budapest Domestic Service, 1815 GMT, October 14, 1973, in *FBIS, DR, EE* (October 16, 1973), pp. F2–5. The joint military exercise referred to by Kadar presumably was Vertes 73. See notes 28, 29.

144. Hungary was the only Warsaw Pact member to support Romania's right not to attend multilateral communist party conferences during the 1967 Middle East war.

145. *FBIS, DR, EE* (October 16, 1973), p. F2.

146. Jozsef Palfy commentary, Budapest Domestic Service, 1335 GMT, October 13, 1973, in *FBIS, DR, EE* (October 15, 1973), pp. F1–3.

147. See note 58.

148. "Solidarity and Diplomacy," *Nepszabadsag*, October 20, 1973, in *FBIS, DR, EE* (October 23, 1973), p. F1.

149. See note 112 in Chapter 2. Budapest Domestic Television Service, 1900 GMT, October 30, 1973, reported a dispute between the Algerian and Romanian delegations at the World Peace Congress in Moscow. *FBIS, DR, EE* (November 2, 1973), p. F1. *Magyar Hirlap*, October 29, 1973, also

reported that the Romanian delegate to the Moscow Congress had protested an attempt to adopt a resolution to condemn Israel, proposed by the Algerian delegate. Romanian Situation Report/43, *RFE* (November 5, 1973), p. 14.

150. *FBIS, DR, EE* (October 16, 1973), p. F3.

151. *FBIS, DR, EE* (October 24, 1973), p. F2.

152. *Zycie Warszawy*, September 29, 1973, p. 5, in *FBIS, DR, EE* (October 3, 1973), pp. G1–5.

153. Polish Situation Report/36, *RFE* (October 19, 1973), pp. 5–10.

154. See notes 41 and 84.

155. *FBIS, DR, EE* (October 9, 1973), p. G1.

156. See Polish Situation Report/36, *RFE* (October 19, 1973), p. 4; and "The Need for Several Solutions," *Trybuna Ludu*, October 10, 1973, p. 2, in *FBIS, DR, EE* (October 15, 1973), pp. G1–2.

157. For example, one Soviet commentary compared the Arab fighting to Polish resistance in World War II: "Could the assertions of Israeli propaganda imputing aggressiveness to the Arabs be true? Of course not. . . . Soviet people well understand the just fight of the Arab peoples against alien aggressors. In the same way the resistance movement came into being during World War II against the Nazi occupiers of Poland, Czechoslovakia, France and other European countries." Moscow in Polish to Poland, 1700 GMT, October 17, 1973, in *FBIS, DR, SU* (October 18, 1973), pp. F9–10. See also Yuriy Shalygin commentary in Polish, 1700 GMT, October 24, 1973, for a discussion of the *limits* of détente, in *FBIS, DR, SU* (October 25, 1973), pp. F1–2.

158. PAP, 1410 GMT, October 16, 1973, in *FBIS, DR, EE* (October 17, 1973), p. G1.

159. "Arab Countries' Drive toward Full Control of Resources," *Trybuna Ludu*, November 12, 1973, in *FBIS, DR, EE* (November 12, 1973), p. G1.

160. M. Berezowski, "Toward Solving the Conflict," *Trybuna Ludu*, October 23, 1973, p. 2, in *FBIS, DR, EE* (October 25, 1973), p. G2.

161. Polish Situation Report/38, *RFE* (November 2, 1973), p. 14. See also Zygmunt Broniarek, "Summit Meetings," *Trybuna Ludu*, November 6, 1973, p. 5, in *FBIS, DR, EE* (November 12, 1973), pp. G2–3.

162. *FBIS, DR, EE* (October 26, 1973), p. G1.

163. Polish Situation Report/38, *RFE* (November 2, 1973), p. 14.

164. Warsaw PAP, 1340 GMT, November 8, 1973, in *FBIS, DR, EE* (November 8, 1973), p. G13. The Poles did not report events surrounding Watergate.

165. *Trybuna Ludu*, October 12, 1973, pp. 1–2, in *FBIS, DR, EE* (October 18, 1973), pp. G3–5.

166. The translation of Gierek's speech, covering 33½ pages, contained only an 11-line reference to the Middle East. Warsaw Domestic Service, 0730 GMT, October 22, 1973, in *FBIS, DR, EE*, Supplement 41 (November 2, 1973), p. 29.

167. *Trybuna Ludu*, October 27, 1973, p. 1, in *FBIS, DR, EE* (November 2, 1973), pp. G7–8.

168. *Trybuna Ludu*, October 30, 1973, p. 1, in *FBIS, DR, EE* (November 2, 1973), p. G5.

169. During his visit, Dent reportedly expressed the desire "to double Polish–American trade exchanges within two years." *Zycie Warszawy*, September 29, 1973, p. 4, in *FBIS, DR, EE* (October 3, 1973), p. G5.

170. See *Trybuna Ludu*, October 8, 1973, pp. 1–2, in *FBIS, DR, EE* (October 11, 1973), p. G4; Warsaw PAP, 1349 GMT, October 20, 1973, in *FBIS, DR, EE* (October 24, 1973), p. G8; Warsaw PAP, 1632 GMT, October 29, 1973, in *FBIS, DR, EE* (October 30, 1973), p. G5; and *Trybuna Ludu*, November 11, 1973, p. 2, in *FBIS, DR, EE* (November 13, 1973), p. G10.

171. JG, "A Special Place," *Zycie Warszawy*, October 2, 1973, p. 4, in *FBIS, DR, EE* (October 5, 1973), p. G1.

172. Polish Situation Report/40, *RFE* (November 23, 1973), pp. 8–9. Also, *Zycie Warszawy* reported that Poland was "Albania's third partner in trade relations." *FBIS, DR, EE* (November 30, 1973), pp. G1–2.

173. Speech to the First National Party Conference, October 22, 1973, in *FBIS, DR, EE*, Supplement 41 (November 2, 1973), p. 29. The media followed a similar pattern at the time of Nixon's visit

to China, refraining from criticizing China until Gierek's catalytic speech on 21 February, 1972 (see note 91 in Chapter 5).

174. M. Berezowski, "Polish Foreign Policy—An Active Role," *Trybuna Ludu*, November 2, 1973, p. 5, in *FBIS, DR, EE* (November 7, 1973), pp. G2–3.

175. Warsaw PAP, 1330 GMT, October 11, 1973, in *FBIS, DR, EE* (October 11, 1973), p. G6. At the same time, Olszowski met with Marshal Yakubovskiy, commander of the Warsaw Pact Forces, in Moscow. See *FBIS, DR, SU* (October 12, 1973), pp. D1–6.

176. See note 157.

177. During the military celebrations, the Polish government presidium met in Warsaw to discuss "problems related to the implementation of [economic] agreements concluded between Poland and the USSR." PAP, 1845 GMT, October 12, 1973, in *FBIS, DR, EE* (October 17, 1973), p. G6.

178. First stated by Premier Ion Gheorghe Maurer in a speech to the UN General Assembly, 23 June, 1967; see note 43 in Chapter 2.

179. After frequent consultations in Bucharest with Gideon Raphael in June 1968, Gheorghe Macovescu visited Cairo to convey the Israelis' desire to negotiate. Heikal claims that Nasser effectively ended Romanian attempts at mediation by telling Macovescu: "What I want from the Israelis is a map showing what they think the final frontiers of Israel should be." Heikal, *The Road to Ramadan*, p. 60.

180. During this visit, Ceausescu also provided Nixon with the "Romanian channel" to the PRC, thereby implementing a foreign policy increasingly antithetical to Soviet interests; see note 13 in Chapter 5.

181. Romanian Situation Report/14, *RFE* (April 20, 1972), p. 15.

182. Although Ceausescu had entertained a number of Third World leaders in Bucharest, the African trip was his first multinational tour of developing countries. It marked the turning point in the identification of Romania with the Third World. See Robert R. King, "Romania and the Third World," *Orbis* 21 (Winter 1978): 880.

183. *FBIS, DR, EE* (April 6, 1972), pp. H1–6. Ceausescu had met PLO leader Arafat on 5 April and reasserted Romania's solidarity with the "righteous struggle of the Palestinian people." Romanian Situation Report/13, *RFE* (April 13, 1972), pp. 4–5.

184. Bucharest Domestic Service, 1515 GMT, April 6, 1972, in *FBIS, DR, EE* (April 7, 1972), p. H4.

185. Bucharest Domestic Service, 0500 GMT, April 20, 1972, in *FBIS, DR, EE* (April 20, 1972), p. H9.

186. Romania had sought for several years to obtain status as a developing country, largely for economic reasons. To this end, it had applied in 1972 to join the UN Group of 77 and to obtain preferential treatment from the EEC. Following Ceausescu's 1972 African tour, the claim that Romania deserved developing status was made with increasing frequency, including in Ceausescu's report to the National Party Conference in July 1972.

187. Bucharest Agerpres, 0927 GMT, September 5, 1973, in *FBIS, DR, EE* (September 6, 1973), pp. H2–3.

188. Romanian Situation Report/40, *RFE* (October 11, 1973), p. 1.

189. Bucharest Domestic Service, 1600 GMT, October 8, 1973, in *FBIS, DR, EE* (October 9, 1973), p. H2. Romania was the only Warsaw Pact member to stress in its initial official declaration Israel's right to exist.

190. Romanian Situation Report/41, *RFE* (October 18, 1973), p. 3.

191. Bucharest Domestic Service, 0500 GMT, October 12, 1973, in *FBIS, DR, EE* (October 15, 1973), p. H1.

192. Bucharest Agerpres, 1905 GMT, October 13, 1973, in *FBIS, DR, EE* (October 15, 1973), p. H2.

193. Kissinger worked until 1:30 AM Saturday organizing the U.S. airlift to Israel and was scheduled to attend a 10:30 AM emergency meeting on the airlift at the White House. See Kalb and Kalb, *Kissinger*, p. 539.

194. According to Heikal, "the position on the Syrian front was giving rise to grave anxiety. By the 13th, messages from Damascus calling on Egypt to draw off Israeli pressure took on a sharper note. . . . It was partly in response to these appeals that on the 14th the commanders of both the Second and Third Armies were ordered to mount offensive eastwards with their armour." Heikal, *The Road to Ramadan*, p. 225.

195. On 13 October at Tirgu Mures. *Scinteia*, October 14, 1973, p. 3, in *FBIS, DR, EE* (October 17, 1973), p. H5. Ceausescu mentioned the Middle East in only one other speech (of eight) made during the conflict—at Braila on 9 October. *Scinteia*, October 10, 1973, p. 4, in *FBIS, DR, EE* (October 12, 1973), p. H7.

196. Romanian Situation Report/41, *RFE* (October 18, 1973), p. 2.

197. *FBIS, DR, EE* (October 17, 1973), p. H1; (October 18), p. H2; (October 19), p. H1; and (October 23), p. H1.

198. *Scinteia*, October 20, 1973, in *FBIS, DR, EE* (October 23, 1973), pp. H3–4.

199. See note 128 in Chapter 2.

200. On 7 October (Harvest Day), Ceausescu spoke in Bucharest; on 9 October, in Galati and Braila; on 12 October, at the Ministry of Interior; on 13 October, at Tirgu Mures; on 17 October, at Buzau; on 18 October, at Ploesti; and on 21 October, at Lutita. The Galati, Braila, Tirgu Mures, Buzau, and Ploesti speeches dealt with regional development. See *FBIS, DR, EE* (October 12, 1973), pp. H5–11; (October 17), p. H6; (October 26), pp. H8–15; and (October 29), pp. H5–12. Only the Braila and Tirgu Mures speeches contained references to the Middle East.

201. "By Joint and Insistent Efforts toward a Just and Durable Peace," *Scinteia*, October 24, 1973, in *FBIS, DR, EE* (October 25, 1973), pp. H1–3.

202. *FBIS, DR, EE* (October 26, 1973), p. H2.

203. *FBIS, DR, EE* (November 6, 1973), pp. H1–4. Eban and his entourage spent nearly 24 hours in Brasov (see *FBIS, DR, EE* [November 7, 1973], p. H1), and some journalists speculated that he may have met secretly with high Soviet officials. A Romanian foreign ministry spokesperson said, however, that the visit to Brasov was "only a sightseeing trip." Romanian Situation Report/44, *RFE* (November 12, 1973), p. 4.

204. The text of the communiqué appeared in *Scinteia*, November 9, 1973, p. 5, in *FBIS, DR, EE* (November 21, 1973), p. H13.

205. Romanian Situation Report/44, *RFE* (November 12, 1973), p. 2.

206. The text of the declaration appeared in *FBIS, DR, EE* (December 6, 1973), pp. H5–6. Ceausescu's visit also led to the granting of most-favored-nation status and the establishment of mixed U.S.–Romanian industrial and commercial enterprises. See Romanian Situation Report/48, *RFE* (December 18, 1973), pp. 4–8.

207. See notes 82 and 83 in Chapter 3; note 105 in Chapter 4; and note 5 in Chapter 5.

208. See notes 122 and 123 in Chapter 2.

209. "Friendship Yesterday, Today and Tomorrow," *Vecernje Novosti*, November 29, 1973, in *FBIS, DR, EE* (December 5, 1973), p. H9.

210. The Soviets refused to sell Boumediene additional arms until he offered cash; see note 59.

211. See note 61.

212. See discussion of the convergence of the Romanian and Yugoslav views regarding Nixon's trip to China, note 140 in Chapter 5.

213. Telegram from Ceausescu to Mao, Bucharest Agerpres, 2015 GMT, September 1, 1973, in *FBIS, DR, EE* (September 4, 1973), p. H1.

214. Bucharest Agerpres, 1905 GMT, November 23, 1973, in *FBIS, DR, EE* (November 26, 1973), p. H2.

215. See above, note 3 in Chapter 5.

216. International Institute for Strategic Studies, *The Military Balance, 1975–76* (London: International Institute for Strategic Studies, 1975), p. 14.

7

Sadat's Visit to Jerusalem, November 1977

U.S., SOVIET, AND ROMANIAN
MIDDLE EAST INITIATIVES

In the late 1960s and early 1970s, the USSR wavered between two seemingly irreconcilable goals: détente with the United States and the consolidation of Soviet influence in the Middle East. Egypt was the political–military base from which the USSR sought to expand into both East Africa and the Arabian peninsula. In pursuit of this goal, the Soviets supplied Egypt and Syria substantial military aid, including specifically the arms to attack Israel in October 1973. But the recipients proved ungrateful,[1] and the Soviets' investment benefited them surprisingly little.[2] In the end, President Anwar el-Sadat concluded that he could come to terms with Israel by other means and through other channels.

The October 1973 war had a positive effect on the U.S. position in the Middle East. After the United States and Egypt reestablished diplomatic relations on 7 November 1973, Kissinger began concerted efforts to achieve a settlement between the Israelis and Egyptians. In December, the United States and USSR made one more joint attempt to negotiate a settlement in Geneva, but the conference broke up after two days over the issue of Palestinian participation. Thereafter, despite their complaints, Kissinger pursued his shuttle diplomacy with no more than perfunctory discussion with the Soviets. Although his diplomatic efforts did not achieve an overall Middle East settlement, they contributed to a basic reorientation of Egyptian foreign policy, and Sadat turned increasingly to the United States.[3]

As Soviet influence waned, Romania, which enjoyed excellent relations with the United States, played an increasingly important role in Middle East politics, including serving as a broker between Egypt and Israel. Describing itself as a "socialist developing country," Romania pursued a foreign policy combining neutrality and active diplomacy, based on two themes: First, small and medium countries (like Romania) should contribute to the solution of international problems; second, developing countries should demonstrate solidarity in their efforts to narrow the gap between themselves and the advanced industrial countries.

Romania maintained good relations with many of the Arab Middle East countries and the Palestine Liberation Organization (PLO), with several members of the Organization of Petroleum Exporting Countries (OPEC), and with the United States and Israel. Leaders of these countries exchanged state visits, issued joint statements, signed economic agreements, and discussed ways to bring peace to the Middle East.[4]

On 26 June 1974, Sadat revealed that the Egyptians had not received any arms from the Soviets since the end of the October war and that the Soviets were upset over Egypt's decision to diversify its arms sources.[5] Immediately afterward, he went off to visit Ceausescu (27–30 June 1974). Their joint communiqué called for an equitable political solution in the Middle East conflict and contained the pledge to maintain permanent contacts and to consult bilaterally whenever possible.[6] That this development exacerbated Soviet–Romanian tensions was indicated by Ceausescu's failure to attend the annual July meeting of communist party secretaries in the Crimea.[7]

Assad visited Yugoslavia in August and Bucharest at the beginning of September 1974. Syria and Romania signed economic accords on the exploitation and use of natural gas and oil and on the construction of the Banyas refinery.[8] Foreign Minister Gheorghe Macovescu's arrival in Israel on 9 September for four days of talks suggests that he may have briefed the Israelis on what the Syrians had said about Middle East problems.

Kissinger visited Bucharest on 3 November, before going on to Yugoslavia. The exchange of speeches at dinner that night reflected the depth of USA–Romanian relations. Ceausescu referred to Kissinger's visit as a "new moment in the expansion of cooperation between our countries."[9] Kissinger responded: "I had the privilege to visit Romania five years ago, together with my President. I had then one of the most important talks I remember to have ever had while accompanying the President, talks . . . *even going beyond the framework of our bilateral talks*" (emphasis added).[10] In 1974, as in 1969, top U.S. officials had discussed Middle East policy with the Romanian leaders.

Soviet–Romanian relations remained tense. Ceausescu's foreign policy report to the Eleventh Romanian Communist Party Congress in November indicated that although Romania wanted to maintain correct relations with the USSR, it would not concede basic issues. He said that Romania (1) wanted to develop military relations not only with all socialist states (that is, including Yugoslavia and the PRC) but with other friendly (that is, Third World and capitalist) states and (2) remained committed to national control of its own military assets.[11]

STRAINS ON SOVIET–ROMANIAN RELATIONS

In April 1975, Ceausescu toured Asia, returning via Jordan and Tunisia, where economic cooperation and probably the political situation were discussed.[12] Several days later, he paid a surprise visit to Egypt and Syria, where he also met with Arafat. Joint Romanian communiqués with Egypt and Syria called for "all interested parties, including the PLO,"[13] to attend the Geneva peace conference. By implication, Romania would also attend. The Soviets demolished the Romanian efforts by rejecting an enlarged list of participants.[14]

Undeterred, the Romanians began a new round of diplomatic activity. Yigal Allon, Israeli deputy prime minister and foreign minister, visited Romania from 27 May to 1 June 1975 to discuss bilateral relations and Middle East matters.[15] Then, while Ceausescu was in the Western Hemisphere on a previously scheduled official visit to Brazil and Mexico, Bucharest Domestic Service announced on 9 June that he would visit President Ford in Washington.[16] The United States and Romania had agreed in April to grant each other most-favored-nation status, and on 11 June, Ceausescu discussed bilateral economic relations and Middle East diplomatic efforts with Ford and Kissinger.[17]

On the same day, Radio Bucharest announced that Romanian Foreign Minister Macovescu would visit Egypt on 17–19 June.[18] A joint Romanian–Egyptian communiqué at the end of the visit noted

> with satisfaction that the meetings and understandings between Presidents Ceausescu and Sadat, in 1972, 1974 and 1975, have led to the steadily ascending course of the relations of friendship and collaboration between the two countries.[19]

It stated also that bilateral economic relations were progressing well and that Middle East political issues had been discussed.

The close political relationship between Romania and the United States continued. President Ford visited Romania on 2–3 August, on a trip that also included the FRG, Poland, and Yugoslavia, and signed the USA–Romanian trade agreement granting most-favored-nation status.[20] Ford may have been referring to Romania's independence of the USSR and its activities in the Middle East when he said: "We realize the importance of close relations with a country that asserts itself with such independence and vigor."[21]

Meanwhile, Kissinger had been actively engaged in shuttle diplomacy in the Middle East, and on 1 September 1975 he announced in Jerusalem that Israel and Egypt has reached an accord on the Sinai. Israel agreed to withdraw from some occupied territory in the Sinai in return for modest Egyptian political concessions and pledges of major U.S. support.[22]

The USSR criticized the agreement[23] but never publicly attacked Sadat. He openly criticized the USSR.[24] While the rest of the Warsaw Pact countries supported the Soviet position (to varying degrees),[25] the Romanians once again exhibited a fundamental deviation, backing the United States and Egypt.[26]

Romania's stand did not seem to undermine relations with the other Middle East states, although it obviously aggravated tension with the USSR. Ceausescu attempted to pacify the Soviets in a speech to the Romanian Grand National Assembly on 18 December by reiterating Romania's obligations to the Warsaw Pact. But he still refused to modify his position.

> As a member of the Warsaw Pact and considering the fact that international circumstances persist in being complicated, Romania is constantly concerning itself with strengthening the combat capacity of its national army that is ready to always do its duty and to act in cooperation with the armies of the other Warsaw Pact states in fulfilling the obligations it has assumed.
>
> At the same time, we maintain and continue to develop relations of friendship and cooperation with the armies of all socialist countries *and with armies of other friendly states that speak out for a policy of independent development, for the respect of each nation's right to independently decide its destiny* [emphasis added].[27]

Romania again became active in Middle East diplomacy as 1976 began. On 27 December, Deputy Foreign Minister Cornel Pacoste arrived in Israel for a five-day visit. On 2 January, Hani Hassan, Arafat's political adviser, met with Ceausescu in Bucharest to discuss a political solution to the Middle East conflict.[28] Between 8 and 18 January, Romanian party secretary Stefan Andrei held talks with leaders in Syria, Egypt, Jordan, and Libya, and with Arafat.[29]

The USSR suffered a significant symbolic and practical setback in the Middle East on 16 March 1976, when Egypt unilaterally abrogated its treaty of friendship and cooperation. Just days earlier, at the Twenty-fifth CPSU Congress (24 February–5 March), Brezhnev had praised the treaty as a model for Soviet–Arab relations. Its abrogation meant the closure of Alexandria port facilities to the Soviet fleet.

TASS characterized the Egyptian act as "good news for the enemies of the Arab east."[30] Sadat, it said, "presented a disturbed picture of . . . Soviet–Egyptian relations."[31] The Warsaw Pact allies supported the Soviet stand to varying degrees,[32] except for Romania, which reported the news factually (quoting from the Soviet and Egyptian news agencies, TASS and MENA) but avoided comment.[33]

Romania's failure to criticize Egypt was the least of its deviations from the Soviet stand. A month later (12–16 April 1976), Egyptian Minister of War Muhammad al-Jamasi, on an official visit to Bucharest, met with Ceausescu and Romanian Defense Minister Ion Ionita. Western news agencies reported from Cairo that on 16 April Jamasi described his visit as opening up new opportunities for cooperation in the production of military equipment.[34]

Public expression of the smoldering tension between the USSR and Romania emerged with Romania's challenge of the Soviet concept of proletarian internationalism, which it countered with the Romanian ideological concept of *nation*.[35] According to Ceausescu, the historical mission of the nation does not end with the achievement of socialism, as the Soviets contended. Rather, the proletariat, after becoming the dominant class in society, also assumes the responsibility for the national and social liberation of other peoples. In a major speech to the Romanian Trade Union Congress on 26 April, Ceausescu said, without specifically naming the USSR:

> Invoking the Marxist–Leninist theory and proletarian internationalism, some philosophers and theoreticians are trying to demonstrate that the nation has ended its historical mission and that it no longer has any future under socialism. I cannot refrain from observing the obvious, namely that such reasoning is absolutely erroneous. Strengthening proletarian internationalism and international solidarity depends on the strength of the working class in each country and on the authority and confidence which it and its revolutionary party enjoy among the ranks of their own people; it does not depend on ignoring and sacrificing national interests in the name of certain theses and principles which are flagrantly at variance with the objective requirements of life and with historical development itself.[36]

The Soviet–Romanian dispute climaxed when the Romanians, apparently in response to Soviet mobilization along their common border (17–20 May), called up reservists and mobilized the Patriotic Guards.[37] On 19 May, Gheorghe Badrus, the Romanian ambassador to Moscow, met with K. Katushev, CPSU secretary in charge of relations with the ruling communist parties.[38] The crisis was apparently resolved the following week, when Aleksey Yepishev, chief of the Main Political Administration, Ministry of the Armed Forces, and then Katushev[39] went to Bucharest to confer with Ceausescu.

Ceausescu, in a major address to the Congress of Political Education and Socialist Culture, indicated that the crisis had passed but again reiterated the Romanian position on pact obligations:

> The Socialist Republic of Romania has no territorial or other problems with the Soviet Union or with the other neighboring socialist countries.
>
> As a member of the Warsaw Pact, Romania is consistently concerned with strengthening the combat capabilities of its national army. It is cooperating with the armies of the other member states and is prepared to always fulfill the obligations assumed.
>
> At the same time, we are consistently developing our cooperation with the armies of all socialist countries and with the armies of other friendly countries, which are in favor of free and independent development for each nation.[40]

A few days later, Minister of Defense Ionita reaffirmed the army's support of Romanian party policy and determination to defend Romania against *any* aggression:

> All our army's activities are marked by unflinching faith in the party and by the determination to unabatedly implement its policy. . . . The Romanian Army

will never stage a war of aggression against anyone. But any aggression against our country will meet with the armed resistance of the entire Romanian nation.[41]

In June and July, the Romanians exchanged a number of political and military visits. A Yugoslav military delegation led by Colonel General Dane Petkovski met in Bucharest with Colonel General Ionita on 9 June and with Ceausescu on 11 June. "During the talks, the sides broached aspects of the current international situation."[42] French Foreign Minister Jean Sauvagnargues visited Bucharest on 9–11 June;[43] the Romanian defense minister went to Britain;[44] and Stefan Andrei, a Romanian party secretary, met with Ford and Kissinger in Washington.[45]

Soviet–Syrian relations began to deteriorate in 1976 as a result of Syria's intervention in Lebanon. The USSR issued a public warning to Syria, as well as to the United States and France.[46] Almost simultaneously, Romania and Yugoslavia took a pro-Syrian position.[47] Assad visited Tito on 25–26 June and Ceausescu on 26–28 June. The joint Romanian–Syrian communiqué of 28 June said in reference to the resolution of the Lebanese situation that the Romanians and Syrians "hope that the Arab League initiative will help achieve this purpose, through cooperation with Syria, by restoring peace in Lebanon in an effective manner."[48] Syrian Prime Minister Khleifawi visited Bucharest in December to negotiate new political and economic agreements, and Assad went in February for talks with Ceausescu.[49]

Although the Soviets had replenished Syrian arms inventories on a large scale following the October 1973 war,[50] Assad cut the number of Soviet military personnel from 3,500 in 1973 to 1,800 at the beginning of 1977 and began to buy helicopters and antitank missiles from France.[51]

By the end of 1976, Soviet influence in the Middle East—despite the massive commitment of military assets—exhibited a significant decline, while Kissinger's step-by-step diplomatic efforts had increased U.S. influence in the region. More important in terms of this analysis, Soviet frustrations in the Middle East seemed to spill over into the Warsaw Pact, contributing to further tension among the member states. Romania's expanded military contacts with all socialist states (Yugoslavia and China) had now been broadened to include all friendly states (the United States, the United Kingdom, France, Italy, the FRG, Third World states, and Arab states).

THE 1 OCTOBER COMMUNIQUÉ: ITS CREATION AND COLLAPSE

The Carter administration, inaugurated in January 1977, rejected the step-by-step diplomacy of the Nixon–Ford–Kissinger era in favor of reconvening the Geneva peace conference under joint USA–USSR sponsorship. Concomitantly, the idea that the PLO might be an appropriate participant in negotiations that would lead to the creation of a Palestinian homeland received some high-level consideration.[52] In mid-February, Cyrus Vance, the new U.S. secretary of state, visited the Middle East.[53]

Mikhail Sytenko, head of the Middle East department of the Soviet foreign ministry, toured the Middle East at the same time as Vance. A 19 February *Pravda* editorial, thought to represent the sensitivities of the Soviet leadership, indicated that the Soviet–Egyptian talks had not gone well. An article that accompanied the editorial reviewed the support that the Soviets had given the Egyptians in the 1967 and 1973 wars against Israel and criticized Sadat's ingratitude. Pointing out that the USSR had "responded to a pressing appeal of the Egyptian leadership and assumed the defense of Egyptian airspace,"[54] the review concluded:

> Today A. as-Sadat "does not remember" all this. . . .
> What has changed since? There has been a change in the political line of the Egyptian leadership. It is in pursuit of this new line that one anti-Soviet lie is piled on top of another. In his unfriendly attitude to the Soviet Union A. as-Sadat goes far beyond the limits of elementary propriety and norms generally accepted in relations among states.[55]

President Carter, at a 10 March press conference, introduced a plan to reconvene the Geneva Conference to seek a comprehensive Middle East settlement.[56] On 16 March, he made the first public accommodation of Palestinian aspirations by an American president when he called the establishment of a homeland "for the Palestinian refugees who have suffered for many, many years"[57] a prerequisite for peace.

The Soviets, eager to participate in a Middle East settlement, immediately adopted a conciliatory position. In a speech to the Sixteenth Congress of Trade Unions on 21 March, Brezhnev called for a Geneva conference and proposed a step-by-step Israeli withdrawal from the Arab territories occupied since 1967, demilitarized zones on Israel's borders, and international pressure to curb the Middle East arms race.

Two points of the Brezhnev plan in particular signaled the new, conciliatory approach. First, Brezhnev said that "the inalienable rights of the Palestine Arab people should be ensured, including its right to self-determination, to the creation of its own state."[58] But he did not refer specifically to the PLO, a Soviet client. Second, softening on the issue of an imposed peace settlement, he said that "the drawing up of peace terms in all their details is primarily a matter for the conflicting sides themselves."[59]

The Soviets pressured Syria and the PLO to attend the proposed Geneva conference. Brezhnev met with Yasser Arafat on 7 April (their first public meeting)[60] and with Assad on 18–22 April to convince them to accept the Soviet

Middle East peace plan. The joint Soviet–Syrian communiqué announcing the agreement of the two states to cooperate in the search for a Middle East settlement indicated the improvement in their relations.[61]

Sadat, after discussing the peace plan with Carter in early April, seemed inclined to go along. At a 13 May press conference, with Ceausescu present, Sadat said: "Although there have been some coldness and some critical periods in our relations with the Soviet Union, we have never disagreed on how to solve the Middle East crisis."[62]

Egyptian Foreign Minister Ismail Fahmy went to Moscow in June with two major objectives: the resumption of Soviet arms deliveries and the rescheduling of Egypt's debt payments, estimated at $4.0 billion.[63] In return, the Soviets wanted an Egyptian pledge to allow the Soviets a direct voice in the settlement of a reconvened peace conference in Geneva.

Initial optimism notwithstanding, Egyptian–Soviet relations remained tense. On 24 June, the Egyptian Information Ministry announced that "no progress" had yet been made toward solving the outstanding problems with the USSR. It was also reported that Sadat was seriously concerned that Soviet and Cuban activities in Africa (particularly in Ethiopia, Libya, and Uganda) threatened Egypt and its closest ally, the Sudan.[64] On 16 July, Sadat told the central committee of the Arab Socialist Union that the USSR had cancelled all Soviet–Egyptian military contracts and demanded the restoration of the Soviet–Egyptian Friendship Treaty, which Egypt had abrogated in March 1976. He then accused the Soviets of delivering "two ultimatums": (1) that the Soviets would not be excluded from Middle East peace efforts and (2) that the Soviets would support Ethiopia against the Sudan.[65]

Egyptian–Soviet relations went from bad to worse. In early August, Sadat claimed that, during a recent Egyptian–Libyan clash, 12 helicopters from the Soviet carrier *Moskva* interfered with Egyptian radio communications.[66] On 17 August, Egypt (1) charged that the USSR had "deliberately delayed delivery and slowed down the shipment of goods" under their 1977 trade agreement and (2) suspended its commitments to the USSR "for the time being."[67]

The breakdown in relations with Egypt may have created further Soviet suspicions about U.S. intentions. Soviet leaders met with Arafat again at the end of August. TASS reported the talks and distributed an interview with Arafat in which he accused the United States of attempting to exclude the Palestinians from Geneva and of "striving to bar the Soviet Union from participation in the Middle East settlement."[68] The Soviets claimed to be confused as to U.S. intentions.[69]

Relations between the United States and USSR peaked on 1 October 1977, when Vance and Gromyko issued a joint statement calling for a specially convened and jointly chaired Geneva peace conference before the end of the year.[70] The statement envisaged a comprehensive Middle East settlement, to include such key issues as the withdrawal of Israeli armed forces from territories occupied in 1967, the resolution of the Palestinian question, and the guaranteed security of the border between Israel and the neighboring Arab states; it appealed to all parties in the conflict to consider each other's "legitimate rights and interests and to demonstrate mutual readiness to act accordingly."

Both sides compromised in issuing the joint statement. The United States agreed to joint sponsorship with the USSR despite the latter's declining influence in the region and accepted the idea of Palestinian rights; the USSR agreed to call for peaceful relations among the parties and did not mention the PLO.

Major issues remained to be resolved. The most difficult involved the Palestinians: Which Palestinians should attend the Geneva conference, what role should they play in the negotiations, and what should be negotiated? The USSR and the Arab countries supported the PLO as the representative for the Palestinians; Israel refused to accept either the PLO or the idea of a Palestinian homeland. In addition, the Arabs continued to insist that Israel should return all the land it occupied in 1967; Israel refused to return all of it. The Soviets sided with the Arabs on the return; the United States argued that Israel should return most of the land.

The United States began a significant diplomatic effort during October to placate the Israelis[71] and to convince all parties to attend the Geneva conference. The United States and Israel made some proposals that Arafat rejected on the ground that they neglected the Palestinian question as a whole.[72] Meanwhile, the Soviets were attempting to get the PLO to create a government-in-exile as a means of breaking the deadlock on the question of their representation at Geneva.

Although U.S. officials remained optimistic about the chances for a Geneva conference, other disconcerting signs began to develop. Sadat announced on 28 October that Egypt would unilaterally postpone its debt repayment to the USSR. Two days later (reminiscent of his behavior in June 1974 and of Jamasi's in April 1976), Sadat went to Bucharest to talk with Ceausescu, who was acting as a go-between for the Egyptians and Israelis.[73] Convinced by Ceausescu that Israeli Prime Minister Begin wanted peace,[74] Sadat decided to take the initiative to obtain a Middle East settlement.

On 6 November, the PLO launched a rocket attack against Israel from southern Lebanon (the first shelling of Israel since 26 September), killing two Israelis. Israel warned the Palestinians in southern Lebanon of a reprisal unless they withdrew some 15 miles behind the border area. Arafat refused, supported by Presidents Sarkis of Lebanon and Assad of Syria, who argued that the Palestinians should not withdraw until there were real prospects of a Geneva conference.[75]

In an apparent last-ditch effort to save the fragile Middle East diplomatic effort, Hussein, after speaking with Sadat, went to Syria to calm Assad. At the same time, Sadat tried to get Arafat to agree to the conference. Although this effort succeeded, the Israelis now balked at going to the conference and objected to Carter's support of a Palestinian homeland. Israel then (9 November) launched a retaliatory attack against two villages in southern Lebanon, killing 60 civilians.

On the same day, in a speech to the Egyptian parliament, Sadat called for Arab unity and an all-out drive to convene the Geneva conference. In the course of his address, Sadat praised the U.S. diplomatic effort and said that, if necessary, he would go to Jerusalem to get a settlement. Arafat was present in the parliament at the time.[76]

The next day, while the Israelis were again raiding Palestinian camps in southern Lebanon, Begin publicly welcomed Sadat's statement, appealed to the "citizens of Egypt" to join Israel in a pledge to have "no more wars," and invited Sadat to Jerusalem.[77] Begin's formal invitation was transmitted on 16 November through the American ambassador in Cairo. Sadat flew to Damascus to get Assad's support but failed. On 19 November 1977, Sadat went to Jerusalem.

Sadat's visit—blessed by the United States—created a crisis for the Soviets. The Egyptian leader's initiative threatened Soviet diplomacy in the Middle East, complicated USA–USSR relations, and exacerbated tension within the Warsaw Pact over the question of how best to achieve a Middle East settlement.

THE SOVIET RESPONSE
TO SADAT'S VISIT TO JERUSALEM

The extensive Soviet media coverage of Sadat's visit to Jerusalem reflected the Soviets' fears that the United States, Israel, and Egypt would work out a separate peace, that the Geneva conference would not be held, and that they (the Soviets) would be excluded from participation in an overall Middle East settlement.

Izvestiya's report on Sadat's address to the Egyptian parliament in which he offered to go to Jerusalem revealed the Soviet apprehension:

> Analyzing the Egyptian President's speech, political commentators draw attention to the fact that Egypt's position is somewhat at variance with the universal desire for a resumption of the work of the Geneva conference. In particular, it is being noted that As-Sadat is obviously striving to exaggerate the role of the American administration in a Near East settlement, letting it be known that the Egyptian leadership, as before, will orient itself mainly toward the United States in the solution of the Near East problem.[78]

On 13 November, *Izvestiya* charged Israel with relying on the support of "those figures in the United States who are known for their links with extremist circles in Israel."[79] According to the government organ, two motives underlay this conspiracy: first, to undermine the "cooperation between the USSR and the United States to achieve a comprehensive peace settlement in the Near East" and second, to "distract public attention from . . . the Israeli military's continuing occupation of Arab territories."[80] Over succeeding days, the Soviet media portrayed Israel as "deliberately building up tensions in southern Lebanon when the Geneva peace conference is in sight" and using U.S. guarantees to legitimize their expansion into southern Lebanon.[81] On 15 November, *Pravda* was still charging the Israelis and the "forces behind them" with trying to involve the Egyptians in separate negotiations.[82]

When it became known that Begin had invited Sadat to Jerusalem, the Soviets responded not with their own condemnation but with criticisms originating in the Arab world (a technique that they had used during the October 1973 war).[83] The Soviet media reported on 17 November that Egyptian Foreign Minister Fahmy had resigned in protest,[84] and *Pravda* cited a statement by the ruling Syrian Ba'ath party warning that a separate settlement would harm the Arab cause:

> It would be a serious mistake to go for a separate or bilateral solution . . . as this would have a pernicious effect on the future of the Arab liberation movement and would promote the implementation of the aims of imperialism and Zionism.[85]

On 18 November, TASS linked Sadat with the Israeli raids in Lebanon: "Characteristically, As-Sadat's overtures to Israel coincide with the escalation of Israeli aggressive actions against its neighboring state, Lebanon."[86]

The day Sadat arrived in Jerusalem (19 November), the Soviets themselves declared that Sadat was betraying the Arab cause and that Israel was planning an attack against Syria:

> Tel Aviv is well aware of the fact that the shortsighted policy of the Egyptian leadership has weakened the combat efficiency of the Egyptian Armed Forces. Taking advantage of this situation, the Begin government would like to conclude a separate deal with Egypt, to take it away from the joint front of states opposed to Israel's aggression and then strike the main blow against the Syrian Arab Republic.[87]

Krasnaya Zvezda implicated the United States as the supplier of military aid to Israel: "While carrying out brigandage in south Lebanon, Tel Aviv is at the same time continuing to build up its military potential with U.S. assistance at an accelerated pace."[88]

On 21 November, when Sadat left Israel, *Pravda* condemned the separate peace talks and the continued occupation of Arab land:

> A bilateral communiqué on the results of the Egyptian–Israeli meeting has been published in Jerusalem. It is completely silent on the problem of resuming the work of the Geneva peace conference on the Near East, makes no mention of the Palestine Liberation Organization and reduces everything to the continua-

tion of bilateral contacts—in other words, separate talks between Israel and Egypt while the occupation of the Arab territories continues.[89]

The Soviet press continued to portray Sadat's policy as a "threat to Arab unity"[90] and concluded that "the Israeli–Egyptian talks have not changed—and could not change—the situation in the Near East for the better."[91]

The Soviets attempted to capitalize on opposition to Sadat's initiative, in the hope of regaining some of their influence in the Middle East. To this end, they set themselves up as the protectors of the PLO and Syria. On 24 November, *Pravda* reported the expulsion from Cairo of Jamal al-Sawrani, the PLO representative, implying that Egypt was a traitor to the Arab cause.[92] On the same day, PLO representative Faruq Qaddumi met with Andrey Gromyko in Moscow. A subsequent PLO communiqué called for "continuous consultations" with the USSR and condemned "imperialist and Zionist plots" to divide Arab countries fighting against Israel.[93] Gromyko's 29 November meeting with Syrian Foreign Minister Khaddam indicated a new closeness in Soviet–Syrian relations.[94]

On 26 November, Sadat invited all concerned parties to send representatives to Cairo to prepare for a Geneva conference. Israel immediately accepted; the PLO and Syria refused. TASS reported that in the speech containing the invitation Sadat had spoken of the Palestinians' right to establish their own state but had not specifically mentioned the PLO.[95] TASS claimed also that the United States was behind Sadat's visit to Jerusalem.[96] On 27 November, the Soviet news agency quoted Sadat as saying in a television interview with the National Broadcasting Company (NBC) that the Cairo meeting would be held even if Israel alone came. TASS interpreted Sadat's statement as an indication that he sought a separate peace: "Thus as-Sadat has admitted that he strives to conclude an agreement with Israel outside the framework of the Geneva conference and attaches to it only the role of a cover for the separate Egyptian–Israeli talks."[97]

As during the 1973 war, Moscow was apparently trying to protect both its remaining Arab ties and, at the same time, the détente with the United States.[98] To this end, although the Soviets refused to go to Cairo, they reiterated their willingness to go to Geneva. The day before the United States accepted Sadat's invitation to Cairo, Dobrynin privately told Vance that the USSR would refuse it. The Soviet ambassador stressed, however, that, although the Soviets disapproved of Sadat's initiative, they still strongly supported a Geneva conference.[99] A Soviet–Syrian communiqué of 30 November made the Soviet position public:

> The mutual determination of the Soviet Union and Syria to strive to achieve a comprehensive Middle East settlement in circumstances which reject the possibility of separate deals, to which some Arab leaders continue to adhere. . . . If it should happen that the Geneva conference should be foiled, those who set their hands to this will bear a severe responsibility.[100]

Middle East political relations suffered another blow when a 2–5 December summit meeting in Libya of hard-line Arab countries denounced the

Egyptian–Israeli talks. The participants signed a mutual defense treaty, announced a boycott of Egyptian companies dealing with Israel, and offered economic, political, and military assistance to Syria.[101] Egypt responded by severing diplomatic relations with Syria, Libya, Algeria, Yemen, and Iraq. Then, to retaliate against the USSR for backing the hard-line Arabs at Tripoli, Egypt closed all Soviet cultural centers in Cairo, Alexandria, and Port Said.[102]

Soviet–American relations, mirroring Middle East events, took a turn for the worse. The Soviet media continued to attack the United States, suggesting again that it had conceived and directed Sadat's trip to Israel and the separate Cairo conference. *Pravda* wrote: "It is clear that the Soviet Union could not agree to participate in such unseemly deeds."[103] A TASS commentary accused Sadat of selling out the interests of the PLO and of acting in collusion with Israel and the United States.[104]

American leaders openly criticized Soviet officials for their failure to discourage or at least to cool the Arab countries' rejection of Sadat's proposal for a conference in Cairo. One U.S. official was quoted as saying on 6 December: "The United States hoped to keep the Syrians, at least, away from the 'rejectionist' conference in Libya this past week and instead of that, the Soviets urged them on."[105] On the same day, Vance criticized the USSR, noting that recent Soviet comments "have not been helpful to the cause of peace" and that the Soviets' diplomatic behavior had "raised questions about what their ultimate objectives are" in the region.[106] Vance indicated that the Carter administration was no longer committed to holding a Geneva conference, but that it was receptive to any approach that produced results.

From this point onward—although negotiations have continued with the purpose of achieving an overall peace settlement in the Middle East—the concept of a Geneva conference was dead, and relations between the United States and the USSR never again reached the high point of the USA–USSR joint statement of 1 October 1977.

We shall now examine the responses of the other Warsaw Pact members to these events in an attempt to determine how the events affected relations between the USSR and its allies.

THE ORTHODOX RESPONSE:
BULGARIA, CZECHOSLOVAKIA, AND THE GDR

Bulgaria, Czechoslovakia, and East Germany generally followed the Soviet line, as they had done in the Middle East crises of 1967 and 1973. A minor difference that became apparent in 1973 appeared to develop further in 1977: The Czechoslovak media tended to overstate the issues and the East German to ignore them.

The press of all three countries described the 1 October USA–USSR joint statement on the Middle East a step in the right direction, stressed the USSR's role, and expressed concern about what they called the antidétente forces in the

United States which sought to undermine the effort. Support for a Geneva peace conference sponsored by the USSR as well as the United States underlay the media commentaries. *Rabotnichesko Delo* wrote:

> The joint Soviet–U.S. declaration on the Middle East confirms the correct approach of Soviet foreign policy to the complicated conflict in the Middle East. Since the very first day Israel and the pro-Zionist circles in the United States have carried on a vast campaign against this declaration. The campaign is headed by notorious anti-Communists and opponents of the Soviet peace policy, such as Senator Henry Jackson and trade union boss George Meany.[107]

Official Bulgarian, Czechoslovak, and East German support of a cochaired Geneva conference was articulated by the foreign ministers of those countries at the UN General Assembly.[108] The foreign ministers also called for the participation of the PLO in the conference. A joint Czechoslovak–East German communiqué issued by Gustav Husak and Erich Honecker after talks in Berlin on 5 October affirmed that their countries "supported the proposals of the USSR for the resumption of the Geneva Middle East conference with the PLO participating on a basis of equality from the start."[109]

When the fragile Middle East diplomacy unravelled in late 1977, leading Sadat to offer on 9 November to go to Jerusalem, the orthodox states mirrored the content and form of the Soviet response. Their media criticized Sadat, questioned Israel's motives, and ultimately implicated the United States. Before the visit, they tended to cite Arab criticisms; during the visit they injected their own commentary; and after the visit they increasingly employed ideological rhetoric.

The Bulgarian press accused Israel of wanting "to preserve the present situation—a greater Israel with expanded boundaries,"[110] warned of the visit's possible consequences, and blamed U.S. Zionists. While Sadat was in Jerusalem, *Narodna Armiya* cautioned that "The decision of Anwar Sadat to have direct talks with Tel Aviv . . . is a step in the wrong direction which can have a dangerous post-effect on a national and all-Arab scale."[111] The next day, the press implicated the United States:

> This step of the Egyptian president to a great extent justifies the hopes of the U.S. government, which is conducting an insincere and hypocritical pro-Israeli policy dictated by the interests of the powerful Zionist lobby in the United States.[112]

The Bulgarian line hardened after Sadat returned to Egypt. The party organ attributed the visit to "Israeli–American schemes."[113]

Although Stefan Todorov, the Bulgarian delegate to the UN, continued to urge that the Geneva conference be held, he saw the Sadat–Begin meeting as undermining the chances of its success:

Unfortunately, certain unilateral and separate initiatives for partial settling . . .
not only hamper the integral settling of the Middle East crisis but also undermine the possibilities for success of the Geneva peace conference on the Middle
East.[114]

The Czechoslovaks, chastened by the Warsaw Pact invasion of their country
in 1968 and Husak's replacement of Dubcek the following year, outdid the Soviets and Bulgarians in their invective. Radio Prague claimed on 17 November
that Sadat's policy was part of a "conspiracy between Zionism and Arab reaction" and on 18 November that his conduct was "vain and perfidious."
Bratislava *Pravda* commented that "the Arab world regards the meeting in Jerusalem as a knife in the back of its just struggle."[115]

Czechoslovak television criticized Carter's part in the affair and concluded
that Sadat was "an Arab statesman in the hands of the U.S."[116] After Sadat
returned to Egypt, *Rude Pravo* (1) compared his going to Jerusalem to Chamberlain's going to Munich just before World War II and (2) reiterated Czechoslovak
support for a Geneva conference as the only formula for a settlement.[117]

Although the SED party officially supported the USSR, the East German
media (as in 1973, 1975, and 1976) tended to ignore the Middle East. The SED
politburo, however, reported to the seventh session of the central committee on
24 November:

> The competent body to review and decide these issues is the general Middle East
> peace conference. We support the Soviet Union's attitude which is aimed at
> smoothing the way, by means of its initiatives, to a resumption of the Geneva
> Middle East conference. The GDR backs the demand by the only legitimate
> representative of the Arab people of Palestine, the PLO, that it should, in ac-
> cordance with the UN resolutions, have an equal right to participate in this
> conference.[118]

The Orthodox states mirrored the Soviet position for salvaging the Geneva
conference with the Soviets cochairing. After Sadat's call for a Cairo conference
and the subsequent Arab hard-liner summit meeting in Tripoli, the Bulgarian
and Czechoslovak media held the United States and Israel responsible for the
Egyptian attempt to achieve a separate peace that would split the Arab national
movement. *Rabotnichesko Delo* predicted a separate settlement:

> Anwar As-Sadat . . . in addition to all other things proceeded along the line of
> conspiracy and capitulation before the Israeli invaders and American imperial-
> ism. A split was introduced into Arab unity. It was precisely this split that the
> United States and Israel wanted to achieve. Their goal is to disunite the
> frontline countries. . . . A perfidious, Zionist-imperialist conspiracy is being im-
> plemented at this moment with the direct participation of an Arab country. The
> political foundation of this conspiracy is an anti-Soviet one.[119]

Rude Pravo claimed that the settlement would impose an unjust peace:

> It is obvious that [the Cairo meeting] is to take place instead of the Geneva conference and to serve as a cloak for the continuation of the separate Israeli–Egyptian talks. . . . The Middle East which is now at a dangerous crossroads needs peace but not at all a separate, superimposed, unjust peace.[120]

The East German media ignored the matter.

When prospects for a Geneva conference were finally dashed with Sadat's closing of pact member cultural centers in Egypt on 7 December, the orthodox states officially condemned this action, holding the Egyptian government alone responsible.[121]

HUNGARY PORTRAYS
THE UNITED STATES SYMPATHETICALLY

Although the Hungarian media generally supported the 1 October 1977 communiqué, they exhibited a number of significant deviations from the orthodox line. First, they did not refer specifically to the USSR's efforts to achieve a Middle East settlement, nor did they refer to what the orthodox Eastern European media had called the antidétente elements in the United States. Rather, the Hungarian press noted sympathetically the change in U.S. policy and the problems that the U.S. government would be likely to have with its intransigent client, Israel:

> Washington has intimated its willingness to seek a solution to the Palestinian problem which would recognize the equal rights of the Palestinian people. However, . . . it seems obvious that Washington has the responsibility of persuading its ally [Israel] to face up to reality.[122]

The Hungarian commentaries on Sadat's Jerusalem visit also evidenced careful reporting and moderation. On 17 November, Radio Budapest broadcast an interview with Hamid Huad, editor of the leading Cairo daily *Al Ahram*, who was to accompany Sadat to Israel. The Hungarian populace was told that the Syrian president had objected to Sadat's visit, "probably because he was not informed beforehand,"[123] and that Nicolae Ceausescu had acted as an intermediary between Egypt and Israel. Finally, on 22 November *Magyar Hirlap* guardedly suggested that, although Sadat had abandoned Arab unity, it did not accuse him of betraying the Arab cause:

> By his present visit, As-Sadat has abandoned the Arab countries' coordinated triple principle, according to which they do not negotiate with Israel, do not recognize it and do not make peace with it as long as it holds Arab territories under its occupation.

Just as before the trip, the Egyptian president declared on several occasions also during his visit that his country does not want a separate peace with Israel. For the time being, there are no indications of preparations for such a separate agreement. However, the negotiations—perhaps by a visit by Begin to Cairo and the inclusion of President Carter—will continue. Therefore, speculations regarding a separate peace are premature, but by no means unfounded.[124]

While the orthodox states were criticizing the United States for its "manipulative policy of conspiracy and collusion," Budapest domestic service commented on 27 November that as a result of the visit "the U.S. will no longer play a key role in a Middle East settlement" and that "an outside mediator, or more precisely mediators, is not essential to negotiations."[125] Three days later, Radio Budapest quoted President Carter to the effect that the United States was not at that time seeking a separate peace between Egypt and Israel:

> Carter affirmed that, like Egypt and Israel, the U.S. government does not yet—
> the stress is on the word yet—aim at a separate agreement because it would
> exclude the other partners concerned with the settlement and would lessen the
> possibility of a comprehensive solution.[126]

In early December, while their hard-line Warsaw Pact allies were condemning Sadat's "capitulation before the . . . Zionist-imperialist conspiracy."[127] the Hungarians took a somewhat less critical stand. One commentator, for example, questioned what the effect of the U.S. position would be on détente:

> I do not know who is or was doing what in Washington in the interests of the
> series of actions by As-Sadat, but I am sincerely afraid that the well concealed—
> or perhaps not so well concealed—intention affects the whole order of
> Soviet–U.S. relations and East–West détente.[128]

After Vance criticized the USSR and indicated that the United States was no longer committed to a Geneva conference, the Hungarian radio reported only that "the U.S. Government has backed down from its former stand, or rather pledge, that the road to a lasting settlement in the Middle East leads through Geneva."[129]

After the Egyptians closed down their cultural offices in Cairo, the Hungarians scored the Egyptian move as unwarranted[130] but noted the fact that the United States had disagreed with the expulsion and expressed concern to the Egyptians:

> There is agreement in every part of the world that As-Sadat's Jerusalem trip
> served the Mediterranean policy of the United States. However, now one hears
> that the United States did not react gladly to As-Sadat's diplomatic and consu-
> late gambits.[131]

Over the following weeks the Hungarian media continued to portray the United States positively, focusing on the U.S. decision to return the Crown of St. Stephen to Hungary. While the orthodox states were arguing that the United States was directing a separate peace, the Hungarian media reported that Carter was puzzled by the Egyptian–Israeli dialogue and was continually being surprised by Middle East developments. Hence, they concluded, the United States could not be conspiratorially directing Egypt and Israel.[132]

In summary, the Hungarians played down the role of the USSR, refrained from declaring Sadat a traitor, and portrayed the United States more favorably than did the Soviets, Bulgarians, Czechoslovaks, and East Germans. Hungary's positions during the 1977 Middle East events were thus quite consistent with its moderation during the 1967 and 1973 wars and with its long-term national commitment to détente.

POLAND PURSUES DÉTENTE

Poland continued to evidence a restraint that distinguished it from the more orthodox Warsaw Pact members. For Poland, the pursuit of détente appeared to take precedence over the support of Soviet Middle East policy. The national (independent of the USSR) orientation of Polish domestic and foreign politics— including Polish alignment with Romanian (and Yugoslav) positions—just becoming apparent in 1972 at the time of Nixon's trip to China and during the October 1973 Middle East war in 1977 assumed the form of an overriding commitment to the expected economic benefits of ties with the West.

Poland's rapprochement with the United States and Western Europe had produced an increase in trade from $5.7 billion in 1973 to $10.4 billion in 1976.[133] At the same time, Poland's hard currency debt jumped from $770 million in 1970 to $12.8 billion by the end of 1977.[134] Growing debt service obligations, coupled with rising consumer expectations that led to riots in Warsaw and Lodz in June 1976 (reminiscent of those in December 1970),[135] forced PUWP leaders to seek financial support from Moscow. Although the USSR provided $1.326 billion in aid, [136] Poland's Western political and economic orientation remained unchanged.

Polish Foreign Minister Emil Wojtaszek, stressing Poland's commitment to détente in a speech to the UN General Assembly on 29 September, described his country's Middle East position as follows: "We are concerned about the lack of progress in solving the Middle East conflict. . . . We are for a rapid convocation of the Geneva conference on the Middle East with the participation of the PLO."[137] Meeting with Soviet Foreign Minister Gromyko and U.S. Secretary of State Vance at the United Nations the following day, Wojtaszek reiterated Poland's interest in détente.[138]

The Polish press coverage of the 1 October joint USA–USSR statement on the Middle East stressed the importance of détente and the need for the two superpowers to work together for its success but virtually ignored the Middle East situation. *Polityka* wrote:

> The recent talks that Andrey Gromyko, minister of foreign affairs of the USSR, had with the U.S. leaders and the communiqué on these talks bear witness to the fact that the two powers, while not concealing the contradictions between them, are for the continuation of the policy of détente.
>
> What is worth stressing is not only the loyalty to this aim, but also the militancy that [Poland's] political leadership displays in strengthening the political and economic foundations of détente. The state of the bilateral relations between Poland and the capitalist countries is also a tangible sign of this militancy.[139]

Similarly, in a number of widespread public appearances in early October, PUWP Secretary Edward Gierek called for détente as a means of furthering Polish economic policy but ignored it as a means of achieving peace in the Middle East.[140]

Several weeks later, after Sadat had announced his intention to go to Jerusalem, *Zycie Warszawy* characterized the Egyptian leader's initiative as "one of the most spectacular and most risky gambles made in the long history of the Middle East conflict," adding that the idea had received a "mixed reception" in the Arab world.[141] The same day, an article in *Trybuna Ludu* dealing with Polish foreign policy called for détente but did not specifically mention the Middle East.[142]

On 21 November, when Sadat was in Jerusalem, Gierek, in presenting the new state budget to the Council of Ministers, again noted the relationship between détente and Poland's economy, but avoided any reference to the Middle East.[143] That same day, FRG Chancellor Helmut Schmidt arrived in Poland on a state visit. Neither the press commentaries during Schmidt's visit nor the final communiqué (which dealt at length with the desirability of increasing trade between the two states and extending economic and political détente to the military sector) referred to the Middle East.

A youth newspaper offered the most critical Polish press analysis of Sadat, accusing him of flaunting an anticommunist, anti-Soviet policy. But in contrast to the orthodox media, which claimed that the United States had staged the Sadat–Begin exchange, *Sztandar Mlodych* described the visit as an Egyptian initiative that had surprised the entire world:

> Faced with a difficult internal situation and a lack of successes in the political sphere, As-Sadat decided on a spectacular and also dangerous step: a trip to Israel. This decision was a surprise for the whole world and, for the Arabs, also a source of bitter disillusionment. . . . The visit of Egypt's president to Israel not only did not clarify the situation in the Middle East, but still further complicated it.[144]

Trybuna Ludu, however, that same day sustained the impression of Poland's neutrality. After citing what had been said in the Knesset during Sadat's visit, and in the Egyptian–Israeli communiqué, the article noted only that "it will take at least several days before the results of President Sadat's visit to Israel can be discerned."[145]

The fairly extensive press coverage of Gierek's official visit to Italy and the Vatican (28 November–1 December) gave no indication that Middle East problems had been discussed;[146] the Polish–Italian joint communiqué of 29 November on mutual relations and international problems indicated, however, that the two countries continued to support the idea of peace negotiations at a Geneva conference:

> The two sides exchanged views on the situation in the Middle East and agreed that there is an urgent need to establish as soon as possible a just, lasting and total peace in that region on the basis of Security Council Resolutions 242 and 338. In this connection they emphasized the necessity for prompt negotiations concerning all aspects of the conflict with the participation of all sides involved and expressed their desire for the Geneva conference to resume its work as soon as possible.[147]

On 3 December, *Polityka* presented what was for a Warsaw Pact country an impartial and balanced analysis of the Middle East situation. Following the Romanian style, *Polityka* indicated what had been said about Sadat's trip by both TASS and U.S. news sources and how the various Arab countries had reacted to the visit. In contrast to the media of the orthodox states, *Polityka* did not accuse Sadat of conspiracy and appeasement, but instead recognized his courage and achievement:

> The President of Egypt has thrown onto the Middle East chessboard an enormous, courageous and risky challenge. It does not seem, however, that even the most spectacular gesture can unlock the deep impasse. Too many mutual resentments have gathered together and too many conflicting interests grind against one another. Despite this, As-Sadat has shaken the Middle East and it is difficult to foresee the further repercussions. It is certain, however, that nothing will ever be the same since the Jerusalem meeting.[148]

Only after Egypt closed Polish cultural centers on 8 December did Poland's political position harden, and then only temporarily. A Warsaw radio commentator on 11 December quoted at length from *Pravda*, which claimed that the United States and Egypt were attempting to eliminate the USSR from the Middle East.[149] Criticism of the United States stopped almost immediately afterward as the Polish media began to focus on the United States in anticipation of President Carter's visit to Poland on 31 December. And on 16 December, Foreign Minister Wojtaszek, addressing the Sejm, discussed the Middle East impartially, ignored the U.S. role, and extended the olive branch to Egypt.[150]

In summary, Poland reacted much more moderately than the orthodox Warsaw Pact states to developments involving the Middle East. The Polish media never directly criticized the United States. The Polish leadership appeared willing if not eager to allow the pursuit of the economic benefits of détente to take precedence over the support of Soviet Middle East policy.

CEAUSESCU'S MEDIATION
RUNS COUNTER TO SOVIET INTERESTS

Romania continued to play the role of intermediary in the Middle East. Ceausescu favored "the resumption of the Geneva conference, in which all concerned countries should participate with equal rights, including the PLO."[151] In relations with Egypt, the Romanians had greater influence than the Soviets.

Sadat clearly trusted Ceausescu and took advantage of the Romanian leader's advice and support in dealing with the USSR, the other Arab countries, and—ultimately—Israel.[152] When in March 1977 Carter and Brezhnev separately called for the resumption of the Geneva conference, Sadat discussed the plan first with Carter and then with Ceausescu.[153]

At a joint press conference with Ceausescu in Cairo on 13 May 1977, Sadat revealed the depth of his relationship with the Romanians:

> For many years now, dating back to President Nasser, . . . [Ceausescu] has been making big efforts remarkable in their sincerity and consistency. These efforts have won our complete trust, in everything that President Ceausescu has said and done.
>
> Although there are a few difficult elements in our relations with the Soviet Union, I want to clearly state that there is no conflict between us and the Soviet Union on aspects concerning the Middle East problems, i.e., on actions and need to reestablish peace in this area. . . . Thus, despite the situation created, we hope that further positive results will be obtained. *We will remain in contact with President Nicolae Ceausescu on this matter* [emphasis added].[154]

Ceausescu also maintained good relations with the Israelis. Prime Minister Menachem Begin visited Ceausescu on 25–30 August 1977. The Romanians and Israelis differed on a number of issues. The Romanian position, as stated in Cairo, called for PLO participation in the Geneva conference; Romania also sought the withdrawal of Israeli troops to the pre-1967 borders. The Israelis opposed both conditions. The two sides adhered steadfastly to their positions but also reaffirmed the cordiality of their relations and the need for peace in the Middle East.[155]

Foreign Minister Macovescu actively involved himself in Middle East diplomacy at the United Nations. On 28 September, in an address to the General Assembly, he elaborated on Romania's Middle East policy:

Romania acts for intensified efforts for the settlement in the Middle East based on the withdrawal of the Israeli troops from the Arab territories occupied following the 1967 war, the recognition of the Palestinian people's right to self-determination, including the right to set up its own Arab Palestinian state, ensuring the independence and sovereignty of all states in the region. Romania declares for the fastest possible convening of the Geneva conference, with the participation of all countries concerned, including that of the Palestine Liberation Organization—sole representative of the Palestinian people. The U.N. must have an even more active role than hitherto in the political settlement of the issues in that part of the world, just as the secretary general is called upon to be present at all actions taken for peace to be arrived at in the Near East.[156]

Macovescu also met with a number of high-level diplomats in New York: Egyptian Foreign Minister Fahmy on 29 September; Gromyko, Vance, Qaddumi of the PLO, and Khaddam of Syria on 1 October; and Huang Hua of the PRC on 3 October. Macovescu dined with President Carter on 4 October and met with Mahmud Riyad of the Arab League on 5 October and Moshe Dayan of Israel on 6 October.

The Romanian press played up Macovescu's activities at the United Nations and, at the same time, virtually ignored the 1 October USA–USSR joint statement calling for a Geneva conference by the end of the year. Although Romania supported the proposal in principle, the press chose to show Romania pursuing its own policy, as a small or medium-sized power, of playing a major role in international conflict resolution.

The Geneva conference seemed possible. On 26 October, however, it was announced that the PLO would send a delegation to Moscow; the Soviets wanted the PLO to create a government in exile to represent all Palestinians at the conference. On the same day, the Romanians announced that Sadat, at Ceausescu's invitation, would visit Bucharest at the end of October.[157]

On 28 October, just before his arrival in Romania, Sadat had made public Egypt's intent unilaterally to postpone its debt repayment to the USSR. After morning talks with Ceausescu on 30 October, Sadat told Egyptian journalists that the Romanian leader had briefed him in detail on the eight hours of discussions that he (Ceausescu) had held with Begin. Sadat implied that he was reconsidering the Egyptian position and making his own preparations for the peace conference:

> I consider that the most important thing at this stage is good preparation for the Geneva conference. As I have told President Ceausescu, I prefer not to go to Geneva if there are not good preparations for the conference, because I do not want a conference along the pattern of the disarmament conference which has been going on for 25 years in Geneva.[158]

He added that "his talks with Ceausescu covered Egyptian–Soviet relations. . . . We also discussed the Soviet Union's role in a Middle East settlement."[159]

Ceausescu also insisted on proper preparations for the conference: "The resumption of the Geneva conference, of a well-prepared conference, can mark an important point."[160]

Begin later said that the exchange of views between Ceausescu and Sadat in Bucharest had been "of great significance" in convincing the Egyptian leader to go to Jerusalem.[161] Sadat confirmed Ceausescu's decisive role, saying that he had asked Ceausescu whether he thought that Begin "really wanted peace" and whether Begin was "a strong man, capable of making a decision and then persuading his people to accept it."[162] Ceausescu's affirmative answers evidently convinced Sadat.

The Romanians remained in close touch with the Egyptians and also conferred with other Middle East officials. The Egyptian Chief of Staff, Lieutenant General Muhammad Ali Fahmi, visited Bucharest on 8–15 November to meet with Ion Hortopan of the Romanian General Staff, Defense Minister Ion Coman, and Ceausescu. It was apparent that they discussed the Middle East and that the two countries participated in joint military activities as well.[163] Other visitors to Bucharest included Kuwaiti Minister of Oil 'Abd al-Mutalib al-Kaziric, Iraqi Minister of Youth Karim Mahmud Husayn, Libyan Minister of Maritime Transport Mansur Muhammad Badr, and Israeli Minister of Industry, Commerce, and Tourism Yigal Hurwitz. Romania's attempt to maintain good relations with all Middle East countries appeared to be succeeding.

In a speech on 19 November, the day Sadat arrived in Jerusalem, Ceausescu, without mentioning Sadat by name, indicated his support of the Egyptian leader's initiative:

> We have acted and are acting for the settlement of the Middle East problems through negotiations designed to lead to the establishment of a just and lasting peace. . . . We believe that this is in keeping with the interests of all peoples and of the general cause of peace. We also believe that everything should be done along these lines to bring about the faster resumption of the Geneva conference, so as to insure that the countries directly interested reach the appropriate agreements and peace, something which is much required not only by the Middle East but by the entire world.[164]

The Romanian media commented on the visit only after Sadat had left Jerusalem and even then said nothing of Ceausescu's role in bringing the two traditional enemies together.

Whereas the Soviet press accused Sadat of betraying the Arab cause by seeking a separate peace, the United States and Romania supported the Egyptian–Israeli bilateral effort as a possible avenue to a multilateral Geneva conference. On 23 November, Romanian Foreign Minister Macovescu paid a surprise visit to Washington to confer with President Carter. According to Bucharest radio:

The two sides [the United States and Romania] emphasized the desire of both
countries to make an active contribution to a political solution of the Middle
East situation, something which can lead to a just and lasting peace in the
area.[165]

A major article in *Scinteia* on 24 November gave clearer scope to the revision of
the Romanian formula as a result of Sadat's visit to Jerusalem:

The resumption and successful unfolding of the Geneva conference require appropriate preparations so that the countries directly concerned . . . may discuss
and establish by themselves the principles of the agreements to be concluded,
the practical way in which relations are to develop in the region.
In this context, the Israeli visit by President Sadat—although it was surprising even to public opinion in Romania—was viewed in this country from the
angle of the need for practical measures of offering a way out of the deadlock
things are in now, favoring the actions and processes directed towards peace.[166]

An editorial in *Lumea* the same day also outlined the revised Romanian formula for Middle East peace. After noting that "President Sadat's visit to Israel
has generated both approval and disapproval, especially in a number of Arab
countries and circles," *Lumea* called for the resumption of the Geneva peace conference, with all concerned parties participating:

A new situation has arisen following President as-Sadat's visit to Israel, new
opportunities have emerged that must be utilized in the interest of resuming the
Geneva conference and of the overall solution of the Middle East problems. . . .
What is essential now is to take firm action to rapidly resume the Geneva peace
conference, with the participation of all sides concerned, including the PLO.[167]

Macovescu met with Vance on 25 November to discuss the need "for new
gestures to prepare the convening of the Geneva conference."[168] Later that day,
Macovescu discussed the Middle East situation also with UN Secretary General
Kurt Waldheim. Ion Dactu, the Romanian ambassador to the UN, speaking to
the General Assembly that same day, referred to new diplomatic efforts and
reiterated the Romanian formula for a Middle East peace.[169] Bucharest radio announced that "some new steps" had been taken to foster "the new spirit" and
"the realistic attitude."[170] Meanwhile, Gromyko and Qaddumi of the PLO had
met in Moscow and condemned the "imperialist and Zionist plots" to split the
Arab countries fighting against Israel.[171]

The Romanian press made no comment on Sadat's 26 November invitation
to the interested parties to a meeting in Cairo to prepare for a Geneva conference. The Yugoslav news agency reported, however, that Mircea Malita, an adviser to Ceausescu, would be a special observer at the Cairo meeting.[172] Egyptian
acting Foreign Minister Butros Ghali immediately denied the Tanjug report, as
did the Romanian press agency ten days later.[173] Radio Bucharest reported the

opening of the Cairo meeting without comment.[174] The media of the other Warsaw Pact states took note of the absence of many of the concerned Arab countries.

Tito, the leader of the nonaligned movement, visited Ceausescu on 3–4 December 1977, among other reasons to be briefed on developments in the Middle East.[175] The press coverage of the meeting indicated the enduring closeness of the relationship between the two countries, both of which continued to distance themselves from the USSR[176] and to maintain high-level contacts with the PRC.[177] Furthermore, in active and apparently coordinated pursuit of establishing a peace zone in the Balkans, Romania and Yugoslavia had expanded their political and military contacts with Greece and Turkey, both NATO members.[178]

Ceausescu presented a clear formulation of the Romanian Middle East position in his report to the Romanian national party conference on 7 December:

> As a matter of fact, it is known that Romania has always spoken out for resolving disputes by negotiations among the directly interested countries. This is a sure guarantee that the solutions that will be agreed upon will be viable and will lead to the establishment of a lasting peace. It is actually known that even *since 1973, actually beginning with the Geneva conference, there have been direct contacts between Arab countries and Israel. It is true that they have had talks through intermediaries, but in fact they have discussed and directly voiced their views.* This is why Romania, not only in the case of the Middle East but in all areas and corners of the world, believes that doing away with intermediaries and that talks between those directly concerned is the safest way to resolve problems and to insure peaceful cooperation and a lasting peace in the world [emphasis added].[179]

Ceausescu's reference here to direct meetings between Arabs and Israelis is the closest that the Romanian leader has come to admitting publicly his role in bringing about these meetings. The Egyptian government implicitly acknowledged Romania's role on 7 December 1977 when it closed Soviet and Warsaw Pact—except Romanian—consulates and cultural centers in Egypt.

An article by Foreign Minister Macovescu in *Lumea* summing up Romania's foreign policy in 1977 again illustrated his country's Middle East position to be closer to that of the United States than to that of the USSR:

> Since the 1967 war, Romania has continually advocated solving the problems through direct discussions between the sides involved in the conflict, as this is the course leading to an atmosphere of trust and capable of facilitating solutions. . . . The recently established summit contacts between Egypt and Israel constitute an act of special importance in Middle East developments: they outlined the possibility for a new means of solving the problems in the area with the direct participation of all the interested sides.[180]

In conclusion, throughout the negotiations and preparations for the Geneva conference and Sadat's visit to Jerusalem, Romania pursued a policy differing fundamentally from that of its Warsaw Pact allies. Romania vigorously maintained the neutrality that it had declared in connection with the June 1967 and October 1973 wars. Its diplomatic actions, embodying the concept of small and medium-sized states contributing to political, rather than military, conflict resolution, often brought it into alignment with U.S. and opposition to Soviet policy. Romania also expanded its military contacts and arms sales with communist states ouside the Soviet sphere of influence (Yugoslavia and the PRC), with non-aligned nations (especially Egypt), with its Balkan neighbors (including NATO members Greece and Turkey), and with European capitalist states (France, the FRG, the United Kingdom, and Italy).

SUMMARY

Soviet diplomatic activities and media coverage of events related to the Middle East indicate that the Soviet leaders considered the USA–USSR jointly sponsored Geneva conference a high-priority policy. Under these circumstances, the Soviets could perceive Sadat's decision to go to Jerusalem in November 1977 only as a threat to their political influence and prestige.

The USSR's Warsaw Pact allies supported to varying degrees—ranging from total acceptance to virtual indifference—the 1 October USA–USSR joint proposal for a Geneva conference and the Soviet condemnation of Sadat's trip to Israel. The reactions of several Soviet allies suggest that the trend toward Warsaw Pact dissension created by the October war and earlier crises continued into 1977 and, in some cases, increased. These reactions suggest also that the more that *national* interest enters into the foreign policy of a Warsaw Pact country, the less cohesive the Warsaw Pact becomes.

Among the more reliable Soviet allies, Bulgaria continued to offer the most consistent and orthodox support of Soviet policy.

As in 1973, the Czechoslovak media followed a harder ideological line than the Soviet press, leading to a situation similar to that witnessed in the GDR under Ulbricht in the 1967, 1968, and 1969 crises. The Soviet leaders had eventually been forced to replace Ulbricht because his orthodoxy had in some measure forced Soviet policy and hampered Soviet pursuit of détente with the West. There is no indication, however, that the Soviets may have begun to fear that Husak might also at some future time stand in the way of Soviet policy, or that the Czechoslovak people might rebel against such strict official orthodoxy.

The East German media showed restraint in supporting the Soviet line in 1977. This restraint, which had been developing since the 1973 war (several months after the GDR had signed a peace treaty with the FRG and joined the United Nations), marked a shift from the GDR's behavior under Ulbricht, especially during the 1967 Middle East war.

Hungary deviated in minor, but potentially significant, particulars from the Soviet position. Its media played down the Soviet contribution to the hopeful atmosphere created by the 1 October joint proposal to resume the Geneva conference, referred to the United States in more favorable terms than did the Soviet, Bulgarian, Czechoslovak, and East German press, and did not brand Sadat's visit to Jerusalem a betrayal of the Arab cause. These moderate reactions, because they were consistent with Hungary's behavior during the five earlier crises, probably did not surprise or concern the Soviets.

The independence of Poland's present leadership and the volatility of Polish society, on the other hand, probably do concern the Soviet leaders. The development of a distinctly national Polish outlook, noted during earlier crises, had led to Polish alignment with Romanian, Yugoslav, and Chinese positions and to a pro-Western orientation. By 1977, Poland's commitment to détente and its expected economic benefits dominated that country's foreign policy. The Soviets must now take into account how these factors would affect Polish official and popular support of a Soviet policy that the Poles might consider antithetical to their own national interests.

Romania's position continued to differ fundamentally from those of its Warsaw Pact allies as it actively pursued its own policy, as a small or medium-sized state, of participating alongside the superpowers in trying to settle the Middle East conflict. The Romanians supported the 1 October proposal for a Geneva peace conference; their insistence on the attendance of *all* concerned parties, however, brought them into conflict with the Soviets, who favored limited participation. Ceausescu's role in convincing Sadat to approach the Israelis placed Romania on the side of the United States, Egypt, and Israel and again in opposition to the Soviets, who backed the other Arab countries.

Romania's disregard of Soviet interests in 1977 was consistent with its earlier behavior and probably did not surprise the Soviet leaders. It did, however, exacerbate already strained Soviet-Romanian relations. The Soviet leaders would doubtless like to put an end to Ceausescu's independence.

NOTES

1. Neither President Sadat of Egypt nor President Assad of Syria publicly thanked the Soviets, and other Arab leaders openly castigated Moscow for insufficient support of the Arab cause. Criticism was most vehement from Libya, Morocco, and Algeria; protests were heard also in Tunisia, Iraq, and Kuwait.

2. The USSR benefited indirectly, however, from the oil embargo and fourfold price increase levied by the Organization of Petroleum Exporting Countries (OPEC), which shook Western Europe (and Japan). The Soviets were able to sell oil at the new, inflated prices (while urging OPEC to continue the embargo). See Arthur Jay Klinghoffer, *The Soviet Union and International Oil Politics* (New York: Columbia University Press, 1977), pp. 174-76; Marshall I. Goldman, "The Oil Crisis in Perspective: The Soviet Union," *Daedalus*, No. 104 (Fall 1975): 137-39.

3. Sadat claims that his relationship with Kissinger and the United States "was regarded by the Soviet Union as an end to my relationship with them. . . . From that moment . . . I have been denied everything Russian. The Soviet Union would not sell me weapons to compensate for my war losses as happened in Syria's case, nor supply me with the necessary spare parts or anything else. The Soviet attitude has hardened to the verge of hostility." Anwar el-Sadat, *In Search of Identity* (New York: Harper & Row, 1978), p. 292.

4. Ceausescu visited the United States on 4–8 December 1973; a joint U.S.–Romanian declaration expressed the desirability of a Middle East peace conference and increased trade. King Hussein of Jordan went to Bucharest in January 1974. Ceausescu toured the Middle East from 12 to 21 February, visiting Libya, Lebanon (where he met with PLO leader Yasser Arafat), Syria, and Iraq. Sadat visited Yugoslavia in March. Nixon went to Egypt and then to Moscow in June.

5. Romanian Situation Report/23, *RFE* (July 18, 1974), p. 10.

6. Sadat and Ceausescu created a joint committee, headed by the two foreign ministers, to examine all aspects of their relations periodically. Ibid., p. 13. Tito visited Ceausescu July 9–11 and was briefed on Sadat's visit.

7. Romanian Situation Report/40, *RFE* (December 19, 1974), p. 2.

8. Romanian Situation Report/28, *RFE* (September 13, 1974), p. 2.

9. Bucharest Agerpres, 0917 GMT, November 4, 1974, in *FBIS, DR, EE* (November 4, 1974), pp. H1–2.

10. Ibid.

11. "We believe that relations of cooperation must be developed among the socialist member states of the Warsaw Pact and between the armies of these states, proceeding from the need to develop and strengthen each national army and the defense and combat potential of each people. . . . At the same time, Romania has acted and will continue to act to expand cooperation between our army and those of all the socialist countries, as well as with the armies of other friendly states." *FBIS, DR, EE* (November 27, 1974), p. H9.

12. Romanian Situation Report/15, *RFE* (April 24, 1975), pp. 2, 4.

13. *FBIS, DR, EE* (April 28, 1975), pp. H1–3.

14. Romanian Situation Report/15, *RFE* (April 24, 1975), p. 6. A further indication of tension in Romanian–Soviet relations occurred on the thirtieth anniversary of Victory in Europe Day. The Romanian media, which pointed out the decisive role played by the USSR in World War II, also noted in great detail the Chinese efforts against Japan. In addition, *Scinteia* (April 27, 1975) claimed that the Romanian armed forces during the insurrection of 23 August 1944 "sided, to a man, with the allied armies." Radio Moscow, on the other hand, broadcasting in Romanian, quoting from Soviet General Sergey Shtemenko's book, *The General Staff During the War*, asserted that "many [Romanian] units did not lay down their arms, but continued their struggle side by side with the Hitlerites." See Romanian Situation Report/18, *RFE* (May 15, 1975), pp. 1–11.

15. See the 1 June Romanian–Israeli joint communiqué. Agerpres, 1920 GMT, June 1, 1975, in *FBIS, DR, EE* (June 2, 1975), p. H6. At a press conference the same day, Allon, referring to the Middle East situation, noted that "small and medium countries, like Romania . . . can play a role," adding that Romania's good relations with both Israel and the Arab countries "prove positive in all domains: economic, cultural, scientific, political, which is a very great contribution to the stabilization of the situation in the Middle East." Ibid., p. H5.

16. Bucharest Domestic Service, 1600 GMT, June 9, 1975, in *FBIS, DR, EE* (June 10, 1975), p. H1.

17. For text of the "Communiqué on Romanian President's Visit to USA," Agerpres, 0928 GMT, June 12, 1975, see *FBIS, DR, EE* (June 12, 1975), pp. H2-3. Romania was the first communist country to negotiate a commercial agreement that was in accord with the 1974 U.S. Trade Act; the USSR had cancelled its trade agreement with the United States in January 1975.

18. Agerpres, 0913 GMT, June 11, 1975, in *FBIS, DR, EE* (June 11, 1975), p. H4.

19. Text of communiqué, Agerpres, 1953 GMT, June 20, 1975, in *FBIS, DR, EE* (June 24, 1975), pp. H13–15.

20. Tito had visited Washington in 1974, Gierek in 1974, and Ceausescu in 1973 and 1975—and these were the only communist states to be granted most-favored-nation status.

21. Romanian Situation Report/30, RFE (August 7, 1975), p. 2.

22. For the text of the agreement, see The New York *Times*, September 2, 1975, p. 16.

23. I. Kalita, "A Complicating Element," *Pravda*, August 30, 1975, p. 5, in *FBIS, DR, EE* (September 2, 1975), pp. F2–3.

24. On September 5, Sadat accused the USSR of trying to divide the Arab countries by staying away from the signing of the Egyptian–Israeli disengagement agreements. The New York *Times*, September 5, 1975, pp. 1, 5.

25. The orthodox media response supporting the USSR was as follows: For Bulgaria, see Radoslav Tsnachev, "Alleviation or Aggravation of the Crisis?" *Rabotnichesko Delo*, September 5, 1975, p. 5, in *FBIS, DR, EE* (September 10, 1975), pp. C11–12. For Czechoslovakia, see Milan Jelinek, "Misgivings and Uneasiness," *Rude Pravo*, September 4, 1975, in *FBIS, DR, EE* (September 8, 1975), pp. D1–2. The East German media (as in 1973) said little about the Middle East. For example, Erich Honecker, in a 5 September address on international affairs, while expressing general support for the USSR, avoided any mention of the Middle East. See *Neues Deutschland*, September 6–7, 1975, pp. 3–4, in *FBIS, DR, EE* (September 9, 1975), pp. E4–5. In Hungary, neither *Nepszabadsag* nor *Magyar Hirlap* condemned the accord, but they expressed anxiety about the future and called for a resumption of the Geneva conference. *FBIS, DR, EE* (September 5, 1975), p. F1.

In Poland (in marked contrast to the USSR), *Zycie Warszawy* contended on 5 September that "although these are little steps, there is a glimmer of hope, at least as far as intentions are concerned." Ibid., p. G12.

26. V. Alexandrescu, "Toward a Political Solution of the Conflict and a Just and Lasting Peace in Middle East," *Scinteia*, September 4, 1975, in *FBIS, DR, EE* (September 5, 1975), p. E1.

27. Bucharest Domestic Service, 0805 GMT, December 18, 1975; *Scinteia*, December 19, 1975, in *FBIS, DR, EE* (December 19, 1975), p. H9.

28. Romanian Situation Report/1, RFE (January 15, 1976), pp. 11–12.

29. Romanian Situation Report/3, RFE (January 29, 1976), pp. 8–10.

30. TASS, 1530 GMT, March 16, 1976, in *FBIS, DR, SU* (March 17, 1976), pp. F3–7.

31. Ibid.

32. The orthodox media response supported the USSR as follows: Bulgaria noted the "efficient and wide-ranging Soviet aid" and the "anti-Soviet propaganda campaign launched in Cairo." Miladin Kunev, "A Gross Distortion," *Narodna Mladezh*, March 17, 1976, in *FBIS, DR, EE* (March 18, 1976), p. C1. The Czechoslovak media charged that "the hostile policy of Anwar Sadat toward the USSR is in harmony with the plans of certain circles of imperialism and Arab reaction." Milan Jelinek, "We Comment," *Rude Pravo*, March 17, 1976, p. 7, in *FBIS, DR, EE* (March 19, 1976), pp. D2–3.

The East German media again avoided specific mention of the Middle East, but *Neues Deutschland* carried extensive articles supporting the USSR and highlighting the recent Twenty-fifth CPSU Congress.

The Hungarian media, without mentioning the USSR or imperialism, noted only that Sadat was "opening the path of foreign policy toward the right." Gyorgy Onodi commentary, Budapest Domestic Television Service, 1730 GMT, March 16, 1976, in *FBIS, DR, EE* (March 17, 1976), p. F1.

The Polish media noted only that it was "an arbitrary infringement of bilateral relations, clearly disadvantageous to the Arab interests." Warsaw PAP, 1117 GMT, March 16, 1976, in *FBIS, DR, EE* (March 17, 1976), pp. G1–2.

33. Bucharest Domestic Service, 1400 GMT, March 16, 1976, in *FBIS, DR, EE* (March 17, 1976), pp. H6–7.

34. It is noteworthy that Jamasi had been in Yugoslavia and France—apparently on a similar mission—immediately before Sadat terminated the treaty.

35. The "debate" was stimulated by the conference of communist and workers' parties to be held in East Berlin in June. *Scinteia*, April 24, 1976, in *FBIS, DR, EE* (April 26, 1976), pp. H1–6. The Yugoslavs supported the Romanian concept of nation.

36. Bucharest Domestic Service, 0706 GMT, April 26, 1976, in *FBIS, DR, EE* (April 27, 1976), p. H11.

37. Hamburg DPA, 1014 GMT, June 3, 1976, and Madrid Domestic Service, 0600 GMT, June 4, 1976, in *FBIS, DR, EE* (June 4, 1976), pp. H8–9. The Soviet and Romanian media apparently did not report the mobilization, but Western observers noted public hoarding in Romania. See Rudolf Woller, *Warsaw Pact Reserve Systems: A White Paper* (Munich: Bernard & Graefe Verlag, 1978), p. 113. The Romanians had reactivated the Patriotic Guards as a result of the Warsaw Pact invasion of Czechoslovakia. The size of the force reached 50,000 in 1968; 125,000 in 1969; 540,000, in 1970; and 700,000 in 1976. See International Institute for Strategic Studies, *The Military Balance: 1969–1970; 1970–1971; 1971–1972;* and *1977–1978* (London: International Institute for Strategic Studies, 1969, 1970, 1971, and 1977). Yugoslavia's similarly structured Territorial Defense Force experienced the same relative growth.

38. Bucharest Domestic Service, 1730 GMT, May 19, 1976, in *FBIS, DR, EE* (May 20, 1976), p. H6.

39. Agerpres, 1958 GMT, May 27, 1976, in *FBIS, DR, EE* (May 28, 1976), p. H1; Bucharest Domestic Service, 1100 GMT, May 28, 1976, in *FBIS, DR, EE* (June 1, 1976), p. H7.

40. Bucharest Domestic Service, 0709 GMT, June 2, 1976, in *FBIS, DR, EE* (June 3, 1976), pp. H2–3. Ceausescu's speech of 29 June at the conference of communist and workers' parties reiterated the Romanian national policy. See Bucharest Domestic Service, 1600 GMT, June 29, 1976, in *FBIS, DR, EE* (June 30, 1976), pp. CC5–17. For discussion of differences among the Warsaw Pact members at the conference, see Jeffrey Simon, *Comparative Communist Foreign Policy, 1965–1976*, The Rand Corporation, P-6067 (August 1977), pp. 99–112.

41. "The Army—Trustworthy Defender of the People's Revolutionary Achievements and of National Independence," *Romania Libera*, June 14, 1976, pp. 1, 3, in *FBIS, DR, EE* (June 30, 1976), p. H6.

42. Bucharest Domestic Service, 1400 GMT, June 11, 1976, in *FBIS, DR, EE* (June 14, 1976), p. H1. The Yugoslavs also evidenced renewed concern about defense. On 9 June, they held the Cevo 76 military exercise. It was reported that regular army units, some territorial defense units, and a number of reservists took part. See B. Pusanjic report, *Politika*, June 10, 1976, p. 13, in *FBIS, DR, EE* (June 22, 1976), pp. I6–7.

43. The joint communiqué noted the French and Romanian concern with "insuring conditions under which all the countries can develop protected against any form of limitation of their national independence and sovereignty, or of interference in their internal affairs." *Scinteia*, June 12, 1976, p. 5; see also *FBIS, DR, EE* (June 15, 1976), p. H2.

44. Agerpres, 0947 GMT, June 24, 1976, in *FBIS, DR, EE* (June 24, 1976), p. H6. Coman visited Rolls-Royce and the British Aircraft Corporation, which were involved in the joint Romanian–Yugoslav *Orao* fighter aircraft project. (See note 4 in Chapter 5.)

45. Agerpres, 0915 GMT, June 23, 1976, in *FBIS, DR, EE* (June 24, 1976), p. H1.

46. On 9 June, TASS issued the following statement: "As for the powers who allude to interest in the situation established in Lebanon and threaten direct military interference in the affairs of Lebanon, the Soviet Union is forced to declare in this connection that: The Middle East is much closer to the Soviet Union than to those who issue such threats and, in any case, the Soviet Union is not less interested in how the situation in Lebanon and around it develops and continues to develop. Nobody should lose sight of this." *FBIS, DR, SU* (June 10, 1976), pp. F1–2.

47. Romania and Yugoslavia apparently were acting together. Yugoslav Foreign Minister Milos Minic visited Assad with a message from Tito on 10 June. Belgrade Domestic Service, 1400 GMT,

June 11, 1976, in FBIS, DR, EE (June 14, 1976), pp. I7-8. Minic then met with Romanian Foreign Minister Gheorghe Macovescu on 12-13 June, and both countries announced that Assad would visit within two weeks. Bucharest Domestic Service, 1730 GMT, June 12, 1976, in FBIS, DR, EE (June 14, 1976), p. H6; Tanjug Domestic Service, 1114 GMT, June 12, 1976, in FBIS, DR, EE (June 14, 1976), p. I8.

48. Damascus Domestic Service, 1815 GMT, June 28, 1976, in FBIS, DR, EE (June 30, 1976), p. H9. For the 26 June Yugoslav-Syrian communiqué, see FBIS, DR, EE (June 28, 1976), pp. I20-23.

49. FBIS, DR, EE (February 17, 1977), pp. H1-3.

50. Galia Golan, Yom Kippur and After: The Soviet Union and the Middle East Crisis (Cambridge: Cambridge University Press, 1977), p. 137.

51. See "Syria Is Said to Reduce Military Role of Soviet," The New York Times March 4, 1977, p. 10.

52. Zbigniew Brzezinski, the new U.S. national security adviser, had suggested in 1975 that a jointly sponsored Geneva conference be reconvened and a Palestinian state be created in the West Bank and Gaza. See Zbigniew Brzezinski, Francois Duchene, and Kiichi Saeki, "Peace in an International Framework" Foreign Policy (Summer 1975), pp. 3-17.

53. Between 16 and 23 February, Vance visited Israel, Egypt, Jordan, Saudi Arabia, and Syria.

54. "A. as-Sadat's 'Memoirs' Are a Blow at Soviet-Egyptian Friendship," Pravda, February 19, 1977, in FBIS, DR, SU (February 22, 1977), p. F5.

55. Ibid., p. F6.

56. The New York Times, March 10, 1977, pp. 10, 26. See also George Ball, "How to Save Israel in Spite of Herself," Foreign Affairs (April 1977), pp. 453-71.

57. Weekly Compilation of Presidential Documents (March 21, 1977), p. 361.

58. TASS, 0730 GMT, March 21, 1977, in FBIS, DR, SU (March 21, 1977), p. R14.

59. Ibid.

60. "Yasser Arafat Is Openly Received by Brezhnev," The New York Times, April 8, 1977, p. 8.

61. Text of joint Soviet-Syrian communiqué, Moscow TASS, 1812 GMT, April 22, 1977, in FBIS, DR, SU (April 25, 1977), p. F2.

62. Henry Tanner, "Sadat Hints a 'New Development' in Relations with Soviet Union," The New York Times (May 14, 1977), p. 3.

63. Christopher Wren, "Improvement in Soviet-Egyptian Ties Seen after Talk," The New York Times, June 12, 1977, p. 8.

64. In late June, President Nimeiry of the Sudan expelled all Soviet military advisers and ordered the Soviets to reduce the number of their diplomats in Khartoum. For Sadat's relations with Nimeiry, see Sadat's, In Search of Identity, pp. 226, 311.

65. "Sadat Says Soviet Has Cancelled Its Military Contracts," The New York Times, July 17, 1977, p. 13.

66. "Sadat Asserts Soviet Interfered in Fighting," The New York Times, August 1, 1977, p. 1.

67. Marvine Howe, "Egypt, Charging Default by Moscow, to Suspend Trade," The New York Times, August 18, 1977, p. 14.

68. Christopher Wren, "Moscow Steps up Its Diplomatic Efforts on the Middle East," The New York Times, August 31, 1977, p. 5.

69. After meeting with Brezhnev in Moscow, Kurt Waldheim, UN secretary general, said at a press conference that the Soviet leadership told him that "they are confused . . . and don't know what is America's real foreign policy." The New York Times, September 13, 1977, p. 3.

70. The text of the communiqué appeared in The New York Times October 2, 1977, p. 16.

71. The Israelis resented not being consulted about the language of the U.S.-Soviet statement, the involvement of the USSR (with whom they did not have diplomatic relations), the elevation of Palestinians to a party to be represented at Geneva, the reference to Palestinian "rights," and the omission of any mention of UN Security Council Resolutions 242 and 338. See Raymond Cohen, "Israel and the Soviet-American Statement of October 1, 1977: The Limits of Patron-Client Influence," Orbis, 22 (Fall 1978): 613-33.

72. Fahmy publicly claimed that the U.S.–Israeli formula should specify the PLO, not Palestinians, to attend the Geneva conference. The New York Times, October 19, 1977, p. 3. Fahmy said the next day that the U.S. agreed to supply Egypt with $260 million in weapons. See The New York Times, October 21, 1977, p. 9.

73. "Sadat Arrives in Bucharest," The New York Times, October 30, 1977, p. 8.

74. Sadat wrote in his memoirs: "Ceausescu sounded very confident, and I trust that man's judgment. Besides, the Romanian president has maintained a consistent link with the Israelis. His emphasis on Begin's desire for peace, on Begin being a 'strong man,' confirmed my conclusion that a change was urgently needed—a change in the positions of both sides. On board the plane that took me to Iran an initiative emerged clearly before my eyes and took definite shape." Sadat, In Search of Identity, pp. 305–06.

75. The New York Times (November 7, 1977), p. 2.

76. The New York Times (November 10, 1977), pp. 1, 3.

77. The New York Times (November 12, 1977), p. 1.

78. R. Moseyev, "Opening of Session," Izvestiya, November 11, 1977, p. 5, in FBIS, DR, SU (November 16, 1977), p. F2.

79. V. Matveyev, "Who is Disrupting a Settlement," Izvestiya, November 13, 1977, p. 3, in FBIS, DR, SU, pp. F4–5.

80. Ibid.

81. Moscow TASS, 1856 GMT, November 15, 1977, in FBIS, DR, SU pp. F3–4.

82. FBIS, DR, SU (November 18, 1977), p. F5.

83. Surprise may have also been a factor in the Soviet response. It was reported in the Yugoslav press that: "It is learned in unofficial circles in Moscow that the Soviet side has not been informed or warned at any time from any place that As-Sadat's visit to Israel was being prepared." D. Cukic, "Report from Moscow," Borba, November 22, 1977, in FBIS, DR, EE (November 25, 1977), p. 13.

84. FBIS, DR, SU (November 18, 1977), p. F1.

85. Pravda, November 17, 1977, p. 5, in FBIS, DR, SU (November 22, 1977), p. F6.

86. "About As-Sadat's Voyage to Israel," Moscow TASS, 1709 GMT, November 18, 1977, in FBIS, DR, SU (November 21, 1977), p. F6.

87. Sergey Losev, "Farce and Reality," Selskaya Zhizn, November 19, 1977, p. 5, in FBIS, DR, SU (November 23, 1977), pp. F6–8.

88. Major Yu. Gavrilov and V. Vinogradov, "Near East: Situation Grows in Complexity," Krasnaya Zvezda, November 20, 1977, p. 3, in FBIS, DR, SU (November 23, 1977) pp. F5–6.

89. "Threat to Arab Unity," Pravda, November 23, 1977, p. 5, in FBIS, DR, SU (November 29, 1977), p. F8.

90. Yuriy Glukhov, "The Realities Remain," Pravda, November 25, 1977, p. 5, in FBIS, DR, SU, p. F7.

91. V. Matveyev, "Israel from One Crisis to the Next," Izvestiya, November 29, 1977, p. 4, in FBIS, DR, SU (November 30, 1977), p. F8.

92. "Characteristic Hushing Up," Pravda, November 24, 1977, in FBIS, DR, SU (November 25, 1977), p. F5.

93. Paris AFP, 1205 GMT, November 25, 1977, in FBIS, DR, SU (November 28, 1977), p. F1.

94. Moscow Domestic Service, 1130 GMT, November 29, 1977, in FBIS, DR, SU (November 30, 1977), pp. F1–3.

95. "As-Sadat's Statement," Moscow TASS, 1650 GMT, November 26, 1977, in FBIS, DR, SU (November 28, 1977), p. F2.

96. Moscow TASS, 2248 GMT, November 26, 1977, in FBIS, DR, SU (November 28, 1977), p. E9.

97. Moscow TASS, 1548 GMT, November 27, 1977, in FBIS, DR, SU (November 28, 1977), p. F3.

98. Apparently reflecting the administration's concern over the TASS reportage, Ambassador to Moscow Malcolm Toon reportedly told a Soviet journalist that Moscow should be taking a more

responsible stand in cochairing the Geneva conference. The Russian said he was taken aback because he thought the Soviet statements had been restrained, given the circumstances. See David K. Shipler, "Soviet Said to Fear Arab Split Imperils Geneva Talks," The New York *Times*, November 24, 1977, p. 5.

99. Bernard Gwertzman, "Soviet Informs U.S. It Won't Take Part in Parley at Cairo," The New York *Times*, November 30, 1977, p. 1.

100. Moscow Domestic Service, 1100 GMT, November 30, 1977, in *FBIS, DR, SU* (December 1, 1977), p. F1.

101. For the Final Resolution of the meeting, see Moscow TASS, 1856 GMT, December 5, 1977, in *FBIS, DR, SU* (December 6, 1977), pp. F1–2.

102. Christopher S. Wren, "Egypt Orders Soviet and 4 Allies to Shut All Culture Offices," The New York *Times*, December 8, 1977, p. 1. Czechoslovak, East German, Hungarian, and Polish consulates were also closed.

103. Moscow TASS, 0721 GMT, December 4, 1977, in *FBIS, DR, SU* (December 6, 1977), pp. F6–7.

104. Yuriy Kornilov, "Cairo: Staking on Quislings," Moscow TASS, 1323 GMT, December 5, 1977, in *FBIS, DR, SU* (December 6, 1977), pp. F7–8.

105. Craig R. Whitney, "Key Vance Aide Sees Gromyko on Mideast," The New York *Times* (December 7, 1977), p. 1.

106. Bernard Gwertzman, "Vance Rebukes Soviet on Mideast, Says Anti-Sadat Drive Hurts Peace." Ibid., pp. 1, 10.

107. "Positive Initiative," *Rabotnichesko Delo*, October 4, 1977, p. 6, in *FBIS, DR, EE* (October 11, 1977), pp. C1–2.

108. The text of Bulgarian Foreign Minister Petur Mladenov's 30 September speech was published in *Rabotnichesko Delo* (October 1, 1977); GDR Foreign Minister Oskar Fischer's speech appeared in *Neues Deutschland* (September 30, 1977); and Czechoslovak Foreign Minister Bohuslov Chnoupek's 4 October address was broadcast by Prague CTK, 0800 GMT, October 5, 1977. See *FBIS, DR, EE* (October 6, 1977), pp. C4, E10, D1–2.

109. East Berlin ADN, 1731 GMT, October 5, 1977, in *FBIS, DR, EE* (October 6, 1977), p. E3.

110. *Rabotnichesko Delo*, November 18, 1977, in *FBIS, DR, EE* (November 18, 1977), p. C1.

111. *Narodna Armiya*, November 19, 1977, in *FBIS, DR, EE* (November 21, 1977), p. C1.

112. Katya Yencheva, *Narodna Mladezh*, November 20, 1977, p. 3, in *FBIS, DR, EE* (November 25, 1977), p. C2.

113. *Rabotnichesko Delo*, November 24, 1977, in *FBIS, DR, EE*, p. C3.

114. Sofia BTA, 845 GMT, December 2, 1977, in *FBIS, DR, EE* (December 2, 1977), p. C2.

115. J. L. Kerr, "East European Media and the Sadat Visit to Israel," Eastern Europe BR/234, RFE (November 29, 1977), p. 3.

116. Ibid., p. 4.

117. Milan Madr, "As-Sadat Recalls 'Peacemaker' Chamberlain," *Rude Pravo*, November 23, 1977, p. 7, in *FBIS, DR, EE* (November 30, 1977), p. D2.

118. East Berlin ADN, 1801 GMT, November 24, 1977, in *FBIS, DR, EE* (November 25, 1977), p. E5.

119. George Kaloyanov, "Conspiracy and Reaction against It," *Rabotnichesko Delo*, December 7, 1977, p. 6, in *FBIS, DR, EE* (December 12, 1977), p. C1.

120. Milan Madr commentary, *Rude Pravo*, December 7, 1977, p. 7, in *FBIS, DR, EE* (December 15, 1977), pp. D4–5.

121. See Sofia Domestic Service, 2000 GMT, December 7, 1977, in *FBIS, DR, EE* (December 8, 1977), p. C1; East Berlin ADN, 1809 GMT, December 7, 1977, in *FBIS, DR, EE* (December 9, 1977), p. E1; and Prague CTK, 1003 GMT, December 9, 1977, in *FBIS, DR, EE* (December 12, 1977), p. D1.

122. MTI, 1200 GMT, October 7, 1977, in *FBIS, DR, EE* (October 12, 1977), pp. F4–5. Hungarian Foreign Minister Frigyes Puja reiterated his country's official position in the UN General Assem-

bly on 7 October. See *Magyar Hirlap*, October 8, 1977, pp. 1, 3, in *FBIS, DR, EE* (October 12, 1977), pp. F1–4.

123. See J. L. Kerr, "East European Media and the Sadat Visit to Israel," Eastern Europe BR/ 234, *RFE* (November 29, 1977), p. 4.

124. Jozsef Szaszi, "As-Sadat Has Abandoned Arab Stand," *Magyar Hirlap*, November 22, 1977, p. 2, in *FBIS, DR, EE* (November 30, 1977), p. F6.

125. J. L. Kerr, in Eastern Europe BR/234, *RFE* (November 29, 1977), p. 5. This implicitly denied the need for a Geneva conference to settle the Middle East conflict.

126. Budapest Domestic Service, 1730 GMT, November 30, 1977, in *FBIS, DR, EE* (December 1, 1977), p. F1.

127. See note 119.

128. Budapest Domestic Television Service, 1800 GMT, December 4, 1977, in *FBIS, DR, EE* (December 9, 1977), pp. F2–3.

129. Budapest Domestic Service, 0500 GMT, December 7, 1977, in *FBIS, DR, EE* (December 8, 1977), pp. F1–2.

130. Budapest Domestic Service, 1730 GMT, December 8, 1977, in *FBIS, DR, EE* (December 9, 1977), pp. F2.

131. Budapest Domestic Service, 1000 GMT, December 10, 1977, in *FBIS, DR, EE* (December 13, 1977), p. F1.

132. Budapest MTI, 1020 GMT, December 21, 1977, in *FBIS, DR, EE* (December 22, 1977), pp. F1–2.

133. Central Intelligence Agency, *Handbook of Economic Statistics, 1978*, Central Intelligence Agency, ER 78-10365 (October 1978), Tables 66 and 67, pp. 67 and 68, respectively. This trend first became apparent in 1971, after the Polish and FRG treaty of December 1970. See also Simon, *Comparative Foreign Policy, 1965–1976*, pp, 33, 71.

134. Central Intelligence Agency, *The Scope of Poland's Economic Dilemma: A Research Paper*, Central Intelligence Agency, ER 78-1034OU (July 1978), Table 6, p. 8.

135. See notes 80 and 81 in Chapter 5.

136. After the December 1970 riots, the Soviets gave Poland $1.11 billion in economic aid. *Handbook of Economic Statistics, 1978*, p. 75.

137. *Trybuna Ludu*, September 30, 1977, pp. 1, 2, in *FBIS, DR, EE* (October 6, 1977), pp. G3–5.

138. Warsaw PAP, 1815 GMT, September 30, 1977, in *FBIS, DR, EE* (October 4, 1977), p. G8.

139. MFR commentary, *Polityka* (Warsaw), October 1, 1977, p. 2, in *FBIS, DR, EE* (October 6, 1977), p. G2.

140. Gierek spoke at the Adam Mickiewicz University in Poznan on 1 October and in Piotrkow on 3 October; visited Hungary on 5–6 October; delivered the opening and closing speeches to the Ninth Plenum of the CC PUWP on 7–8 October; and hosted the official visit of the King and Queen of Belgium on 10–11 October.

141. J. L. Kerr, Eastern Europe BR/234, *RFE* (November 29, 1977), p. 5.

142. Ryszard Drecki, *Trybuna Ludu*, November 17, 1977, p. 2, in *FBIS, DR, EE* (November 21, 1977), pp. G1–2.

143. The full text of Gierek's address was published in *Trybuna Ludu*, November 22, 1977, p. 2, in *FBIS, DR, EE* (December 1, 1977), pp. G1–6.

144. Antoni Olczak, *Sztandar Mlodych*, November 22, 1977, p. 5, in *FBIS, DR, EE* (December 7, 1977), pp. G3–4.

145. J. L. Kerr, Eastern Europe BR/234, *RFE* (November 29, 1977), p. 6.

146. See *FBIS, DR, EE* (November 29, 1977), pp. G1–2; (December 2, 1977), pp. G1–3.

147. *Zolnierz Wolnosci*, December 1, 1977, p. 2, in *FBIS, DR, EE* (December 6, 1977), pp. G7–10.

148. Tadeusz Pasierbinski, "Betrayal or Chance?" *Polityka*, December 3, 1977, pp. 12–13, in *FBIS, DR, EE* (December 12, 1977), pp. G1–5.

149. See Jacek Kalabinski commentary, Warsaw Domestic Service, 1105 GMT, December 11, 1977, in FBIS, DR, EE (December 12, 1977), pp. G5–6.

150. Wotjaszek said: "Concerning the Middle East, . . . we consider that a permanent and peaceful solution of the conflict should be achieved on the basis of the familiar UN resolution." Trybuna Ludu, December 17–18, 1977, p. 3, in FBIS, DR, EE (December 21, 1977), p. G5.

151. See Ceausescu's toast at dinner with Sadat, May 11, 1977, Scinteia, May 12, 1977, p. 13, in FBIS, DR, EE (May 16, 1977), p. H2. The USSR, wanting to exclude Romania, objected to the formulation "all concerned countries."

152. In 1974, Sadat and Ceausescu had pledged to maintain permanent contacts and to consult bilaterally whenever possible. See note 6.

153. See note 62.

154. Scinteia, May 14, 1977, p. 3, in FBIS, DR, EE (May 19, 1977), p. H5.

155. Jerusalem Post, August 31, 1977, in FBIS, DR, EE (August 31, 1977), p. H1.

156. Agerpres, 1975 GMT, September 28, 1977, in FBIS, DR, EE (September 29, 1977), p. H3.

157. Bucharest Domestic Service, 1730 GMT, October 26, 1977, in FBIS, DR, EE (October 27, 1977), p. H2.

158. Cairo MENA, 1500 GMT, October 30, 1977, in FBIS, DR, EE (October 31, 1977), p. H6.

159. Ibid.

160. Bucharest Domestic Service, 1500 GMT, October 30, 1977, in FBIS, DR, EE (October 31, 1977), p. H4.

161. AFP, Jerusalem, November 18, 1977, in Romanian Situation Report/36, RFE (December 23, 1977), p. 26.

162. December 11, 1977. Ibid. Also see note 74.

163. After General Fahmi met with Ceausescu, Bucharest Domestic Service (1730 GMT, November 14, 1977) noted: "In this connection, they emphasized the relations of friendship existing between the armies of the two countries." FBIS, DR, EE (November 15, 1977), p. H15. Lumea (March 10, 1978), said that Romania had set up an assembly line for the ARO-240 military vehicle in Cairo.

164. Bucharest Domestic Service, November 19, 1977, and Scinteia, November 20, 1977, pp. 1, 5, in FBIS, DR, EE (November 23, 1977), p. H1.

165. Bucharest Domestic Service, 2000 GMT, November 23, 1977, in FBIS, DR, EE (November 25, 1977), p. H5.

166. "A Demand of the Cause of International Peace and Security," Scinteia, November 24, 1977, in FBIS, DR, EE (November 25, 1977), p. H4.

167. "The Just and Political Settlement of Interstate Disputes," Lumea, November 24, 1977, pp. 9–10, in FBIS, DR, EE (November 29, 1977), p. H2.

168. Bucharest Domestic Service, November 26, 1977, in Romanian Situation Report/36, RFE (December 23, 1977), p. 27.

169. Bucharest Domestic Service, 1100 GMT, November 26, 1977, in FBIS, DR, EE (November 28, 1977), p. H5.

170. Romanian Situation Report/36, RFE (December 23, 1977), p. 27.

171. Paris AFP, 1205 GMT, November 25, 1977, in FBIS, DR, SU (November 28, 1977), p. F1.

172. Belgrade Tanjug Domestic Service, 1459 GMT, November 30, 1977, in FBIS, DR, EE (December 1, 1977), p. H1.

173. Romanian Situation Report/36, RFE (December 23, 1977), p. 26.

174. Radio Bucharest, December 15, 16, 1977.

175. The Middle East figured in both the dinner toasts and final joint communiqué. See FBIS, DR, EE (December 5, 1977), pp. H1–10; (December 6, 1977), pp. H1–3.

176. Scinteia, (December 6, 1977), also reported that "Nicolae Ceausescu and Josip Broz Tito expressed the determination of the RCP and LCY to ensure the observance of every party's right to elaborate its revolutionary strategy and tactics, its home and foreign policy." FBIS, DR, EE (December 7, 1977), p. H1.

177. Tito visited Chairman Hua Guofeng in September, and Ceausescu's son Nicu headed a Romanian delegation to China. Romanian Situation Report/35, RFE (December 6, 1977), p. 2. After Mao's death in September 1976, the exchange of Romanian and Chinese delegations intensified. *Frankfurter Allgemeine Zeitung*, October 17, 1977.

178. In May 1975, Greek Premier Constantine Karamanlis visited Romania and with Ceausescu signed a "joint solemn declaration." In December, Greek Minister of Defense Evangelos Averof agreed to purchase 2,000 Romanian jeeps for Greece's armed forces. *Scinteia*, December 3, 4, 6, 1975. This was the first time a NATO country had placed an order for military equipment with a Warsaw Pact state.

Ceausescu went to Greece on 26–29 March 1976, the first visit of a Warsaw Pact chief of state to Greece. (Tito followed in May.) Romania pursued a similar campaign with Turkey. In August 1975, Turkish Premier Demirel visited Romania, and another solemn declaration was signed. Ceausescu visited Turkey in June 1976, shortly after Tito had been there.

179. Bucharest Domestic Service, 0712 GMT, December 7, 1977, in *FBIS, DR, EE* (December 8, 1977), p. H31.

180. Gheorghe Macovescu, "Romania: A Dynamic and Principled Foreign Policy," *Lumea*, No. 1 (January 1, 1978), pp. 5–9, in *FBIS, DR, EE* (January 16, 1978), p. H7.

8

Conclusion

This book has traced the development of differences in foreign policy outlook of Warsaw Pact countries by examining the increasing dissension and deviation from critical Soviet policies toward the Middle East, the PRC, NATO, and regional security during the 1967–77 period. First, between the 1967 Middle East war and Sadat's visit to Jerusalem in 1977, the USSR's Warsaw Pact allies demonstrated increasing reluctance to support Soviet policy on the Middle East, and Romania, identifying itself with U.S. policy, effectively undermined Soviet influence in that area. The USSR's influence in the Middle East in 1977 resulted from circumstances that were largely unrelated to Soviet efforts and commitments to the Arabs since 1967.

Second, the more independent pact members (Poland and Hungary) refused to support Moscow's condemnation of the Chinese and Yugoslav brands of socialism; Romania, in outright defiance, developed closer political, economic, and military ties with both Yugoslavia and the PRC. Ignoring Soviet fears of facing hostile forces on its eastern and western frontiers, Romania then played a major part in the establishment of diplomatic relations between the USSR's major adversaries, the United States and China.

Third, Soviet concerns for regional security and efforts to strengthen the pact command structure were blocked by Romania and, to varying degrees, Poland and Hungary. Soviet concerns for security led to changes in military deployments during the period in question. Believing hostilities with China to be a real possibility, the Soviets strengthened their combat units along the border with the PRC. Also, internal Warsaw Pact dissidence led to the pact invasion of Czechoslovakia and, on several occasions, the concentration of forces along Romania's (and recently Poland's) borders. Romania, for its part, vowed to defend itself against any invasion of its territory and established a sizable self-defense force for that purpose. Yugoslavia took similar measures.

Ironically, the USSR's outstanding foreign policy success during the ten-year period studied—the Soviet–FRG peace treaty and détente with Western Europe—which eventually received full Warsaw Pact support, also undermined pact unity. Coming to terms with West Germany decreased the dependence of the Eastern European allies (in particular, Poland and the GDR) on the USSR and encouraged all of them (except Bulgaria) to develop their own economic and political ties with the West.

Further evidence of challenges to Soviet authority developed during the Warsaw Pact's November 1978 PCC conference in Moscow when the USSR pressed its allies to declare their opposition to the Sadat–Begin peace efforts in the Middle East; to implicitly condemn China by declaring solidarity with Vietnam; and to increase their defense expenditures to meet NATO increases. Pact members acceded to these Soviet requests at the Moscow conference to varying degrees: Poland and Hungary opposed some, Romania opposed them all.

Then, between July 1980 and December 1981, Poland's Solidarity exhibited a Western gravitation, a degree of social mobilization, and an open challenge to the Soviet "order" much greater than what Poland had experienced during the 1970s. The martial law mechanism for reestablishing social control (in contrast to military intervention) may have been utilized, in part, due to a recognition of varying degrees of opposition not only inside Poland, but also among the NSWP (and West).

The responsiveness of the individual Warsaw Pact countries (listed in descending order of political reliability) to Soviet policy during the six crises is summarized below.

BULGARIA: A MODEL ALLY

Bulgaria proved to be the USSR's most consistent and compliant ally in the six crises examined, never faltering in its adherence to the Soviet line. In 1967, it supported the Arab cause and condemned Israeli aggression. In 1968, a token force of Bulgarian troops invaded Czechoslovakia alongside Soviet forces. Bulgaria was also rumored in 1968 to have allowed Soviet troops to mass on its border with Romania in preparation for a possible invasion of that country. Finally, the Bulgarians condemned both the "rightist revisionism" of Yugoslavia and the "leftist revisionism" of the People's Republic of China and Albania.

In 1969, Bulgaria blamed the Chinese for the Ussuri incident and, like the East Germans, compared Chinese territorial claims against the USSR to West German "revanchist" claims against Eastern Europe. The harshness of the Bulgarian criticism implied that the Bulgarians (1) supported the Soviet attempt at the 17 March, 1969, meeting of the Warsaw Pact PCC in Budapest to engineer an official Warsaw Pact condemnation of China and (2) may also have agreed to an alleged Soviet demand for the PRC's expulsion from the socialist movement. Although the Bulgarians supported the Soviet-sponsored détente and the Budapest PCC appeal for a European security conference, evidence suggests that the conservative Bulgarians sympathized with, if not supported, East Germany's opposition to a European security conference. Continuing to depend chiefly on the USSR even during détente, Bulgaria was the only Warsaw Pact member not to increase its political and economic ties with the West during the 1970s.

In 1972, the Bulgarian media criticized Nixon's *U.S. Foreign Policy for the 1970's*[1] as anti-Soviet, used Nixon's planned trip to China as the basis for linking U.S. and Chinese anti-Sovietism, and charged the Chinese with betraying socialism.

Knowing that Egypt and Syria intended to attack Israel, Brezhnev visited Todor Zhivkov, the Bulgarian leader, in September 1973, probably to caution him against raising the Macedonian issue with Yugoslavia (which Bulgaria did periodically) at a time when the USSR was seeking permission to fly over Yugoslavia to supply its Middle East clients in the imminent war. At Soviet behest, the Bulgarians tried (not entirely successfully) to come to terms with Yugoslavia. In October, the Soviets sent Zhivkov to Prague to moderate the Czechoslovaks' position and to encourage them to seek rapprochement with Yugoslavia. The Bulgarian media continued to criticize the Chinese—this time for their stand on Arab issues.

Again in the crisis created by Sadat's visit to Jerusalem in 1977, Bulgaria remained the USSR's most consistent and reliable ally. The Soviets are probably convinced, on the basis of these six experiences, that they can rely on Bulgaria in any crisis.

CZECHOSLOVAKIA:
LOYAL BUT INCONSISTENT

Czechoslovakia proved to be an inconsistent but reliable Warsaw Pact ally. Following the orthodox line on the 1967 Middle East war, the Czechoslovaks supported the Arabs and condemned Israeli aggression. Several months later, however, Czechoslovakia challenged the USSR and threatened Warsaw Pact unity with its attempted economic and political reorganization. In early 1968, Dubcek replaced Novotny as head of the Czechoslovak Communist Party, promising "democratization," but also loyalty to the USSR. Thereupon, an unprecedented public debate (including even noncommunist groups), joined in by the media, revitalized political life in Czechoslovakia.

The liberalization spilled over from Czechoslovakia into Poland, where public political unrest contributed to a factional feud in the Polish party. Increasingly concerned over the contagion of Czechoslovak liberalism, Gomulka, the Polish leader, and Ulbricht, the East German leader, urged the Soviets to contain Czechoslovakia.

After months of attempts at political resolution, during the night of 20–21 August, Warsaw Pact troops invaded Czechoslovakia. The Soviets, still fearing Czechoslovak liberalism, had probably been egged on by Ulbricht to take decisive action. Dubcek was taken forcibly to Moscow but was spared the fate of Nagy, the Hungarian party leader who was tried and executed following the 1956 Hungarian uprising. Dubcek returned to Prague still in control. His apparent success may have been due in part to the fact that the Czechoslovak party and populace had united solidly behind him and that the Romanian and Yugoslav (as well as the French, Italian, and Spanish communist party) leaders had supported him.

Czechoslovak reactions to the events of March 1969 must have been a source of Soviet consternation. In every area where the Soviets expected Warsaw Pact support, the Czechoslovaks failed to meet Soviet expectations. They only reluctantly admitted that the Chinese had been the aggressors in the Ussuri incident, continued to regard the PRC as a member of the socialist community, and joined the Romanian refusal to condemn China at the Budapest PCC session. The Czechoslovaks also adopted the Romanian position on the reorganization of the Warsaw Pact as proposed at the Budapest PCC session. They joined the Budapest appeal for a European security conference not to support the Soviets but to further their own national interests. Finally, the media praised and expressed friendship for Yugoslavia despite Soviet criticism of that country. The Czechoslovak show of independence, added to the tensions remaining between Soviet and Czechoslovak leaders as a result of the August 1968 invasion and continued Warsaw Pact occupation of Czechoslovakia, probably led to the Soviet decision to remove Dubcek.

Husak's replacement of Dubcek in April 1969 marked the "normalization" of Czechoslovakia and its return to Soviet orthodoxy. Czechoslovak reluctance to condemn the Chinese and to support the Soviets in the Ussuri incident turned into unquestioning defense of the Soviet and rejection of the Chinese position at the time of the USA–PRC rapprochement in 1972. The Czechoslovak media charged the Chinese with practicing anti-Sovietism, betraying socialism, and colluding with the United States on issues involving Vietnam, India and Pakistan, and the Middle East. Linking the Romanians with the Chinese, the Czechoslovak media also rejected the Romanian positions that they had espoused in 1968 and early 1969.

On the other hand, the zealousness of Czechoslovakia's criticism of the United States, Israel, and China at the time of the October 1973 Middle East war appeared to worry the Soviets, and they sent Zhivkov to Prague to moderate the Czechoslovak position and to encourage the Czechoslovaks to seek rapprochement with the Yugoslavs. The Czechoslovaks, however, now appeared unable to accept Yugoslavia's rightist revisionism.

The Czechoslovaks "overreacted" also to Sadat's visit to Jerusalem in late 1977. Surpassing the invective of the Soviet and Bulgarian media, the Czechoslovak press described the visit as part of a "conspiracy between Zionism and Arab reaction" and compared Sadat's going to Jerusalem to Chamberlain's going to Munich before World War II. Czechoslovakia's hard ideological line led to a situation similar to that witnessed in the GDR under Ulbricht in the 1967, 1968, and 1969 crises. There is no indication, however, that the Soviets may have begun to fear that Husak might also in some future crisis stand in the way of Soviet policy, or that the Czechoslovak people might rebel against such strict official orthodoxy. On balance, the Soviets must now consider Czechoslovakia to be a reliable, albeit inconsistent, ally.

EAST GERMAN LEGITIMACY
BRINGS RESTRAINT

At the time of the 1967 Middle East war, the GDR depended entirely on the USSR for its security and legitimacy. Strategically located but politically isolated, the GDR shared full diplomatic relations only with other communist states. Ulbricht, the most doctrinaire of the Warsaw Pact leaders, had opposed the establishment of diplomatic relations between Romania and West Germany in January 1967 and thereafter had done his best to prevent the other Warsaw Pact states from recognizing the FRG. Although the GDR supported all of the USSR's positions in connection with the June 1967 crisis, East German hatred of the FRG, desire for diplomatic recognition and antipathy for Romania were beginning to threaten the unity of the Warsaw Pact.

Fearing the spread of Czechoslovak liberalism in 1968, Ulbricht was reported to have urged the Soviets to contain Czechoslovakia and to have played a role in the subsequent Soviet decision to invade. Although the East German hatred of the FRG and distrust of Romania and Czechoslovakia coincided with Soviet interests in August 1968, Soviet leaders, who were probably already contemplating a shift in policy toward the FRG, could only have seen Ulbricht as a liability.

The East German press, which had singled out West German aggressiveness as the root of the June 1967 Middle East war and the 1968 attempted counterrevolution in Czechoslovakia, also portrayed the PRC and the FRG as acting in concert in the Ussuri incident. At the Budapest PCC meeting, the GDR faithfully supported the USSR against China, probably even to the point of agreeing to a Warsaw Pact condemnation of the PRC, acceded to the Soviet-inspired Warsaw Pact military reorganization, and followed the Soviet line with regard to Yugoslavia. But it attempted to balk the Budapest appeal for a European security conference, as it had opposed earlier attempts at rapprochement with West Germany.

Despite Ulbricht's opposition, the Soviets and West Germans signed a peace treaty in August 1970. Ulbricht's perceptions of East Germany's national interests finally forced his retirement in May 1971. Honecker's succession at the Eighth German Socialist Unity Party Congress was orderly and prearranged with the Soviets.

Détente and the new leadership apparently modified the GDR's behavior. The East Germans accepted the Soviet interpretations of Nixon's February 1972 foreign policy statement, his trip to China, and the Shanghai communiqué. The most significant aspect of their reaction was the decoupling of European (specifically West German) from Asian issues. The tension that had developed between the GDR and USSR over the rapprochement with the FRG apparently had been resolved with Ulbricht's removal.

The June 1973 treaty between East and West Germany and the admission of both to the United Nations in September marked the end of the GDR's political isolation and its integration into the world diplomatic community. The GDR supported the Soviet position on the October 1973 Middle East war and the convening of a peace conference and sought to cultivate relations with Yugoslavia. The East German media, however, reacted with restraint, repeating Soviet criticisms of the United States, Israel, and China.

At the time of Sadat's trip to Jerusalem, the GDR officially supported Soviet Middle East policy, while the media, again showing the restraint that had been developing since the 1973 war, tended to ignore the Middle East. This restraint marked a shift from the GDR's behavior under Ulbricht, especially during the 1967 Middle East war.

HUNGARY: A "SOFT" ALLY
IN THE CENTRAL TIER

The Hungarians began to diverge from the Soviet line on the 1967 Middle East crisis soon after the fighting began. Only a step or two behind the Romanians in their readiness to recognize the FRG, the Hungarians were less inclined than their orthodox Warsaw Pact allies to associate West Germany with U.S. and British imperialism in the Middle East. Although Hungary officially sided with the Arab cause, it severed relations with Israel only with hesitation and qualification. The press hinted at popular opposition to official support of Soviet policy on Israel, insisted on Israel's right to exist, supported Romania's right to act independently of the other socialist countries, and ignored China.

Hungary participated reluctantly in the invasion of Czechoslovakia in 1968. The Hungarians sympathized with the Czechoslovak reforms, particularly the economic experiment, which resembled both their own so-called new economic mechanism, launched in January 1968, and the Yugoslav economic system. The Hungarian leaders appeared to be trying to balance interest in the Czechoslovak reforms and détente with the FRG, on one hand, against loyalty to the USSR on the other. In recognizing its responsibilities to the USSR and the other Warsaw Pact countries, the Hungarian leadership was doubtless motivated by the hope of preserving the benefits of the liberalization that had been allowed to develop in Hungary following the return to orthodoxy after the 1956 rebellion.

Kadar, the Hungarian leader, trying to mediate between Czechoslovakia and the other Warsaw Pact partners, counseled caution and moderation. Although the Hungarians reluctantly supported the 18 August decision made in Moscow to invade Czechoslovakia, Kadar tried to persuade the others (USSR, Bulgaria, GDR, and Poland) to reverse that decision. The Czechoslovak ambassador in Budapest was probably informed of the imminent attack, and he presumably warned Dubcek.

The Hungarian press coverage of the invasion was more sympathetic to the Czechoslovaks than that of the other Warsaw Pact states (except Romania). First, while the orthodox press portrayed the Czechoslovak leadership, and especially Dubcek, as treacherous and revisionist, the Hungarians refrained from comment. Second, while the orthodox press suggested that the Warsaw Pact should be the instrument to correct the state of affairs in Czechoslovakia, the Hungarians expressed the view that it was up to the Czechoslovaks to solve their own problems. Third, while the orthodox press described open hostility on the part of the Czechoslovak populace and suggested that a long occupation would be required, the Hungarian press reported that the streets of Prague were returning to normal and that there were no incidents of violence, and the Hungarian government began to withdraw its troops from Czechoslovakia. Furthermore, the Hungarian press criticized neither the rightist revisionism of Yugoslavia nor the leftist revisionism of the PRC.

The Soviets were not unaware of Hungary's special relationship with Czechoslovakia during the 1968 crisis (for example, the warning to the Czechoslovak ambassador in Budapest that the Warsaw Pact forces were about to invade), nor were they blind to Hungary's pursuit of relations with the FRG and support of Romanian independence in 1967. In fact, the Soviets had probably not completely trusted the Hungarians since the 1956 uprising. The Hungarians' performance during the Czechoslovak crisis doubtless reinforced this evaluation of Hungary as an ally.

The Hungarians may therefore have felt the need in 1969 to demonstrate their loyalty to the Soviets, at least to the extent that Soviet positions did not conflict with Hungary's own. To this end, Hungarian reports of the Ussuri incident branded China the aggressor and attributed the attack to Mao's domestic problems; they did not, however, link China and West Germany or accuse Mao of betraying socialism. The moderation of this criticism suggests that the Hungarians opposed the Soviet demand at the 17 March PCC meeting in Budapest to condemn the PRC. Their enthusiasm for a European security conference reflected Hungary's earlier rapprochement with the FRG and a more sincere commitment to European détente (including with Yugoslavia) than that of its more orthodox Warsaw Pact partners.

The Hungarian critique of Nixon's address to the Congress in February 1972 did not contain charges of U.S. anti-Sovietism or collusion with the PRC; instead, it emphasized the future role of the United States in Europe. Hungary's long-standing relationship with the Italian Communist Party, whose views on Nixon's China trip conflicted with those of the USSR, may have contributed to Hungary's restraint in criticizing Nixon's visit. The Hungarians did not see evidence of USA–PRC collusion in the Shanghai communiqué, nor did they accuse China of no longer being socialist. By their moderate course, the Hungarians evidently hoped to maintain cordial relations with the United States and with the Romanian and Italian communist parties and avoid straining relations with the USSR.

Pursuing its own interests in deepening détente, as it had done in earlier crises, Hungary diverged in small but meaningful ways from the Soviet position on the 1973 Middle East war. The Hungarian media credited the United States as well as the USSR with attempting to resolve the Middle East crisis, played down the U.S. worldwide military alert, hinted at Arab and Warsaw Pact disunity, and minimized criticism of China. The Hungarians did not have to follow the Soviets in seeking rapprochement with Yugoslavia—their sympathy for the Yugoslav economic system had long been evident.

Hungary again deviated in minor but meaningful particulars from the Soviet position on the Middle East in 1977. Its media played down the Soviet contribution to the hopeful atmosphere created by the 1 October joint proposal to resume the Geneva peace conference, referred to the United States in more favorable terms than did the Soviet, Bulgarian, Czechoslovak, and East German press, and did not brand Sadat's visit to Jerusalem a betrayal of the Arab cause. These moderate reactions, because they were consistent with Hungary's behavior during the five earlier crises and with its long-term national interests (economic reform and détente), probably did not surprise or concern the Soviets.

On balance, Hungarian behavior has been consistent (that is, predictable) during the six crises. The Soviets probably expect Hungarian reluctance, but they also expect Hungary's ultimate support and compliance.

UNPREDICTABLE POLAND: AN UNRELIABLE ALLY IN THE NORTHERN TIER

Polish government policy diverged in several particulars from that of the USSR at the time of the 1967 Middle East war. When the fighting began, the Polish media, following the Soviet line, condemned Israel as the aggressor and criticized the United States, Britain, and West Germany for aiding Israel. Popular sentiment, however, which ran strongly in favor of Israel, evidently persuaded the Polish government to soften its stand. The effect of public opinion on the official line could be seen in the hesitancy and qualifications with which the Polish government broke diplomatic relations with Israel. It could be seen also in what Gomulka, the hard-line Polish leader, said in a major speech: Answering a Catholic deputy to the *Sejm* (National Assembly) who had criticized the government's failure to reaffirm Israel's right to exist, Gomulka publicly acknowledged that right. At the same time, he lectured Polish Jews on their rights and duties as Polish citizens.

Other deviations from the Soviet line at the time of the 1967 Middle East war involved Poland's (1) dissociating France from Israeli activities so as to protect the traditional Polish–French relationship and (2) ignoring the China problem, possibly in part because the PRC–USA talks were being held in Warsaw and in part because the Poles and Chinese were in the process of negotiating a trade agreement.

Internal forces beyond the control of the Polish leadership significantly affected Polish policy again during the 1968 Czechoslovak crisis. But whereas in 1967 those forces had limited Polish support of Soviet policy, in 1968 they contributed to it. One such force was the liberalism that spilled over into Poland from Czechoslovakia, leading to antigovernment protests in March 1968. The protesters included prominent intellectuals whose liberalism combined Polish nationalism, resentment of Soviet hegemony, and the desire for political and economic reforms. Another such force was the ensuing power struggle within the Polish party that compelled Gomulka to seek Soviet support. One may speculate, then, that internal troubles drove Gomulka to back the Soviet invasion of Czechoslovakia (to the extent of contributing the second largest force after the USSR) as a likely way to preserve the status quo in Eastern Europe and his own power in Poland.

Following the Soviet line, the Polish media justified the invasion of Czechoslovakia primarily in terms of West German revanche (Poland and East Germany had yet to settle their post–World War II boundaries with the FRG), denounced Romania's support of Czechoslovakia in defiance of Warsaw Pact policy, and condemned Yugoslavia's criticism of the invasion. But again they ignored China's leftist revisionism.

The Czechoslovak crisis seemed, at least superficially, to have returned Poland to the orthodox fold. From the Soviet perspective, however, this crisis, like that in 1967, demonstrated the effect of unpredictable and uncontrollable domestic pressures on Polish policy and political reliability as an ally.

The unpredictability of Polish official and popular support of Soviet policy in the Middle East and Czechoslovak crises carried over to the issues related to the Ussuri incident in March 1969. While the Polish media sided with the USSR against the Chinese, the moderation of their response, noted in earlier crises, was again apparent. This moderation made it appear unlikely that Poland had joined the Soviet attempt at the Budapest PCC meeting to engineer a Warsaw Pact condemnation of the PRC or its expulsion from the socialist movement.

Poland might have been expected, in the context of unresolved territorial issues with the FRG, to have opposed the March 1969 Budapest appeal for a European security conference. But again Poland acted unpredictably. As a result of domestically initiated changes in its foreign ministry two months earlier, Poland had revitalized its foreign policy and had called for a European security conference and the resumption of political dialogues with Western Europe, including the FRG. Although Poland enthusiastically supported the Budapest appeal, the openness of the Polish press in referring to internal Warsaw Pact opposition to the appeal contrasted markedly with the attempt of the Soviet media to convey the impression of unanimity.

Polish unpredictability continued. Initiatives toward the FRG culminated in a treaty in December 1970. Also in December, spontaneous popular riots led to the Soviet-approved ouster of Gomulka. His successor, Gierek, needing Soviet economic assistance, was anxious to prove his loyalty to Soviet leaders. But although the Polish media in most particulars followed the Soviet line on the USA–PRC rapprochement, they continued to exhibit a distinct national orientation during 1972. This independence was apparent in Polish support of Nixon's offer to increase economic and cultural links with Eastern Europe and in the continued Polish softness on the China issue. From the Soviet perspective, the volatility and uncertainty of Polish domestic politics, coupled with the apparent national orientation of its media (necessitating Soviet broadcasts in Polish to Poland), probably raised further questions about Poland's political reliability.

Poland's foreign and domestic policy acquired an increasingly nationalistic orientation as its contacts outside the Warsaw Pact increased. Throughout the crisis engendered by the October 1973 Middle East war, Polish economic expansion and détente took precedence over the war in Polish policy. The Polish media showed great restraint in the criticism of Israel and were quick to praise the U.S. peacemaking role. At the same time, Poland maintained better relations with Yugoslavia than did any other Warsaw Pact country except Romania. The Soviets betrayed some concern regarding Poland's moderation: They beamed a number of Polish-language broadcasts to that country to correct the Polish interpretation of events in the Middle East and, perhaps more significantly, sent Marshal Grechko and other high-ranking political–military officers to Warsaw during the critical period of the Middle East war, ostensibly to attend the thirtieth anniversary celebration of the Polish People's Army, but perhaps also to indicate Moscow's concerns to the Polish leadership.

The national orientation of Polish domestic and foreign policy—including Polish alignment with Romanian and Yugoslav positions—just becoming apparent in 1972 at the time of Nixon's trip to China and during the October 1973 Middle East war, in 1977 assumed the form of an overriding commitment to the expected economic benefits of ties with the West. Before and after Sadat's visit to Jerusalem, the Polish media stressed the importance of détente and the need for the two superpowers to work together for its success. But they wrote sparingly and relatively uncritically of events in the Middle East and never directly criticized the United States.

Ever since July 1980, the Solidarity movement, which exhibits a Western gravitation and degree of social mobilization much greater than anything Poland experienced during the 1970s, has driven Polish politics. It contributed to the downfall of two PUWP first secretaries: Edward Gierek and Stanislaw Kania. Even after Wojciech Jaruzelski imposed martial law in December 1981, policy decisions were limited, to a degree, by the anticipated response of Solidarity.

From the Soviet perspective, it remains quite clear that Poland's popular and official unpredictability creates a question mark in the strategically important Northern Tier. Poland's domestic volatility, leadership instability, economic liability, and social mobilization with a strong Western gravitation make it an ally of questionable political utility.

ROMANIA'S PREDICTABLE UNRELIABILITY NEUTRALIZES THE SOUTHERN TIER

During the period under analysis, Romania effectively undermined the USSR's hegemony over the Warsaw Pact, its China policy, and its position in the Middle East. In so doing, Romania demonstrated unreliability as a Soviet ally and, with increasing support from Yugoslavia, called into question the effectiveness of the Warsaw Pact's Southern Tier.[2]

Romania first challenged the USSR in April 1964 by declaring its right to national sovereignty within the communist movement and its intention to pursue an independent foreign and domestic policy. The declaration was followed by (1) the establishment of diplomatic relations with West Germany in January 1967 in direct contravention of Soviet and Warsaw Pact policy and (2) the refusal to attend international communist conferences at which Romania might be forced to support Soviet positions.

Under the leadership of Nicolae Ceausescu, the independent and ambitious general secretary of the Romanian Communist Party, Romania then challenged the USSR on the theoretical issue of the limits of Soviet authority in the communist movement, Warsaw Pact, and Romania. On a practical level, Ceausescu sought to establish Romania's right to act independently and to circumscribe its political and military obligations to the Warsaw Pact and communist movement. At the same time, Ceausescu continued to profess complete loyalty to the Warsaw Pact and to the traditional goals of communism.

Challenging the CPSU's hegemony over international communism, on 7 May 1967, Ceausescu reiterated his determination to pursue independent bilateral relations with *other communist and socialist parties*. On 31 May, he identified the improvement of relations with *all socialist countries* as the major goal of Romanian foreign policy but also indicated Romania's interest in establishing ties *with all states, regardless of their social order.*

In implementing this independent policy, Romania challenged for the first time the USSR's Middle East position. In April 1967, when the USSR was supplying arms to the Arabs, Romania signed a sizable trade agreement with Israel. After the June 1967 war broke out, Romania was the only Warsaw Pact state to appeal to both sides to cease hostilities, to refuse to sign the 9 June Moscow statement condemning Israel, and to neither break nor threaten to break diplomatic relations with Israel.

Romanian Premier Maurer, in the United States to attend the UN General Assembly emergency session on the Middle East, engaged in some extraordinary diplomacy for a Warsaw Pact representative. Interacting with Western leaders (including the president of the United States) independently of his Soviet and pact counterparts, Maurer became deeply involved in seeking a compromise solution.

The day after President Johnson and Premier Kosygin ended their 25 June meeting in Glassboro, New Jersey, Maurer became the first communist head of government to be received by Johnson in the White House. On 28 June, he met with de Gaulle in Paris. On 4 July, he arrived in Peking. Maurer was the only communist leader other than Kosygin to have contact with both Johnson and de Gaulle and the only one then dealing with the Americans, Soviets, and Chinese.

Challenging Soviet hegemony over the Warsaw Pact, on 17 June 1967, Ceausescu called for the abolition of both the North Atlantic and Warsaw treaty organizations, but pledged that as long as the pact existed Romania would participate in its activities, including joint combat training—provided that each member state retain command of its own army. On 14 August 1968, a week before the invasion of Czechoslovakia, Ceausescu repeated the demand for national control of Warsaw Pact member forces and warned against pact military intervention in the internal affairs of member states.

The invasion of Czechoslovakia involved Romania in another head-on confrontation with Soviet policy, this time involving international communist relations, the Warsaw Pact, and China. In condemning the invasion, Romania aligned itself with the non-Warsaw Pact socialist states—Yugoslavia, Albania, and China—and with the French, Italian, and Spanish communist parties, with which the Romanians maintained close ties. The Soviets rebuked the Romanians for their relations with rightist (Yugoslav) and leftist (Chinese) revisionism and accused the Chinese of having encouraged the Czechoslovaks to revolt against the Warsaw Pact.

Soviet measures to suppress Romanian dissidence led Ceausescu to challenge Soviet hegemony over Romania. After the unsuccessful Soviet attempt to engineer Ceausescu's ouster in 1967, the Romanian party chief built up popular support for his policies and strengthened Romania's internal security ministry.

In August 1968, when the Soviets appeared prepared to invade Romania, Ceausescu, with the full support of the armed forces general staff, proclaimed Romania's determination to defend itself and announced the establishment of a self-defense force, the Patriotic Guards, for that purpose. In Peking, Premier Chou En-lai promised the Romanians China's military support if the Soviets invaded.

The Czechoslovak crisis fundamentally altered Romania's relationship with the Warsaw Pact. It edged Romania into closer relationships with Yugoslavia and China. It led Romania to expand its trade with the West and the nonaligned nations, clearly with the intention of reducing its economic and political dependence on the USSR. And finally, it caused Romania to expand the Patriotic Guards and to again refuse to allow joint Warsaw Pact maneuvers on Romanian territory. At the same time, Romania continued to balance its assertions of independence and sovereignty with the reaffirmation of its adherence to the principles of socialism and to the Warsaw Pact.

The Romanians challenged the USSR's Warsaw Pact and China policies again when the Soviets tried to involve their allies in their dispute with the PRC over the Ussuri incident of early March 1969. At the 17 March session of the PCC in Budapest, the Romanians were among those opposing the Soviet demand for a pact condemnation of China. To avoid having to support a future Soviet political or military action against the PRC, Romania argued for limiting the Warsaw Pact's sphere of influence to Europe. Romania also continued to demand control of its own armed forces. Finally, it enthusiastically supported the Soviet-inspired Budapest appeal for a European security conference—in the hope that a settlement would bring the end of great-power bipolarization of Europe and the concomitant relaxation of Soviet control over Eastern Europe. In all of these challenges, Romania found support in Yugoslavia.

Romania continued to defy Soviet demands with regard to the Warsaw Pact and China even though Sino–Soviet hostilities appeared to have been a real possibility during the second half of 1969 and the Soviets continued to feel seriously threatened from both east and west. Although after prolonged hesitation Romania renewed its friendship pact with Moscow in July 1970, it refused to agree to compulsory military assistance to the Warsaw Pact or to consultation with the USSR before making military decisions. Two weeks later, openly flouting Soviet policy, the Romanian minister of defense visited Peking, where the Chinese promised fraternal help in the defense of Romanian sovereignty should the USSR threaten Romania.

Ceausescu himself went to Peking in June 1971, the first visit of a Warsaw Pact party leader to the PRC since the Sino–Soviet rift ten years earlier. While he was there, the Soviets strongly criticized China's foreign policy, citing specifically the dangers of a USA–PRC rapprochement, and beamed broadcasts to the Romanians warning that Peking's policies undermined communist unity. At the same time, the Soviets allegedly moved Warsaw Pact troops to the Romanian border in anticipation of a military coup. The Romanians (along with the Yugoslavs) in response began large-scale mobilization.

Its long-standing relationship with China led to Romania's role in the Nixon administration's move toward diplomatic recognition of the PRC. Nixon had discussed with Ceausescu the normalization of USA–PRC relations—in 1967, before his election to the presidency, in August 1969, and again in October 1970. After their 1970 talks, Ceausescu had relayed Nixon's desire for diplomatic relations to the Chinese, who then responded that Nixon would be welcome to visit Peking. The Romanians were the only Warsaw Pact state to react favorably (as did the Yugoslavs) to Nixon's public acceptance of the invitation on 15 July 1971.

In fact, the Romanians (and Yugoslavs) opposed the Soviet line on nearly every issue connected with Nixon's February 1972 trip to China. Where the Soviets saw in Nixon's foreign policy address to the U.S. Congress a continuation of the U.S. position of strength policy, an imbalance in his treatment of the USSR and China, and the desire to undermine communist unity by expanding trade with Eastern Europe, the Romanians saw a U.S. policy based on negotiations rather than confrontations, a balance in Nixon's treatment of the two communist superpowers, and the call for increased trade with Eastern Europe as a manifestation of détente. Where the Soviets saw in the Shanghai communiqué collusion and secrecy cloaking parallel USA–PRC interests in a Munich-like Vietnam-for-Taiwan deal, as well as China's betrayal of socialism, the Romanians saw no secrecy, no collusion, no deals, and no Chinese betrayal of socialism. Moreover, the Romanians considered the United States to have taken a positive step to further the cause of détente and peace.

Romania again played an active intermediary role in Middle East relations in connection with the October 1973 Yom Kippur war. In this case, however, Romanian diplomacy probably did not unduly concern the Soviets because it was consistent with Romanian behavior in earlier crises and because it sought some of the same goals as Soviet diplomacy in 1973—namely, an end to the Middle East fighting and, more important, the preservation of détente with the United States. Nor, apparently, did Ceausescu fear Soviet reprisals in 1973.

In mediating the October 1973 war, however, Romania laid the groundwork for preempting the Soviet role in future Middle East negotiations. Long a friend of Israel and the United States, Romania also maintained good relations with many of the Arab countries and the PLO. As Soviet influence in the Middle East declined, Romania (coordinating its policy with Yugoslavia) became increasingly active in the search for a Middle East settlement.

Ceausescu once more challenged Soviet hegemony by declaring in November 1974 and again in December 1975 that Romania wanted to expand *military relations* not only with all socialist states but with other friendly states as well. Adding to the challenge, in April 1976 Ceausescu countered the Soviet concept of proletarian internationalism with the new Romanian concept of unity (which also received the support of Yugoslavia). But Ceausescu's rhetoric—both military and ideological—boiled down to the demand for Romanian sovereignty, independence, and control of its own armed forces.

The Soviet-Romanian dispute climaxed when the Romanians, apparently in response to Soviet mobilization along their common border in May 1976, called up reservists and mobilized the Patriotic Guards. (Yugoslavia's territorial defense forces also mobilized.) Although the Soviets and Romanians settled the crisis and Ceausescu expressed Romania's desire for peace with its socialist neighbors, he again called for military cooperation with socialist and other friendly countries. A few days later, the Romanian defense minister reaffirmed the army's support of Romanian party policy and determination to defend Romania against any aggression.

Egypt's relations with the USSR had foundered following the Yom Kippur war, and Sadat, clearly trusting Ceausescu, took advantage of the Romanian leader's advice and support in dealing with the USSR, the other Arab countries, and finally Israel. In June 1974, Sadat revealed that Egypt had received no arms from the USSR since the end of the war. Immediately afterward, he visited Ceausescu; the two leaders pledged increased trade and consultation. Similarly, after Egypt unilaterally abrogated its friendship and cooperation treaty with the USSR in March 1976, Sadat turned to Romania for support. Finally, two days after announcing in October 1977 that Egypt would unilaterally postpone its debt repayment to the USSR, Sadat went to Bucharest to consult with Ceausescu. On this occasion, convinced by Ceausescu that Israeli Prime Minister Begin wanted peace, Sadat decided to take the initiative. On 9 November, he announced that, if necessary, he would go to Jerusalem to obtain a Middle East settlement. The next day, Begin invited him to Israel. Ceausescu never publicly admitted his role in bringing Sadat and Begin together.

The USSR could not conceivably count on Romania, which has preempted its influence and subverted its policy in the Middle East, works and votes against the USSR in the United Nations, refuses to permit Warsaw Pact exercises on its territory and to cede control of its armed forces to Warsaw Pact command, and has coordinated its policy with the USSR's two major adversaries, the United States and China. Soviet tolerance may also indicate that the close coordination between Romania and Yugoslavia is deterring the Soviets by raising the political costs, particularly with the nonaligned countries. In effect, the Romanian–Yugoslavian nexus (despite the reliability of Bulgaria) effectively denies the Soviets the support of the Southern Tier.

LESSONS FOR THE FUTURE

Between 1967 and 1977, four major stresses developed within Eastern Europe:

1) The development of the policy of détente (particularly with the FRG and United States) increased the security of the NSWP and correspondingly diminished the threat posed by NATO.

The resolution of World War II boundary questions (between the FRG and the USSR and Poland in 1970 and the FRG and GDR in 1973) and public embrace of détente by the United States did lower the visible threat posed by NATO to Eastern Europeans—the threat of U.S.-backed FRG revanche was transformed into a much desired USA–FRG economic presence. This change has been most perceptible among those East European states—Romania, Yugoslavia, Poland, and Hungary—enjoying most-favored nation status with the United States.

In the wake of the Soviet invasion of Afghanistan and establishment of martial law in Poland, the United States must fight the temptation to bury détente. The United States should recognize some of détente's successes in Eastern Europe, and our purpose should be to further increase the gap between Soviet exhortations about the threat posed by NATO and the symmetry between the values shared by the peoples of some of the NSWP states and the West.

More than ever should we heighten the differentiation between our treatment of certain East European states (such as Romania, Yugoslavia, Poland, and Hungary) and our treatment of the Soviet Union and some of its subservient allies (such as Bulgaria, East Germany, and Czechoslovakia). A permanent part of U.S. political policy should be to deepen mutual relations with Romania, Yugoslavia, Hungary, and Poland through various types of economic (credits and trade) and social (cultural) activities—and "to neglect benignly" those NSWP allies willing to engage in greater subservience to Soviet needs.

2) The use of the pact in the invasion of Czechoslovakia and in pressuring Romania (and recently Poland) has led to varying degrees of NSWP opposition in its use as an instrument in pressuring wayward allies.

The military intervention forced the Romanians to recognize that it was the Warsaw Pact that posed the principal threat to its independent policies: It prompted them to denounce the use of force against a fraternal ally, adopt the Yugoslav doctrine of territorial defense, develop a credible Patriotic Guard, and broaden economic, political, and military ties with the West, the PRC, and the nonaligned Third World in order to demonstrate to the Soviets that a repeat performance (in Romania) would likely be very costly. To the degree that Romania (in conjunction with the West, the PRC, Yugoslavia, and the Third World) has influence among other NSWP members (notably Hungary and Poland), they, too, are likely to demonstrate more restraint in the future. In fact, the lessons of 1968 (and Polish popular resolve) were partly responsible for Soviet hesitancy during an 18-month period (July 1980–December 1981) and utilization of the martial law mechanism instead of military invasion to restore socialist order in Poland.

3) The development of Sino–Soviet tensions particularly since the Ussuri conflict and the Soviet (mis)handling of the China question has also led to major stresses within Eastern Europe.

China has been an East European issue not only to the extent that the Soviets have attempted to acquire NSWP support against the PRC but also to the extent that Romania and Yugoslavia have utilized the PRC to deter the USSR from a Southern Tier adventure and provide a focal point for opposition to Soviet desiderata (for example, Cambodia–Vietnam, the Indo–Pakistani war, and the warming of USA–PRC relations). The issue of China, then, in itself is neither a constant nor a major issue within Eastern Europe; it is, though, an area of underlying stress that continues to surface and may be subject to outside manipulation.

4) The development of Middle East policy and planning has likewise contributed to differences within Eastern Europe.

Romania's independent Middle East diplomacy, first evident during the 1967 war, contributed to great tension not only with the USSR but also with Yugoslavia. Coordinated Romanian-Yugoslav diplomacy was becoming apparent during the 1973 war, and close coordination was quite evident during Sadat's visit to Jerusalem. Romania's (and Yugoslavia's) independent diplomatic activity in the Middle East appeals to Romanian (and Polish and Hungarian) national interests, enhances its prestige and responsibility in the international community, and contributes to the exclusion of Soviet influence from both the Middle East and the Balkan peninsula.

In sum, political differences in foreign policy outlook among East European countries not only exist, but they also have increased between 1967 and 1977. Some of them, notably those that the Soviet Union has attempted to coordinate with Eastern Europe, are quite significant: the issue of European (and U.S.) détente, the Soviet use of the Warsaw Pact as a political–military instrument against wayward allies, and policies toward the PRC and the Middle East. The result has been the creation of a very delicate balance of forces that can easily become upset.

NOTES

1. *U.S. Foreign Policy for the 1970's: The Emerging Structure of Peace*, Report to the Congress by Richard Nixon, 9 February 1972 (Washington: Government Printing Office, 1972).

2. This book does not try to answer how Romania escaped the fate of Hungary in 1956 and Czechoslovakia in 1968, or why Ceausescu was not forced from power as were Nagy, Dubcek, and Ulbricht when they threatened Soviet policy.

Index

Budapest PCC meeting, (March 1969), 69, 71, 75, 77, 78, 80, 81, 83, 86, 88, 89, 90, 91, 127, 208–209, 210, 213

Bulgaria, 17, 24, 33, 34, 43, 48, 57, 62, 71, 79, 84, 91; Chinese relations, 18; Czechoslovak, GDR and, response to 1977 Sadat visit to Jerusalem, 183–186; expulsion of Albanian ambassador, 48; as model ally of USSR 208–209; response to Czechoslovak crisis (1968), 47–49; response to Middle East War (1967), 17; response to Middle East War (1973), 141–143; response to Nixon visit to China (1972), 107–109; response to Ussuri crisis (1969), 73–75

Bulgarian-Yugoslav debate over Macedonia, 84

Carrillo, Santiago, 57, 125

Carter, Jimmy, 6, 176, 177, 187

Ceausescu, Nicolae, 12–13, 14, 16, 22, 27, 28, 29, 30, 31, 44, 45, 47, 53, 55, 57, 58, 59, 82, 85, 92, 93, 101, 119, 128, 154, 155, 156, 157, 160, 186, 191; address to Congress of Political Education and Socialist Culture, 175; foreign policy report to Eleventh Romanian Communist Party Congress (1974), 172; refusal to criticize Israel, 28–33; role in bringing Sadat and Begin together, 221; speech to Romanian Trade Union Congress (1976), 175; support of Arabs, 28; visit to

China (1971), 102, 125, 219; visit to U.S. (1975), 173

Central Committee (CC) of the Romanian Community Party (RCP), 12, 31

Chiao Kuan-hua, 147

China, 4, 13, 14, 25, 45, 57, 72, 73, 78, 79, 82, 83, 86, 87, 88, 89, 91, 92; attacks on Damanskiy Island (March 1969), 70–73, 77, 81; collusion with U.S. on Vietnam, India and Pakistan, and Middle East issues, 210; "cultural revolution," 71; response to Czechoslovak crisis (1968), 62; two-superpower theory, 109, 110, 120, 127

Chinese-Indian border clashes, 81

Chnoupek, Bohuslav, 143

Chou En-lai, 32, 47, 61, 102, 108, 110, 116

Christian, George, 33

Cierna nad Tisov, 44

Comintern, 83; failure of, 1943, 13

control mechanisms, 2–3

Council of Mutual Economic Assistance (CMEA), 17

crisis importance, 6–8

Crown of St. Stephen, U.S. return to Hungary, 188

Cyrankiewicz, Josef, 23

Czech manifesto (1968), 44

Czechoslovak Communist Party (CPCS), 4, 19

Czechoslovakia, 4, 9, 18, 19, 33, 34, 42, 43, 71, 80, 81, 87, 88, 89, 91, 93; challenge to USSR, 42–45; condemnation of Israel aggression, 209; as loyal but inconsistent ally of USSR, 209–211; liberalization, 6,

42–45; new economic model, 42; response to Middle East War (1967), 18–20; response to Middle East War (1973) 143–145; response to Nixon visit to China (1972), 111–114; response to Ussuri crisis (1969), 81–84, 89; support of Arabs, 209

Czepuk, Harry, 49

Czinege, Lajos, 52

Dactu, Ion, 194

Damanskiy Island, 4, 70, 71, 74, 90

data limitations, 8

Dayan, Moshe, 192

Defcon 3, 140

Dent, Frederick, 153

Dobrynin, 139

Dolanc, Stane, 147

Dubcek, Alexander, 42, 43, 44, 45, 46, 47, 51, 52, 53, 61, 62, 81, 82, 83, 84, 89, 92, 93, 111, 209; trip to Moscow (1968), 43

Dzhurov, Dobri, 47

East Germany, 22, 57, 71; developing restraint as ally of USSR, 211–212; response to Czechoslovak crisis (1968), 49–50; response to Middle East war (1967), 20–22; response to Middle East War (1973), 145–148; response to Nixon visit to China (1972), 109–111; response to Ussuri crisis (1969), 76–77

Eban, Abba, 32, 154, 156, 157

Egypt, 5, 7; abrogation of treaty of friendship and cooperation with USSR, 174

Eighth SED Congress, 109

Einheit, 110

Engels, Friedrich, 13

Ethiopia, 178

European Security Conference (ESC), 75, 85, 91, 92–93, 100, 109, 117, 209, 219

extraregional influences, 1

Fahmi, Muhammad Ali, 193

Fahmy, Ismail, 178, 181

Federal Republic of Germany (FRG), 42, 45, 48, 49, 51, 72, 74, 82, 90, 92, 93, 145, 159

Feher, Lajos, 53

Fock, Jeno, 26, 53

Ford, Gerald R., 173

France, 23, 58

Gabelic, Andro, 88

deGaulle, Charles, 32

Geneva peace conference, call by U.S. and USSR, 178, 191, 192, 196

Geneva talks, Middle East, 171, 180, 183

German Democratic Republic (GDR), 13, 20, 21, 33, 49, 52, 72, 76, 77, 145, 159

Ghali, Butros, 194

Gheorghe, 58

Gheorghiu-Dej, 12

Gierek, Edward, 100, 114, 116, 127, 152, 189; address to the First National Party Conference, 1973, 152–153; visit to Italy (1977), 190

Giscard d'Estaing, Valery, 153

Gliga, Vasile, 85

Gomulka, Wladyslaw, 12, 23, 24, 25, 28, 43, 44, 50, 63, 77, 100,

About the Author

Jeffrey Simon is a senior analyst at Analytical Assessments Corporation, Arlington, Va. Previously he was a senior member of the research staff at System Planning Corporation, and he has held research positions at the Rand Corporation and the American Enterprise Institute for Public Policy Research. From 1972 to 1979, he was an assistant professor in the Department of Government at Georgetown University. Among his publications are *Ruling Communist Parties and Détente* (Washington: American Enterprise Institute, 1975), *Comparative Communist Foreign Policy, 1965-1976*, The Rand Corporation, P-6067 (August 1977), and *Warsaw Pact Reliability*, System Planning Corporation, SPC620 (September 1980). Dr. Simon holds a Ph.D. from the University of Washington and an M.A. from the University of Chicago.

DATE DUE